Case Studies in Political Economy: Japan 1854–1977

Bruce R. Scott

John W. Rosenblum

Audrey T. Sproat

Division of Research   Harvard Business School

Boston • 1980

Publisher Division of Research, Harvard Business School

Distribution Soldiers Field
Boston, MA 02163
Order No. 9-980-003

© **Copyright** 1980 by the President and Fellows of Harvard College

Library of Congress Catalog Card No. 80-80126

Printed in the United States of America

ISBN No. 0-87584-153-8

Case Studies in Political Economy: Japan 1854–1977

Preface

This is a book about political economy. It deals with major economic and political problems that have faced the Japanese government. It is organized historically to permit study of the evolution of the Japanese economy and its major political and economic institutions. This historical material forms the background or context in which to evaluate successive crisis or opportunity situations requiring the Japanese government to make fundamental choices of far-reaching importance to Japan and her major trading partners.

The Course Module consists of seven case studies; these trace the evolution of Japanese economic policy from the opening of Japan in the 1850s to the frictions between Japan and some of her principal trading partners in the late 1970s. These primary cases are supplemented by five additional cases, not included here. (Supplemental cases are printed separately[1] in order to encourage unprejudiced thinking about the policies the Japanese government might pursue in coping with the various problems confronting it.) This Course Module also contains a section entitled Country Analysis. It provides a framework with which to analyze all of the case studies. The material is designed as a vehicle for teaching political economy to graduate students, business executives, and government officials. Further, it is designed primarily for generalists rather than for specialists on Japan. It has relevance for Americans for three specific reasons. First, Japan has developed a more coherent and operational economic strategy than the United States. Second, Japanese business–government relations have developed in a way which supported much closer cooperation in designing such a strategy; and, finally, the Japanese strategy has had an ever-increasing impact on economic performance in the United States. As a major industrial competitor, the one with the most rapid economic growth over the last 30 years, the one which expanded its share of US imports from zero in 1945 to 20 percent in 1977, Japan merits serious study by all who are interested in the performance of the US economy and manufacturing industry.

The cases were developed for a course in business, government, and the international economy at the Harvard Business School. This course, as presently conceived, is built upon comparative analysis of the major industrial nations of the western system as seen through the historical evolution of their economic strategies. It is a 54-session course required of all MBA students. The cases on Japan occupy nine of those sessions, an amount roughly equal to that accorded to the US and much larger than that accorded any other country. Japan, as seen through those cases, becomes a standard against which other countries are compared and evaluated.

[1] Both this Course Module and the supplementary materials are available from the Intercollegiate Case Clearing House, Soldiers Field, Boston, MA 02163.

The case studies of Japan entered the course in the 1973-74 academic year as part of a change in basic course design. In previous years the emphasis had been largely on the US business environment as seen from the viewpoint of various business firms. Antitrust, labor relations, and economic regulation were major segments, as was business planning or forecasting. In 1973-74 the course shifted to an international perspective and to countries as the basic unit of analysis. An administrative viewpoint was retained by looking at an economy from the point of view of its "manager"—which was government rather than a firm. These changes required the development of new teaching materials and a new analytic framework. The result to date, as represented in this Course Module, reflects the contributions of the fifteen faculty members who have thus far participated in teaching this new course.

The idea for the course came from a school research project on French national planning conducted by John H. McArthur and Bruce R. Scott from 1963 through 1968. Professor Scott supervised the case and course development effort. Audrey Sproat shouldered the principal responsibility for research and case writing. The Japanese cases have also had inputs from a number of Japanese-speaking assistants including Toshio Gotoh, David Baskerville, and Stephen E. Marsland. Mr. Marsland made especially important contributions to the sections on labor and early industry. John W. Rosenblum took the lead in developing the analytic framework and wrote the section on country analysis. Professors Scott and Rosenblum also shared the responsibility for managing the course during these formative years.

Hugo E. R. Uyterhoeven and George C. Lodge deserve special recognition for their roles in the development of this new course. As the first chairman of the new General Management area, Professor Uyterhoeven played a key role in organizing the team which conceived and developed the course. He subsequently joined the teaching group and for two years was an active participant in the process. Professor Lodge played a unique role in this faculty group, not only as a source of continuity with the work of preceding years but as a major contributor of ideas and cases.

At this point in time the cases on Japan represent our most significant investment in terms of time and effort and in terms of developing distinctive teaching materials to help non-Japanese gain a rapid introduction to Japan and the evolving Japanese economic strategy. They have been revised in light of suggestions by faculty colleagues, by MBA students, and by participants in our executive programs, notably a number of Japanese business executives who took valuable time to offer their comments. They also reflect the stimulus of outside sources such as the writings of Norman Macrae of *The Economist*, James Abegglen of the Boston Consulting Group, and Peter G. Peterson, formerly US Secretary of Commerce.

Finally, we owe special thanks to Dean John H. McArthur and former Dean Lawrence E. Fouraker for their unfailing support of this academic venture.

B. R. Scott
J. W. Rosenblum
A. T. Sproat

Soldiers Field
Boston, Massachusetts
May 1980

Introduction

POLITICAL ECONOMY AS A FIELD OF STUDY

> There is a lot of politics in economics these days, although this is hardly surprising when political survival so often seems tied to government action. As economists, we are hardly to blame for this state of affairs. But, having bolted from the seminar room to the policy scene, we can, it seems to me, be more effective in our contributions if we think of ourselves as engaged in—to use the words of an earlier day—political economy. This is more than a call for a greater overlay of common sense, uncharacteristic humility, and renewed attention to the analysis of policy issues; it is a call for an extension of institutional analysis beyond the firm and the union so that we might better understand—and thereby affect economic decision-making by government.
>
> George P. Schultz, "Reflections on Political Economy," *Challenge*, March/April 1974.

Political economy is the study of economic policy making as it takes place in its political and institutional context. Typically it is the study of economic policy making at the highest levels of government of the nation state. The problems considered have to do with choice of goals, formulation of supporting policies, development of institutions, and mobilization of resources. Government, and particularly the executive branch of government, is charged with influencing or "managing" an economy, and it is this managerial role of government which is the subject of this book.

Political economy as defined above is the active province of a relatively small number of people at high levels in government. It is nonetheless the business of all responsible managers, whether in public service, state-owned corporations, or the private sector. The key decisions, usually thought of as policy decisions when seen separately, or as an economic strategy when seen as a totality, affect the business environment for firms large and small, public or private, and likewise affect the context in which government agencies operate. As such, an understanding of their meaning is important to all managers. Some managers will be able to distinguish themselves from others through a capacity to diagnose some of the basic problems facing government and thereby anticipate not only some of the policy changes but also the implications for their own firm or agency. Given the growing importance of government in the management of economic activity, it behooves all responsible managers to become familiar with the basic concepts of political economy as well as with the specifics of how these apply in their national and industrial context.

This Course Module is a vehicle for teaching political economy to managers, whether in the public sector or private. It does so by presenting case studies of problems facing a government in the management of its economy and asking the reader to work through these problems. In order to gain a better understanding of how government can and does influence an economy it asks the reader to identify and evaluate the problems facing the government policy maker, to formulate options for dealing with these problems, and then to think through the implications of these policy options for various interested parties. The options may be primarily economic in character, as in a devaluation or an increase in the rate of growth of the money supply. The implications are also bound to be political in part. This process of case analysis provides practice in combining economic and political considerations in an evaluation of what the problem is, what has caused it, and how various options might help to resolve or reduce it. It is the opportunity for economic and political analysis in a single evaluation that is the basic rationale for these case studies.

CASE STUDIES IN COUNTRY ANALYSIS

Case studies in political economy might choose to look intensively at fragments of a system; alternatively, they might attempt an overview, sacrificing something in depth. The second approach is chosen here in order to draw attention to the nation state as an economic environment. Thus, our case studies are concerned with "country analysis," not with how the various departments of government work, how government manages a particular segment of the economy, or how state or local government works.

Three axioms have guided the case development. First, the nation state, rather than component states or regions, is the basic unit of analysis. Although areas such as Texas, California, or even Iowa are larger than most nation states, their governments have fewer policy options to influence their economies. For example, the interstate commerce clause of the US Constitution prohibits the states from imposing tariffs or quotas on imports or controls on the movement of capital. For this reason, as well as others rooted in history, nation states are much more distinctive economic environments than the various states or regions of which they may be composed. They are managed by governments through more or less distinctive institutions toward more or less explicit goals. The evaluation of performance, goal setting, and policy formulation at the national level is the subject of these cases.

The second axiom is that the reader is asked to identify with the administrative point of view: in these case studies the administrator is the government of the particular country, especially its executive branch. The idea is to portray the situation as it confronts the administrator who has responsibility for influencing, if not really "managing," the outcomes. The reader is asked to identify with the manager and to evaluate possible solutions from his or her point of view, not from that of a journalist, a professor of economics, or an impartial observer. By identifying with and understanding the administrator's point of view, the reader can better understand government's point of view and may thereby become more effective in anticipating changes in public policy.

Third, the cases are designed to permit comparative analysis both across countries and over time within a country. They have a standard format to facilitate this comparison, a format explained in the section on country analysis. Use of this framework facilitates analysis through comparison and the recognition of policy options for similar situations.

TEACHING AND LEARNING OBJECTIVES

The basic objective is to introduce a practical framework for country analysis: practical in the sense of dealing with economic, political, and social data relevant to policy formulation by a national government and also practical in the sense of providing a framework in which the data can be assimilated and analyzed by the intelligent layman. This objective stands in contrast to current trends in economics, where simplifying assumptions facilitates quantitative analysis of problems abstracted from their social and political setting. It also contrasts with the teaching of political science, with its emphasis on theories, ideology, and institutions in isolation from their impact on economic performance. The basic objective is to bring economic and political analysis back together again in a practical framework not unlike that used by many experienced practitioners in this field. This objective does not include developing a theory of economic growth. Rather, it attempts to develop a framework for analyzing some of the basic options confronting economic policy makers.

SUBSTANTIVE KNOWLEDGE

The basic concept employed here is that of national economic strategy: a statement of broad goals and policies that orients the government's influence, not only on the domestic economy but also on its trade and financial relations with other countries. Borrowed from the Business Policy teaching area, where it has proved to be a powerful concept for understanding the functions of top management in a firm, the concept of "strategy" is extremely valuable as a guide to in-depth research on the influence of government on business. It was first used in a study of the impact of the French government on the French business environment.[1] This use of the concept suggested its wider applicability for teaching and research. It subsequently proved successful as a way of selecting, organizing, and analyzing data on some twelve countries.

The case studies on Japan will introduce basic concepts from economics, including national income, balance of payments, and monetary and fiscal policy. From political science the studies introduce concepts such as interest groups, the structure and functioning of the executive and legislative branches, and the ideology or the prevailing beliefs about how a society should be organized. In addition to conceptual knowledge, the cases aim to impart a great deal of institutional knowledge. They trace the evolution of government in Japan from the Shogunate through the Restoration, the years of limited democracy, the takeover by the military, the US Occupation, and the period of full democracy since 1952. They sketch the origins and evolution of major economic institutions such as the *zaibatsu*, the banking system and labor unions. They also trace Japan's relations with its major trading partners.

These institutional data are essential for reasoned analysis of the case problems, on the one hand; on the other, they provide valuable background knowledge for executives in business or government who deal with the modern multinational corporation or the impact of foreign trade. It is part of a basic economic literacy, valuable in its own sake and valuable once again in helping to interpret the daily news or magazine articles.

---

[1] John H. McArthur and Bruce R. Scott, *Industrial Planning in France.* Boston: Harvard University, Graduate School of Business Administration, Division of Research, 1969.

ATTITUDES

In addition to concepts and facts, certain attitudes or frames of mind are valuable to the analyst of national economic strategies. The cases presented here encourage the reader to take the point of view of the generalist rather than the specialist. Understanding the issues requires consideration of economic, political, and social data. It requires breadth of analysis and the capacity to integrate disparate ideas and information. The cases also encourage the reader to take an "inside point of view"— to see the problem as a practitioner might have seen it in that situation at that point in time. In analyzing the problems confronting Finance Minister Inouye in 1929, for example, it is important to look at them from his point of view and not from the view of an American in San Francisco or Washington D.C. Since political economy is based on a pluralistic view of the world, one with multiple decision centers each with its own strategy, it is important that each new situation be viewed as the insiders or decision makers might view it, not in terms of one's own interests or some abstract notion of a world order. Analysis of multiple decision centers, such as are involved in US–Japanese trade relations, therefore requires the extra effort of seeing several different points of view at once.

Recognition of different viewpoints and interests helps one to accept the idea that "where you stand depends on where you sit." In the field of political economy it may also help one to realize that the economic ideas one works with also depend in part on where one sits. In the United States, for example, the notion of comparative advantage is a static concept little changed from the first formulation in terms of wine growing in Portugal versus sheep raising in England. Comparative advantage is seen as based on factor endowments taken as givens. Many American economic textbooks continue to treat them that way. For the

Japanese, on the other hand, a desire to "catch up with the West" led to a dynamic notion of investing in technology and thereby eventually achieving a comparative advantage—even though the starting point was one of significant disadvantage. Japan's economic strategy has been based on a different concept of comparative advantage, as well as on the development of novel institutions to implement this concept. An example is the Japan Development Bank. Some official American thinking—even in 1980—seems rooted in the earlier conception as expounded in American textbooks.

Third, the cases encourage the reader to take the point of view of the *responsible analyst*,[2] perhaps an assistant to the decision maker. Because they cover so much ground, space does not permit them to develop the depth necessary to understand internal administrative processes—let alone office politics or personal psychological profiles. As a result, the analyst is not asked to decide what a particular minister "should" do. He or she is asked instead for an identification and evaluation of the broad issues, for the formulation of options that the administrator might consider, and for an evaluation of the implications of the various options.

ANALYTICAL SKILLS

Political economy draws upon analytical skills of various types and levels. In economics, for example, the cases in this Course Module provide an opportunity for first-order analysis of balance-of-payments statements; they also provide an opportu-

---

[2] We say *responsible analyst* because we wish to encourage the reader to weigh possible domestic political gains versus international commitments, and short-term expedients versus long-term gains and costs. We try to encourage the reader to take the role of a chief economic advisor, not that of a political speechwriter.

nity for analyzing different financing strategies including foreign debt, foreign equity, domestic savings, or domestic inflation of the money supply. At yet another level they provide a vehicle for practice in identification of an over-all economic strategy encompassing not only broad goals but a broad range of economic policies including monetary, fiscal, foreign trade and investment, and incomes policies, as well as sectoral policies toward industry, banking, labor, and agriculture. Somewhat similar opportunities exist for practice in political analysis, including opportunities to identify changing relationships between executive and legislative branches, the changing roles and influence of different interest groups, and the changing role of a particular country in an international political and economic order.

The heart of what this Course Module and the course from which it is drawn provide is the opportunity for *practice* in identifying and evaluating a total economic strategy for a particular country at a particular point in time. The idea is to practice analyzing totalities, bringing in additional concepts in successive case situations. The historical organization of the materials suits this approach: the world continues to increase in complexity, and the concepts used for formulating economic and political analysis become more complex over time.

Practice in strategic analysis is greatly facilitated by comparisons: several countries at a point in time, for example, or several points in time for the same country. Both types of comparison are valuable, and our experience to date suggests that the two types strongly reinforce one another. Thus to compare the Inouye options in 1929 with those of Matsukata in 1881 is instructive, but it is still more instructive to compare the Inouye options with those of Hoover or FDR in 1932 or 1933. To achieve both longitudinal and horizontal comparison takes one beyond the confines of Japan and into other countries.

JAPAN AS A CASE STUDY

Japan was given top priority as a case study because we believed there was a great deal to be learned from Japanese experience. In the last 30 years Japan's economic growth has outdistanced that of any other country for any recorded time period of comparable length. This period has seen Japan transformed from a war-devastated producer of low-quality goods, sustained by low wages and a low standard of living, to one of the foremost economic powers, highly respected for the quality and workmanship of its products and for wage levels roughly comparable to those of western Europe. This rapid transition represents a degree of success that is the envy of many industrial societies and most of the less developed countries.

This success is all the more remarkable because the Japanese have had so little by way of natural resources to build upon. Japan must import about 99 percent of the oil it needs, about 95 percent of the iron ore, half the coal, all of the bauxite for aluminum, and all of the cotton for its textile industry. In addition, it must import much of the food needed to feed a population of over 100 million crowded into an island archipelago whose area is about equal to Finland or the state of California, but only 15 percent of which is habitable. With more than 2000 people per square mile of habitable land, Japan is the most densely populated land in the world, with all the attendant problems of congestion, pollution, and need for infrastructure. In order to progress and to pay for the food and capital equipment needed to sustain its drive for industrialization, Japan had to import raw materials, transform them, and sell them abroad.

On numerous occasions western experts studied Japan, only to conclude that her prospects were dim and her ambitions unrealistic. As recently as the 1950s her circumstances were compared with those of Britain and found to be much less promising. These analyses focused on Japan's natural resources and existing facilities and cost levels. They did not take account of the possibility of an economic strategy which, over time, might radically alter those relative technological and cost positions. Indeed, many of the analysts came from the United States, a country noted for its skepticism about economic strategies and where—in any event—rivalries between business and government leaders made implementation of any national strategy problematic indeed. Japan, it seems, was able to develop a strategy and an *organization* for implementing it and changing it as needed.

If Japan's achievements are largely the result of strategy and organization rather than of natural resources, then other countries might look to it for lessons. This is indeed what has happened. For many countries Japan is a model, a role once accorded to the United States. Besides teaching about Japan for its own sake these cases allow the reader to explore those aspects which seem most important for those who would use Japan as a model.

Japan presents some particularly important questions for Americans. Recent Japanese history, since Admiral Perry's arrival in Tokyo Bay in 1853, has been closely intertwined with American history. Trade relations have been important from the outset; indeed, Admiral Perry arrived as the first US special trade representative, with a fleet of warships to back up his request for an "open door" for American merchants in Japan. Since that time trade and diplomatic relations have seen their ups and downs, including an open confrontation from 1941 to 1945.

Since World War II Japan has become a key partner in the western military, political and economic system. It was brought in under American auspices, following a US occupation and a US "reform" and reorganization of many of Japan's basic institutions.

By the 1970s Japanese-US relations reflected growing tensions in the areas of trade and international payments despite Japan's growing role in the western system. Indeed, tensions in the trade and payments area seem to some to be approaching a point where they may compromise that partnership. To others it seems that the partnership may have blinded the US to its real interests in trade and payments, thereby allowing Japanese business to compete unfairly with American business in America. An understanding of these issues requires far more than repeating old slogans such as "free trade." It requires a careful attempt to understand Japanese economic strategy and American options for dealing with it constructively. This Course Module gives particular attention to Japanese-American trade relations, so as to help American readers develop a better understanding of Japanese strategy and official American reaction to it.

Japan's economic policies and institutional organization have evolved over time, sometimes as a result of unforeseen or unfortunate events such as wars. The present is firmly rooted in the past and in the accidents of history as well as in the design of her leading citizens. The cases in this volume trace that evolution from 1853 to 1977 and focus on critical moments or turning points. They attempt to give a balanced picture of the actions of people and the sweep of events more or less beyond their control. From this selection of events and source material, the reader should be able to extract his or her own analysis of "how Japan ticks" and, by analogy, to consider constructively how much may be applicable in another national setting at another point in time.

Country Analysis

General managers have a tendency to leave country analysis to the experts. Specialists' judgments about the future direction of national economies are accepted without critical examination. Executive attention is focused on the implications of the predictions for their firm. The problem with this management strategy, however, is that when left to experts alone, the analysis often becomes an exercise in applying conventional wisdom to pieces of the environment.

During the early 1930s, for example, many economists were recommending strict adherence to the concept of the balanced federal budget. Common sense, some economists, and some politicians argued for increased government spending to stimulate demand. Such a policy would have certainly been in business' best interest, yet public policy and many business executives accepted the economic thinking even as the reality of the situation showed that 25 percent of the working population was unemployed.

In the 1960s and 1970s substantial expert opinion existed to support the notion that oil was overpriced, since it sold for prices well above marginal costs. OPEC was viewed as a cartel that could not hold together. Many public policy makers and oil company managers acted on the basis of the judgment. A carefully reasoned country analysis of the major producing and consuming countries, however, would have shown the expert judgments to have been highly questionable.

In order to develop a country analysis, the business manager or analyst must be able to read and use the data and judgments provided by the experts. This literacy requires familiarity with the language and concepts of economists and social scientists and the institutional arrangements of different countries and international agencies. For example, what does an economist mean by investment? Money? GNP? How does the Japanese banking system work? What decisions are made by the International Monetary Fund, and how?

An intelligent consumer needs to do more than read the labels. The manager needs to organize and relate the data in a way that allows him or her to reach his or her own conclusions with respect to the future shape of national economies. The remainder of this chapter describes such a framework for managerial country analysis.

COUNTRY ANALYSIS

To accomplish this analysis, it is useful to regard the nation state as a purposeful entity, in much the same way that many analysts choose to view the firm. In both instances, of course, an extraordinary simplification is involved. Decisions, public and private, are the outcome of complicated processes of bargaining and negotiating and the use of power which we call politics. To posit a rational manager of the processes is certainly not of much descriptive value or perhaps of much normative value. On the other hand, this assumption and the framework of analysis that it facilitates provide a significant aid to business managers in improving their predictions about the future directions of national economies. The framework offers a useful format for the organization of data and a place to start in analyzing national policy.

The basic concepts of the framework are three in number: performance, strategy, and context.[1] By performance we mean how well the economy has been doing along such dimensions as real growth in GNP, inflation, unemployment, and balance of payments. Strategy includes the implicit or explicit choice of national goals as well as the policies (Industrial Organization would label these as conduct) being followed by the national government in pursuit of these goals. Context denotes the institutional, ideological, political, and physical "givens" that shape a government's strategic choices and the outcomes of these choices.

Thus, the first step in analysis is to organize information about the national environment into the analytic categories of performance, strategy, and context. This procedure is not a mechanistic or simple activity. Performance trends must be calculated. Causal relationships and policy implications must be established. Official statements need to be distinguished from and compared to actions. Judgments must be made about what data are important and what are not.

Having analyzed a national environment in terms of its performance, strategy, and context, country analysis turns next to relating these data to one another. The consistencies and inconsistencies that appear provide excellent clues as to what is likely and what is not likely to change in the future.

Performance

Since everything seems to be related to everything else, it is difficult to decide where to begin the description. The easiest place to start is economic performance, however, because relevant standard statistical series are usually available. On the other hand, the performance variables that should be studied, the time period over which performance should be measured, and the criteria against which performance should be evaluated are not the same for each situation.

Moreover, given a calculator and a series of numerical exhibits there is, unfortunately, almost no limit to the amount of time one can spend manipulating the numbers. The question is how far to go. Our advice is to start with some basic indicators of national economic performance. Calculate the level and trends for real GNP, inflation, unemployment, unit labor costs, if available, and balance of trade. See what pattern emerges.

For example, if inflation seems high and unemployment low, you would consider the possibility of "demand-pull" as the cause of rising prices. You might then examine the capacity-utilization figures for corroboration of your hypothesis. If demand-pull continued to look like a good diagnosis, you could study the components of GNP for insight into the causes of excess demand. Has government deficit spending played an important role in creating demand?

On the other hand, if an initial survey of economic performance reveals relatively high inflation and high unemployment,

---

[1] These concepts are derived from the Harvard Business School courses in Business Policy and Industrial Organization. (An alternative framework for analysis might be that provided by the descriptive decision theory of H. A. Simon.)

one could look for "cost-push" inflation. An investigation of the relation between changes in wages and productivity would be a logical next step, and one would expect to find compensation per hour growing faster than output per hour. One might then examine investment data (Is productivity suffering because of lagging business investment?), information on organized labor (Are wage demands likely to slow down in the face of high unemployment?), and information on the unemployment compensation scheme (How much does one lose, after tax, if unemployed?).

The country analyst is much like a doctor who is giving a patient a general physical examination. Begin with a standard series of questions. The direction and intensity of further diagnosis is a function of the answers obtained to the initial questions. The basic indicators of economic performance may lead to examination of other, more detailed indicators. They may also highlight important aspects of strategy (e.g., deficit financing), and context (e.g., extent of union activity). Having pursued the leads that have been generated by the initial survey of performance, the analyst can turn to strategy.

Strategy

As was the case with performance, some standard questions can be asked.

1. What are the economic goals? Which ones are of high priority?

2. What noneconomic goals are important to the government? How do these goals relate in terms of priority to the economic ones?

3. What major economic policies does the government employ to implement its goals?

Many dimensions of a country's economic performance may please or concern a business executive, but if that executive wishes to predict future economic policies and performance, his preferences are of little importance. The critical relation is between performance and the strategy of the government.

Goals. Many examples could be cited to show the importance of government's goals, including goals that are non-economic. The Canadian government's action in establishing the Canadian Development Corporation and the Foreign Investment Review Agency is a case in point. These moves came as a result of the growing economic role of foreign direct investment, the behavior or performance of the foreign subsidiaries in Canada, and a shift in national goals away from improved standard of living at all costs to a desire for more control by Canadians over Canada's economic development. The business executive may question the wisdom or feasibility of the new goals, but it is clear that changing national goals did result in new policies toward foreign-owned enterprise.

Another example of the importance of non-economic goals in analyzing a national environment is provided by the Johnson administration. In an effort to maintain public support for both the Great Society and the war in Vietnam, President Lyndon B. Johnson was reluctant to increase taxes. This fiscal policy was changed only after a change in US economic performance—growing inflation—became an even greater threat to public support than taxes. The importance of the non-economic goals of world leadership and social welfare at home was so great, however, that it did not allow any retreat from the Great Society or Vietnam, and the new taxes were imposed—although billed as temporary.

Economic Policies. The second component of a national strategy is the economic policies of the government. Shaped by the goals and context, these policies are valuable keys to predicting future economic performance. As was the case with performance, however, what policies to study in what detail is the challenge to the analyst. The best way to begin is to group government actions into five categories: fiscal, monetary, incomes, foreign trade and investment, and structural.

Fiscal Policies.   Data on fiscal policy—even just data on government income less expenditure—throw important light on the way the economy is being managed. Yet the analyst must go beyond the levels of budget surplus or deficits, since built-in stabilizers such as income tax and unemployment insurance tend to create budget deficits during recessions and surpluses during periods of expansion. The fiscal policies of a particular administration, therefore, are best appreciated by studying the discretionary moves that it makes. Are tax rates being raised or lowered? Is the tax burden being shifted from one segment of society to another? What areas are being affected?

Fiscal actions are also excellent indicators of national direction. A review of the sources and uses of government funds based on the US federal budget in the 1960s and 1970s reveals that the country's national priorities and problems shifted in a dramatic fashion. Similarly, a comparison between tax structures and social welfare expenditures in Japan and Great Britain provides insight into the difference between the national development strategies of those two countries.

Monetary Polices.   Monetary policies are a second major component of a government's economic strategy. By influencing bank reserves, money, and credit, governments can influence demand for goods and services and the level of investment at both an aggregate and industry level. The tight money policies of the US Federal Reserve in 1969, for example, made a significant contribution to the US recession in 1970.

On the other hand, the Japanese government's willingness and ability to allocate credit selectively is viewed by many as a key factor in implementing that country's successful postwar development strategy.

To identify a government's monetary policies, the analyst can begin by calculating how fast the money supply has been growing relative to changes in real and nominal GNP. Changes in the money supply, however, are a result of market forces and government policies, not government policies alone. A thorough description of monetary policy will include government actions in areas such as open market operations, discount rates, reserve requirements, exchange rates, and capital controls.

Incomes Policies.   Many nations have experimented with various forms of "wage price policies" or efforts by the government to influence directly the rate of change in prices, wages and other income shares. Common during periods of war, these direct limits on the growth of wages and prices (and therefore incomes) are turned to when the now traditional macroeconomic fiscal and monetary tools are not getting the desired performance. (The growth of big labor and big business has introduced an inflationary bias into many economies, and floating exchange rates have seemed to add to the problem.)

The US experiment with an incomes policy in the early 1970s illustrates some of the administrative and political problems associated with this approach to economic management. Canada and Great Britain have experienced similar problems in trying to resolve who is to be covered, how wage and price limitations are to be justified and enforced, and what is to happen when the incomes policy is lifted.

Income maintenance programs are another important component of a government strategy. US government policies in areas such as unemployment insurance, welfare, food stamps, medicaid, disability allowances, and minimum wages have had a significant impact on the business environment. Many critics feel these efforts have reduced both the incentives and opportunities to work.

Foreign Trade and Investment Policies. Foreign trade and investment policies are also a controversial area. Economic theory suggests that a one-world economy with each nation specializing in products where it has a comparative advantage would be to all countries' benefit. On the other hand, foreigners do not vote in national elections, and in the short run jobs speak louder than economic theories and future performance. Non-economic factors such as the Cold War also play a role.

After World War II, for example, Japan was able to protect its home market through a series of tariffs, quotas, subsidies, and foreign exchange and investment controls. US concern about Communist China, Japan's modest initial market share, and the rapid growth in over-all world trade after World War II led the US policy makers to overlook these violations of the international rules of the game. As US feelings toward China moderated and the balance-of-payments situations of Japan and the United States changed, however, US policy makers began to put pressure on Japanese officials to modify their foreign trade and investment policies.

In the current climate of world economic slowdown and potential resource shortages, the foreign trade and investment policies of many countries are being re-examined. The future of regional economic integration arrangements such as the European Economic Community are being questioned. Voluntary "import quotas" and "orderly marketing agreements" are being proposed for a variety of commodities and products in an attempt to forestall a return to full-scale protectionism.

A government's foreign trade and investment policies can be identified by considering the various balance-of-payments categories. For example, what actions are being taken to influence the level, composition, and direction of trade? How are current-account deficits being financed? What restrictions, if any, are being placed on foreign investment and borrowing?

Structural Policies. Unsatisfactory economic performance often leads governments to change the structural arrangements of the economy. The New Deal in the United States was such a response. No sector of the economy was ignored. Banking, agriculture, industry, and labor were affected by new legislation. Concern about US economic performance in the 1970s has also resulted in proposed structural changes: Senator Philip Hart has proposed stronger antitrust regulations; Senators Hubert H. Humphrey and Jacob Javits have proposed more active national planning. Many legislators would like to have the independence of the Federal Reserve reduced. And there is a widespread belief that the workings of the independent regulatory agencies need to be reformed.

Much current public debate in western Europe also centers on the appropriate organization for national economies. Capitalism is being challenged by the Socialists and Communists. The efficiency and effectiveness of state enterprise is questioned by the Conservatives.

To identify a government's structural policies, an analyst can ask the following questions: Which industries receive government support? (At what level? In what form?) On what basis are these industries chosen? What is government policy toward competition? What other restrictions, if any, does government place on the management of business enterprise? Is there anti-pollution regulation, for example? Must management bargain with labor unions?

Context

The last major analytic category for country analysis relates to the context within which the goals and policies of a government are formulated and implemented: the opportunities for and constraints on public action. For analytic purposes, this context can be segmented into a domestic and an international component. The domestic context can be thought of in terms of its institutional, ideological, political, and physical dimensions. The international context consists of the economic performance, strategic profiles, and contexts of other countries as well as the international economic system within which nations have agreed to compete.

Think about a nation's context as if it were the environment facing the country's chief executive officer. In the US the context is the environment that faces the president and associates in the executive branch. In countries with parliamentary forms of government, the point of view is that of the prime minister and his or her cabinet.

The analyst approaches a description of the context by trying to gain insight into the policy options open to the executive branch of government and the likelihood that these policy options will be pursued successfully. What are the domestic and international pressures for and constraints on executive action? How well equipped is the nation to pursue various options? What are its strengths and weaknesses relative to its major competitors?

Institutional Context.   Begin a description of the domestic context with the governmental setting. The constitutional power of the executive branch of government varies from country to country. The zone of discretion open to a US president is far less than that of the British prime minister. The power of the executive in the Fifth French Republic was substantially greater than in the Fourth.

Government regulation of the economy is an important aspect of the context. Government regulation is today one of the top "growth industries" in the US, for example. In 1965 industries subject to pervasive federal regulation accounted for roughly 7 percent of US GNP. By 1978, the growth of regulation was such that heavily regulated industries accounted for over 30 percent of GNP. But even firms producing the remaining 70 percent of US output have not escaped the escalating costs of complying with government regulation, for regulatory scrutiny has extended to cover hiring and promotion decisions, workplace safety, pension plans, capital financing, product design, plant location, and emission, effluent, and other waste disposal practices.

The relative strength of the nation's industrial system is another institutional reality. The problems and options facing the West German government with its profit-oriented industry and cooperative business–labor relations are far different than those facing the French government with "pre-Capitalist" management traditions and hostile business–labor relations. A great deal of Japan's postwar economic success has been attributed to the characteristics of "Japan, Inc.," the pattern of relationships between government agencies, the major banks, and the large industrial firms.

Ideological Context.   A second important component of the domestic context is the country's ideology: the dominant set of ideas about what constitutes legitimate behavior and appropriate national goals. In the United States and Canada, for example, most people feel the government that governs least governs best and the rights of the individual are paramount to those of the community at large. The growing role of government in managing economic activity and legislating regulations to protect the rights of the community (environmental protection laws, for example) makes these citizens uncomfortable.

In a country like Japan, on the other hand, a consensus exists that the community needs are more important than those of the individual. Moreover, it is legitimate for government to play an active role in achieving strong national economic performance. These different attitudes toward the role of the individual and the state have had significant impact on national strategies.

US President Herbert Hoover excluded a number of policy options in 1930–1932 because they were not consistent with his and the country's ideology. Japanese economic strategy after 1931 was not constrained by such an ideology and therefore took a more pragmatic and successful path. The history of US demand management also shows the power of ideology to influence strategy. The notion that the US government could and should take an active role in managing aggregate demand was born during the Depression and the Second World War. It was first institutionalized with the Employment Act of 1946 but not fully implemented until the Kennedy administration in the early 1960s. President Dwight D. Eisenhower and his Treasury Secretary George M. Humphrey continued to resist active demand management for reasons similar to Hoover's.

The choice of national goals is also influenced by ideology. The United States and Canadian emphasis in the 1960s on improved individual standard of living is in stark contrast to the Japanese pursuit of national economic success. In the 1970s, however, North Americans seem to be increasingly concerned with community needs along with individual rights. A slowdown in world economic growth, high levels of environmental pollution, shortages—both actual and forecasted—of natural resources, and rising prices appear to have led many North Americans to question traditional ideologies and, therefore, national goals.

Political Context.   Political factors also play an important role in shaping executive action. Election year decision making in the US, for example, tends to "give" rather than "take." Administrations with small congressional or parliamentary majorities (or even minorities) often pursue "compromise" strategies.

The interests of such major interest blocks as business and labor nearly always have to be considered. For various countries at various times, other interest groups, such as the church and the military, also play important roles in the formulation of national policies. Population control efforts in many low-income countries are limited by church policy and influence. Military expenditures account for a substantial percentage of government budgets, and foreign economic policies often have a national defense motivation.

The farm block is also a significant economic and political factor in most countries. A continuing problem for the European Economic Community, for example, has been its Common Agricultural Policy. And agricultural reform is one of the most sensitive political issues for the low-income countries. Structural changes aimed at improved productivity are slow in coming, even though these countries face the possibility of a long-term food shortage.

Physical Context.   A fourth dimension of the domestic context is the country's natural attributes, the kinds of data in which a demographer and a geographer would be interested. Where is the country located? What natural resources are available? How many and what kind of people live and work there?

Differences of opinion within OPEC, for example, can be understood in terms of the oil reserves and populations of its different members. North Sea oil and gas are key factors in any appraisal of the United Kingdom's long-term prospects. Japan's large, well-educated population, limited natural resources, and strategic island location have had a strong influence on its economic strategy. Canadian economic development has been shaped by that country's small population, large natural-resource base, and proximity to a giant neighbor to the south.

International Context.   If one thinks about the international economic system as a number of nations linked together by some economic rules of the game, then the international context for any individual country is the performance, strategy, and domestic context of all other nations plus the international rules of the game. Japanese economic strategy and performance is certainly part of the context for the US president. US political concerns with respect to the Soviet Union are an important dimension of the West German context. The economic performance of western Europe in the 1970s is material to countries as diverse as the United States and Saudi Arabia.

The international rules of the game are also important. The ways in which international liquidity is created and individual country currencies are valued have a significant influence on world trade and national economic performance. The Bretton Woods system, for example, greatly benefited Japan and western Europe. The currencies of these countries were allowed to remain undervalued relative to the US dollar thus providing those nations with a significant trading edge. Eventually, however, continued US deficits resulted in an inflationary level of world liquidity. The conduct of the US as the world banker and the value of the dollar were questioned in the late 1960s and early 1970s.

Another aspect of the international system is trade and tariff agreements. The memory of the extreme protectionist policies of the

1920s and early 1930s resulted in a steady decline in tariff barriers after the mid-1930s. With most countries taking part in the General Agreement on Trade and Tariffs (GATT), it was hoped that quotas and tariffs would become an even smaller part of national economic strategies. The world slowdown of the 1970s seems to have challenged that assumption, however, and the left in Great Britain has argued for withdrawal from the Common Market. Labor union leaders and industrialists in the United States are putting pressure on the US government to negotiate agreements with various countries that would limit the amount of certain products imported into the United States.

COUNTRY EVALUATION

The analysis of a national environment can be organized and displayed on a chart such as the one given here. Organizing the information in this way facilitates an evaluation of the country's situation, the objective of which is a forecast of what changes, if any, can be expected to take place in the country's performance, strategy, and context. Which dimensions of performance will the government attempt to modify? Will these policies be successful? What impact will they have on the national context?

How Serious Is the Situation?

The prediction process begins with a comparison of national performance and goals. If the government is satisfied with the country's economic performance, new policy initiatives are unlikely. A European businessman might view 5 percent US unemployment as extraordinarily high and therefore expect reflationary policies from Washington. The US president might very

Performance	*Strategy*	*Context*
GNP	**Goals**	**Domestic**
Personal consumption	Autonomy	Institutional
Investment	Growth	Government
Government consumption	Income redistribution	Industry
		Banking
Inflation	**Policies**	Agriculture
	Fiscal	Labor
Unit labor costs	Monetary	Ideological
Wages	Incomes	Political
Productivity	Foreign trade	Physical
	and investment	
Capacity utilization	Structural	**International**
		Other countries
Unemployment		Trade blocs
		GATT, IMF
Balance of payments		
Trade		
Imports		
Exports		
Current account		
Capital account		
Exchange rates		

well view the same figures as unfortunate but unavoidable and therefore take no action at all.

Similarly a US observer might expect West Germany to reflate its economy in order to stimulate world demand. After all, the observer might argue, Germany's balance-of-payments picture is strong and its inflation low relative to other nations. The memories of hyperinflation after both world wars make German policy makers risk-averse when it comes to inflation, however. Moreover, the strategy of export-led growth that was so successful in the 1960s became institutionalized and therefore hard to modify.

On the other hand, when economic performance and government goals diverge, significant policy changes do occur, as evidenced by FDR's economic program in the 1930s and Richard Nixon's new economic game plan in 1971. Moreover, inconsistencies between a country's performance and the international context can also lead to pressure for policy changes. Japan's prob-

lems in the late 1960s and early 1970s are good examples of such a situation. Had Japanese performance continued at its previous level, Japan would have had to take shares of world trade and resources that were unacceptable to other nations, particularly the United States. The Japanese were not unhappy with their economic performance, but there was strong impetus for change coming from outside.

The balance-of-payments performance of some other countries is another example of potential inconsistencies between national performance and the international context. The development aspirations of many countries led them to "live beyond their means." Large current account deficits were incurred in the process, and these deficits were financed with short- and long-term debt at high rates of interest. As long as the banks and other international sources of financing continued to roll the debt over, the performance picture did not become an unsatisfactory one from the national government's viewpoint. There is little domestic support for austerity and a "pay-as-you-go" development strategy, as evidenced by recent events in a country like Peru.

The question is how long the "international bankers," be they Citibank or the IMF, will be able and willing to play the game. For some small nations like Sri Lanka the answer might be "not very much longer." On the other hand, many other nations with similar performance records seem to have a good chance of escaping a cutoff. Countries like Egypt, Great Britain, and Italy may be too important economically and politically to countries such as the United States to be allowed to fail.

Is the Situation Likely to Improve?

After assessing the pressures for improved economic performance, the analyst must evaluate whether the current government policies are likely to bring performance into a better fit with goals and the international context. One test, of course, is the fit between the policies and the problem. Tight money can slow the growth of investment and consumption, but if the causes for inflation are institutional—administered prices and wages, for example—the impact on performance may be to increase unemployment with marginal (if any) improvement in the rate of inflation. Devaluation is another popular government response to performance problems. If, however, the supply or demand for a country's imports and exports are not very price-elastic, such a policy may hurt rather than help the nation's balance-of-trade performance.

A second test of economic policies is their fit with the context. The aspirations and policies of many LDCs in the early 1970s were fashioned after those of Japan. In spite of valuable natural resources in some cases, however, these ambitious policies seemed to conflict with the domestic context. In-

come distribution and the level of education were poor. These countries lacked the kind of domestic market and skilled labor and management force upon which Japan built its economic success.

Administrative feasibility is the third test. Some actions are relatively easy for a government to implement: not many people are involved in devaluing a currency or increasing a nation's money supply. On the other hand, an effective incomes policy or structural reform of the industrial sector is a complicated managerial undertaking. Even if ideologically and politically acceptable, the tasks of setting and monitoring wages and prices or designing and developing a competitive industrial system are quite challenging. Such policies may be appropriate given the context and performance of the country, but how likely are they to succeed?

If current government policies are judged to be inadequate for any reason, the next step in country evaluation is to decide whether effective new policies can be expected. Perhaps a change of government is likely, bringing with it fiscal and monetary policies more suited to the country's situation. The trade balance may be suffering from an overvalued currency that the government is willing to devalue.

In many cases reasonable options to current policy can be identified, but there seem to be ideological constraints on their implementation. The rules of the game under the gold standard, for example, were seen as excluding devaluation as a policy option. Balanced budgets were part of the economic theology of the twenties and thirties. Rationalization of industry and more active government planning have always been resisted in the United States because such policies conflict with commonly accepted notions of a limited state and the power of competition to provide superior economic performance.

Other constraints on action are political. The growing concern with environmental pollution in Japan during the 1970s, for example, constrained that country's product/market choices. Strong resistance to serious austerity reduced the likelihood of a tough energy conservation program in the United States or an effective incomes policy in the United Kingdom.

In some instances, the gap between performance and goals is so large that countries are forced to re-examine goals. There seems to be no reasonable way to get there from here. During the 1960s, Great Britain was forced to abandon the goal of being a major military force, and during the 1970s she reduced her expectations with regard to the standard of living.

THE FUTURE BUSINESS ENVIRONMENT

Having assessed the likelihood that the economic performance of a country will improve, stand still, or deteriorate, the final step in country evaluation is to forecast the future domestic and international context. If Japan's economic growth slows down and her economy continues to open, for example, what will Japan, Inc. look like in ten years? If Great Britain's postwar performance trends continue, what will the institutional context of that country look like a decade from now? If the price of oil continues to rise, what form will the international economic system take? Are we headed for a period of protectionism as in the 1930s?

The evaluation process just described can be summarized in terms of a series of analytic questions.

1. Is the country's economic performance consistent with its goals?

2. Is the country's economic performance consistent with the international context?

3. Are the government's economic policies likely to bring economic performance into a better fit with goals and the context?

   a. Do the policies address the causes of the performance problems?

   b. Are the policies consistent with the context?

4. Are policy changes reasonable to expect? How will these new policies influence performance?

5. What shape will the future domestic and international context take? How well prepared is the government to meet such changes?

Japan A: 1853–1881, The Challenge to the Old Order

After being a "closed" society for more than two centuries, Japan was opened to outside influence in 1854. Rapid changes followed, especially after 1868. But change proved costly in economic as well as psychic terms. By 1881, a new finance minister, Prince Matsukata—who had "started his career as a sword-wielding page" [16, p. 86]— had to decide what to do about Japan's first "modern" economic crisis. His problems were inflation and a trade deficit large enough to threaten Japan's capacity to keep on buying critical imports from the West.

THE CHALLENGE TO A "CLOSED" SOCIETY

In 1854 Japan had been closed or all but closed to foreign influence for two centuries. After 1638, a small Dutch trading post on a tiny harbor island and an occasional licensed Chinese trader were the only legal sources of outside contact. Missionaries, originally welcomed in 1549, had been driven out; Christianity had been made a crime and many converts martyred; expatriate Japanese had been forbidden to come home; ships big enough to brave the open sea were not allowed to be constructed; and all travel from the islands had been stopped. The purpose of this isolation was to ward off any unsettling influence. The

Shoguns (barbarian-subduing generalissimos) of the noble House of Tokugawa were determined to preserve the hard-won central power and stability which they had given Japan since 1603, thereby putting an end to "centuries of anarchic division" [14, p. 7].

Nevertheless, Japan's "forbidding and forbidden coast" intrigued all trading nations, especially the Americans. Since her islands lay athwart their route to China, "They in particular hoped for open ports in Japan in which to refit their ships and replenish their stores" [14, p. 9]. Coal was especially needed by the new and inefficient steamships of the day, and in the 1840s Secretary of State Daniel Webster declared the rumored coal fields of Japan to be "a gift of Providence, deposited by the Creator of all things in the depths of the Japanese islands for the benefit of the human family" [12, pp. 22, 23].

Besides economic motives, missionary zeal and concern for shipwrecked sailors fueled US interest in opening Japan. After many peaceful efforts had failed, the US government finally commissioned Commodore Matthew C. Perry to enter Japanese waters with a squadron.

At home, Perry's mission was greeted with joy, one California paper even going so far as to enthuse, "Hurrah for the universal Yankee Nation, Commodore Perry, and the new prospective State of Japan" [12, p. 28]. In Tokyo, of course, the reaction was far different:

> Tokyo's reaction to Americans began with panic. Terrified families gathered their household goods and fled to the hills as news spread of a foreign invader. Four black ships had sailed into the Bay of Tokyo, two of them belching black smoke, the first steamships to visit Japan. The date was July 8, 1853. Commodore Matthew C. Perry had arrived to open Japan to the commerce and culture of the western world [12, p. 1].

Having communicated US demands, Perry sailed away, but promised to return the next year for an answer.

A DILEMMA FOR THE SHOGUN: 1853–1854

At a loss as to what he could do, the Shogun and his principal advisors spent several months in sounding out the opinions of the *daimyo* (vassals or territorial lords). The Shogun found the lords and their retainers split into two camps: one group demanded that Perry be kept out; the other disagreed, but only on tactics, not objectives. Pessimistic about success against Perry, the latter group favored "temporary concessions and a quick build-up of military forces" [12, p. 8].

Those who wanted to resist Perry were not entirely unready to do so. Having watched with alarm as the West started to carve up China in the early 1840s, the Shogun had ordered the daimyo to build coastal forts and outfit them with the cannon which Japan had long since copied from an old-style European design. So well was this order obeyed that the price of brass for cannon rose out of sight, whereupon one of the daimyo—with nothing but a translated Dutch book to help him—mastered both western-style iron technology and the engineering needed to cast iron cannon. Similarly, another daimyo managed to produce two bark-style vessels and a paddle-wheel vessel with nothing to help him except Dutch books on steam engines and ships. Still other daimyo had geared up to make mortars and howitzers out of iron produced by traditional methods [24, pp. 2–4]. By 1854, however, these efforts were only starting to bear fruit. Some daimyo hoped that mock wooden forts would be enough to scare Perry away, but this idea found limited favor. As one Japanese observer later put it, "There is no point in criticizing the mediocrity of lower officials. But what is to be done if even those who ride on golden saddles . . . who wear brocade and feast on meat, and call themselves 'high class'" propose such follies [23, p. 615]?

On his return, Perry brought nine warships "all equipped with big guns ready for firing" and so huge that their wake almost swamped the Japanese ships sent out to meet them. After hearing an eleven-gun salute and "marveling" at the discipline of the US sailors, Japan's negotiators agreed to sign a treaty. This met the needs of US sailors and ships, but not the needs of traders. As a stimulus to a future trade treaty, Perry left the Shogun gifts: a one-third sized model railroad and its track, a mile-long telegraph system, and—on request—side arms, a recipe for percussion caps, and a ship's launch with a howitzer [22, pp. 290, 291].

THE "UNEQUAL TREATIES": 1858–1865

The Shogun could present the concessions of 1854 as minor humanitarian moves. Not so a trade treaty, particularly inasmuch as Britain, Russia, France, and the Netherlands would demand any rights that might be granted to the United States. Yet, looking across the sea to mainland Asia, Japan's leaders saw how readily—and successfully—the West might back up its demands with force.

> Already, in 1842 [Manchu China] had lost the "opium war." This resulted in the Nanking Treaty whereby Hong Kong was ceded to England, and Shanghai and four other cities were permitted to be made open ports. In 1851, England seized Rangoon and used it as a base for the colonization of Burma. In 1857, the allied forces of England and France seized Manchu China's Canton, and in the following year they took Tientsin, forcing the signing of the Tientsin Treaty. Also, in 1858, England formally made India a colony by taking over direct government control. Then, in 1860, by declaring the Chinese counterattack to be a violation of the Tientsin Treaty the Allied English and French armies occupied Peking and forcibly exacted the Peking Treaty. Later on, the great European powers used these Tientsin and Peking Treaties as the basis of their semi-colonization of China. Then, by taking advantage of unequal treaties, the powers were able to have Tientsin, Hankow, and four other cities named as open ports. They also won the freedom to engage in Christian evangelization. England also won the concession of the Kowloon peninsula on the shore opposite Hong Kong. Furthermore, in the previous year (1859), France occupied Saigon, and in 1862 it made Cambodia a protectorate. Then in 1873, France attacked Tonkin and also converted this territory into one of its protectorates. In another region, Russia put pressure on Manchu China so that in 1858 the Aijun Treaty had to be signed. This allowed Russia to occupy the region north of the Amur River, while the area between the Ussuri River and the eastern sea coastline was to be mutually shared by China and Russia. But then, in 1859, Russia took over this common territory [21, pp. 12, 13].

Clearly it was fortunate for Japan that Europe was soon busy fighting in China and that the United States, still claiming to be nonimperialistic, was soon busy with a civil war. Even so, trade treaties could not be resisted. By 1858 the Shogun had been prevailed upon to sign treaties giving the five western powers the right to set up missions and to trade in certain ports. By 1865 the Shogun had also signed away the right to levy import duties of more than 5 percent *ad valorem* [14, pp. 8–10]. Since the West made no parallel concessions, these treaties became known as the "unequal treaties."

Whether Japan would face still more demands and perhaps be forced down the same route as China would depend on her own resources and behavior. These in turn were shaped by her heritage from the past.

JAPAN'S HERITAGE FROM THE PAST

Institutions and Aims

Before 1603, when the noble house of Tokugawa seized control, Japan had experienced centuries of intermittent warfare. The country was split into scores of territories, each ruled by a different clan. Each territory had its own government and laws, its own money, and its own army. One territorial lord challenged another for local supremacy, and when a lord was victorious he was instantly checked by an alliance of his neighbors. The emperor, while respected, held no real economic or military power.

When Ieyasu Tokugawa conquered Japan in 1603, his ambition was to structure the country in such a way as to preserve his family's rule forever. Besides isolating Japan, he confiscated the territories of many lords who had opposed him and gave these lands to his supporters. He seized all precious metals mines in Japan and reserved to his government the right to coin specie.

He forbade construction of bridges across major rivers, kept roads too narrow for the movement of armies, and established checkpoints at all major crossroads, fords, towns and mountain passes. Lords were forbidden to undertake military operations of any kind, and they were required to be in attendance at the Tokugawa stronghold of Edo (present-day Tokyo) every other year. When a lord was not in Edo, his family served as hostages there. Territorial lords were subject to surprise inspections by Tokugawa officials, and Tokugawa spies were everywhere. Lords continued to rule their own territories, however, within these restrictions.

Japan's population in the Tokugawa era was "stagnant" at about 30 million, since the mainly agricultural economy proved unable to support a larger number. The people were divided into four social classes. At the top—about 7 percent of the total—were the *samurai*, whose different ranks included all territorial lords, Tokugawa officials, and military men. Next were the peasants, about 80 percent of the population; third, laborers including various craftsmen. The last group were merchants and townsmen.

The samurai, who numbered roughly two million, composed the traditional military caste. Since not all samurai were needed as warriors during the era of Tokugawa peace, they had become increasingly involved in managing territorial enterprises, such as salt mines, and in government administration. Yet, suitable employment could not be found for all, and the samurai "constituted the major nonproductive class of the society" [11, pp. 541–543; *cf* 17, pp. 19–23]. Their support was provided either by land holdings of their own or by an allowance paid in rice by the lord to whom they owed allegiance. Under these circumstances, some members of this top class had sunk into poverty, and some were heavily in debt to rich merchants.

Peasants, who numbered roughly 24 million, owed allegiance to their lords. They paid taxes to their lords in kind, usually 30 to 50 percent of their rice crop. Although peasants were the second highest class, their life was not easy, as attested by the frequency of peasant uprisings or "smashings" and also because famine, infanticide, and abortion played a role in keeping the population steady. In addition, peasants were subject to numerous restrictions. For example, they were not allowed "to move, to change professions, to sell arable land, to partition holdings into parcels smaller than a certain minimum, or to change their crops at will" [11, pp. 541–543]. Restrictions touched even their daily life. They were, for example, "ordered not to eat much rice and never to use silk, never to purchase tea and sake, never to live in a luxurious home" [11, pp. 541–543].

On the other hand, Japan's peasants were not serfs. Although they could mortgage their fields and sink to tenant farmer status, they had property rights to their land. Nor was the peasants' output limited to crops, for they produced rice wine, tea, and silk. In addition, merchants sometimes organized peasant households to produce umbrellas, paper lanterns, and cotton yarn. Peasants received cash for these goods, and they purchased fish, salt, and cloth on the market.

Although merchants were looked down upon, they gradually became wealthy through trade and finance and by acting as middlemen between the peasants who produced the goods and samurai who consumed them. Merchant families developed close ties with the territorial lords for whom they marketed the excess rice that had been collected as taxes. Merchants also financed peasant purchases of seeds and samurai purchases of luxuries, charging high interest rates for this service.

Despite tolls and other restrictions that were imposed on trade, national markets developed in indigo, sugar, paper, and rice. The national road system, although narrow, was very extensive and well-traveled. The concentration of administration in the castle towns of the territorial lords fostered rapid urbanization. Owing to the requirement that the lords or their families be constantly at the seat of government, Edo grew especially rapidly, its population sometimes reaching 1.3 million. Such concentrations of population allowed merchants to organize large-scale production of rice wine, earthenware, and sugar. The need for credit by both peasants and samurai stimulated the growth of financial markets, and Japanese merchants accordingly developed sophisticated credit instruments. Finally, education, always respected by all classes, was fairly widespread: an estimated 40 percent of the boys and 15 percent of the girls were in some kind of school in the late Tokugawa period.

By 1854 cracks had started to appear in the Tokugawa system of control. Peasants had little incentive to be productive since they were forbidden to buy luxuries and taxes were high. Merchants contented themselves with monopoly profits and high interest rates to peasants and samurai, and did little to promote productive investment. Craftsmen operated within the confines of restrictive guilds. Many samurai borrowed in times of need and remained in debt. The treasuries of the territorial lords were depleted by natural disasters, the construction of public works ordered by the Shogun, and the suppression of increasingly frequent peasant uprising [14, p. 7ff.]. The house of Tokugawa itself was in weak financial condition, owing in part to its top-heavy bureaucracy and in part to poor money management.

As a result of the growing financial weakness of the Shogun and the Shogun's efforts to keep the territorial lords weak and poor, many samurai were critical of the Tokugawa. Aware of the growing strength of the West and of western encroachments in

Asia, many samurai also believed that the Tokugawa were keeping Japan militarily weak and incapable of resistance [11, pp. 541–543; 16, pp. 106–107].

Summing up the institutions of Tokugawa times, western observers reached different conclusions. According to one view, Japan's old order constituted "one of the most conscious attempts in history to freeze society in a rigid hierarchical mold" [10, p. 15]. According to another, the prevailing opinion that Japan "stagnated" under the Shoguns is quite wrong. Rather, "Tokugawa seclusion allowed Japan, slowly and peacefully, to reach a base point from which it could leap into industrialization" [15, p. 86].

Values and Beliefs

A main cementing force in traditional Japan was its values and beliefs. The family, hierarchical but supportive, was the basic institution on which other institutions were modeled. As in the feudal West, vows of loyalty bound the samurai to his daimyo and the daimyo to the Shogun.

Elaborating on loyalty, traditional Japan stressed other cognate virtues and duties which found their expression in the terms *giri* and *on* and in *Bushido*, the "Code of the Warrior." *Giri* might be defined as a duty of open-ended reciprocal benevolence within any relationship. *On* implied benevolence within a relationship between unequal individuals. Significantly, the obligation lay upon superiors as well as inferiors: it was obligation down as well as up. The code of *Bushido*, as modified by Confucianism, stressed absolute loyalty to one's lord and unswerving filial piety. It also extolled scholarship and learning. Through an extension of its influence, the code of Bushido not only served the samurai class, it also provided a model by which artisans, farmers, and merchants structured the relationship between master and apprentice or master and servant [26, pp. 2-5].

In addition to giri, on, and Bushido, the *Chu Hsi* school of the Confucian religion helped to shape the value system of Japan. This belief, adapted from China, was favored by the Shoguns over native *Shintoism* (originally, mainly awe of nature), largely because many of its tenets helped to make the people easy to rule [26, pp. 2-5]. As described by Edwin O. Reischauer, Confucianism aimed, not at creating a "universal ethic . . . which equates all individuals" but rather at building "a more perfect society" through the "proper regulation" of particular relationships, for example, those between ruler and ruled, husband and wife, father and son. "Here," he added, "is the fundamental ethical difference between the Far East and Europe." In the East "There is no universal ethic" [14, pp. 135, 136]. Reprinted by permission of Harvard University Press.

Looking at this absence of a "universal ethic," Michael Y. Yoshino spelled out some of its implications, especially for social control versus individualism.

> Obviously, the traditional Japanese society must have had a substitute for a universal code of ethics or religious sanctions. The concept of shame was the substitute. Shame enforced the very particularistic ethical code and prompted one to rigid adherence to specific rules of conduct.
>
> . . . Shame usually had two related aspects: personal shame—the disapproval of the society heaped upon oneself and "we-group" shame—dishonor to one's collectivity and the accompanying fear of rejection by the group. The latter was particularly powerful because of the great importance attached to collectivity in traditional Japan. . . .
>
> Traditional Japan has often been characterized as a collectivity-oriented society. In fact, the individual hardly existed in it as a distinct entity. In every aspect of life, he

was tightly bound to a group and had virtually no individual freedom. Indeed, the basic political, economic, and social unit in traditional Japan was the collectivity rather than the individual. . . . The most important criterion for judging actions and behavior was whether they were right and best for the group [26, pp. 9-11].

THE RESTORATION OF THE EMPEROR: 1868–1869

When he signed the unequal treaties, the Shogun knew he lacked the strength to expel the "barbarians" from the West. He also knew, however, that expulsion was by far the more popular course. Among its proponents were the strong, so-called "outside" lords, descendants of the 17th century vassals who had pledged themselves to the Tokugawa only after their resistance had been crushed. These traditionally least loyal lords controlled some of the largest domains, the farthest from Tokyo, and the most involved in foreign trade and western knowledge. Thus, these lords had been in the vanguard of rearming. What was more, the outside lords had a rallying point in the person of the emperor of Japan. Unlike the Shogun, the emperor could not be blamed for the opening of Japan, since his ancestors had been shorn of power in 1192 A.D. "What is the use of a 'Barbarian-subduing generalissimo,'" asked these critics (referring to the Shogun's full title), "if he cannot subdue the barbarians?"

Imperial Britain and France knew of the rift between the emperor's party and the Shogun, and, although busy elsewhere, each sought to make allies of one side or the other. Under these circumstances, the Shogun, especially, might have been tempted to make western help decisive, but he did not. He concentrated instead on acquiring western-style weapons and ships and even a shipyard modeled on the big French shipyard at Toulon. The Shogun also tried to prevent disruptive attacks by the hostile outside lords on westerners already in Japan. When such attacks did occur, the West responded not only by reducing the offending stronghold to rubble but also by demanding large indemnities which the Shogun had to pay.

The Shogun's growing financial weakness and his concessions to the West spurred the emperor's supporters into action. Early in 1868, a coup was engineered under the leadership of Takamori Saigo of Satsuma. A council of those favorable to the coup was summoned, and a decree was approved stripping the Shogun of his lands and office. A decision was also taken to return formal authority to the emperor.

When the Shogun's adherents responded violently and the fighting threatened to spread, the Shogun vacillated: he wished to save Japan from civil war, but he also wished to preserve his own leadership. With his country at risk and his treasury depleted, he hit upon a plan in 1869. Formally, at least, he would return his mandate to the emperor, for reasons he declared to be as follows:

> Now that foreign intercourse becomes daily more extensive, unless the government is directed from one central authority, the foundations of the state will fall to pieces. If, however, the old order of things be changed, and the administrative authority be restored to the Imperial Court, and if national deliberations be conducted on an extensive scale, and the Imperial decision be secured, and if the empire be supported by the efforts of the whole people, then the empire will be able to maintain its rank and dignity among the nations of the earth [13, p. 20].

In giving up his formal authority, the Shogun reportedly expected to retain strong *de facto* power but found himself excluded by the outside lords who had backed the emperor and now meant to rule. Fighting then continued between the Shogun's and the emperor's parties, but the former were quickly defeated.

At first the Shogun's followers could not be reconciled to seeing the emperor move into the Shogun's Tokyo palace. According to a contemporary, "The most ardent" of the Shogun's "loyal partisans . . . would not even eat a piece of cake if it came from Tokyo," or lie in bed at night "with their heads pointing to the capital," [23, pp. 633–635]. After a year or so, however, these dissidents returned to the seat of government where they joined the throng of office seekers, "all swarming together like insects around some fragrant food" [23, pp. 633–635].

MEIJI JAPAN: "RICH COUNTRY, STRONG ARMY"

With the Shogun out of the way and the outer lords in power, Japan's new leaders quietly dropped their stated commitment to expelling the barbarian and agreed that their opened country should stay open. In fact, the young emperor[1] was given the name *"Meiji"* meaning "enlightened rule," and was made to promise in his Charter Oath that "intellect and learning should be sought throughout the world in order to establish the foundation of the empire" [10, p. 9].

At the same time, a new slogan or motto was adopted: "Rich country, strong army." The revolution in goals thus implied has been spelled out as follows by Dr. Reischauer:

---

[1] According to rumor, the Emperor Meiji's father had been assassinated in order that the emperor's advisors would have a young and maleable person to advise.

The securing of military equality with the Occident was, of course, the clearest and most understandable objective of Japan's new leaders, because Japan's helplessness in the face of Western naval power had been made all too clear to them. They were all obsessed with the fear that Japan, too, might go down the road toward colonialism already being followed by so many other Asiatic peoples. But they did not simply set their sights at military reform. With surprising perspicacity, they saw that military strength in turn depended upon industrial power, technical knowledge, and administrative efficiency and that it would not be enough merely to acquire the new Western weapons. Instead they embarked upon a broad and intensive program of economic, political and even social reform, such as the world has rarely seen [14, pp. 10, 11]. Reprinted by permission of Harvard University Press.

At first it was questionable whether all elements in Japan would stay in line behind this rallying cry. It led to sacrifice and thus to unrest. Even among the Meiji themselves, the influential Saigo saw its two objectives as over-ambitious and thus as conflicting. For example, when the cabinet was voting to build railroads, he warned his colleagues not to go ahead.

If in our envy of the greatness of foreign nations, we rush ahead without regard to the limitations of our own strength, we will end by exhausting ourselves without accomplishing anything. We must immediately dismiss the matter of constructing steam railways and concentrate on increasing our military strength [20, p. 42].

GOVERNMENT AS A CHANGE AGENT

With ambitious goals like "strong army, rich country," Japan would need change agents. As in many developing countries,

government rather than private enterprise played the major role, at least in the opening Meiji years. An economic historian from Harvard University, Henry Rosovsky, suggests the following explanation:

Comparative economic history tells us that countries beginning industrialization in a setting of relative backwardness require leadership and strong action to get started. More or less spontaneous modern economic growth may have been the case in Great Britain, but it is difficult to find elsewhere. Government, and to a greater or lesser degree private or semi-private banks, supplied the necessary push in Prussia and Russia. This alone would warrant a close look at what the government was doing in Japan, but the situation goes deeper than that. The genesis of Japanese industrialization naturally coincides with events which affected other aspects of society: a new political system, a new class structure, and participation in international affairs. Especially during the years of transition, when changes came in rapid succession, the private sector—individuals without a policy—played a less active role. . . . The main impetus for action had to come from the government. None of this means that in viewing a century of modern economic growth one should ascribe all success to government and a minor and inactive role to the private sector. It does mean, however, that in the very early stages of growth government performed the more important tasks [16, p. 14, 15].

CHANGING GOVERNMENT INSTITUTIONS

With the end of the Shogunate, Japan's so-called "dual" system of government was replaced with a single central authority: the emperor and his advisors. To help achieve a transfer of public loyalty, the emperor's advisors even went so far as to restore the nation's ancient traditional religion, Shintoism, which preached the emperor's divinity along with love of nature. This move was made without undermining prevailing Confucian values and beliefs, since Shintoism had become infused with Confucian ideas. The change, however, warranted confiscation of Buddhist temples and other wealth, thus easing for the moment the new central government's revenue problem.

Although presented as divine, Japan's emperor was not made an absolute monarch. Rather, he acted with consent of his advisors, who ruled Japan as a sort of cabinet. These leaders were drawn from among the outside lords or more commonly from among the lords' more talented samurai. Dominant among them were members of the great outside domains of Satsuma, Chosu, Hizen, and Tosa. Reflecting the primacy of the first two, the government of early Meiji Japan soon came to be known as the "Sat-Cho" government [4, pp. 99-110; 18, pp. 26-70 *passim*; 29, pp. 111-117].

Changing the form of the central government was not a major problem for the Meiji elite. A much more difficult question was changing central-local relationships. For as long as the lords had the right to levy taxes, the new central government would remain impoverished and weak.

By force of argument, threat, and example, between 1868 and 1871 Japan's new leaders gained agreements from all the other feudal lords for a major change in the old system. The lords transferred their taxing power and other rights to the central government in return for a yearly money allowance payable from the central treasury. This allowance was to be split among all the classes who had formerly lived off the rice tax, and it was to be proportional to former income. This stipend, while it lasted, was a heavy drain. From 1872 to 1876, lords and samurai, who constituted only 6 to 7 percent of the population, received payments

amounting to more than 34 percent of total current expenditures by central and local governments combined [16, p. 116].

Once the pension system was established, the central government moved forward on a plan to restructure central-local government relations. The French prefectural system was chosen as a model, and Japan emerged with its local governments playing a relatively minor role. Speaking of the early political setup, Dr. Reischauer saw it as undemocratic: western institutions, he said, had been grafted onto eastern autocracy, not so much to moderate the latter as to make it more efficient. "The Occident provided the rulers of Japan with better tools than they had ever known before to enforce abject obedience, and, more important, to inculcate blind loyalty" [14, pp. 186-187]. Reprinted by permission of Harvard University Press.

The new government was not only powerful but also entrenched. There was no mechanism by which it could be changed or removed. The Meiji elite divided up spheres of authority in the government and gave their supporters government positions. They controlled the emperor and his decisions and the power to make political appointments. There was no constitution, no elections, and—so far—no political parties. The only source of opposition to the government was within it. Cabinet members did not always agree on the proper course of action.

Virtually everyone was thus excluded from a voice in the government: landholders and farmers, businessmen, converts to western liberalism, and ex-samurai. Yet, early in the Restoration era, the emperor in his Charter Oath had promised that a national "assembly" would be created and all decisions reached "by discussion." Critics seized upon this promise and agitated for a more representative government. The Meiji elite moved to still this discontent and, at the same time, to delay fundamental changes. Accordingly, the emperor announced in 1881 (thirteen years after the fall of the Shogun) that a lengthy study would be made to design a constitution for Japan.

CHANGING THE SOCIAL ORDER

With a new relationship between the central government and the domains, feudalism was partly dismantled. How much farther the Meiji elite would go was not easy to predict. On the one hand they were beneficiaries of the feudal system; on the other, as pointed out by Henry Rosovsky:

> [i]t must have been obvious soon after the Restoration that this class structure was a major obstacle to modern growth. It was too rigid and froze society into an agricultural mold; it was a wasteful arrangement in that the best educated and most able section of the population was largely underemployed [16, p. 114].

In any event, the Meiji leaders decided to dismantle the rest of feudalism, and by 1873 the new government had forced through major changes. As a result, three new classes emerged. At the top was a small open-ended nobility into which successful businessmen, statesmen, and military leaders could aspire to make their way. Next came the class of ex-samurai, but membership in this no longer conferred any special privilege, only a courtesy title. All the rest of the people comprised the third class.

Other changes gave meaning to this new class structure: restrictions on movement by farmers, craftsmen, and city dwellers were ended. Individuals were allowed to buy or sell land. Members of the feudal ruling classes were freed to participate legally in such formerly forbidden activities

as agriculture, commerce, and industry. Restrictive guilds were dissolved and long-term apprenticeship contracts and other forms of servitude were abolished. Abridgement of special privileges extended even to the symbolic level, as evidenced by a ban placed on the wearing of swords. This ban did away with the main status symbol of the old warrior caste, and little imagination was needed to realize the impact of such a deprivation. Thus, a "simple listing" of the decrees doing away with feudalism "does not do justice to the resentment, conflict, and confusion" they must have engendered [1, p. 31; 16, pp. 114, 115].

REVAMPING THE MILITARY

If the new government was to maintain its power, it could not allow its military strength to depend on the arms of the samurai, whose loyalty had always been with their clans. Thus, an edict of 1872 inaugurated universal military service. "Samurai are not the samurai of old," the edict stated, "and commoners are not the commoners of the past. They are all equally subjects of the Imperial nation and there should be no difference in their service of gratitude to the country" [6, pp. 29, 134].

It was not long before the new army was tried in combat. In 1874 an expeditionary force was prepared to strike against Formosa (Taiwan) where natives had massacred shipwrecked Japanese. Despite objections by western powers and a postponement of the expedition by the central government, the local commander set sail. His pretext: morale was pitched so high that the soldiers were uncontrollable. The expeditionary force quickly conquered the island and made China pay ¥500,000 to get it back. The prestige of the new government was greatly enhanced, and the government was emboldened to wrest the

Ryukyu Islands from China, a deed accomplished by 1879 [6, pp. 141–144].

INTRODUCING WESTERN TECHNOLOGY

Besides abolishing the old political and social order at high emotional and financial cost, the Meiji leaders moved quickly toward their goal of introducing western technology. Japanese were sent to study abroad and foreign specialists were brought to Japan. Even ordinary trade in goods played a part in introducing western knowledge. In 1887, for example, half the value of Japan's total imports was made up of textiles, but "Much of the remainder was virtually a sample list of western factory goods. . . . These cargoes were made up of things, but they were also transmitters of ideas" [10, p. 324].

To one high Meiji government leader, foreign travel seemed so important that he originated a broad travel program. Generous subsidies for study abroad were granted to commoners as well as to samurai. Japanese students "by the score" took advantage of this opportunity, and as early as 1872, 380 of them were in foreign universities [10, pp. 12, 510]. Businessmen and officials also made frequent visits to the West. Thus, in 1871, "almost the entire Meiji government" sailed to Europe and the United States in order to study public finance, insurance, the postal service, factories, factory regulation, etc. The "objective of all this" was to see how all these things could be "applied and implemented" in their own country [7, pp. 122, 123].

More important than foreign travel was the import into Japan of foreign technical experts and teachers. Here again government took the lead. For example, between 1870 and 1885 the newly-formed Ministry of In-

dustry employed over 500 foreign engineers and technical instructors, of whom almost four-fifths were British. Railways received the largest contingent, 256, followed by machine shops with 81 and mining with 76. Before 1880 the government also imported 34 experts on agriculture, and a partial list of foreign instructors employed by the government before 1900 numbered 151 names. Private schools and private industry also employed some foreigners, but these were few in number except in shipping, where most of the cost was actually footed by the government via heavy subsidies [7, pp. 127–131].

Total expenditures for all foreign experts is unknown, but costs ran high; for example, 130 instructors and technicians at Tokyo's Technical University cost the Ministry of Industry ¥341,000 (about $300,000), or over half its budget in 1879. Such high salaries hurt both government finances and the feelings of domestic personnel. "The most important function of the foreigners, therefore, was to make themselves superfluous as quickly as possible" [7, p. 122].

With a view to freeing Japan from her galling and expensive dependence on outsiders, the Meiji leaders were quick to sponsor local technical training. Thus, from 1871 to 1883 the central government established two new technical schools at the university level, a number of technical training programs, schools of navigation and marine engineering, a school of banking and finance (closed in 1893), a school of business patterned on American models, and three agricultural schools. Of the latter, one, headed by an American, was entrusted with the task of pioneering agricultural development in Hokkaido, the northernmost and most recently settled of the four main islands of Japan.

Only in commercial training did the central government fail to take the lead, "probably because the officials felt that trade wasn't really difficult to learn and that instruction in it could be left in private hands." Thus, of seven commercial colleges established in Japan by 1883, "all but one was private or prefectural" [7, pp. 128, 129].

CHANGING SCHOOLS AND EDUCATION

Going beyond technology, the Meiji rulers also moved in other areas of education. Under their leadership, the year 1872 saw a relatively early commitment to a four-year system of free, compulsory schools [10, p. 511].[2] The curriculum was radically changed from Tokugawa times, when the emphasis had been on classic Chinese language and the favored Chu Hsi School of Confucianism, which put a special stress on loyalty. At least temporarily, this orientation was replaced by a practical orientation. The prime minister himself issued the directive creating the change, and he obviously had great expectations.

> There is no other way for men to elevate themselves, to manage their property, to be prosperous in their affairs, and so to succeed in life than by disciplining themselves, giving heed to wisdom and enlarging their talents. But without schooling one can do none of these things. . . . Therefore, learning can be called the source of the riches of self-reliance, and hence every man should have schooling. . . . While higher education should be left to individual ability, still if little children—boys and girls alike—do not go to primary school, their parents are making a mistake [21, pp. 166, 167].

---

[2] Not until 1876 was attendance at school made compulsory for children up to twelve in England, and not until 1890 was elementary education made generally available at public expense.

IMPROVING COMMUNICATIONS AND TRANSPORT

A system of communications to link regional garrisons and to permit rapid mobilization was essential for national defense. The government's top priority, after military industry, was the rapid extension of a telegraph network throughout Japan. Within fifteen years of the fall of the Shogun, Japan had a national telegraph system over 2000 miles in length [31, pp. 477, 478].

Merchant Shipping

Following the opening of Japan to trade, most Japanese coastal traffic was carried by western companies in western ships, which were larger and faster than their Japanese counterparts. This arrangement posed a threat to the Japanese economy in case of war with a western power; it also meant that foreign companies were being paid to move Japanese goods. Moreover, Japanese overseas military operations, already on the drawing board, required extensive shipping for supplies and troop transport. Western companies could not be relied upon for such operations. A strong domestic merchant marine was therefore of primary importance to the Meiji elite.

Circumstances thus provided the perfect opportunity for a bold and daring shipping entrepreneur with excellent government contacts, Yataro Iwasaki. He started his company in 1870 by leasing three steamers from a territorial lord, buying them the next year. In a very short time, owing to Iwasaki's management ability and generous government support, his firm, the Mitsubishi Company, came to dominate the Japanese shipping industry.

In 1874, when Japan invaded Taiwan, the government purchased thirteen steamers to facilitate transport and supply, and entrusted them to Mitsubishi. These steamers were later given to the company for nothing. In 1875 Iwasaki forced a rival firm out of business and took over its eighteen steamers. When Mitsubishi entered into keen competition with the Taiheiyo Kisen Kaisha, the government bought the latter's steamers for over ¥800,000[3] and gave them to Iwasaki.

During the samurai rebellion in 1877, the government advanced $700,000 to Mitsubishi to purchase steamers and expand its business, since Mitsubishi was strained to the limit in transporting and supplying government troops. During the 1870s the government gave Mitsubishi, under various names, ¥8 million of which half was a subsidy and half was a loan repayable in ten to fifteen years, almost without interest. The Mitsubishi Company thus became a near-monopoly in this period.

Later, when Mitsubishi's monopolistic operations aroused strong public resentment, the government helped to found a rival firm in 1882. Keen competition arose between this company and Mitsubishi. By 1885 the competition reached extremes, and the economy class fare from Yokohama to Kobe, which had been ¥5.5, dropped to less than one yen. The government-backed shipping firm lost nearly ¥700,000 in six months.

The government promptly stepped in and encouraged Iwasaki to buy up the majority of the rival firm's stock. The merged firm which resulted from this buyout was protected by the government by an 8 percent

dividend guarantee for fifteen years [19, pp. 373–378].

The opponents in the price war were animated not just by self-interest but by different views of what constituted a sound political economy and a viable Japanese "champion" in the competitive race with foreign shipping. As Johannes Hirschmeier put it:

> In the last analysis, this fight was between two opposing principles: [Iwasaki's rivals] believed in an economic order ruled by cooperation, with joint-stock companies and fair competition. Iwasaki believed that the strong should rule and that monopoly was a good thing because private profits would eventually also benefit the nation; what was good for Mitsubishi was bound to be good for Japan [7, p. 224].

The Mitsubishi Company expanded its operations into related enterprises: a subsidized marine academy; a "documentary bill company" whose customers "were obliged to ship their goods in Mitsubishi bottoms, to insure them with a Mitsubishi Maritime Insurance Company, and to store their freight in Mitsubishi godowns"; a shipyard, purchased cheap from the government, into which ¥6 million were poured within a few years to make it the nation's most efficient; plus large interests in coal mining [1, p. 91; 7, pp. 233, 234]. Summing up Iwasaki's strenuous career, Dr. Hirschmeier wrote

> Iwasaki was probably the boldest of all Meiji entrepreneurs. On his deathbed in 1885 he claimed before his friends that he was "The Man of the Far East" . . . His quest for power and greatness, combined with samurai patriotism, are reflected in his Mitsubishi family rule: "Do not take up small projects, engage only in large enterprises. Once you begin something, see to it that it becomes a success. Do not engage in speculation. Do business with a patriotic attitude" [7, p. 224].

---

[3] The yen averaged $1.02 in 1874, declined to $0.961 in 1877, and to $0.887 in 1879. Hit by the drop in world prices for silver, it continued to decline irregularly until 1896, when its value was pegged at US $0.496.

Railroads

Less important than the merchant marine was rail transportation. Japan's cities were virtually all seaports or located near the sea, and the inland areas were mountainous. Nevertheless, as part of a long-range plan to build a national rail net for troop mobilization and movement of goods, the Japanese soon became involved in building railroads.

Since railroads were capital-intensive, requiring advanced technology and massive sums in start-up costs, no private investors were willing to become involved at first. The government, therefore, built two short stretches of railroad linking Japan's two largest cities with their seaports (Tokyo with Yokohama and Kyoto with Osaka). Thereafter railroad building lagged. What lines were built served primarily to supplement existing shipping lines—linking the Sea of Japan, Lake Biwa, and the Pacific, for example. As late as 1882 the total Japanese rail "network" amounted to only 174 miles, all government-owned [1, p. 41; 7, pp. 136-141; 15, p. 25].

BUILDING AN INDUSTRIAL BASE: STATE CAPITALISM

With the restoration of the emperor, the new government of Japan inherited a number of modern enterprises which had been set up by the Shogun and the territorial lords. These included several cotton-spinning mills, precious metals mines, coal mines, and a number of munitions factories and shipyards [9, p. 31; 19, pp. 306, 307, 347-348, 351, 352; 28, p. 14].

Since national defense was the primary concern, the new government first reorganized the armaments works. By 1877 all of

these had been consolidated into two large arsenals and two large shipyards. Each was a complex of many factories which produced more than just weapons. In 1875, for example, the Tokyo Armaments Works had an arms plant, a smithy, a saddle plant, a carpenters' shop, an iron puddling plant, a foundry, and a gunpowder plant. While the government placed top priority on achieving independence from foreign sources of munitions, military industry also produced quantities of civilian goods [19, pp. 308-315, 327].

Although military industry grew slowly because of its capital-intensive nature, the lack of skilled workers, and the need to keep up with rapid western technological advances, Japanese military plants chalked up an impressive record. Thus, in 1870 the Yokosuka Navy Shipyard advertised that it could repair any kind of naval craft in the country. In 1880 the first Japanese-built iron warship was launched, and in 1881 the first Japanese ship made with a Japanese engine was completed. The army also performed impressively. By 1886 every Japanese division was equipped with Japanese-made rifles and artillery [19, pp. 304, 308, 313-314, 327-329].

Besides its efforts in the military area, the government turned its attention to two industries critical to the balance of trade: silk reeling and cotton spinning. State intervention in silk reeling was designed to support rather than supplant flourishing private investment and production. Since this industry was labor-intensive and required little capital investment or managerial skill, major intervention was not needed. Even so, the state established three large mills to demonstrate advanced techniques and to train workers who were then sent to new private mills as instructors. More importantly, the government took steps to insure that all reeled silk was of the uniform quality required in export markets. Thus, it licensed all silkworm egg raisers, assisted the formation of trade associations devoted to improving silk quality, supported the establishment of reliable testing and conditioning facilities in the ports, and encouraged the concentration of ownership in both egg-raising and silk-reeling production. The government's impact was therefore important, even though government-owned mills in 1879 constituted less than one percent of all silk-reeling mills [1, pp. 69–70; 30, p. 395; 32, pp. 303–304; 33, pp. 2–38].

State intervention in cotton spinning was motivated by the desire to substitute local production for imports. Since Japan's cotton was inferior in quality and her hand-spinning process was relatively costly, local production could not compete with a flood of British goods. When no private investors appeared right away to modernize this capital-intensive and relatively demanding industry, the government floated a ¥10 million loan, bought equipment and set up thirteen small spinning mills of about 2,000 spindles each. These mills were put into private hands but made no headway owing to their relatively small size (the average British mill had 10,000 spindles), poor location, and high labor costs [27, pp. 1–6]. It was not until 1883 that the first competitive Japanese cotton spinning plant was set up (by Eiichi Shibusawa) to become the precursor of a major industry.

Other government initiatives included re-equipping major precious metals mines and many coal mines, plus creating at least one model plant in several industries. The government built one glass plant, one cement plant, one brick plant, one agricultural development station, and even one sugar refinery for making sugar out of Japanese beets. Although these ventures lost money and some had to be discontinued, the Japanese government showed that it was aggressively attempting to introduce modern industries into the economy [20, pp. 46–55, 59–65; 21, pp. 231–234].

Besides producing selected products, government plants helped to supply examples of mechanization and large scale. Thus, in 1881 government mines numbered only six out of a total of about 2000, yet they produced 90 percent of the silver and gold for the year, 41 percent of the lead, 23 percent of the iron, and 6 percent of the copper. The large government machinery plant employed 531 people in 1881, at a time when most of Japan's enterprises were still home workshops of fewer than five people [20, pp. 46, 47, 55].

As for the accomplishments of these enterprises, these were to be measured not in profits but rather in models provided, in start-up difficulties overcome, and in employment opportunities made available to the impoverished but capable and often restive samurai. According to one of the earlier analysts, Thomas C. Smith, the government's achievement could be summarized as follows:

> What did government enterprise accomplish between 1868 and 1880? Quantitatively, not much: a score of so of modern factories, a few mines, a telegraph system, less than a hundred miles of railway. On the other hand, new and difficult ground had been broken: managers and engineers had been developed, a small but growing industrial labor force trained, new markets found; perhaps most important, going enterprises had been developed to serve as a base for further industrial growth.

It may be argued that this growth would have come without government enterprise, and that by far the most important achievement of the first fifteen years of the Meiji period was the creation of an institutional environment favorable to economic development. No one would deny the importance of this achievement, but it is doubtful that it would have brought the rapid development it did after 1880 without the experience, organization, and plant contributed by more than a decade of government enterprise. And the speed of development was crucial; for the traditional economy was already failing fast under the destructive impact of foreign trade, threatening prolonged social and political instability. Had it given way, economic development would almost certainly have been delayed or arrested—with political consequences we may surmise from modern Chinese history [20, p. 103].

More briefly, another historian concludes, "In spite of business failures among the early state enterprises, we might describe this episode as a glorious defeat of a reconnaissance force, which eventually led to victory in war" [8, pp. 171, 172].

DEVELOPING FINANCIAL INSTITUTIONS

Creating enterprises, paying samurai pensions, building telegraph systems and railroads, spreading education, bringing in technical knowledge, importing strategic arms and other products were all costly policies for the Meiji leaders to pursue. Thus, immediate financial needs, in combination with the long-term goal of becoming a strong modern nation, led the Meiji to turn their attention to currency, fiscal policy, and banking.

Currency Reform

From Tokugawa times, the Meiji had inherited a variety of coins—more or less debased—plus more than 1600 different kinds of notes issued by the Shogun and the daimyo. An early objective, therefore, was to create a single national currency, including notes that would be "convertible" into precious metals, preferably gold.

The government decided in 1871 to standardize the currency, but the goal of making all paper currency convertible was not accomplished so easily. In fact, before they got nationwide taxing power, the Meiji themselves resorted to the printing press for money. Thus, by 1873 they already had ¥88.3 million of nonconvertible paper notes outstanding. After small additions, this figure stood at ¥106.9 million in 1876 [16, p. 126].

Luckily for the Meiji leaders, however, no significant inflation had so far resulted. Western commentators, noting this outcome, wondered why. Perhaps the reason lay in the rising need for currency of any sort as Japan increasingly replaced rice with money as her medium of exchange. Perhaps, less tangibly, the reason lay only in the "immaturity of the capitalistic milieu in Japan" [1, p. 41; 16, p. 130].

Fiscal Policy

Beyond getting hold of the taxing power, which they did in 1871, the Meiji were interested in making tax reforms. One of these was to simplify taxes. Thus, they cut the number of types from nearly 1600 to 74. Another reform was to put the major tax on land on a money basis rather than on a rice basis and to stabilize the income from this source by basing the tax on the value of the land instead of on the fluctuating value of the harvest. In pursuit of this objective, the land was valued at a level such that a 3 percent tax rate would yield approximately the same revenue as the old rice tax had produced. Landholders objected so strongly, however, that a rate reduction to 2.5 percent was promised for 1879 [10, pp. 98, 521–523].

Although the land tax was changed in form, it still remained the principal tax.

Thus, from 1877 through 1880 the land tax accounted for an annual average of ¥41.1 million out of ¥56.1 million total, or 74 percent of all revenues [16, p. 130].

Banking System

To issue Japanese currency—whether convertible or not—as well as to accommodate business needs, the Meiji wanted banks. This western import came in two types. First, there might be a single central bank of issue (which could also perform other central bank functions) as in the British model.[4] Second, there might be a number of so-called "national" banks, all of which were authorized to issue notes as in the US model.[5] In the face of some internal dissent, the Meiji adopted the US pattern. Any institution meeting the requirements of the Bank Act of 1872 was authorized to issue notes. These requirements included raising capital, 40 percent of which must be specie while up to 60 percent might be the government's nonconvertible notes. On buying up the latter and turning them in to the state, the bank was to receive bonds in return, and it could issue notes against these bonds—an activity that was expected to be profitable. The specie in the bank's capital

was to serve as a reserve to make the notes convertible.

Had this scheme worked as planned, the government's nonconvertible notes would all have been recalled and a convertible currency established. But it did not work. Since a bank operating under this system in Japan's current environment soon saw all its specie disappear, only four banks were founded under the Banking Act of 1872 [2, p. 6].

Under these circumstances the Meiji decided in 1876 that the banking act must be amended. Amendment, however, became one facet of a dual-purpose plan that aimed not only to create more banks but also to end the great yearly drain on government resources involved in making feudal pension payments. The scheme called for capitalizing the pension obligations by means of a ¥172.9 million bond issue (the bonds to be divided among the pensioners in lieu of future annual payments) and granting permission for recipients to use these bonds as banking capital, against which notes could be issued—this time, nonconvertible notes—up to a total of ¥34 million.

In part, this scheme worked as hoped, for new banks quickly sprang up, 153 of them by 1879. In part the scheme did not work as hoped because it helped to fuel a samurai rebellion.

---

[4] As summed up by a Bank of England official, a modern central bank should:

. . . have the sole right of note issue; should serve the needs of commercial banks and other financial institutions; should be the principal fiscal agent of its government; should have the main responsibility for the maintenance of the gold and foreign-exchange reserves of the nation; and should have principal responsibility for the control of the volume and use of money in the interests of economic stability and growth [5, p. 1].

[5] Dating back only to 1863–1864, the US model was the brainchild of a government that wanted banks to help finance the Civil War and that, like the Meiji, expected banks to help redeem the paper money (greenbacks) which the government had issued in its emergency.

DISSENSION AND REVOLT: THE SATSUMA REBELLION OF 1877

Even before their controversial commutation of the feudal pensions in connection with the Banking Act of 1876, the Meiji leaders ran into opposition. Thus, within the first ten years there were over 200 local peasant uprisings or "smashings"—"more by far than in any decade of the Tokugawa era" [20, p. 30]. There were also three samurai revolts. Commutation of the pensions helped cause a fourth, the Satsuma Rebellion of 1877. Another motive was dissension over the cautious foreign policy adopted, in the face of provocations by Taiwan and Korea, by the then-dominant Meiji clique.

Although the Satsuma Rebellion was by far the most serious threat to date, it was decisively put down within months. Victory proved that Japan's new army of largely peasant conscripts was able to outfight the old warrior class. The effort proved expensive, however. To pay for it the state had to issue ¥27 million of added paper money and to borrow ¥15 million paper from a bank [16, p. 127].

DOMESTIC INFLATION: 1877–1881

With the state forced to issue paper money to put down costly revolts, one likely result was inflation. Just how quickly this developed is subject to dispute, but analysts agree that by 1881 inflation was a serious problem (see Exhibit 1). Inflation brought different results to different groups, and some domestic interests benefited.

> The profit inflation which accompanied these financial disturbances gave a temporary stimulus to certain branches of industry. . . . Enterprises in many sections of manufacture and mining were newly established or were reorganized and expanded. The farmers are said to have benefited greatly. While the burden of their debts and taxes payable in paper money remained constant, their money receipts from sales of rice and silk were augmented. New farm houses sprang up in every province; new clothes and ornaments were freely purchased; landed property came into great demand . . . and in general everybody rejoiced in hope and a sense of prosperity.

The landlords, in particular, received a windfall, for their rents were paid in rice while their tax obligations were expressed in the depreciating currency [1, p. 45]. Reprinted by permission of Macmillan, London and Basingstoke.

Exhibit 1

Trends in Money Supply, Prices and Interest Rates

Year	Non-convertible Notes in Circulation (¥ million)	Specie and Convertible Notes/Total Currency (%)	Wholesale Price Trends— Shigedo Estimates (% change)	Interest Rate (%)
1868	65.4	75.1	+12	14.0
1876	106.9	40.1		12.1
1878	165.7	25.6	+52	10.4
1881	153.3	19.1		14.0

SOURCE: H. Rosovsky [16, pp. 124–129]. Reprinted with permission.

BALANCE OF TRADE AND PAYMENTS PROBLEMS

However pleasing inflation might be to farmers and businessmen, from the government's point of view it could only exacerbate one of Japan's major problems, namely, a near-chronic deficit in the nation's balance of trade. From 1868 through 1880 the cumulative deficit came to approximately ¥77 million. This was close to one-tenth of national income according to one estimate, which put the 1880 figure at ¥799 million [3, p. 32: table 10]. Moreover, the higher domestic prices rose, the more attractive imports would become and the harder it would be for Japan to export, unless she devalued the yen. Imports, moreover, would continue to include not just the strategic goods essential to the government's program but goods in competition with the products of Japan and even nonessential luxuries.

To check an influx of unwanted imports, most governments could raise their tariffs. The Meiji, however, could not do so, for in the "unequal" treaties the Shogun had signed away the nation's right to increase the tariff rate beyond 5 percent *ad valorem*.

Another way to help the balance of trade would be to increase exports. So far, however, Japan had only two products, tea and silk, in which the West took much interest. The national dependence on these two products is illustrated in Exhibit 2.

To some extent, the market for silk fluctuated in response to factors beyond Japan's control. For example, the recent completion of the US transcontinental railway was extremely helpful to this market, but in 1868 European silkworm raising started to recover from a ten-year blight, just as the new Japan got under way. Within two years, the price of Japanese silk had fallen about 45 percent [24, pp. 9, 10].

Until exports could be increased, the remaining ways to pay for imports were to pay in specie or to borrow the needed foreign exchange from abroad. As for paying in specie, Japan was more fortunate than some developing countries in that she had inherited a fair-sized stock of gold and silver from Tokugawa times. But this was rapidly melting away. From 1872 to 1881 the drain on gold and silver was ¥71 million; by 1884 an official report on the Japanese economy stated that precious metals were exhausted. "What we send abroad henceforth," it added, "will necessarily be what at present remains underground" [10, pp. 15, 16; 20, p. 25].

As for borrowing abroad to pay her bills, Japan had so far managed to finance most of her programs from her own resources. Two modest foreign loans had been floated to start her railroads and assist her pension plan, but further foreign borrowing had been eschewed since the Japanese were "wary" of what they saw as "financial imperialism" [10, p. 253].

THE FINANCIAL CRISIS OF 1880–1881

By 1880–1881 Japan was deep in a financial crisis. The deficit in the balance of trade stood at a tenth of the national income; gold and silver stocks were melting away; the dollar value of the yen had slipped from over $1 to under 90 cents; no more than 20 percent of the currency was made up of specie or convertible notes; the national debt stood at ¥245 million or three times the government's yearly revenue; interest rates had moved up to 14 percent; according to one estimate at least, average prices had risen 52 percent in the last three years; and the price of rice, the chief food staple, had doubled [16, p. 129, 136].

Under these circumstances the time had come for new policies, perhaps even for the foreign loans of which Japan had so far been so leary. The only alternative was to

Exhibit 2

Exports of Tea and Silk as a Share of Total Exports

	1868–1872	1873–1877	1878–1882
Raw silk/total exports, value (in percent)	56.89	45.97	43.20
Tea/total exports, value (in percent)	24.48	25.86	21.99
Average annual value of total exports (millions)	¥15.60	¥22.14	¥30.74

SOURCE: T. Smith [20, p. 58]. Reprinted with permission.

try to tighten the belt at home, in spite of all the hardships this would involve for the beneficiaries of inflation.

So deep was the cabinet cleavage on these choices that a dramatic new step was taken: the issue was referred to the emperor himself. After thinking it over, the emperor opted against borrowing abroad. In explaining his reasons, he quoted advice he had earlier received from US President Ulysses S. Grant. "Look at Egypt, Spain, and Turkey," Grant had said on a visit to Japan, "and consider their pitiable condition. . . . Some nations like to lend money to poor nations very much. By this means they flaunt their authority and cajole the poor nation. The purpose of lending money is to get political power for themselves" [21, p. 185, 186].

Differences between US and Japanese statistics underscore the relevance of this advice. The US population in 1880 was later estimated at 50.26 million compared with 36.65 million for Japan. Estimated US total and per capita gross national product averaged $7.4 billion and $170 for the decade 1869–1878, compared with perhaps $735 million and $20 for Japan in 1880.[6]

---

[6] Based on a K. Ohkawa's estimate of ¥799 million for Japan's national income in 1880, when yen values ranged between US $0.9525 and US $0.8925. All these estimates are in current values [3, p. 12: table 1, p. 32: table 10, p. 318: table 121; 25, pp. 8, 24].

CHANGE OF LEADERSHIP

Following the emperor's decision, a different clique from within his inner circle took control in October 1881. This group was more conservative than its predecessors, and it was inclined to substitute German influence for French. The dominant figure in this new clique was the finance minister, Prince Matsukata. It was his main task to decide what to do about the financial crisis that had evolved by 1880, a crisis which he himself was later to describe in the following terms:

> At that time we fell into a condition which filled all classes . . . with anxiety. . . . The farmers, who were the only class to profit from these circumstances, took on luxurious habits, causing a great increase in the consumption of luxury goods. . . . Consequently imports . . . were increased and the nation's specie supply further depleted. Merchants, dazzled by the extreme fluctuations in price, all aimed at making huge speculative profits and gave no heed to productive undertakings. As a result, interest rates were so high that no one could plan an industrial undertaking that required any considerable capital. . . . Moreover, the depreciation of paper money revealed the disorganization of our finances to foreign countries and did much to undermine confidence in our government [20, pp. 96, 97].

REFERENCES

In English

1. Allen, George C. *A Short Economic History of Modern Japan, 1867–1937*. London: Allen and Unwin, 1962.

2. Bank of Japan. Economic Research Department. *Money and Banking in Japan*, translated by S. Nishimura. Tokyo: Credit Information Company of Japan, 1973.

3. ————. Statistics Department. *Hundred-Year Statistics of the Japanese Economy*. Tokyo: 1966.

4. Beasley, William G. *The Modern History of Japan*. New York: Praeger, 1963.

5. Beckhart, Benjamin H. *Federal Reserve System*. New York: Columbia University Press, 1972.

6. Fujii, Jintaro. *Outline of Japanese History in the Meiji Era*, translated and adapted by Hattie K. Colton and K. E. Colton. Tokyo: Obunsha, 1958.

7. Hirschmeier, Johannes. *The Origins of Entrepreneurship in Meiji Japan*. Cambridge, Mass.: Harvard University Press, 1964.

8. Klein, Lawrence and K. Ohkawa (eds.). *Economic Growth: Japanese Experience Since the Meiji Era*. Homewood, Ill.: Richard D. Irwin, 1968.

9. Koh, Sung Jae. *Stages of Industrial Development in Asia, A Comparative History of the Cotton Industry*. . . . Philadelphia: University of Pennsylvania Press, 1966.

10. Lockwood, William W. *The Economic Development of Japan: Growth and Structural Change, 1868–1938*. Princeton, N.J.: Princeton University Press, 1954.

11. Miyamoto, M., Y. Sakudo, and Y. Yashuba. "Economic Development in Pre-Industrial Japan: 1859–1894," *Journal of Economic History* (December 1965), p. 541 ff.

12. Neumann, William L. *America Encounters Japan: From Perry to MacArthur*. Baltimore, Md.: Johns Hopkins, 1963.

13. Quigley, Harold S. *Japanese Government and Politics*. New York: Century, 1932.

14. Reischauer, Edwin O. *The United States and Japan* (3d ed.). New York: Viking, 1964. (Original edition, Cambridge, Mass.: Harvard University Press, 1950.)

15. Rosovsky, Henry. *Capital Formation in Japan, 1868–1970*. New York: Free Press, 1961.

16. ———— (ed.). *Industrialization in Two Systems: Essays in Honor of Alexander Gerschenkron*. New York: Wiley & Sons, 1966.

17. Sansom, George. *A History of Japan 1615–1867*. Stanford, Calif.: Stanford University Press, 1963.

18. Scalapino, Robert A. *Democracy and the Party Movement in Prewar Japan*. Berkeley, Calif.: University of California Press, 1953.

19. Shibusawa, Keizo. *Japanese Society in the Meiji Era*, translated and adapted by A. H. Culbertson and Michiko Kimura. Tokyo: Obunsha, 1958.

20. Smith, Thomas C. *Political Change and Industrial Development in Japan*. Stanford, Calif.: Stanford University Press, 1955.

21. Takahashi, Kamekichi. *The Rise and Development of Japan's Modern Economy*. Tokyo: Jiji, 1969.

22. Takekoshi, Yosaburo. *The Economic Aspects of the History of the Civilization of Japan* (vol. III). New York: Macmillan, 1930.

23. Tsunoda, Ryusoku (ed.). *Sources of Japanese Tradition*. New York: Columbia University Press, 1958.

24. Tsurumi, Yoshi. "Japanese Efforts to Master Manufacturing Technologies, An Historical Review." New York: Queens

University, 1970. Distributed by the Intercollegiate Case Clearing House, Soldiers Field, Boston, Mass. 02163.

25. United States, Bureau of the Census. *Historical Statistics of the United States* (part I). Washington: U.S. Government Printing Office, 1975.

26. Yoshino, Michael Y. *Japan's Managerial System: Tradition and Innovation.* Cambridge, Mass.: MIT Press, 1968.

In Japanese

27. Eto, Tsuneharu. "Koyu no Mengyo to Yoshiki Mengyo no Ishoku" (The Traditional Cotton Industry and the Importation of the Western Cotton Industry), *Keizai Shi Kenkyu 19* (June 1938), pp. 1–16.

28. Iijima, Banji. *Nihon Boseki Shi* (History of the Japanese Spinning Industry). Tokyo: Osaka Sogensha, 1949.

29. Oka, Yoshitake. *Kindai Nihon no Keisei* (The Foundation of Modern Japan). Tokyo: Kobundo, 1947.

30. Takahashi Keizai Kenkyujo. *Nihon Sanshigyo Hattatsu Shi* (History of the Development of the Japanese Silk Industry) (vol. 1). Tokyo: Seikatsusha, 1941.

31. Tokei Kyoku. *Nihon Teikoku Tokei Zensho* (A Volume of Complete Statistics on Imperial Japan). Tokyo: Tokei Kyoku, 1902.

32. Tsuchiya, Takao and H. Ouchi (eds.). *Meiji Zenki Zaisei Keizai Shiryo Shusei* (Collected Documents on Economics and Finance in the Early Meiji Period) (vol. 17). Tokyo: Nihon Hyoron Shinsha, 1931.

33. Yamamoto, Itsuji. "Tomioka Seishijo Seiritsu to Shoki no Jotai" (The Establishment and Early Condition of the Tomioka Silk Reeling Mill), *Rekishigaku Kenkyu* (Tokyo) 6 (November 1936), pp. 2–38.

Japan B: 1881–1930, The Military Challenge to Civilian Control

In the 50 years between 1880 and 1930, Japan quintupled her real GNP and more than doubled the size of her empire through victory in three wars. This expansion taxed her resources. On three occasions—1913, 1920, and 1927—a balance-of-payments crisis forced the government to consider another Matsukata-style deflation. Each time, however, events intervened to make deflation unnecessary (1913) or domestically unacceptable (1920 and 1927). Not until booming 1929 did the government believe that the time was right for another dose of "hard medicine."

Hardly was deflation under way in Japan when the start of a worldwide depression threatened her farmers and businessmen with ruin. In addition, cutbacks in the military budget and the government's moderate foreign policy led to military opposition. By 1930 the armed services increasingly appeared ready to challenge not only the civilian government's strategy but also civilian control of the state.

INSTITUTIONAL BACKGROUND

The Constitution of 1890

The democratic government structure that was destined to be challenged in the 1930s traced its beginnings to the Constitution of 1890. This has been described as "an attempt to unite two concepts which . . . were irreconcilable: Imperial absolutism and popular government." The closest model was the constitution designed by Germany's autocratic Frederick the Great [20, pp. 56, 82, 83, 150].

"Popular" elements were relatively minor: the constitution called for a Diet (legislature) made up of two equal houses, only one of which was elected, the other being a House of Peers. The Diet was not strong in any case: it could be prorogued at any time, and if it refused to vote a budget, the old budget could simply be renewed. Most important, the Diet was not given the right to choose the members of the cabinet, and the cabinet itself was held in check by a sharing out of political power among institutions it could not control. These included the House of Peers, the Privy Council, the top levels of the bureaucracy (which tended to feel "officials' honored, people despised"), and—most important of all—the emperor's informal circle of advisors [5, pp. 143–148, 156, 157; 20, pp. 82–87, 148, 149].

As for the place of the people, the franchise was limited at first to only 1.5 percent of the population. Personal and property "rights" were granted, but were made subject to vague and hence "open-ended" limitations. There was nothing to compare with such US safeguards as due process or judicial review [8, pp. 5, 6; 20, pp. 113, 114].

In contrast to "popular" elements, "imperial" elements were pronounced in the 1890 constitution. Formally at least, the emperor was "sovereign," with all the attributes thereby implied. He "gave" Japan its new constitution, and his consent was necessary to amend it. The emperor was also "sacred" and "inviolable." As such, he was supposed to be shielded from all responsibility for error. Thus, his broad powers were, as in the past, exercised not by himself but by advisors acting in his name [20, pp. 85, 86, 149-151, 194].

Under these circumstances, who would be the emperor's close advisors was a key constitutional issue, for they would decide on major policies and appointments. The Meiji elite (or Sat-Cho oligarchs) played this role when the constitution came into force, and they intended to keep on playing it. Moreover, they intended to pass on their powers to their own handpicked successors. Collectively these successors were known as the *Genro* (elder statesmen). In support of such an arrangement, the oligarchs argued that government ought to be in the hands of a "transcendental body"—one speaking for "all the emperor's subjects" rather than for any limited group representing only particular interests [20, pp. 42, 43, 153-156, 164, 168].

In implementing this design, the Meiji elite faced a challenge from political parties that had developed in the Diet by the early 1880s. The constitution gave Japan the form of a parliamentary system, and the parties were determined to have the substance, too. Since the Diet had limited but meaningful powers over the budget, the parties' demands could not be ignored [6, p. 13; 20, pp. 155, 156].

Yet the Genro found ways of getting party cooperation that fell far short of letting the parties choose the cabinet and the cabinet run the government. The Genro were able to get at least enough cooperation by corrupting or co-opting the parties. Money, peerages, and political posts were the usual

counters in this game. If essential (at least until 1913) the Genro could also get cooperation by having the emperor issue an "Imperial Rescript" [20, pp. 164-166, 191-195].

The events of 1913 were an important step in Japan's slow progress towards democracy. They began with a budget quarrel. Military outlays had been cut severely after the Russo-Japanese War, and by 1911 the army was determined to have two more divisions. It was in a strong position to achieve its will in this matter. Peculiar features of Japan's constitution gave the army and navy ministers the right of "direct access" to the throne. In addition, both ministers had to be chosen from among the top two ranks of active service officers. As a result, either service could force a government to fall by pulling its minister out of the cabinet [5, pp. 144-146; 20, pp. 174, 175]. The army chose this course in 1911. In the protracted crisis that followed, the pro-army faction of the Genro had to use imperial rescripts several times. Finally, the Diet refused to respond to a rescript asking it to rescind a vote of censure. This refusal put the Genro on notice that resort to imperial rescripts risked weakening the emperor's position. If the emperor was to serve as a rallying point for patriotic fervor and the "Japanese spirit," he must be above politics. From this point on and for this reason, open intervention by the emperor "practically ceased" [6, pp. 13-15; 20, pp. 191-195]. Party government had won a signal victory, but even so the Genro did not lose their power.

New Educational Goals

Besides choosing a German model for their new constitution, the Meiji leaders of the 1880s also followed German inspiration in setting new educational goals. Gone were the liberal French ideals originally voiced in

1872.[1] According to Hugh Borton, "The initial emphasis on the needs of the individual . . . was gradually but effectively replaced by an educational system whose purpose was to train the individual to serve the state" [5, pp. 176–178]. In 1890 this trend found expression in a new Imperial Edict on Education. Here the "mania" for practical western knowledge had clearly been "replaced by a conscious effort to teach the old concepts of morality based on Confucian doctrine and national patriotism" [5, pp. 176–178]. Calling the "way" that he proposed "infallible for all ages and true in all places," the emperor exhorted his subjects not only to "pursue learning and cultivate the arts" but also to be "filial" and "harmonious," to "advance the public good," and—"should emergency arise"—to offer themselves "courageously to the state" [5, pp. 176–178].

Despite this old–new stress on ethical behavior, Japan did not reduce her strong commitment to having a literate working population. The percentage of attendance for compulsory (male primary) education reached 50 percent by 1891, 80 percent by 1900, 95 percent by 1905, and 99 percent by 1920 [2, p. 368]. By way of comparison, in 1920 or 1921 male literacy was around 94 percent in the United States, Canada, and Belgium; 77 percent in Italy; 71 percent in Poland; 53 percent in Portugal; 48 percent in Mexico; and 16 percent in India [11, pp. 46, 47].

EMPIRE BUILDING

In addition to using German models for Japan's constitution and schools, the oligarchs in power after 1881 also brought in Germans to guide their military strategy. These advisors focused national apprehension on Korea. Although the so-called "hermit kingdom" was still undeveloped, ill-ruled, and weak, its geographical location made it a "dagger at the heart of Japan." Furthermore, as the Germans pointed out, the "key" to the control of Korea was control of Liaotung, a small peninsula with a large ice-free harbor [22, p. 277].

Against this backdrop, when China moved to reassert her ancient "suzerainty" over "independent" Korea, China and Japan were soon at war. The fighting started in mid-1894, and Japan emerged the victor early the next year.

The treaty ending the Sino-Japanese War reaffirmed Korean independence and gave Japan the coveted Liaotung Peninsula which was the "key" to Korean defense; the large coastal Island of Formosa (now Taiwan), which guarded the southern sea approaches to Japan as well as the sea lanes of the China trade; and an indemnity of ¥366 million in gold.

Just at her moment of triumph, however, Japan suffered the first of several diplomatic defeats that cut into her military gains and shaped her international relations. Russia, supported by France and Germany, demanded from a now-exhausted Japan that she return Liaotung to China. Ostensibly, the purpose of this "retrocession" was to show respect for China's "territorial integrity," but only two years later Russia moved into Liaotung herself. Here she would be able to realize her goal of building an ice-free port on the Pacific, well south of her Siberian port at Vladivostok. Bitterness in Japan ran deep. As one contemporary put it, "The retrocession of Liaotung shaped the destiny of my whole life. After I heard of it I was spiritually a different person. . . . As a result of the triple intervention, I was baptized to the gospel of power" [17, p. 180].

Even western observers saw the triple intervention as a deep affront to Japan. They predicted war and they wondered what

[1] One factor in the rise of German influence over French was the German victory over France in the War of 1870.

would happen to the small island chain if she ventured to take on mighty Russia. Meanwhile, Japan made ready for revenge. In 1896 she started to double her army and navy; in 1900 she won friends and admiration by her behavior during China's Boxer Rebellion, and in 1902 she reaped the reward for which she had been hoping—namely, a prestigious alliance with England. England had the largest battle fleet in the East, and her neutrality would be essential to Japan's success in any war with Russia [22, pp. 279–280].

While readying for war, Japan used diplomacy, too, in an effort to settle her differences with Russia. But in 1904, after Russia had rejected ten proposals in six months, Japan broke off negotiations. War was soon declared on both sides.

Since Russia's army (a million men to Japan's 270,000) was mainly in the West, her strategy was to delay a major engagement until she had achieved numerical superiority by moving men from the West to the East. Partly for this very purpose, she had forced China to rent her a zone through which she had constructed a north–south Manchurian railway to link her ice-free port in Liaotung with her east–west railway across Siberia. Japan's opposing strategy was to force a quick decision in Liaotung, before a Russian buildup could occur. Moving quickly, Japan defeated the local Russian force, captured Russia's ice-free port (Port Arthur), and took the rest of the Liaotung Peninsula. Seeking to reverse this initial outcome, Russia then dispatched her fleet to the East, but—to the amazement of the western world—the Japanese surprised and sank this armada [7, vol. XV].

Nevertheless, the Japanese had lost over 20,000 troops and they still faced a formidable foe in the remainder of the Russian army. Both contestants also faced a shortage of money, military equipment, and supplies. Under these conditions, when US President Theodore Roosevelt offered his good offices for arriving at a settlement, his

offer was accepted by both sides. A peace treaty signed at Portsmouth, New Hampshire, gave Japan (1) Russia's 25-year lease on Liaotung from China, together with its provisions for renewal; (2) Russia's rights, good to at least 1938, to the South Manchurian Railway Zone (a corridor 60 miles wide wherein the leasor had not only a railroad but also mining rights and rights of political administration); (3) the southern half of the Island of Sakhalin, which Japan had only recently ceded to Russia; and (4) Russian recognition of "paramount" Japanese interests in Korea—political, military, and economic. In 1907, a similar recognition having been obtained from Europe and the United States, Japan assumed control of Korea, and she formally annexed it in August 1910.

POLITICAL AND DIPLOMATIC REPERCUSSIONS: 1907–1913

Following the annexation of Korea, Japan's new empire totaled 112,000 square miles compared with 147,000 for her homeland. She had greatly strengthened her credit with the West, had made herself the idol of the undeveloped world, had raised the pride of her own people to a pitch not experienced since Perry's "black ships," and had stored up credit for her Genro leaders which would long protect them from political critics.

Nevertheless, the Russo-Japanese War, like the Sino-Japanese War before it, brought a diplomatic defeat to Japan. This time the offender was the United States, and its fault lay in supporting Russia against Japan's demand for the whole of the Island of Sakhalin instead of just the southern part of it.[2]

---

[2] Popular resentment ran high because the Japanese people had not been informed of the military and financial problems of continuing the fight with Russia. Thus they saw only the victories achieved on the battlefield and at sea.

Moreover, as the new possessor of Russia's former rights in Manchuria, Japan soon came into conflict with the US policy of the "Open Door" for China. As reaffirmed publicly in 1899, this policy demanded equal rights for all nations in China, including equal rights for all the powers in each particular power's special "sphere of influence." Still another cause for Japanese hostility toward the US was the latter's acquisition in 1899 of Hawaii and the Philippines. The Japanese navy already could foresee their use as future US naval bases.

After these events the United States joined Russia as one of Japan's least favored western nations. While Japan's army directed its thinking to China, the possibility of colonies in China, and the risk of a Russian war of revenge, Japan's navy—not unlike Britain's—focused on the possible threat to the seaways of their small, trade-dependent island homeland. "In 1907," said Admiral Shigeru Fukudome, "the Imperial Navy made the United States its sole strategic enemy" [6, pp. 6–10; 22, pp. 281, 282].

These considerations gave rise to enduring but divergent concerns on the part of Japan's armed services. The army demanded 25 divisions to man the broad areas for which it was responsible. The navy demanded enough ships to forestall US aggression in the West Pacific. Economy-minded civilian governments incurred the army's wrath by allowing only nineteen divisions, but the navy at first had no compelling reason for resentment. Despite budget cutbacks, it had as many battleships as the United States until World War I, and it still gained strength from an alliance with Great Britain [6, pp. 6–14].

Battleship Ratios, 1905 and 1914

Year	UK	US	Japan	France	Germany
1905	39	11	11	12	20
1914	39	10	10	12	19

SOURCE: J. Crowley [6, p. 7]. © 1966 by Princeton University Press. Reprinted by permission.

ECONOMIC GAINS FROM WAR AND CONQUEST: 1897–1913

Besides significant political results, military success and conquest and Japan's new status as a world power brought a number of economic gains. In 1897, making use of the indemnity paid by China, Japan was able to go on a modified gold standard and to peg the yen at almost US $.50. In 1899 she succeeded in obtaining a major revision of the old "unequal treaties" that had troubled and angered her since the 1850s. In 1911 these treaties were finally terminated. Financing, too, was eased. No longer was it deemed essential to maintain a *superbalanced* budget. Yet, despite a shift to deficit financing, Japan could now borrow abroad more cheaply than at home. The old prohibition on foreign borrowing could therefore be profitably abandoned [2, p. 318; 14, pp. 240, 588, 589].

In addition, Japan's colonies brought certain economic gains. They supplied her with significant imports, notably rice, iron ore, and sugar, which otherwise would have to be purchased abroad. Japan's colonies also acted as a guaranteed market for Japanese exports of textiles and manufactured goods.

Government's expansionist policy also stimulated growth in heavy industry. In 1901 the government added to its holdings a giant iron and steel works at Yawata. By 1913 Yawata was a significant factor in Japanese domestic steel output of 255,000 tons—up from zero in 1896, or 34 percent of Japanese domestic consumption of steel [1, pp. 79, 80].

Shipbuilding, reacting to government incentives legislated in 1896, 1899, and 1909, grew rapidly as well. Japanese military and engineering industry also grew, owing to the impetus of military expansion and extremely high military demand. By western standards, however, the heavy industry sector was still small, even ten years after the Russo-Japanese War. Even in 1914 the total number of operatives in factories that employed five or more persons was only 950,000, of whom 560,000 were females" [1, pp. 70, 71, 79–90]. Japan was now a "dual" economy, one with large modern plants in a few industries and small firms and traditional technology in others.

OTHER UNDERLYING SOURCES OF GROWTH

Although preparedness, war, and conquest stimulated growth and industrialization, these were not the only or even perhaps the most basic causes of Japan's advance (*see* Exhibits 1, 2, 3, and 4 for details).[3]

Seeking to explain Japanese development, economists pointed to three underlying factors needed by any developing country. First, Japan was able to borrow from a pool of advanced technologies already in existence elsewhere. Second, she had some surplus for investment, since from the 1870s through the early 1900s agricultural output increased by about 1.7 percent a year, without itself demanding any capital-intensive kinds of changes. Third, the people were prone to save, since the poor lacked other sources of security and business saw chances for high potential profit. Moreover, once the farm surplus shrank, business stood ready to take over as a new source of surplus for investment [15, p. 13].

COST OF GROWTH AND CONQUEST: THE FINANCIAL CRISIS OF 1913

Besides bringing economic gains, growth and conquest also brought costs. In preparing for their wars with China and Russia, the Japanese had poured resources into the military. Expenditures on the army, just under ¥15 million in 1893, rose to ¥53 million in 1896 and remained at that level until 1904. Naval expenditures also rose rapidly. The war with Russia alone cost ¥1730 million—over one-half of Japan's GNP [3, pp. 159, 160, 170, 175, 176].

A large empire also proved costly. Japan's new colonies required considerable investment, diverting funds from Japan proper. Infrastructure had to be built up and potential resources exploited. Much of this investment would not pay off for years. The government imposed new taxes and raised taxes on land, *sake,* and personal income in the early 1900s in order to help pay for Japan's expanded military and colonial administration.[4] Even so, Japan's national debt quintupled between 1900 and 1913 [1, pp. 48, 49; 12, pp. 521–523].

Other signs of strain emerged in these years. Wholesale prices rose relatively rapidly (*see* Exhibit 5). Government finances were often in the red, and currency in circulation almost doubled (*see* Exhibits 6 and 7). The cumulative balance of payments showed a heavy deficit in visible and invisible trade as well as substantial foreign obligations derived from foreign loans and investments in Japan (*see* Exhibit 8).

How serious these trends looked to Japan was described by Junnosuke Inouye, one-time head of the Yokohama Specie Bank (in control of foreign exchange transac-

---

[3] In the absence of GNP accounting (which had not yet been developed), various estimates have been made of Japan's GNP before World War II. Those used here are from K. Ohkawa and H. Rosovsky [15, *passim*].

---

[4] Japan had adopted a personal income tax in 1887, compared with 1911 in the United States.

Exhibit 1

Gross National Expenditures (Product) in Current Prices, 1887–1930
(millions of yen and percentage breakdown)

Cal Year	Prvt Consump Expndtr ¥	%	Gnrl Govt Consump Expndtr ¥	%	Gross Domest Fxd Cap Formation ¥	%	Exprt Gds & Servs & Factor Inc Rec'd fr Abroad ¥	%	Less Imprt Gds & Servs & Factor Inc Pd Abroad ¥	%	GNE at Mkt Prices ¥
1887[a]	682	80.2	61	7.2	115	13.5	55	6.5	63	−7.4	850
1902[a]	2,140	77.7	283	10.3	375	13.6	335	12.2	380	−13.8	2,754
1905	2,351	74.5	626	19.8	516	16.3	401	12.7	738	−23.4	3,156
1906	2,461	71.3	485	14.1	540	15.6	540	15.6	575	−16.7	3,451
1907	2,672	73.6	338	9.3	634	17.5	617	17.0	633	−17.5	3,628
1908	3,060	77.6	307	7.8	663	16.8	506	12.8	594	−15.1	3,942
1909	3,060	77.3	320	8.1	598	15.1	539	13.6	556	−14.0	3,961
1910	3,145	76.7	339	8.3	689	16.8	586	14.3	656	−16.0	4,103
1911	3,488	74.9	407	8.7	860	18.5	618	13.3	718	−15.4	4,655
1912	3,855	77.6	370	7.4	857	17.3	723	14.6	837	−16.8	4,968
1913	4,128	79.2	339	6.5	860	16.5	836	16.0	951	−18.2	5,212
1919	11,072	72.8	881	5.8	2,937	19.3	3,230	21.2	2,909	−19.1	15,211
1920	11,075	70.8	1,085	6.9	3,596	23.0	2,968	19.0	3,094	−19.7	15,630
1921	11,286	75.4	1,120	7.5	2,868	19.2	1,998	13.3	2,303	−15.4	14,969
1922	11,719	74.8	1,198	7.6	2,975	19.0	2,309	14.7	2,538	−16.2	15,663
1923	11,921	79.5	1,164	7.8	2,500	16.7	2,095	14.0	2,681	−17.9	14,999
1924	12,274	78.5	1,187	7.6	2,930	18.7	2,561	16.4	3,324	−21.3	15,628
1925	12,863	78.9	1,073	6.6	2,704	16.6	3,167	19.4	3,497	−21.4	16,310
1926	12,496	77.8	1,133	7.1	2,826	17.6	2,880	17.9	3,283	−20.5	16,052
1927	12,283	75.2	1,391	8.5	2,892	17.7	2,857	17.5	3,080	−18.8	16,343
1928	12,370	74.7	1,668	10.1	2,743	16.6	2,900	17.5	3,131	−18.9	16,550
1929	11,942	73.1	1,612	9.9	2,815	17.2	3,160	19.3	3,182	−19.5	16,347
1930	11,001	74.5	1,479	10.0	2,323	15.7	2,358	16.0	2,395	−16.2	14,766

SOURCE: K. Ohkawa and H. Rosovsky [15, pp. 10, 286]. Reprinted with permission.
[a] The figures for 1887 and 1902 are five-year averages centered on the years shown.

Exhibit 2

Gross National Expenditure (Product) in Constant 1934–1936 Prices, 1887–1930 (millions of yen and percentage breakdown)

Cal Year	Prvt Consump Expndtr ¥	%	Gnrl Govt Consump Expmdtr ¥	%	Gross Domest Fxd Cap Formation ¥	%	Exprt Gds & Servs & Factor Inc Recvd fr Abroad ¥	%	Less Imprt Gds & Servs & Factor Inc Pd Abroad ¥	%	GNE at Mkt Prices ¥	GNP (% Chnge)	Implicit Deflator (Aggregate)[a]
1887[b]	3,737	86.3	291	6.7	383	8.8	91	2.1	178	4.1	4,330	—	19.6
1902[b]	5,440	81.8	719	10.8	679	10.2	325	4.9	631	9.5	6,650	2.8[c]	41.4
1905	5,272	79.1	1,552	23.3	688	10.3	346	5.2	1,196	18.0	6,662	0.0[c]	47.3
1906	5,238	77.5	1,136	16.8	866	12.8	443	6.5	923	13.6	6,760	1.5	51.0
1907	5,378	82.0	755	11.5	926	14.1	451	6.9	955	14.5	6,555	-3.0	55.2
1908	6,015	83.0	691	9.5	1,035	14.3	440	6.0	933	12.8	7,247	10.6	54.3
1909	6,132	82.6	719	9.7	991	13.3	492	6.6	917	12.3	7,417	2.3	53.3
1910	6,389	80.9	734	9.3	1,146	14.5	579	7.3	951	12.0	7,897	6.5	51.9
1911	6,306	79.0	815	10.2	1,389	17.4	601	7.5	1,133	14.2	7,978	1.0	58.3
1912	6,487	81.1	719	9.0	1,271	15.9	697	8.7	1,181	14.7	7,993	0.2	62.1
1913	6,692	82.9	657	8.1	1,297	16.1	779	9.6	1,358	16.8	8,067	0.9	64.6
1919	8,813	75.8	1,032	8.9	2,283	19.6	1,323	11.4	1,826	15.7	11,625	6.3[c]	130.7
1920	8,680	75.0	1,060	9.1	2,471	21.3	1,136	9.8	1,782	15.4	11,565	-0.5	135.0
1921	9,253	75.4	1,045	8.5	2,649	21.6	1,014	8.2	1,689	13.7	12,272	6.1	122.0
1922	9,827	82.1	1,116	9.3	2,381	19.9	1,078	9.0	2,438	20.4	11,964	-2.5	130.6
1923	9,998	87.5	1,099	9.6	1,883	16.5	927	8.1	2,485	21.7	11,422	-4.5	131.1
1924	10,207	79.7	1,116	8.7	2,052	16.0	1,194	9.3	1,761	13.7	12,808	12.1	122.0
1925	10,407	83.7	1,005	8.1	2,215	17.8	1,430	11.5	2,621	21.1	12,436	-2.9	131.0
1926	10,556	83.9	1,084	8.6	2,338	18.6	1,529	12.1	2,924	23.2	12,583	1.1	127.7
1927	10,861	83.9	1,304	10.0	2,395	18.5	1,710	13.2	3,322	25.6	12,948	2.9	126.0
1928	11,177	81.1	1,595	11.5	2,368	17.2	1,824	13.2	3,188	23.1	13,776	6.4	120.2
1929	11,102	80.2	1,531	11.0	2,505	18.1	2,012	14.5	3,315	23.9	13,835	0.4	118.0
1930	11,152	79.8	1,475	10.5	2,430	17.4	2,017	14.4	3,098	22.1	13,976	1.0	105.6

SOURCE: K. Ohkawa and H. Rosovsky [15, pp. 10, 286, 288, 306]. Reprinted with permission.

a Applies for GNP and NNP. Not shown are individual deflators for consumers' goods and services, investment goods, agriculture (including forestry and fishing), mining and manufacturing, facilitating industry, construction, services, and imports and exports.

b The figures for 1887 and 1902 are five-year averages centered on the years shown.

c Average annual rate of change compounded.

Exhibit 3

Sectoral Distribution of Net Domestic Product and Workforce

A. NET DOMESTIC PRODUCT (NDP)[a] BY SECTOR IN CURRENT PRICES (MILLIONS OF YEN AND PERCENTAGE BREAKDOWN)

Year	Agriculture (Incldg Forestry & Fishing) ¥	%	Mining & Mfg ¥	%	Facilitating Industry[b] ¥	%	Construction ¥	%	Services ¥	%	Total NDP ¥
1887[c]	309.9	41.1	102.5	13.6	19.6	2.6	27.1	3.6	294.8	39.1	754
1905	856	31.4	545	20.0	144	5.3	86	3.2	1,095	40.2	2,726
1910	1,104	30.9	715	20.0	231	6.5	157	4.4	1,367	38.2	3,574
1913	1,712	36.5	928	19.8	284	6.1	194	4.1	1,573	33.5	4,691
1919	4,977	35.2	3,780	26.7	778	5.6	478	3.4	4,123	29.2	14,136
1920	3,916	29.1	3,391	25.2	1,086	8.1	699	5.2	4,361	32.4	13,453
1921	3,781	27.3	2,911	21.0	1,231	8.9	673	4.9	5,233	37.8	13,830
1925	4,172	26.5	3,196	20.3	1,595	10.1	852	5.4	5,964	37.9	15,734
1926	3,506	22.6	3,135	20.2	1,646	10.6	862	5.6	6,335	40.9	15,484
1927	3,340	22.3	3,102	20.8	1,528	10.2	820	5.5	6,155	41.2	14,945
1928	3,162	20.4	3,507	22.6	1,608	10.4	844	5.4	6,405	41.3	15,526
1929	3,138	19.8	3,874	24.5	1,653	10.5	836	5.3	6,316	39.9	15,817
1930	2,118	16.0	3,069	23.2	1,575	11.9	727	5.5	5,768	43.5	13,257

B. NET DOMESTIC PRODUCT (NDP)[a] BY SECTOR IN CONSTANT 1934-36 PRICES (MILLIONS OF YEN AND PERCENTAGE BREAKDOWN)

Year	Agriculture (Incldg Forestry & Fishing) ¥	%	Mining & Mfg ¥	%	Facilitating Industry[b] ¥	%	Construction ¥	%	Services ¥	%	Total NDP ¥
1905	1,551	26.8	754	13.0	201	3.5	178	3.0	3,096	53.6	5,780
1910	1,917	26.7	961	13.4	362	5.0	287	4.0	3,639	50.8	7,166
1913	2,206	28.9	1,169	15.3	465	6.1	326	4.3	3,465	45.4	7,631
1919	2,784	23.9	2,035	17.5	653	5.6	344	2.9	5,822	50.0	11,638
1920	2,545	23.5	1,745	16.1	876	8.1	350	3.2	5,322	49.1	10,838
1921	2,519	21.1	1,955	16.3	1,061	8.9	404	3.4	6,009	50.3	11,948
1925	2,749	21.3	2,189	16.9	1,422	11.0	573	4.4	5,975	46.3	12,908
1926	2,565	19.6	2,417	18.4	1,514	11.5	618	4.7	5,979	45.6	13,093
1927	2,742	21.1	2,547	19.6	1,419	10.9	605	4.6	5,659	43.6	12,972
1928	2,635	18.7	2,856	20.3	1,454	10.3	646	4.6	6,459	46.0	14,050
1929	2,960	20.2	3,261	22.2	1,561	10.6	648	4.4	6,233	42.5	14,663
1930	2,664	19.7	3,190	23.6	1,544	11.4	702	5.2	5,383	39.9	13,483

SOURCE: K. Ohkawa and H. Rosovsky [15, pp. 10, 282, 284]. Reprinted with permission.

[a] NDP is GNP less net factor income from abroad and depreciation (provision for consumption of capital).
[b] Facilitating industry includes transportation, communications, and public utilities.
[c] Five-year average centered on the year shown.

Exhibit 4

Population and Labor Force by Sector (totals in thousands and percentage breakdown of persons gainfully employed)

Year	Agriculture (Incldg Forestry & Fishing)	%	Mining & Mfg	%	Facilitating Industry[a]	%	Construction	%	Services	%	Total Gainfully Occpd	Private Nonagriculture	%	Total Population
1887[b]	—		—		—		—		—		—	—		38,703
1902	—		—		—		—		—		—	—		44,964
1905	16,205	64.8	3,094	12.4	625	2.5	538	2.2	4,542	18.2	25,004	7,774	31.1	46,746
1906	16,117	64.2	3,154	12.6	642	2.6	557	2.2	4,637	18.5	25,107	7,841	31.2	47,132
1907	16,126	63.9	3,180	12.6	732	2.9	547	2.2	4,671	18.5	25,256	8,018	31.7	47,654
1908	16,069	63.3	3,248	12.8	713	2.8	613	2.4	4,721	18.6	25,364	8,174	32.2	48,224
1909	15,926	62.7	3,384	13.3	691	2.7	613	2.4	4,805	18.9	25,419	8,369	32.9	48,850
1910	15,943	62.5	3,353	13.1	705	2.7	614	2.4	4,907	19.2	25,522	8,413	33.0	49,489
1911	16,051	62.5	3,373	13.1	687	2.7	637	2.5	4,923	19.2	25,671	8,435	32.9	50,179
1912	16,060	62.1	3,417	13.2	709	2.7	669	2.6	4,991	19.3	25,846	8,596	33.3	50,925
1913	16,094	61.7	3,534	13.6	661	2.5	682	2.6	5,072	19.5	26,043	8,764	33.7	51,671
1919	14,834	54.9	4,764	17.6	972	3.6	690	2.6	5,766	21.3	27,026	10,577	39.1	55,032
1920	14,663	53.9	4,966	18.2	1,043	3.8	701	2.6	5,838	21.5	27,211	10,906	40.1	55,885
1921	14,731	53.8	4,746	17.3	1,020	3.7	707	2.6	6,201	22.6	27,405	10,984	40.1	55,963
1922	14,772	53.4	4,899	17.7	1,023	3.7	730	2.6	6,209	22.5	27,633	11,150	40.4	56,666
1923	14,110	50.5	5,399	19.4	1,089	3.9	745	2.7	6,530	23.4	27,873	12,013	43.1	57,389
1924	14,452	51.8	5,226	18.7	1,102	3.9	767	2.7	6,352	22.8	27,899	11,742	42.1	58,119
1925	14,394	51.2	5,330	19.0	1,118	4.0	790	2.8	6,471	23.0	28,103	11,979	42.6	58,876
1926	14,349	50.5	5,412	19.0	1,099	3.9	825	2.9	6,747	23.7	28,432	12,312	43.3	59,736
1927	14,276	50.2	5,725	20.1	1,091	3.8	802	2.8	6,590	23.1	28,484	12,432	43.6	60,741
1928	14,363	49.8	5,719	19.8	1,121	3.9	839	2.9	6,783	23.5	28,825	12,654	43.9	61,659
1929	14,573	50.0	5,795	19.9	1,135	3.9	853	2.9	6,815	23.4	29,171	12,780	43.8	62,595
1930	14,689	49.6	5,872	19.8	1,162	3.9	846	2.9	7,050	23.8	29,619	13,101	44.2	64,450

SOURCE: K. Ohkawa and H. Rosovsky [15, p. 310]. Reprinted with permission.

[a] Facilitating industry includes transportation, communications, and public utilities.

[b] Five-year average centered on the year shown.

Exhibit 5

Comparative Wholesale Price Indices,
1900–1930
(1913 = 100)

Cal Year	Japan	US	UK
1900	75.6	80.4	88
1901	72.6	79.2	82
1902	73.2	84.4	81
1903	77.9	85.4	81
1904	81.9	85.5	82
1905	88.0	86.1	85
1906	90.6	88.5	91
1907	97.7	93.4	94
1908	94.2	90.1	86
1909	89.8	96.8	87
1910	90.9	100.9	92
1911	94.3	93.0	94
1912	99.8	99.0	100
1913	100.0	100.0	100
1914	95.5	87.5	100
1915	96.6	99.6	127
1916	116.9	122.5	160
1917	147.0	168.3	206
1918	192.6	188.1	226
1919	235.8	198.6	242
1920	259.4	221.2	295
1921	200.4	139.8	182
1922	195.8	138.5	154
1923	199.2	144.1	152
1924	206.5	140.5	164
1925	201.7	148.3	160
1926	178.8	143.3	148
1927	169.8	136.7	144
1928	170.9	140.0	142
1929	166.1	138.3	134
1930	136.7	123.6	113

SOURCES: H. G. Moulton [14, p. 564], reprinted with permission; League of Nations [11(1934–1935), pp. 227, 229: table 112].

tions), later head of the Bank of Japan, and finally in 1929 Japan's minister of finance.

Ever since Japan first entered into her modern commercial relations with the rest of the world, the dominant . . . nature of her foreign trade has been an excess of imports. . . . This has meant that . . . Japan has been engaged in one perpetual struggle to find the money wherewith to meet her obligations abroad.

By the end of 1913 this continued and ever-increasing strain on her resources had very nearly reached a breaking point. . . . She was actually facing the prospect of having to borrow yet further, merely in order to raise the money wherewith to pay the interest on her existing loans [21, p. 871].

SAVED BY WORLD WAR I

Just as Japan seemed close to a crisis, in need perhaps of a second Matsukata deflation, her situation suddenly changed. World War I was declared, and, in the words of Mr. Inouye, "Orders for arms and munitions . . . started to rain down on Japan . . . and all exports from this country [started] to make notable advances" [21, p. 874]. From a trade deficit averaging ¥65 million a year in 1911–1914, Japan moved to a trade surplus averaging ¥352 million in 1915–1918 (*see* Exhibit 8). Japan thus changed from a debtor to a creditor nation and ended the war with more than ¥3 billion in her reserves of foreign exchange [1, p. 98].

World War I brought other benefits. These included another surge of growth, more industrialization, and the penetration of new foreign markets—particularly markets in Asia, since these had been cut off by the war from their usual sources of supply. Japan also made territorial gains. She declared war on the Allied side, seized

Germany's Pacific islands, and invaded Shantung (a Chinese province opposite Liaotung), which had been a German sphere of influence. Taking further advantage of the fact that Europe and America were otherwise engaged, Japan issued a notorious set of Twenty-One Demands on China. These included Chinese acceptance of Japan's takeover of former German rights in Shantung, a 99-year extension of Japan's existing rights in Manchuria and Liaotung, commercial and mining rights in Manchuria and Mongolia, etc. Five especially "oppressive" demands "would have made China a political as well as an economic colony of Japan," but these five demands were withdrawn in the face of strong Chinese and European protests [19, pp. 195-197]. Later, Japan sought other concessions through loans to Chinese warlords, the amounts involved reaching ¥295 million.

Japan's wartime gains were made without the loss of a single soldier. After the war, troops were sent to North Sakhalin and East Siberia as part of a general Allied effort to wrest Russia from the communists. Japan used seven divisions for this purpose, the size of her commitment having been determined by the army rather than by the government [3, pp. 209-212]. Since the Allies had sought only one division to accomplish their limited objectives in the East, Japan's response was seen as "crude imperialism" [6, p. 23]. More goodwill was lost for what turned out to be only temporary gains. In 1922 Japan vacated Russia's territory and Soviet troops moved in.

MORE DIPLOMATIC DEFEATS

Repeating a pattern set in the past, Japan's success in World War I was followed by diplomatic defeats. At the Peace Conference, Europe's secretly promised support for some of the Twenty-One Demands on China proved of no help to Japan, for US President Woodrow Wilson opposed all secret treaties and threw his powerful support behind the principle of national self-determination. In addition, Japan's new islands in the Pacific were classed as "mandates" of the League of Nations, which meant that they should not be fortified. For as long as this prohibition was observed, the islands had as little strategic value as they had economic value. Also at the Peace Conference, six major powers, led by Australia and the United States, refused to insert into the Covenant of the League a clause recognizing racial equality [19, p. 247].

In 1922 a Nine-Power Pact prevailed on Japan to voice support for China's sovereignty, integrity, etc., and to reaffirm the principle of the Open Door in return for nothing more tangible than "recognition" of her "special" position in China. Afterward, Japan vacated Shantung as well as Siberia and North Sakhalin. This left the mandate islands as Japan's sole territorial gain from World War I.

Also in 1922, Britain terminated its prestigious alliance with Japan under pressure from the United States and Canada. Japan was left prey to permanent fears that Britain and the United States might form a two-power alliance against her. In a related Five-Power Pact, Japan was prevailed upon to accept a naval ratio of only six to ten vis-à-vis Britain and the United States, whereas all agreed that seven to ten was the minimum needed to permit Japan to dominate home waters. As a partial offset, Britain and the United States agreed not to fortify their West Pacific outposts (i.e., Hong Kong and the Philippines) [9, p. 226]. But the Japanese became increasingly determined to achieve a seven-to-ten ratio at the next naval conference.

Another blow fell in 1924. Amid much talk of the "Yellow Peril," the United States

Exhibit 6

Revenues and Expenditures on the General Account, the National Debt, and Changes in the Net Financial Position of the National Government, 1892–1930 (millions of yen)

(1) Year (Begin 4/1)	(2) Expndtrs	(3) Nonbor- rowed Revs	(4) Surpl (+) or Defct (−)	(5) Loans Floated for GA[a]	(6) Accumu- lated GA Surpl (Japan Proper)	(7) Chnge in Accum GA Surpl (Japan & Colonies)	(8) Natl Debt	(9) Chnge in Natl Debt	(10) Net Chnge in Govt Finan Position
1891	83.6	78.9	−4.7	—	19.7	—	274.6	—	—
1892	76.7	81.8	+5.1	—	24.7	5.1	277.9	3.3	1.8
1893	84.6	89.0	+4.5	—	29.2	4.5	267.8	−10.1	14.6
1894	78.1	69.0	−9.1	—	20.0	−9.1	326.1	58.3	−67.4
1895	85.3	98.4	+13.1	—	33.1	13.1	409.7	83.5	−70.4
1896	168.9	150.9	−17.9	3.0	18.2	−15.0	410.3	0.7	−15.7
1897	223.7	171.8	−51.8	36.4	2.7	−14.7	421.2	10.9	−25.6
1898	219.8	182.0	−37.8	35.4	0.3	−2.1	413.3	−8.0	5.9
1889	254.2	218.8	−35.4	35.2	0.1	−0.2	506.2	92.9	−93.1
1900	292.8	257.6	−35.1	38.1	3.1	2.7	518.8	12.6	−9.9
1901	266.9	239.5	−27.3	31.7	7.5	4.0	568.5	49.8	−45.8
1902	289.2	277.1	−12.1	12.7	8.1	1.3	584.6	16.0	−14.7
1903	249.6	245.2	−4.4	6.9	10.6	2.3	617.3	32.7	−30.4
1904	277.1	310.3	+33.2	6.6	50.4	42.3	1078.8	461.5	−419.2
1905	420.7	410.9	−9.8	73.9	57.2	8.3	2113.6	1034.8	−1026.2
1906	464.3	457.8	−6.5	15.5	66.0	9.2	2327.1	213.5	−204.3
1907	602.4	791.1	+188.7	—	254.7	192.2	2305.0	−22.0	214.2
1908	636.4	539.4	−96.9	0.8	158.6	−97.2	2292.8	−12.2	−85.0
1909	532.9	516.4	−16.5	2.6	144.7	−10.2	2651.2	358.4	−368.6
1910	569.2	525.4	−43.8	2.8	101.3	−35.6	2780.3	129.1	−164.7
1911	585.4	544.7	−40.6	11.2	71.8	−28.1	2742.1	−38.2	10.1
1912	593.6	597.2	+3.7	18.3	93.8	25.7	2750.7	8.5	17.2
1913	573.6	615.3	+41.7	12.9	148.3	51.1	2686.5	−64.2	115.3
1914	648.4	575.6	−72.8	10.7	86.2	−69.0	2649.7	−36.8	−32.2
1915	583.3	620.7	+37.4	1.7	125.3	40.2	2657.7	8.0	32.2
1916	590.8	686.4	+95.6	1.6	222.5	108.8	2662.7	5.0	103.8
1917	735.0	845.5	+110.4	17.0	349.9	148.5	2872.6	209.9	−61.4
1918	1017.0	1100.9	+83.8	28.4	462.1	131.3	3255.2	382.6	−251.3
1919	1172.3	1327.5	+155.1	19.1	436.3	172.9	3489.7	234.5	−61.6
1920	1360.0	1310.7	−49.3	53.6	640.7	−6.5	4066.4	576.7	−583.2
1921	1489.9	1372.0	−117.9	53.0	575.9	−68.6	4330.7	264.3	−332.9
1922	1429.7	1484.6	+54.9	26.9	657.7	70.4	4601.9	271.2	−200.8
1923	1521.1	1352.6	−168.4	35.0	524.2	−136.0	5049.8	447.9	−583.9
1924	1625.0	1475.2	−149.9	128.0	502.3	−18.1	5163.2	113.4	−131.5
1925	1525.0	1522.4	−2.6	46.6	546.4	55.5	5428.8	265.6	−210.1
1926	1578.8	1475.9	−102.9	34.0	477.5	−46.9	5627.5	198.7	−245.6
1927	1765.7	1524.1	−241.6	61.1	297.0	−179.1	5985.7	358.2	−537.3
1928	1814.9	1551.6	−263.3	157.1	190.8	−107.2	6447.6	461.9	−569.1
1929	1736.3	1535.7	−200.6	99.9	90.1	−119.4	6576.2	128.7	−248.1
1930	1557.9	1468.8	−89.1	38.0	39.1	na	6842.8	266.6	na

Exhibit 6 (continued)

SOURCES: H. G. Moulton [14, pp. 208, 212] for columns 2 through 7, reprinted with permission; column 8 from Bank of Japan [2, table 49]. Column 9 computed from column 8; column 10 computed from columns 7 and 9.

a While the General Account did not comprise the whole of central government revenues and expenditures, it did comprise most of the income and outgo involved in "normal" government activities. Viewing the GA balance as critical, the government often borrowed for this account (column 5) in order to show a surplus in it (column 6). This figure might be misleading as to general trends, especially when extraordinary expenditures occurred (as for wars and earthquake relief), since these did not show up in the GA figures. Expenditures in excess of income were, however, reflected in the total national debt (column 8). Changes in the debt (column 9), adjusted for changes in the GA surplus for Japan and her colonies (column 7), therefore, give a valid indication of trends in the government's financial position (column 10). For further detail, see sources.

passed an Oriental Exclusion Act, which was aimed at preventing immigration from Japan. Since, under a "gentlemen's agreement," no such immigration had occurred for many years, this was simply a gratuitous slap. Moreover, the same kind of slap was being administered in Australia, Europe, Canada, and South America—some of them places to which Japan might have sent some of her fast-growing excess population [9, pp. 103–105].

A further minor setback was the souring of several of Japan's large wartime loans. Those made to Czarist Russia and the Chinese warlords would never be repaid. As banker J. Inouye later put it, "They might just as well have been thrown into the sea" [14, p. 284].

POLITICAL INSTABILITIES

In the 1920s political parties appeared to be winning their decades-long fight to make Japan's government "responsible." This change did not mean that the majority party in the Diet got to choose the prime minister.[5] Nor did it necessarily mean that

the person chosen as prime minister was always the leader of the largest party. What it did mean was that a government would not seek to stay in office if it could not get support from a majority in the lower house.

Noting the rising power of parties and noting, too, that Japan had adopted manhood suffrage in 1925, many analysts at home and abroad now hailed Japan as a new recruit to the democratic fold. At the same time it was realized that Japan's democracy might not prove viable.

Some factors clearly favored democracy. These included the current respect in which this form of government was held. Democracies had won World War I and they now claimed to have fought the war "to make the world safe for democracy." Also favorable were widespread education in Japan, a lively if sometimes intemperate press, and the development of a virtual two-party system, with no major rift between the rather narrow-based and right-wing main parties. One of these, the *Seiyukai*, drew most of its support from the large landed interests; the other, the *Minseito*,[6] drew most of its support from business. Even so, their economic

---

[5] Prince Saionji, one of the Genro, was still alive and he remained "Prime Minister Maker."

[6] These party names meant respectively "Friends of Constitutional Government" and "Constitutional Democrats."

Exhibit 7

Factors in the Money Supply, 1885–1930

(1) At End of Year	(2) Ratio of Specie to Currency in Circulation %	Currency in Circulation		(5) Commercial Bank Deposits[b] ¥ billion	(6) Money Supply[c] ¥ billion
		(3) Total[a] ¥ billion	(4) Note Issue of the Bank of Japan ¥ billion		
1885	1.5	0.15	—		
1886	14.3	0.17	0.04		
1887	18.4	0.17	0.05		
1888	26.1	0.17	0.07		
1889	32.1	0.18	0.08		
1890	22.2	0.20	0.10		
1891	30.3	0.21	0.12		
1892	38.3	0.21	0.13		
1893	37.2	0.23	0.15		
1894	35.5	0.23	0.15		
1895	23.2	0.26	0.18		
1896	48.3	0.27	0.20		
1897	30.2	0.30	0.23		
1898	32.1	0.28	0.20		
1899	32.4	0.34	0.25		
1900	21.2	0.32	0.23		
1901	23.5	0.30	0.21		
1902	31.5	0.32	0.23		
1903	36.0	0.32	0.23		
1904	21.8	0.38	0.27		
1905	27.4	0.42	0.31		
1906	31.4	0.47	0.34		
1907	31.8	0.51	0.37		
1908	33.9	0.50	0.35		
1909	41.8	0.52	0.35		
1910	37.9	0.59	0.40		
1911	36.2	0.63	0.43		
1912	38.1	0.65	0.44		
1913	35.7	0.63	0.43	1.6	2.2
1914	38.9	0.56	0.39		

Exhibit 7 (continued)

Currency in Circulation

(1) At End of Year	(2) Ratio of Specie to Currency in Circulation %	(3) Total[a] ¥ billion	(4) Note Issue of the Bank of Japan ¥ billion	(5) Commercial Bank Deposits[b] ¥ billion	(6) Money Supply[c] ¥ billion
1915	40.0	0.62	0.43		
1916	49.7	0.83	0.60		
1917	58.1	1.12	0.83		
1918	45.2	1.58	1.14		
1919	45.7	2.08	1.56		
1920	69.2	1.80	1.44	7.0	8.8
1921	63.9	1.95	1.55	7.6	9.5
1922	57.2	1.86	1.59	7.7	9.6
1923	48.6	2.20	1.70	7.7	9.9
1924	48.6	2.18	1.66	8.0	10.2
1925	49.5	2.14	1.63	8.6	10.7
1926	51.3	2.06	1.57	9.0	11.0
1927	48.3	2.20	1.68	8.9	11.1
1928	46.4	2.28	1.74	9.2	11.5
1929	49.2	2.18	1.64	9.2	11.4
1930	43.6	1.92	1.45	8.7	10.6

SOURCES: Columns 1 through 4, Bank of Japan [2, p. 166: table 53, pp. 170, 171: table 55]; column 5, League of Nations [11(1928), p. 196: table 98; 11(1933–34), p. 232: table 115; 11(1936–37), p. 254: table 129].

[a] Note issues of the government, national bank notes, the Banks of Japan, Korea, and Taiwan; gold and silver notes of the Yokahama Specie Bank, and subsidiary coins.

[b] Private deposits in ordinary banks. Excludes public deposits and deposits in special and savings banks.

[c] Currency in circulation plus commercial bank deposits.

platforms tended to be "none too clearly differentiated" [14, pp. 20, 21].

Factors unfavorable to democracy included the constitutional arrangements, the lack of any large social class committed to democracy, the importance of the state in the economy and the consequent unwillingness of business to challenge those in actual possession of state power, and the economic setbacks that arrived in the 1920s at the same time as party governments [20, ch. 7, esp. pp. 254–258, 270–281].

Still another threat to democracy was public distrust of political parties. One factor here was a widespread belief that the two largest parties were the creatures of the largest big business combines, known as the zaibatsu. Thus, the Seiyukai and Minseito cabinets were also known as the "Mitsui" and "Mitsubishi" cabinets for the names of their respective zaibatsu supporters. The charge that the two major parties were too subservient to business did not go unvoiced, for Japan had several small but vocal parties of the left. Moreover, this charge could gain

Exhibit 8

Cumulative Balance of Payments for All of Japan, Including Korea and Formosa
(millions of yen)

Item	1904–1913	1914–1919	1920–1923	1924–1929
Merchandise trade (includes specie other than gold)				
Exports	4,519.3	8,373.1	6,502.6	12,714.2
Imports	−5,225.8	−7,175.6	−8,398.5	−15,034.7
Balance of merchandise trade	−706.5	1,197.5	−1,895.9	−2,320.5
Invisible trade				
Interest and dividends				
Received in Japan	13.3	166.5	153.2	117.8
Paid abroad	−650.2	−480.1	−274.3	−600.2
	−636.9	−313.6	−121.1	−482.4
Other (net)[a]				
Undertakings, services	274.2	441.3	405.6	688.3
Freight	252.4	1,356.7	622.7	801.7
Insurance	−17.9	9.8	29.2	51.2
Tourists, missionaries	23.5	66.5	47.3	86.8
Government payments	−329.7	165.5	−74.3	−269.9
Miscellaneous	−1.8	111.3	31.5	79.8
Balance of invisible trade	−436.2	1,837.5	940.9	955.5
Gold movements [b]				
Exports	258.9	242.2	0.3	90.3
Imports	−199.3	−846.2	−541.2	−1.4
Balance of gold movements	59.6	−604.0	−540.9	88.9
Balance of all current items	−1,082.8	2,431.0	−1,495.9	−1,276.1
Capital movements				
Investments, loans		No mean- ingful detail available	No mean- ingful detail available	For detail *see* Exhibit 10
By foreigners in Japan	2,045.3			
By Japanese abroad	−127.5			
Loans redeemed, shares sold				
Foreign	30.2			
Japanese	−270.2			
Balance of capital movements	1,677.8	−2,431.2	1,495.8	1,104.2
Grand totals				
Credits (+)	7,906.6	—	—	19,059.7
Debits (−)	−7,311.8	—	—	−19,231.9
Errors, omissions, and short-term capital (net)[c]	−594.8	—	—	172.2

SOURCE: E. B. Schumpeter (ed.) [21, pp. 875, 880 and appendix tables I, II, III].

NOTE: Compiled from various sources, in some cases long after the event; these figures should be regarded as no more than meaningful estimates.

[a] Debit and credit not shown separately for these items.

[b] Exports of gold, as of other merchandise, are credit items and imports are debit items.

[c] A plug-in figure.

some credence from Japan's slow progress in social legislation. A Factory Act was proposed as early as 1898 but was not enacted until 1911. Even then, application of the act was delayed until 1916. In response to rising labor unrest, a Workmen's Compensation Act was passed in 1922, but its application was delayed until 1927. Similarly, amendments to the Factory Act were passed in 1923 but were not put into effect until after 1926. These amendments cut hours for women and children from 11 to 10 and raised the minimum working age from 10 (boys) and 12 (girls) to 14. Only in 1929 was night work prohibited for women and children [12, pp. 558, 559; 13, pp. 55–62]. Reasons for this slow progress included Japan's low per capita GNP (under $140 throughout the 1920s compared with $776 in the United States); employers' fears that costs would rise too high (especially in textiles which was the largest export industry); the weakness of independent labor unions (which never enrolled more than 6 percent of the workforce) [21, p. 650], and employers' efforts to develop a distinctive Japanese pattern of labor–management relations, one modeled on the family rather than on the western stance of confrontation.

Corruption was another key reason for public mistrust of political parties. Past arrangements had promoted corruption. Governments had not been controlled by parties, but when they were in need of votes in the Diet, they had sometimes purchased party support. Similarly, party leaders had enjoyed no accepted right to join the cabinet, but they had sometimes purchased high office or sacrificed their principles in order to get it [20, pp. 141–143, 157, 158, 166, 169–173, 177–180, 244, 278, 279].

Corruption was also used to get contracts. Perhaps the most famous example dated back to 1910–1913 and involved a contract to build a heavy cruiser. Mitsubishi could have built this ship, but a unit of Mitsui got the job allotted to a British shipyard in re-

turn for a ¥1.5 million fee, of which ¥400,000 went to a vice admiral. When this news leaked, there was rioting "from Kobe to Osaka" [19, p. 188].

More current examples of corruption were disclosed when the Minseito displaced the Seiyukai in mid-1929. Under the Seiyukai, honors had been sold—an especially serious offense given Japanese concern for patriotism and prestige. Also sold were "a dozen or more charters for electric railways" and—in the colony of Korea—"government land, high official posts, water rights, reclamation rights, etc., etc." For every scandal that was revealed, some believed many went unreported. As one journal put it in 1929, scandals were becoming so "numerous" and so "shameless" and extending to such "exalted places" that a "ban" had been placed on the publication of some of the more "unsavoury" examples [10(Sep. 26, 1929), p. 337; 10(Dec. 26, 1929), p. 680].

Finally, behavior in the Diet tended to undermine respect for this key democratic institution.

> The minority groups, unable to do anything constructive, often resorted to the wildest possible scenes in order to distract the steam-roller majority and to get publicity for their cause in the press. So-called *yaji* (jeerers) held attention by hooting down administration spokesmen . . . or actually engaging in free-for-alls. The major parties had copied the old bureaucratic technique of employing *soshi* (strong-arm men) whose chief task was to act as bodyguards to their employers and as "rough men" toward the opposition [20, p. 219].

ECONOMIC INSTABILITIES

The economic problems of the 1920s got their start during World War I, when strong world demand and a fast rising money supply pushed up costs and prices.[7] Even after the war boom collapsed, the index of Japan's wholesale prices stayed above the indices of rival trading nations (*see* Exhibit 5 and Part 1 of Exhibit 9).

Further evidence that Japan's prices were noncompetitive was provided by the trade balance. This turned negative when rival trading nations started to revive, and it stayed negative throughout the 1920s (*see* Exhibit 6 and Part 2 of Exhibit 9). In short, as soon as the war boom was over, Japan was plagued again by the same problem that had been a chief concern throughout the prewar era.

One way to cope with postwar deficits was to draw on the reserves of foreign exchange that Japan had built up during the war. These were still substantial in 1920 despite the soured loans to Czarist Russia and the Chinese warlords. But they were not large enough to finance such substantial and persistent deficits as were experienced in the 1920s. What was needed was a way to end the deficits, not just to finance them.

One possibility for ending deficits was to devalue the yen, making exports cheaper and imports dearer. Yet, prevailing economic wisdom cast doubt on the efficacy of this approach, especially as a long-run solution. In line with current thinking, Japan's leaders favored a strong and stable yen—in fact, a yen still pegged at its old prewar value. This objective was set aside,

but only temporarily, owing to an earthquake in 1923. Lives lost totaled 100,000 and property damage was between ¥3.3 billion and ¥5.5 billion (compared with a ¥15 billion GNP) [12, pp. 42, 43; 14, pp. 305, 306]. Rebuilding "without stint," Japan saw imports soar and the yen plummet (*see* Exhibits 9 and 10).

Government's commitment to a strong yen was next demonstrated in 1925, when Japan took tentative steps toward making the yen convertible to gold.[8] As a result, the yen moved up (*see* Part 3 of Exhibit 9), but an export boom was nipped in the bud.

With devaluation ruled out, another way to fight trade imbalance would be to deflate, that is, to push prices down by putting the economy through "hard times." This was the approach used successfully by Matsukata in the 1880s, and it was the approach in which most Japanese governments believed. Deflations were in fact under way in 1920 and 1925, but they were countermanded before they had gone far enough to make Japan's prices competitive again. On both occasions the government found compelling reasons not to push ahead.

In 1920 the collapse of the postwar boom was so painful for farmers, businessmen, and banks (which had lent money to unsound businesses) that the government "preferred to temporize rather than to incur the social consequences of a violent deliberate deflation" [1, pp. 100, 101].[9] Instead of permitting deflation to continue, the government moved in the opposite direction by instituting price supports for rice and silk and by extending large advances to the banks in order to prevent a panic. Since the cost of these measures was fi-

---

[7] Since Japan had no internal market for discounting export bills and London, the center for such discounting, could not handle the business due to the war, the Yokohama Specie Bank cleared its holdings through New York. When the US embargoed gold shipments in 1917, the bank no longer had any way to settle its holdings of export bills except by selling them to the Bank of Japan. In order to purchase these bills the Bank of Japan issued large amounts of notes [1, pp. 99, 100]. Between 1913 and 1920, the money supply quadrupled, whereas real GNP rose only 44 percent (Exhibits 1 and 7).

---

[8] Britain went back on gold in 1925, pegging the pound at its old prewar value, and Japan, among others, wished to follow this example.

[9] Government's fears of social unrest had been intensified in 1919 near the climax of the wartime boom, when consumers rioted over rice prices.

Exhibit 9

Part 1

Wholesale Price Movements in Selected Countries,
1900-1930
(1913 = 100)

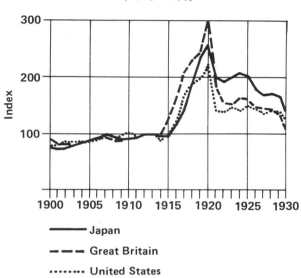

- Japan
- - - Great Britain
- - - - United States

Part 2

Balance of Trade, Japan Proper, 1885-1929

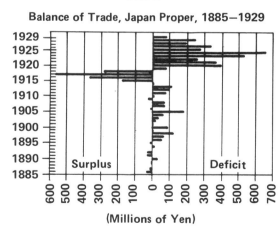

Part 3

Exchange Rates for the Yen
New York, 1913-1930

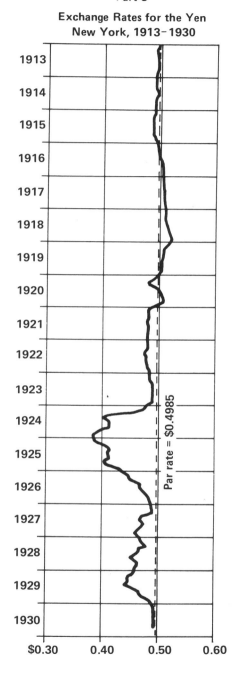

SOURCE: H. G. Moulton [14, p. 152]. Reprinted with permission.

Exhibit 10

Annual Balance of Payments for All of Japan, Including Korea and Formosa: 1924–1930 (millions of yen)

Item	1924	1925	1926	1927	1928	1929	1930
Merchandise trade (includes specie other than gold)							
Exports	1872.0	2378.1	2122.7	2078.7	2041.5	2221.2	1521.0
Imports	−2601.8	−2735.1	−2565.2	−2367.7	−2375.4	−2389.5	−1681.3
Balance of merchandise trade	−729.8	−357.0	−442.5	−289.0	−333.9	−168.3	−160.3
Invisible trade							
Interest and dividends							
Received in Japan	20.4	18.9	13.2	23.1	20.5	21.7	22.4
Paid abroad	−82.5	−106.2	−104.0	−99.6	−98.9	−109.0	−103.1
	−62.1	−87.3	−90.8	−76.5	−78.4	−87.3	−80.7
Other (net)[a]							
Undertakings, services	116.4	126.3	113.2	114.7	101.6	116.1	90.6
Freight	117.8	128.9	125.1	132.5	138.3	159.2	125.3
Insurance	15.2	20.3	2.2	0.6	4.7	8.3	0.4
Tourists, missionaries	19.1	19.7	22.7	17.1	4.9	3.3	0.7
Government payments	−56.5	−66.4	−42.8	−52.5	−28.0	−23.5	−14.2
Miscellaneous	14.3	13.5	10.5	12.2	18.1	11.1	10.9
Balance of invisible trade	164.2	154.9	140.0	147.9	161.2	187.3	133.0
Gold movements							
Exports	—	22.1	32.1	36.1	0.0	0.0	308.6
Imports	—	−0.1	−0.3	−0.1	−0.4	−0.5	−21.9
Balance of gold movements	0.0	22.0	31.8	36.0	−0.4	−0.5	286.7
Balance of all current items	−565.6	−180.0	−270.7	−105.2	−173.1	18.4	259.4
Capital movements (net)[a]							
Long-term capital							
Debt redemption	−71.6	−13.1	−30.2	−21.4	−12.8	60.7	24.2
Purchase, sale of							
Existing securities	−44.3	−72.8	2.5	−95.0	−78.3	−63.9	−143.2
New issues	308.7	137.0	103.9	51.3	180.8	23.0	102.5
Other long-term investments	44.9	12.8	−34.3	−61.1	−36.3	−72.6	−76.1
Short-term capital	309.8	115.7	233.8	172.7	63.1	−4.1	−203.4
Balance of all capital items	547.5	179.6	275.7	46.5	116.5	−56.9	−296.0
Grand totals							
Credits (+)	3372.5	3320.0	3162.1	2956.8	2991.5	3257.1	2734.3
Debits (−)	3389.7	3320.0	3162.1	3015.5	3048.0	3295.6	2770.3
Errors, omissions, and short-term capital (net)[a]	17.2	—	—	58.7	56.5	38.5	36.0

SOURCE: E. B. Schumpeter (ed.) [21, summarized from appendix tables I, II, and III].

NOTE: The figures in the current account are cited from various Japanese sources; the figures in the capital account are from reports to the League of Nations.

[a] Debit and credit detail not shown.

nanced by increased government borrowing, the deflation of 1920 "was arrested at an early stage" [1, pp. 100, 101].

The next effort at deflation started in 1925 when the government became alarmed about the inflationary impact of the earthquake reconstruction boom. Economies were effected and taxes were raised again at the same time as exports were slipping because of the increased value of the yen. Prices were falling when 36 banks—some of them major banks—closed their doors, in part owing to "frozen" earthquake loans. Actions taken to end the banking crisis again postponed the completion of deflation.

Nevertheless, the financial crisis of 1927 strengthened the economy. It served to weed out some of the "unsound" industrial and trading companies left over from World War I. Others passed under more efficient control. The same was true of the banking system: within eighteen months the number of "ordinary" banks declined from 1359 to 1030 [1, p. 103].

LONGER RUN ECONOMIC PROBLEMS

By 1928 issues of immediate economic policy were not the only issues to be faced. Analysts were also drawing attention to such longer run economic problems as population growth in relation to the food supply and the future standard of living, given Japan's limited resources.

Fears About the Future Food Supply

By 1927 Japan's population was increasing by about one million a year while domestic food output was almost static. Looking ahead, Japan's Ministry of Agriculture predicted that about 120 million bushels of rice and wheat combined would have to be imported by 1957, at an estimated cost of ¥0.72 billion [9, pp. 76, 77]. In sum, unless Japan could finance heavy imports of food in addition to all her other needs, population would outrun its means of subsistence.

Four possible solutions were seen: (1) increased agricultural output, (2) birth control, (3) emigration, and (4) increased in-

dustrialization to produce exports to pay for imports and perhaps to finance investments in China from which Japan could get some benefits.

The first three courses faced many obstacles. Japan's farm output was already relatively high per acre, and to increase it further would probably call for an investment in mechanization. This continued to be held back by the small size of the average farm (2.6 acres), the relatively high proportion of farmers who worked all or part of their land as tenants (42.3 percent and 26.5 percent, respectively), the low income of the farmer as determined by his low productivity (only about ¥240 per capita in current values for 1925–1929), and the difficulty of finding jobs elsewhere for many of the 14.7 million people employed, or underemployed, on the land [12, p. 25; 15, pp. 282, 310; 21, p. 129].

As for birth control, the Japanese were a family-oriented and intensely nationalistic people. Only in the 1920s had contraception been legalized, and it had received little publicity. As for emigration, this was largely cut off by exclusion laws except to Japan's own colonies, and these were unattractive because they offered an even lower standard of living than Japan's [9, pp. 89–107].

Japan placed its hope in the fourth alternative, industrialization. In this area her prospects received a close analysis from two US economists whose conclusions are summarized below.

Industrial Prospects: Somber Predictions

Whether or not Japan could solve her problems by increased industrialization was the topic of an often-cited study by Dr. John E. Orchard, a professor at the School of Business of Columbia University. He visited Japan in 1926 and 1927 and published his book in 1930. Dr. Orchard prefaced his account by pointing out that Japan was essentially hoping to follow the British strategy for making a small island rich. This strategy involved importing raw materials and transforming them into manufactures which could then be exported to keep the cycle going. The scheme had worked well for Britain, but could it also work for Japan? Dr. Orchard emphasized that Japan lacked not only Britain's advantages in coal and iron but also its head start. Long before countries like India or China had begun their own industrialization [16, pp. 2, 3].

Elaborating further on what Japan lacked, Orchard turned first to capital. Its scarcity was attested by the interest rate of 10 to 12 percent. As a result, most industrial units were small and much machinery old and obsolete. Even in textiles, the leading industry, Orchard saw machines made in the 1890s that had been imported second-hand from England, and he was reminded of the Tokugawa buying obsolete cannons from the Dutch [16, pp. 242–245].

Power was another scarce resource: Japan had a probable minimum of 14 million horsepower from her streams, but this was inadequate to meet all future needs [16, pp. 267, 269].

Even labor, "the chief industrial asset of Japan," was not in good supply so far as factory work was concerned. In spite of overpopulation, this shortage was attested by the need for continuous recruitment, turnover rates that varied by industry from 35 to 65 percent, and by the short working life of the women employees who made up a large proportion of the total and whose wages were considerably lower than the men's [16, pp. 339, 340].

So far as factory labor was concerned, scarcity was not the only problem. "A most important weakness" was "inefficiency."

This resulted partly from overstaffing and partly from the long nine-to-eleven-hour day. Inefficiency resulted even more from using obsolete machines. Thus, although Japan paid lower wages than the West, when labor costs per unit of output were compared, Japan's relatively low wages gave her little or no advantage. For example, in cotton spinning, "With three times the output and four times the wage, American wage costs per pound of yarn average about 35% greater than the Japanese." In cotton weaving, "Seven and a half times the Japanese output and five and a third times the wage leaves the American manufacturer with a wage cost per pound of cloth that is less than the Japanese. . . . Since the wage costs on American yarn average 35% more . . . and the wage costs on American cloth . . . average 33% less . . . the one nearly balances the other" [16, pp. 362, 371, 374, 375].

Finally, Japan's greatest and most irreversible lack was her scarcity of raw materials. This would be decisive for the future: "Japan has practically no iron ore and her reserves of coal are small and not of the best quality for industrial needs. Her poverty in these two materials must inevitably limit Japan in the realization of her industrial ambitions" [16, p. 276].

As if all these negative factors were not enough, even markets looked precarious because of Japan's great dependence on only two export markets and two export products (*see* Exhibit 11). "Japan's export trade moves in two streams: her luxury product, silk, goes East to the United States; her staple manufactures, chiefly cotton textiles, go toward the West and . . . Asia" [16, p. 448]. The US share, 42 percent in all, was made up of silk (85 percent), a product already threatened by rayon and by the possibility of silk from China.[10] The Asian share, 43 percent in all, was threat-

---

[10] Nylon, the real competition for silk, was not introduced in commercial quantities until after 1939.

ened by the possibility that native industries would be developed and by the hostility of China, endemic since the era of the Twenty-One Demands. Although China (including Liaotung) took 26.6 percent of all Japan's exports, she had mounted boycotts against Japan in at least seven years since 1920 [16, pp. 434-436, 449, 452].

Based on his conclusion that there seemed to be "no prospect" that Japan could attain "a position of major importance as a manufacturing nation," Dr. Orchard urged Japan to abandon her ideal of becoming the England of the East. Rather, his advice for Japan was the same as for China and India, two other "capital-poor" nations whose people "cling to their villages, and even if . . . enticed . . . to the city factory . . . return to their homes after . . . a few months." Instead of trying to emulate the "industrial order" of the West, such countries should decentralize their manufacturing and concentrate on village industry. Further, Dr. Orchard believed that Japan should adopt a more conciliatory stance toward China, in recognition of her "dependence" on this huge Asian neighbor for both raw materials and markets. Even though China was "no match for Japan in open warfare," she had "perfected in the boycott an economic weapon of defense" that struck Japan "in a most vulnerable spot." Hence, "imperialistic" policies toward China should be replaced with "friendly relations" and with "peaceful penetration through the investment of Japanese capital." In sum, for Japan, "The past has been beset with difficulties; the prospect for the future is none too brilliant" [16, pp. 450, 451, 482, 488, 489].

The conclusions of a second major US study of Japan at the end of the twenties were no more optimistic. The study was conducted by The Brookings Institution, and it received assistance from the Bank of Japan whose president, Junnosuke Inouye, had asked the Institution to undertake this work. Mr. Inouye had a number of reasons

for his interest: besides being a leading banker, he was also the author of an influential book on Japan's balance-of-payments problem, and he was transferring his major activity from banking to politics in 1929.

Aided by the Bank of Japan, the Brookings study was rich in analysis and statistics but not particularly rich in suggestions. Unlike Dr. Orchard, the Brookings study did not advise Japan to step backward, but its positive suggestions were relatively few. One course to be avoided was devaluation—something Japan had, perforce, already tried:

> The experience of many countries during the . . . last 200 years shows conclusively that, in the early stages of monetary depreciation . . . business activity is stimulated. But this history also demonstrates conclusively that an enduring prosperity cannot be built upon a policy of fluctuating exchange or continuous monetary inflation, with the exchange steadily going lower. Experience has shown again and again that, after a brief interval . . . progressive disintegration . . . occurs. Inflation is an opiate to the effects of which the economic body eventually succumbs [14, p. 405].

As for solving the population problem by further industrialization, the Brookings study simply pointed to the trends: "Whereas the rate of population growth has been accelerating, the rate of industrial growth has been declining" [14, p. 482]. In order to employ the workers entering the market over the next fifteen years, Japan would need 500,000 new jobs a year, but there was "no assurance" that such a "volume of employment" could be provided:

> In the long run there is no sovereign means for upbuilding the strength of the nation other than by maintaining a proper balance between population and economic resources. The increased effectiveness of the present economic organization of Japan over that of feudal days has permitted a doubling of the population in 60 years and

Exhibit 11

Percentage Distribution of Imports and Exports by Principal Categories and Commodities, Selected Years 1900–1928, Japan Proper and Sakhalin

	Percentages of Total Value of Imports						Economic Categories and Principal Commodities	Percentages of Total Value of Exports					
	1900	1913	1919	1922	1925	1928		1900	1913	1919	1922	1925	1928
	18.1	16.3	16.2	15.4	15.2	13.6	Food, drink, and tobacco	11.1	9.8	7.1	6.4	6.4	8.2
	1.7	1.4	1.6	2.1	2.7	3.1	Beans and peas	—	—	—	—	—	—
	—	—	—	—	—	—	Comestibles, tinned and bottled	0.2	0.5	0.4	0.4	0.6	1.2
	3.1	6.6	7.5	3.2	4.7	1.5	Rice and paddy	—	—	—	—	—	—
	9.3	5.0	2.7	3.4	2.9	3.0	Sugar	—	—	—	—	—	—
	—	—	—	—	—	—	Sugar, refined	—	2.5	1.0	1.2	1.4	2.0
	0.2	1.7	1.8	3.1	2.7	3.1	Tea, green and other	4.4	1.6	0.9	1.1	0.6	0.6
	—	—	—	—	—	—	Wheat	—	—	—	—	—	—
	—	—	—	—	—	—	Wheat flour	—	—	—	0.1	0.6	1.3
	28.0	48.5	50.3	43.8	58.0	53.1	Raw materials	13.6	8.1	5.2	5.2	7.1	4.6
	0.7	0.6	0.9	0.9	1.0	1.7	Coal	9.8	3.7	1.8	1.4	1.4	1.3
	—	—	—	0.3	0.6	2.1	Crude and heavy oil	—	—	—	—	—	—
	—	0.5	0.8	0.6	1.3	1.3	Crude rubber	—	—	—	—	—	—
	0.6	1.0	0.8	1.0	1.2	1.3	Hemp and other vegetable fibers	—	—	—	—	—	—
	1.6	0.5	6.2	5.2	4.2	4.0	Oil cake	—	—	—	—	—	—
	a	0.2	1.0	0.5	0.5	1.0	Ores (iron, zinc, others)	—	—	—	—	—	—
	20.7	31.6	30.7	22.6	35.9	25.1	Raw cotton	—	—	—	—	—	—
	0.3	0.4	0.5	4.5	3.0	5.1	Wood	0.8	1.6	1.1	0.9	0.9	0.9
	1.4	2.3	2.8	2.9	4.7	5.1	Wool	—	—	—	—	—	—
	20.2	17.2	20.8	20.7	12.8	17.4	Semi-manufactured articles	43.8	51.9	43.2	51.4	47.3	43.1
	—	0.1	—	0.8	0.1	—	Cotton yarn	10.1	11.2	5.4	7.0	5.3	1.4
	0.1	—	1.2	—	—	0.6	Copper	6.3	4.5	1.2	0.1	0.1	0.1
	—	—	—	—	—	—	Iron	—	0.1	0.9	3.0	0.3	0.2
	0.3	1.4	2.4	0.9	0.6	1.2	Pig iron	—	—	—	—	—	—
	0.2	0.6	0.5	0.6	0.6	0.5	Pulp (paper and rayon)	—	—	—	—	—	—
	—	—	—	—	—	—	Raw silk	21.8	29.9	29.7	40.9	38.2	38.3
	7.2	6.3	8.4	7.4	3.4	5.7	Steel and other iron (incl scrap)	—	—	—	—	—	—

Finished manufactures	32.1	16.8	12.0	19.3	13.6	15.2	27.8	29.2	43.0	35.5	38.1	42.5
Automobiles and parts	—	0.2	0.5	0.4	0.4	1.5	—	—	—	—	—	—
Cotton piece goods	6.4	1.4	0.3	0.7	0.4	0.3	2.8	5.3	13.4	13.6	18.8	18.4
Cotton piece goods, bleached	—	—	—	—	—	—	0.9	1.0	1.6	0.9	1.4	1.4
Cotton piece goods, gray	—	—	—	—	—	—	0.9	1.8	4.5	4.9	5.9	6.4
Cotton piece goods, other	—	—	—	—	—	—	1.1	2.5	7.3	7.7	11.5	10.6
Iron manufactures	—	—	—	—	—	—	0.2	0.1	1.0	0.6	0.6	0.7
Knitted goods	—	—	—	—	—	—	0.2	1.4	1.9	1.1	1.3	1.7
Machinery and parts	3.4	5.0	4.1	6.0	3.5	4.2	0.1	0.4	0.8	0.9	0.4	0.6
Mineral oils, refined	5.2	1.8	1.3	2.0	1.6	2.0	—	—	—	—	—	—
Paper	—	—	—	—	—	—	0.6	0.4	1.2	1.0	0.9	1.3
Pottery	—	—	—	—	—	—	1.2	1.0	1.1	1.3	1.5	1.8
Silk piece goods (incl cotton mixtures)	—	—	—	—	—	—	9.1	6.2	7.7	7.2	5.1	7.0
Toys	—	—	—	—	—	—	0.2	0.4	0.6	0.4	0.5	0.6
Woolen piece goods	6.2	1.7	0.6	2.6	2.2	1.4	—	0.1	0.5	0.1	0.2	0.2
Miscellaneous	1.5	0.6	0.7	0.8	0.4	0.7	3.6	1.0	1.5	1.5	1.2	1.6
Total value of imports and exports Japan proper and Sakhalin (millions of ¥)	287	729	2173	1890	2573	2196	204	632	2099	1637	2306	1972

SOURCES: Bank of Japan [2, p. 280: table 115]; E. B. Schumpeter (ed.) [21, pp. 830, 831].

a Less than 0.05 percent.

its support at higher levels of living. But the continued rapid increase of population in recent years now threatens the maintenance of these standards. Unless the rate of population growth is restricted and restricted soon, the social outlook for Japan will present itself in somber colors [14, pp. 482, 483].

STRATEGIC GOALS OF JAPAN'S ARMED FORCES

While economists advanced one set of proposals for Japan, her army and navy advanced still others, based in part on economic but more on military considerations. As in earlier years, the army's chief concern was Japan's position in China, while the navy's was Japan's domination of home waters. The navy was also concerned with maintaining access to the South Pacific, since this area produced rubber, oil, and other strategic raw materials.

Besides pursuing individual objectives, the army and navy joined in condemnation of recent cuts in military outlays. Between 1921 and 1923 these had fallen from 49 to 30 percent of the budget. Again, it was the army that found the cuts most galling. In the 1920s the navy was still able to build a new fleet of submarines and heavy cruisers, but the army had to economize on either troops or new weaponry. Since tanks, planes, anti-aircraft guns, and new communications equipment were vital, the army decreased its forces by 38,000 men. Also in 1924, it had to cut the number of its divisions from a "minimal" 21 to only 17 [6, pp. 30, 87, 88].

Army Strategy

So far as China was concerned, past civilian policy could be called "economic penetra-

tion by political intrigue." That is, Japan had sought trade and investment rather than territory. She also sought to protect her interests by "aid" to Chinese leaders such as Chiang Kai-shek, the head of a "Nationalist" movement in the South, and Chang Tso-lin, the most potent warlord in Manchuria [19, pp. 179, 180, 254–256].

Domination by economic means did not satisfy powerful army elements, however, particularly the militant members of the small Kwantung Army which Japan maintained in Liaotung and the Manchurian Railway Zone. "Within the Imperial Army . . . faith in the use of military power as the best method to protect the property and lives of Japanese nationals on the continent had never faltered." The army's most immediate concern was Manchuria. One reason was the Railway Zone and other investments; the other, hatred of communism and Russia. A so-called "Strike North" faction was especially eager for "direct military action" in Manchuria. This group "was convinced of the historical inevitability of a Soviet–Japanese conflict," and it wanted Manchuria in order to achieve a "strategic advantage" against the Soviets [6, pp. 30–33, 110–112].

Although such a policy would be distasteful to Britain and the United States, the Japanese believed that it would at least not provoke armed retaliation. They reasoned that the same might not be true of the course proposed by a rival "Strike South" faction. This group allegedly questioned whether Japan could single out Russia from the rest of the West, and it looked forward to mobilizing the resources of all of China for an eventual comprehensive showdown [4, p. 553].

The army advanced several arguments for the use of force versus diplomacy. Trade most easily followed the flag, it said, and pointed to the frequency of Chinese boycotts. Aid could not be counted on to buy control; otherwise, why would Chiang Kai-shek appear to be attempting to unite all

China? Western views should not be decisive, for in the 1920s Japan had been building a "new fleet" of heavy cruisers and submarines, while US shipyards had been "relatively dormant" [6, p. 30].

After 1927, the militants' views looked particularly compelling, for Chiang Kai-shek turned an army toward Manchuria. (The Japanese moved to head it off by moving troops back to Shantung.) In addition, Russia's latest five-year plan had "greatly augmented the strength of the Red Army" massed along the northern borders of Manchuria [6, p. 111].

Naval Strategy

Like the army, the navy was dissatisfied with civilian military policy, the reason being the low naval ratio (6 to 10) accepted back in 1922. Two facts had helped Japan to live with this decision. The first was that since Britain and the United States had not agreed on ratios for cruisers, ratios had been set for battleships and aircraft carriers only. A second and much more important reason was that the United States had built almost no warships in the 1920s.

By 1929 this situation was clearly going to change: the United States was planning a big new naval building program, and it opened talks with Britain looking toward a second Naval Conference. Here the United States would seek not only to maintain the existing 6-to-10 ratio but also to extend it to all naval ships.

EMERGENCE OF A "RADICAL RIGHT"

As in Italy and Germany, the 1920s saw the emergence of a radical right in Japan. This movement was radical in its condemnation of existing institutions, policies, and performance, but rightist in its anticommunism, imperialism, ultranationalism, and dedication to traditional ideals. Among the chief proponents of such views was Ikki Kita, who made a "tremendous impact" with a book published in 1924. John Roberts summarizes Kita's views as follows:

> Kita, a fanatical imperialist, believed that peace would come only when the Western powers had slaughtered each other and Japan had become "shogun" of the world. However, his domestic policy was humanitarian and, like those of Hitler and Mussolini, bore a superficial resemblance to socialism. A necessary step for achieving his aims was that of breaking the power of big capitalists and landowners by establishing an idealistic form of state capitalism. The middle and lower classes, however, were to retain their property as a sovereign right [19, p. 250].

Kita's views and those of others like him attracted many converts. Some were drawn from a fast-growing number of patriotic societies, many from the ranks of army officers who had been indoctrinated with such traditional ideas and ideals as the "Code of the Warrior," a "mystical belief in the divine qualities of the Imperial institution," and the "unique obligation of the soldier to render absolute loyalty to the Throne" [6, p. 86]. These officers found their "vision of Japan . . . painfully at odds with sordid realities" [19, p. 250].

> Since the army's educational program canonized the unique "spiritual powers" of the Japanese state, implicitly it censured the prevailing notions of parliamentary democracy, armament limitations, and pacifistic approaches to international politics. In the process, the professional officer developed a profound antipathy toward the political scene where, it seemed, politicians and businessmen voiced the principles of European liberalism and workers were beguiled by socialism and communism [6, p. 87]. © 1966 by Princeton University Press. Reprinted by permission.

In keeping with these attitudes, "most officers viewed the army as the last bastion of traditional values." Some even wanted it to engineer a second or "Showa Restoration" to redo the work of 1868 [6, pp. 87, 93].[11]

In assessing the significance of army opinion, observers noted the existence of close ties between the army and the largest social class, that is, the peasantry:

> Most army recruits were peasants. Moreover, the services—particularly the army—were highly exceptional among Japanese institutions in that they provided opportunities for the individual to rise on his own merits. Consequently, many of the officers, especially of the lower ranks, came from peasant families and had poignant memories of rural suffering. In addition, military life was Spartan, and the pay standards of even the high officers were extremely low in comparison with those of the commercial-industrial classes [20, p. 363].

THE CHANGE OF POLICIES: 1927–1930

The civilian policy of dominating a divided China by supporting Chiang Kai-shek in the South and Chang Tso-lin in the North suffered major setbacks in 1927 and 1928. First, Chiang turned his troops toward the north in what looked like a bid to unite all China. Chang Tso-lin at first moved south to meet him, but when Chiang reached Peking it was agreed that the Manchurian warlord should retreat into home territory. Chang Tso-lin then boarded a 20-car troop train to carry out his retreat. Japanese dig-

nitaries who waited to greet him at Mukden were stunned to learn that the car in which Chang was riding had been blown up only a few miles short of the station. Japan's Manchurian ally was dead [19, pp. 363–365]. The assassins and their motives remained a mystery for years, although suspicion fell immediately (and correctly, as history would reveal) on extremists in Japan's Kwantung Army [20, pp. 236, 237].

Public opinion was shocked. The Seiyukai Premier, Giichi Tanaka, went to the War Office "in an effort to get punishment," but because "powerful generals" insisted on making army discipline an internal army affair, "the plotters remained unpunished and the Tanaka cabinet resigned" [20, pp. 236, 237].

On the advice of Prince Saionji, last of the Genro, the Minseito took office in July 1929. This party was less militant than the Seiyukai. Under Yukio Hamaguchi as premier, the post of foreign minister went to Baron Kijuro Shidehara, well known as an advocate of "friendship" with China. The post of finance minister went to banker J. Inouye, well known as a long-term advocate of "balanced budgets and free gold movements" [1, p. 103; 21, p. 9]. Under these leaders, the Minseito program called for purification of politics, reform of China policy, disarmament, a balanced budget and a return to the gold standard. Disarmament was one key step toward balancing the budget, for expenditure on the armed forces had been running about 30 percent of the "General Account" budget for the three years ending March 31, 1929 [14, pp. 578, 579]. Another obvious economy would be to cut the salaries of government employees. The Minseito announced a 10 percent cut in September 1929. This had to be rescinded almost at once, however, because it threatened to precipitate "a general strike in official circles" [10(Oct. 24, 1929), p. 433]. As for returning to the gold standard, the plan was to delay this crucial step until the way for it had been

---

[11] Showa was the official name of Emperor Hirohito, the grandson of Emperor Meiji. He had become Prince Regent in 1922 because his father, Emperor Taisho, was too ill to undertake the duties of emperor. Taisho held office from the time of the death of Meiji in 1912.

prepared by some of the other steps in the program. Yet, the mere promise of going back on gold was enough to make the yen start climbing. It was trading at almost its old prewar rate when Japan went back on gold on January 11, 1930 (*see* Part 3 of Exhibit 9).

Most of the Minseito's economic planks, especially the balanced budget and the return to gold, were designed to push prices down. Japan's index of wholesale prices was still relatively high (*see* Exhibit 5), and considerable hardship would be entailed if such plans were implemented. Yet a price decline was seen as essential to solve the chronic balance-of-payments problem. Moreover, if "hard medicine" must be administered, circumstances looked especially favorable in July 1929. Confidence in the soundness of the banking structure had been restored by the reforms of 1927, and Japanese exports were expanding in response to the stimulus of world prosperity [1, pp. 103, 104].

Yet conditions were changing rapidly. Early 1930—which finally saw the Minseito win a long-delayed election by a decisive 80-seat majority—also saw two developments inimical to the party's policies. One was the advent of the Great Depression; the other was a second Naval Conference.

Impact of the Great Depression

When the boom of 1929 collapsed, it became evident that "no more unfortunate moment" could have been chosen for deflating and going back on gold. On the heels of Japan's self-imposed price decline came a further and much deeper slippage. The price of one main export, silk, fell 50 percent during 1930, silk being a luxury product. In addition, exports to Asia, including cotton textiles, were hit by a "precipitous" decline in the value of silver and thus in the purchasing power of Asian currency, which was silver-backed [1, p. 104; 21, p. 894].

These blows fell especially heavily on farmers, "one of the largest and most vulnerable sections of the Japanese economy." Owing to a series of good harvests, farmers were already suffering from low prices for rice. "The fall in silk prices ruined many of these farmers, while the decline in the cotton trade reduced the opportunities for employment offered to their daughters by the textile mills" [1, pp. 104, 105]. Given the role of silk in exports, "the plight of the raw silk trade . . . affected not only the agricultural classes but the entire commercial and financial world" as well [21, p. 893].

Impact of the Naval Conference

Besides facing a worsening depression, the Minseito also faced the sensitive issue of naval ratios. The US was planning a big shipbuilding program, and in May 1925 cabinet-level talks on naval ratios started between the United States and Britain. The crux of the debate was heavy cruisers, a type of ship on which the two countries had been unable to agree at the 1922 Naval Conference. In 1929 the US had just one heavy cruiser, but Congress had authorized a fleet of twenty-three. Britain saw this number as too many: it would cause Japan to seek at least fourteen, assuming that Japan would be content with a six-to-ten ratio. If Japan had fourteen cruisers, Britain would need more than her present strength of fifteen in order to protect her interests in the South Pacific. Australia and New Zealand would insist. (*See* Exhibit 12 for the relative naval strength of the major powers as of January 1929.)

Largely in the interests of economy, Prime Minister Ramsay MacDonald hoped that

Exhibit 12

Naval Conference: Comparing the Five Large Powers

	Britain	*US*	*Japan*	*France*	*Italy*
Capital ships					
Number	20	18	10	9	4
Tonnage	556,350	506,198	292,400	194,547	86,528
Number after 1942	15	15	9	6	6
Tonnage after 1942	525,000	525,000	315,000	175,000	175,000
Ratio for the above	5	5	3	1.68	1.68
Aircraft carriers					
Number	7	4[a]	4[b]	2[b]	1
Tonnage	120,350	90,086	68,870	32,145	5,315
Ratio[c]	5	5	3	1.75	1.75
Tonnage[c]	130,000	135,000	81,000	60,000	60,000
Large cruisers (age limit: 20 yrs)					
Afloat					
Number	11	1	8	3	2
Tonnage	110,000	10,000	68,400	30,000	20,000
Building					
Number	6	12	4	3	4
Tonnage	56,800	120,000	40,000	30,000	40,000
Projecting					
Number	1	10	—	1	—
Tonnage	10,000	100,000	—	10,000	—
Total					
Number	18	23	12	7	6
Tonnage	76,800	230,000	108,400	70,000	60,000
Small cruisers (age limit: 20 yrs)					
Afloat					
Number	43	10	21	5	9
Tonnage	217,111	70,500	98,415	49,402	40,968
Building					
Number	—	—	—	—	6
Tonnage	—	—	—	—	29,602
Projecting					
Number	—	—	—	—	—
Tonnage	—	—	—	—	—
Total					
Number	43	10	21	5	15
Tonnage	217,111	70,500	98,415	49,402	70,571

Exhibit 12 (continued)

	Britain	US	Japan	France	Italy
Destroyers					
(age limit: 16 yrs)					
Afloat					
Number	150	284	103	61	78
Tonnage	157,585	290,304	108,975	70,752	74,399
Building					
Number	20	—	6	21	11
Tonnage	26,785	—	10,200	44,864	14,620
Projecting					
Number	9	—	6	6	—
Tonnage	12,390	—	10,200	15,413	—
Total					
Number	179	284	115	88	89
Tonnage	196,761	290,340	129,375	131,027	89,019
Submarines					
Afloat					
Number	53	108	64	44	45
Tonnage	45,434	77,062	66,077	31,983	27,840
Building					
Number	10	2	7	47	14
Tonnage	14,750	5,520	11,765	49,780	9,824
Projecting					
Number	6	3	—	11	—
Tonnage	6,080	4,650	—	11,225	—
Total					
Number	69	113	71	102	59
Tonnage	66,364	87,232	77,842	92,988	37,664

SOURCE: *Japan Chronicle* [10(February 20, 1930), pp. 168, 169].

NOTE: The *Asahi* publishes the above table as showing the naval strength of the five naval powers at the end of January 1930.

[a] One projecting.
[b] One building.
[c] Under Washington Treaty.

the US government would agree to settle for eighteen heavy cruisers; if so, Japan might be satisfied with her existing fleet of twelve. "In that event," he concluded, "the United States could still build a fleet of heavy cruisers, and Japan and Great Britain could avoid the necessity of any new construction in this category of warship" [6, pp. 27, 35, 39, 40].

No US–British agreement had been reached on cruiser numbers by January 1930, when the second Naval Conference convened in London. In any case, the two superpowers had erred in supposing that Japan would agree to a six-to-ten ratio. Her hegemony in the Western Pacific was at stake, as other naval experts recognized [6, p. 43]. Thus, Japan's government had made a public pledge to achieve a ratio of seven to ten, calling this "essential" to her security.

> In order to demonstrate the earnest desire of the Japanese government for a real reduction in naval armaments, as well as to indicate the basic unity among all important political and naval groups in Japan, the entire Hamaguchi cabinet, the leaders of the opposition party, the Seiyukai, and the leading members of the Privy Council attended an October 10 [1929] briefing session on national defense policies at the official residence of the naval minister. Following this conference, Premier Hamaguchi advised the press of the government's intention to seek a 10:7 ratio with the United States in the heavy-cruiser category. This ratio, the premier indicated, was indispensable to the security of the empire [6, p. 43]. © 1966 by Princeton University Press. Reprinted by permission.

At the conference, Japan appeared adamant on seven to ten. Finally, the US delegation was compelled to reconsider its initial policy in the interest of making sure that Britain would stick with a united front against Japan. The US target for heavy cruisers—already cut from 23 to 21—was cut again to Britain's preferred figure of eighteen. This done, US Secretary of State Henry Stimpson and British Prime Minister Ramsay MacDonald agreed "that Great Britain and the United States would continue to pursue identical lines with reference to Japan in view of the very strong feelings of Australia of the necessity for keeping Japanese big cruiser figures down" [6, p. 48].

Anglo-American unity was revealed to Japan on February 17, but Japan's delegation refused to back down. Ignoring Britain, spokesman Reijiro Wakatsuki—an ex-premier—addressed his arguments to the US.

> Neither he nor the Japanese people could understand why Japan should not be given a 70 per cent ratio, unless the United States actually harbored the idea of ultimately engaging in a war with the Japanese empire. "As long as America held that ten percent

advantage," concluded Wakatsuki, "it was possible for her to attack. So, when America insisted on sixty percent instead of seventy percent, the idea would exist that they were trying to keep that possibility, and the Japanese people could not accept that" [6, p. 49]. © 1966 by Princeton University Press. Reprinted by permission.

Despite the force of these arguments, Secretary Stimpson believed that Japan would change her tune once her imminent elections were over. If not, and Stimpson quickly learned that he was wrong, Japan could be confronted with the threat of an Anglo-American naval pact as a last resort. This was expected to convince her leaders that the alternative to a three-power treaty would "compromise her security more decisively" than a six-to-ten cruiser ratio [6, p. 52].

Against this backdrop and with the talks temporarily stalled, Japan made it known that she would accede to eighteen heavy cruisers for the US if the last three were deferred until 1935. The US countered with a proposal to defer the last three until 1934, 1935, and 1936, calling this the "maximum concession" possible. The next morning, March 14, Japan was presented with the "final" American proposal [6, p. 54], which worked out essentially as shown below.

	US (tons)	Japan (tons)	Japan/US (%)
Large cruisers	180,000	108,400	60.2
Small cruisers	143,500	100,450	70.0
Destroyers	150,000	105,500	70.3
Submarines	52,700	52,700	100.0
	526,200	367,050	69.75

SOURCE: J. Crowley [6, p. 64]. © 1966 by Princeton University Press. Reprinted by permission.

On receipt of this news, Foreign Minister Shidehara "fired one question at the Japanese delegation: was it possible to obtain further concessions?" The "dreaded reply" was no [6, p. 56], and Japan's government was forced to consider whether to amend its instructions to its spokesmen.

Discussion of this issue started March 15. Since the minister of the navy was at the talks in London and since he made no explicit objection to a change, his subordinates in Tokyo inferred that the ministry supported new instructions. On sounding out the naval general staff and the foreign minister, however, they found an absolute cleavage of opinion. The general staff wanted to cable Japan's delegation that its first instructions were "unalterable"; Foreign Minister Shidehara "countered with the importance of international cooperation and the desire of the government to reduce military expenditures" [6, p. 57].

Before a decision could be reached, other power centers would have to be consulted, including Prince Saionji and members of Japan's Supreme War Council. If concessions were to be made, support must be mustered in high places, since an attack could be expected from the militant Seiyukai in the Diet, and since the treaty must be ratified by the Privy Council.

While this "backstage maneuvering" was going on, the vice-chief of Japan's naval staff went public with his objections, stating that the Japanese navy "by no means" accepted the US proposals. When this news reached London, Stimpson and MacDonald decided to apply maximum pressure. A cable went to the US Ambassador in Tokyo stating that the March 14 proposal was "the fullest concession to which we or the British can go, and if not accepted by Japan, then Great Britain and ourselves see no course open but to make a two-power treaty . . ." [6, pp. 59, 60].

The US Ambassador believed that such an open threat would be counterproductive. As he saw it, US insistence on a six-to-ten ratio had already undermined Japanese support for a foreign policy based on friendly relations with the West and China. Accordingly, the US Ambassador did not show the cable to the Japanese premier, as suggested, but took it to Foreign Minister Shidehara, the chief proponent of the peace policy. Shidehara decided to pocket the cable, lest the military learn of it and use it to mobilize support for an intransigent answer to London [6, p. 60].

The moment of decision had arrived on both the budget and the naval treaty.

REFERENCES

1. Allen, George C. *A Short Economic History of Modern Japan, 1867–1937*. London: Allen and Unwin, 1962.

2. Bank of Japan, Statistics Department. *Hundred-Year Statistics of the Japanese Economy*. Tokyo: 1966.

3. Beasley, W. G. *The Modern History of Japan*. New York: Praeger, 1963.

4. Bergamini, David. *Japan's Imperial Conspiracy*. New York: William Morrow, 1971.

5. Borton, Hugh. *Japan's Modern Century*. New York: The Ronald Press, 1955.

6. Crowley, James B. *Japan's Quest for Autonomy: National Security and Foreign Policy, 1930–1938*. Princeton, N.J.: Princeton University Press, 1966.

7. *Encyclopedia Britannica*. "Russo-Japanese War," *eleventh edition*, 1911.

8. Fahs, Charles B. *Government in Japan: Recent Trends in Its Scope and Operation*. New York: Institute of Pacific Relations, 1940.

9. Hindmarsh, Albert E. *Basis of Japanese Foreign Policy*. Cambridge Mass.: Harvard University Press, 1936.

10. *Japan Chronicle*. Tokyo weekly newspaper.

11. League of Nations. *Statistical Yearbook of the League of Nations*, annual. Geneva.

12. Lockwood, William W. *The Economic Development of Japan: Growth and Structural Change, 1868–1938*. Princeton, N.J.: Princeton University Press, 1954.

13. Marshall, Byron K. *Capitalism and Nationalism in Prewar Japan. The Ideology of the Business Elite*. Stanford, Calif.: Stanford University Press, 1967.

14. Moulton, Harold G. *Japan: An Economic and Financial Appraisal*. Washington: Brookings Institution, 1931.

15. Ohkawa, Kazushi and Henry Rosovsky. *Japanese Economic Growth: Trend Acceleration in the Twentieth Century*. Stanford, Calif.: Stanford University Press, 1973.

16. Orchard, John E. and Dorothy Orchard. *Japan's Economic Position: The Progress of Industrialization*. New York: McGraw-Hill, 1930.

17. Pyle, Kenneth B. *The New Generation in Meiji Japan*. Stanford, Calif.: Stanford University Press, 1969.

18. Reischauer, Edwin O. *The United States and Japan* (3d ed.). New York: Viking, 1964. (Original edition, Cambridge, Mass.: Harvard University Press, 1950.)

19. Roberts, John G. *Mitsui: Three Centuries of Japanese Business*. New York: Weatherhill, 1973.

20. Scalapino, Robert A. *Democracy and the Party Movement in Prewar Japan*. Berkeley, Calif.: University of California Press, 1953.

21. Schumpeter, Elizabeth B. (ed.). *The Industrialization of Japan and Manchukuo, 1930–1940*. New York: Macmillan, 1940.

22. Silberman, Bernard S. and Harry D. Harootunian (eds.). *Modern Japanese Leadership*. Tucson: University of Arizona Press, 1966.

Japan C: 1945–1952, From Occupation to Independence

Midway through 1952 Japan regained the independence she had lost after World War II. Those seven years had been momentous: the War had reduced Japan's economy to ruins; the victors had shorn her empire away; and the US Occupation had required Japan to remold many of her institutions in line with democratic models. But now—if she saw fit—Japan could begin to dismantle these changes.

Besides perhaps remolding her institutions, Japan would have to meet a more familiar challenge: What strategy would best assure the economic future of a population of 85 million, crowded on a small, resource-poor island chain, whose survival would largely depend on foreign trade?

FROM THE DEATH OF TAKAHASHI TO THE END OF WORLD WAR II

With the assassination of Finance Minister Korekiyo Takahashi in February 1936, the last effective civilian restraint on Japan's military elite was removed, and the power to formulate Japanese strategy passed to the military. There followed, starting in 1937, a protracted war with China; the mounting threat of US economic intervention in the form of an oil embargo; Japan's

decision to strike back at Pearl Harbor; and the full-scale expansion of World War II into the Pacific.

Well before the Allies began to win their fight against Japan, they began to announce their postwar intentions, once victorious. Thus, Japan learned from the Cairo Declaration in December 1943 that the Allies meant to "punish" her "aggression" and to take her empire away. Nearer the end of hostilities and after the tide of success had turned, Japan learned more from the Potsdam Declaration of July 1945: "The Japanese military forces . . . shall be permitted to return to their homes." "We do not intend that the Japanese shall be enslaved as a race or destroyed as a nation." "Japan shall be permitted to maintain such industries as will sustain her economy." "The occupying forces of the Allies shall be withdrawn from Japan as soon as these objectives have been accomplished and there has been established in accordance with the freely expressed will of the Japanese people a peacefully inclined and responsible government" [34, p. 236]. Reprinted by permission of Harvard University Press.

A few months later, two atomic bombs ended Japan's hope to resist. She surrendered on August 15, stipulating only that she be allowed to keep her emperor. The Occupation got under way in the first week of September 1945.

AN ECONOMY IN RUINS

By the time Japan sought peace, her economy lay in ruins. Edwin O. Reischauer described the scene as follows:

> Physical destruction alone was enough to change Japan permanently. It is estimated that 1,850,000 Japanese lost their lives during the war, 668,000 of them in Japan proper as a result of the air raids. During the first few years after the war, over 6,000,000 soldiers and civilians who had been abroad, many of them for decades, were dumped back in Japan, providing just that many more mouths for the overtaxed land to feed. Forty per cent of Japan's aggregate urban area was destroyed or damaged. . . .
>
> But the destruction of Japan's cities, while bitter enough . . . was not as serious for the nation as the collapse of the economy. . . . Industrial production . . . in 1946 . . . sank to less than a third of the 1930 total and a mere seventh of the 1941 figure. . . . The production of coal, Japan's largest source of power, had fallen by November 1945 to one-eighth of the monthly average of 1940. Pig-iron production that same month was only a seventieth of the monthly average in 1942. Textile production at the beginning of 1946 was scarcely more than a twentieth of what it had been in 1937. Less than a tenth as many electric motors and truck chassis were being made at the beginining of 1946 as in 1939 and 1941 respectively. Machine production . . . had come virtually to a halt, and the nation had been thrown back on agriculture as its sole support [34, pp. 207–209, *passim*]. Reprinted by permission of Harvard University Press.

Severe as it was, physical destruction did not tell the whole story. In the words of a Japanese participant, "The mental apathy and dejection of the people helped reduce the economic foundation to complete disorder." Moreover, partly because of government actions, inflation was soon "on the march" [37, p. 64].

THE EMPIRE DISMANTLED

As had been decided in 1943, one of the first Allied steps was to carve away Japan's empire. Thus, her area fell from 678,000 square kilometers to 383,000, and her density of population (including refugees from former colonies) rose from 189 per square kilometer in 1941 to 212 in 1947 [3, p. 13; 37, p. 95]. Even though the Cold War was starting to heat up, most of Japan's conquered territories were returned to the neighbors from whom they had been taken. Thus, Formosa, Manchuria, and the Pescadores Islands were returned to China, and South Sakhalin and the Kuriles to Russia. Korea regained independence, while the Marshall, Caroline, and Mariana Islands were temporarily given to the United States as a mandate and later were given to the United Nations.

US POST-SURRENDER POLICY FOR JAPAN

Since the United States would supply the occupying force for Japan under the leadership of Douglas MacArthur as Supreme Commander of the Allied Powers (SCAP), the dominant voice in Japanese affairs was that of the United States. Even as General MacArthur waited aboard ship in Tokyo Bay for the formal Japanese surrender, Washington radioed a set of instructions. Titled *Initial Post-Surrender Policy for Japan*, this document outlined a three-part program targeted at demilitarization, the creation of a "peaceful and responsible" government, and the restoration of the economy to a point that would permit "the peacetime requirements of the population to be met" [34, appendix 2, pp. 341–348].

DEMILITARIZATION

Insuring that Japan "would not again become a menace to . . . peace" [34, p. 341] was the first objective listed for post-surrender policy. Thus, arsenals were closed, naval bases and shipyards destroyed, the armed forces demobilized, and the military ministries in the cabinet abolished. Twenty-five leaders were selected to be tried as war criminals, and about 200,000 other persons were barred from public life in 1946 as having favored militant nationalism and aggression. Additions to this list in the following year reached into local government and 246 major business firms. Plans were also laid regarding reparations, and an ambitious program of industrial limitation was undertaken.

> We eliminated Japan's whole aircraft industry as well as such industries as synthetic oil and synthetic rubber, which were justified only by wartime conditions. We quite stupidly stopped atomic research and banned certain small industries, such as the production of bearings, which are important for military as well as civilian uses. We went still further by putting drastic limits on major industries, such as steel, chemicals, and machine tools, which, while necessary for peacetime economy, had in the past been devoted in large part to direct military purposes [34, pp. 247, 248]. Reprinted by permission of Harvard University Press.

As a final stroke for demilitarization, the Occupation required Japan to renounce war as an instrument of national policy. Accordingly, Article 9 of the new constitution stated, "The right of belligerency of the State will not be recognized" [34, p. 351].

CREATION OF A "RESPONSIBLE" GOVERNMENT

According to *Initial Post-Surrender Policy*, Japan's political system "should conform as closely as may be to principles of democratic self-government." Although it was not "the responsibility of the Allied Powers to impose upon Japan any form of government not supported by the freely expressed will of the people," the Japanese should nevertheless be "encouraged to become familiar with the history, institutions, culture, and the accomplishments of the United States and the other democracies." "Democratic political parties" were also to be "encouraged" [34, appendix 2].

A New Constitution

In line with these policy mandates, the Occupation soon suggested that the Japanese rewrite their constitution. Under US pressure, the Japanese prepared a document that the Allies could approve, which went into effect in May 1947. In contrast to the old constitution, the new one rested sovereignty in the people and extended suffrage to women. In addition, the power of the prime minister was increased by making cabinet members collectively responsible to the Diet instead of individually responsible. A bicameral system was continued, but the upper house of the Diet was no longer equal to the lower house, particularly in budgetary matters.

While following parliamentary models for the most part, the new constitution also reflected US influence. That is, it provided for a judiciary that would be "independent of the executive branch," for a Supreme Court with "full judicial powers," for the assignment of certain powers to elected—not appointed—local governments, and for a Bill of Rights no longer subject to vague and open-ended limitations [6, pp. 409–411, *passim*].

Democratic Political Parties

To encourage "democratic" parties, an election was scheduled for 1946—before the new constitution was completed—in which parties would be able to compete. Besides splinter groups and "independents," four main groupings emerged. From right to left these were: the conservative Liberal Party, the center-to-conservative Progressive Party (which went through several changes of name before merging with the Liberals), the socialist Social Democratic Party (which had split into separate left- and right-wing factions by 1952), and the small Communist Party. In three of the four elections held through 1952, the right-wing Liberals won the largest single block of seats. Thus, under their long-term leader Shigeru Yoshida, they usually formed the government, either alone or in a coalition with the Progressive Party. The one exception came between April 1947 and October 1948 when the Social Democrats won a plurality and participated in a coalition with the Progressive Party. Points of view proved too different, however, for this coalition to remain productive [29, p. 75], and leadership returned to the Liberal Party even before the following election (*see* Exhibit 1).

Commenting on the basis of conservative strength and on its potential durability, one US student of postwar Japanese government, Jerome B. Cohen, wrote in 1958:

> The businessmen, of course, back the conservative party, chiefly with funds. Labor, on the whole, backs the Socialist party. Since labor is more numerous than business, why does the conservative party carry elections most of the time? The answer seems to be that in addition to business managers, former landlords, and wealthy persons, the conservatives have managed to gain wide support among farmers and in the ranks of small business communities which keep them in power. On the whole, the Socialists have made little headway with either of these two key groups. Should either or both, at some point, transfer their political allegiance, the balance of power in Japan would shift from right to left [10, p. 213].

Exhibit 1

Major Party Shares of Seats in Japan's House of Representatives (percentage of 464 to 466 seats)

Election	Liberals[a]	Progressives	Social Democrats	Communist	Other[b]
April 1946	30.2	20.3	19.8	1.1	29.7
April 1947	28.1	26.0	30.7	0.8	15.2
Jan 1949	56.7	14.8	10.3	7.5	10.7
Oct 1952	51.4	18.2	23.8[c]	—	6.6

SOURCE: R. Scalapino [36, p. 159]. Adapted with permission.
[a] Later the Liberal Democratic Party (LDP), the long-time dominant party in Japan.
[b] Includes splinter groups and independents.
[c] This 23.8 percent was made up of 11.6 percent left-wing and 12.2 percent right-wing socialists.

REDESIGN OF EDUCATION

Initial Post-Surrender Policy made no specific mention of education, but, like the Meiji before it, the Occupation pushed through changes in this field. Making education a force for democracy was partly a matter of indoctrinating teachers, rewriting texts, and changing courses. It was also partly a matter of reducing the emphasis on memorization and encouraging freedom of thought. (The Occupation did not, however, go so far as to permit open criticism of its own measures or to allow the open entry into Japan of works of "Communistic propaganda") [34, pp. 267–268]. In addition, the new educational setup also involved a plan to make upper-school and college education more widely available. Under the previous system, "Only about 3.5 per cent of the students who graduated from the sixth year of elementary school went beyond the eleventh grade and only half of 1 per cent went on to the university." The new arrangement created a six-year compulsory grade school and a three-year compulsory junior high school, followed by a noncompulsory three-year senior high school and a four-year college—"in other words, the American educational system" [34, pp. 264, 265].

DEMOCRATIZING JAPAN'S ECONOMY: PROPOSALS FOR STRUCTURAL CHANGE

In the economic area, *Initial Post-Surrender Policy* called not only for "reparation," "restitution," and "economic demilitarization," but also for "promotion of democratic forces" and "resumption of peaceful economic activity."

Under the heading "Promotion of Democratic Forces," it was indicated that "en-

couragement" would be given to the "development of organizations in labor, industry, and agriculture organized on a democratic basis." "Favor" would be shown to "a program for the dissolution of the large industrial and banking combinations," which had earlier "exercised control of a great part of Japan's trade and industry." Favor would also be shown to policies that would permit "a wide distribution of income and of the ownership of the means of production and trade."

Land Reform

On arriving in Japan the Occupation found that, in contrast to prewar times, the farm was less depressed than industry. Whereas in 1946 farm family real income was 9 percent above what it had been in 1934–1936, real wages[1] in manufacturing were only 30 percent of this level in 1947 [2, p. 201; 23 (1955), p. 90: table 60]. This situation reflected not so much an improvement of the farm economy as it did the greater wartime destruction in the cities. As a result, returning soldiers had poured onto the land and many rural workers were underemployed. Farms remained as small as ever (averaging under two acres) in relation to the families they had to support.

After reviewing this scene, the Occupation opted for reforms that would broaden land ownership. According to a plan put through in 1948, absentee landlords were required to sell all their land to the government, and even cultivating landlords in most parts of Japan had to sell any land above ten acres (of which no more than 2.5 acres could be leased to someone else). Once the state acquired the land, it was resold cheap to the tenant farmers by whom it had been worked.

---

[1] Nominal wage index divided by consumer price index.

Pointing out that the "government purchase and resale prices were based primarily on prewar monetary values, without allowances for Japan's runaway inflation," Reischauer noted that the program amounted to "virtual confiscation of the former owners." Thus, the land-reform program was the most "surprising" of the US postwar reforms, yet it was also one of the "least controversial." "Our land reform was, to say the least, drastic, but it has met only with praise. Actually it was based on plans long advocated by certain Japanese and thus from the start had the sympathy and support of most people in Japan" [10, p. 32]; [34, pp. 280–282 *passim*], reprinted by permission of Harvard University Press.

As a result of this change, landless tenant farmers declined from 28 percent of the rural population in 1941 to only 5 percent in 1950, and rent all but disappeared from the farmer's management expenses [13, p. 213; 22(1954–55), p. 29].

Labor Reform

As the Occupation saw it, prewar Japan had been dominated by the military, the bureaucracy, and big business largely because there were no "countervailing forces." Labor unions—never very strong—had been outlawed during World War II, and workers had been mobilized in what was called the Movement to Serve the Country Through Industry, or *Sampo*. All firms with more than 100 wage earners had been forced to establish a company-wide organization that included all workers and managers. These company Sampo units provided for the election of worker representatives, labor-management discussion of working conditions, and joint solution of problems such as turnover, absenteeism, and low productivity. Solidarity between workers and management and worker devotion to productivity were encouraged by

the slogan, "One enterprise, one family" [35, pp. 259, 260; 43, p. 75].

When Japan surrendered, the Occupation believed that a strong and independent union movement was essential to democratization. Accordingly, Sampo was formally abolished, and by 1947 Japan—"hitherto notoriously backward in labor relations"—found herself endowed with "a labor code in accord with the most advanced standards of western nations." Thus, a law patterned after the US Wagner Act guaranteed labor's freedom to organize, to bargain collectively, and to strike. An institution patterned after the US National Labor Relations Board was set up to implement these rights, and an act patterned on proposals of the International Labor Office spelled out the legal protections and working conditions to which labor would be entitled [2, pp. 152, 153].

Encouraged by this change of climate, union membership rose from zero in 1940–1945 to almost 6.7 million in 1946. This was almost 56 percent of all paid employees, or about 26 percent of all employed persons other than proprietors. Groups not organized included mainly farmers, the self-employed, family workers, and workers in small industry and business [2, p. 149; 10, p. 206].

As the labor movement grew, a struggle developed as to who would control it. Socialists and Communists hoped to use defeat and hard times to radicalize Japanese labor. The Occupation expected to see a US-style labor movement in which strong craft and industrial unions would focus on negotiating for improved working conditions and pay. Japanese management hoped to revive as much as possible of the native prewar pattern of labor-management relations. This pattern had been developed in the early years of Japan's industrial era when management sought to cut the high turnover rates that plagued its factories and when it also sought to devise a native pattern of labor relations far different from the western stance of confrontation.

The native pattern, which management and moderate labor favored, was, like Sampo, built on the idea of the company as a family. It thus sought to mobilize some of the oldest and strongest elements in Japan's traditional value system in order to achieve a relationship based not upon class warfare but upon loyalty, mutual supportiveness, and cooperation.

Along with the concept of the firm as a family went a distinctive pattern of remuneration. Originally aimed at cutting turnover as well as at reinforcing the family analogy, this pattern included a substantial bonus element in pay. Further, it based total pay less on the attributes of the job than on the attributes of the worker and those of the company by which he or she was employed. Thus, pay varied by size of firm, by the worker's status as a "regular" or a "temporary" member of the company workforce, and by such personal factors as the worker's age, sex, education, and seniority. Known as *nenko*, this distinctive pattern of pay might be supplemented, in some cases, by another distinctive benefit: the promise of "permanent" employment. Not all companies could afford this promise, so "lifetime" employment had so far been available almost exclusively to "regular" workers in the public services and large enterprises [11, p. 115; 33, p. 37].

SCAP soon discovered that at least the structure of Japan's union movement would depart from the US model. Although Japan's new labor legislation, like the Wagner Act, forbade employers to favor company unions, the sudden call to unionize could most readily be met by organizing on an enterprise rather than a craft or industrial basis [11, p. 227]. Once organized, the enterprise unions kept the key function of collective bargaining in their own hands, instead of turning it over to the loose national confederations that formed to unite the enterprise unions. Since the latter were exluded from the bargaining function, they concentrated on politics [2, pp. 154–158; 12, pp. 8–10, 51, 52; 28, p. 54ff., 115–136, 177, 179].

A more critical issue was control of the union organizations. At the national level, the answer was soon clear. Owing to the extreme privations of the postwar period, the confederation that attracted the largest number of members was the farthest left (Sanbetsu Kaigi). Similarly, the unions of public employees turned radical owing largely to the conjunction of extreme inflation and effective ceilings on their pay. Speaking of this early postwar era, Bronfenbrenner stated, "What the occupation [has] created has become a Frankenstein monstrosity in the form of an anti-capitalist, anti-American union movement of considerable strength" [16, p. 23].

At the more critical company level, the situation was not at first so clear. Radical unionists, whom SCAP itself had freed from prison, urged a vigorous fight for wage increases and union rights. In 1945 and 1946, many plants were seized and run by their workers, and in 1947 and 1948 SCAP was forced to act decisively to avert a general strike [20, pp. 56, 61–63; 28, p. 70].

On the other hand, moderates in many company unions appeared ready to return to old ways. SCAP was disturbed to see some company unions admit management personnel, and like Sampo, seek financing from company funds. Fearing that such unions could not be sufficiently independent, the Occupation responded at first by stepping up its program of labor education. Going further later, SCAP got laws passed against these practices. It even considered outlawing company unions, until dissuaded by the Japanese Justice Department, which pointed out that such a step would violate freedoms guaranteed by the new constitution [20, p. 68; 35, pp. 259, 260].

The motives of moderate labor have been variously assessed. Left-leaning critics have suggested that hard times permitted the employer to trade jobs for control. Without denying this possibility, other analysts have noted that unions organized on a company basis might reasonably be convinced that loyalty and concern for their firm's competitive position were essential to their firm's survival in hard times, and therefore to the workers' own well-being. The early absence of strong state social programs was another reason to think along these lines [11, p. 229; 12, pp. 89, 91; 19, pp. 71, 72, 211–234 *passim*; 28, pp. 69–73].

Business Reform

In prewar times, Japan had a dual economy with some enterprises that were very large and modern and others that were traditional in character. The modern sector was dominated by big-business combines (the *zaibatsu*), each of which operated in a variety of industries, in banking, and possibly in trade. The zaibatsu were mostly under close family control, and they were politically influential owing to their various ties with government. These ties went beyond financial contributions to parties and included a history of business-government favors, frequent movement of personnel between business management and the bureaucracy, and bonds of a social and personal nature. The Occupation tended to ascribe much that it saw wrong in Japan to the zaibatsu. Said General MacArthur, "The world has never seen . . . so abnormal an economic system" [10, pp. 195, 196]. According to a special US Mission on Japanese Combines, "This type of industrial organization tends to hold down wages, to block the development of labor unions, to

destroy the basis for democratic independence in politics, and thus to prevent the rise of interests which could be used as counterweights to the military designs of small groups of ambitious men" [10, pp. 195, 196]. Part of the statistical basis for the Occupation's concern shows up in Exhibit 2.

Against this backdrop, the Occupation's plan for reform included (1) breaking up existing combines, (2) dissolving even single companies that were deemed "excessive concentrations of economic power," and (3) passing antitrust legislation that was even stricter than that of the United States. To implement so complex a program, legislative and other help was needed from the government of Japan.[2] Obliged to assist in a program that it feared would further weaken the economy, the government proved a "balky instrument." It delayed to the point where the last big reform law in the business package was not ready for the books until January 1948 [17, pp. 11, 68, 99].

The goal of breaking up existing combines did not stop with the Big Four as the Japanese had hoped, or even with the Big Ten, although it focused mainly on the latter and their 1200 subsidiaries[3] [17, pp. 22, 26, 68]. Dissolution measures were aimed at getting rid of holding companies and at breaking the ownership and personal ties that held the combines together. Thus, 56 designated zaibatsu family leaders and 83 designated holding companies had to turn over all their stock to a government commission for resale to selected types of investors, prefera-

---

[2] In contrast to postwar plans for Germany, the Potsdam Conference decided that the Japanese Occupation was to work through the Japanese government rather than through a military government of its own. This decision was dictated by language difficulties and by ignorance of Japanese administrative procedures.

[3] The test of domination by a combine was combine ownership of a 10 percent share of company stock.

Exhibit 2

Big Four and Big Ten Shares of Total Paid-in Corporate Capital by Industry Group, 1946 (in percent)

Corporations	Finance	Heavy Industry	Light Industry	Other	All Industry
Four largest[a]	49.7	32.4	10.7	12.9	24.5
Ten largest[b]	53.0	49.0	16.8	15.5	35.2

SOURCE: R. Komiya (ed.) [26, p. 230]. Reprinted by permission.

[a] The "Big Four" zaibatsu. These were Mitsui, Mitsubishi, Sumitomo, and Yasuda.

[b] The "Big Four" plus Ayakawa, Asano, Furukawa, Okura, Yakajima, and Nomura.

bly employees [17, pp. 70, 87]. In addition, zaibatsu family members were excluded from positions in business, and high-ranking zaibatsu appointees were excluded from positions in successor companies of the former combine. As a result of these and other moves—especially a purge of wartime business leaders in January 1947—1575 Japanese executives lost their jobs [17, pp. 92–102], and stock valued at approximately ¥15 billion changed hands. (Depending on the estimate used, this sum amounted to one-third or one-half of the total paid-in value of all stock) [17, pp. 181, 182]. Since big shareholders affected by this plan received their compensation in the form of non-negotiable bonds that depreciated during the inflation, one irreversible outcome of the plan was the loss of the old zaibatsu family fortunes. As one Japanese writer put it, "The former *zaibatsu* . . . sold their stockholdings and then they had to liquidate their real estate and even their art collections to survive in the inflation. Several years ago they became 'the tribe of the setting sun'" [42, p. 12].

The goal of ending "excessive concentration of economic power" went beyond the breakup of the combines to contemplate the breakup of even a single enterprise "which by reason of its relative size in any line or the cumulative power of its position in many lines, restricts competition or impairs the opportunity for others to engage in

. . . any important segment of business." Since this law went beyond even US practice and since the Japanese tended to equate scale with strength, opposition to it was acute [17, pp. 109–111], and the law was not put in final form until December 1947. By that time the Occupation had already identified 325 companies[4] to which it might be applied: 257 in industry and 68 in services and distribution [17, p. 113]. In a controversial decision, no banks or financial companies were named, as had been originally planned, since the problem of bank-combine relations had already come under the purview of a recent Anti-Monopoly Law [17, p. 195]. (This law had forbidden banks to hold any stock in a competitor or more than 5 percent of the stock of any other type of company) [17, pp. 161–165; 42, p. 24].

The goal of making all business more competitive was sought not only by breaking up existing concentrations but also by the Anti-Monopoly Law which was designed to prevent new concentrations from arising [17, p. 123]. This law has been described as "the Sherman Antitrust Act, the Clayton Act, and the Federal Trade Commission Act, all combined into one"—although in some respects it went beyond them [17, p.

---

[4] Of this number, 51 were among the 83 holding companies identified under the zaibatsu breakup plan [1, pp. 91–95].

120].[5] One major chapter of the law spelled out restrictions on intercorporate stockholding, multiple directorates, mergers, and acquisitions of assets—"the major building blocks of combine enterprise." Most of these were either forbidden entirely or forbidden without first obtaining the permission of Japan's new Federal Trade Commission [1, pp. 91–95]. Another major chapter of the law spelled out unfair practices. These included price fixing and price discrimination; restriction of sales or production volume; restraints on the adoption of new methods and technologies and on the construction of new facilities; restrictions on new products, markets, or customers; and resort to boycotts, dumping, exclusive dealing, and tied sales [17, pp. 121–123].

REHABILITATING JAPAN'S ECONOMY

Initial Goals and Tools

Under the heading "Resumption of Peaceful Economic Activity," *Initial Post-Surrender Policy* put the challenge of rebuilding Japan squarely up to the Japanese themselves. "The plight of Japan is the direct outcome of its own behavior, and the Allies will not undertake the burden of repairing the damage." The Japanese would, however, be "afforded an opportunity to develop for themselves an economy which [would] permit the peacetime requirements of the population to be met" [34 pp. 346, 347].

Resources beyond minimal needs were to be devoted to reparations. In order to im-

---

[5] In contrast with US practice, competition was defined to include "potential competition"; companies could be broken up simply on the grounds of "undue disparities of bargaining power"; and a limit was set on stockholding by individuals [32, pp. 288, 310].

plement this objective, it was decided in January 1946 that Japan would be allowed to develop an economy wherein real civilian per capita consumption could reattain the average level of 1930-1934. This was about ¥175 in constant 1934-1936 prices [32, pp. 121-123]. Just what it meant in dollars was open to debate, since from 1930 through 1933 the average exchange value of the yen steadily declined from $0.4937 to $0.2523, then rose to $0.2951 in 1934 when the dollar itself was devalued. This remained its approximate value for as long as an exchange rate was quoted.

On-the-Spot Developments

Once inside Japan, the Occupation found revival complicated by two problems of unforeseen severity: the levels of destruction and inflation. Although rehabilitation was supposed to be up to the Japanese themselves, it would have to be facilitated.

Aid. Viewing the destruction wrought by the war and the collapse of essential trade, the Occupation realized that Japan would soon be starving. Partly for humanitarian reasons and partly to stave off dangerous unrest, the United States decided to send aid. This aid took the form of food, fertilizers, and essential raw materials. The bill for aid passed the billion dollar mark in 1948 and the two billion dollar mark in 1951.

Freeze on Deposits and Currency Exchange. Turning to inflation, the Occupation quickly decided that purchasing power should be siphoned off by a capital levy and other stiff taxes, which would also help to redistribute wealth. Rumors of this plan soon spread, however, and the Japanese responded with a fresh wave of runs on the banks. Although the Occupation countered in March 1946 by temporarily freezing bank deposits and converting old bank notes into a reduced number of new ones, prices did not fall and the volume of money was soon permitted to go up again.

For the next three years, the attack on inflation shifted to means other than monetary [37, pp. 64, 65; 39, p. 7]. Seeking to explain this approach, which "in retrospect" seemed "especially strange," one US participant pointed to the role, among other factors, of economic theory: "The late forties was perhaps the most extreme period of the most extreme form of Keynesian doctrine, prior to the so-called 'rediscovery of money' at the turn of the decade. According to this doctrine, the quantity of money did not really matter." The popularity of Keynesianism in turn reflected the background and experience of operating-level personnel in the Occupation force.[6] "Many ex-OPA[7] economists from Washington brought with them to Tokyo the . . . doctrine that the way to check inflation was price control. . . . These OPA hyper-Keynesians found . . . allies in Japan, where similar doctrine had prevailed among the military and in wartime agencies of economic control" [16, p. 18].

Rationing and Price Controls.   In both Japan and the US price controls had worked well in wartime. After the war, however, sellers diverted their goods to black markets. In an effort to reduce the motive for such action, official prices were increased from time to time, but to no avail. While failing to achieve the desired objective, these official price increases did contribute to a wage-price spiral, with wages rising faster than

---

[6] Operating-level personnel were especially influential because of the lack of direction from above. According to Martin Bronfenbrenner, a one-time junior member of the Occupation forces from whom this account is taken, ". . . the major interest of the General supervising the entire Economic and Scientific Section of MacArthur's headquarters . . . was the revival of professional baseball in Japan" [16, p. 12].

[7] OPA was the US wartime Office of Price Administration.

consumer prices and productivity—although not as fast as wholesale prices rose.

Subsidies and Multiple Exchange Rates.   With costs rising despite price controls, legitimate business was unable to produce at the permitted price and needed subsidies. Similarly, exporters could not meet the world price: they needed both production subsidies and export subsidies. In effect, these export subsidies resulted in a so-called "multiple exchange rate" for the yen rather than a single exchange rate. This system and its implications for costs have been described by Jerome Cohen.

> . . . the Foreign Trade Board would purchase goods for export . . . paying the producer's cost of production plus profit in yen, and would then sell the goods in world markets for the going price in dollars. . . . If the Board paid 6,000 yen for a bicycle and sold it abroad for $20 there was thus established an implicit rate of 300 to 1. If wage and raw material costs of the bicycle producer rose and the Board paid him 8,000 yen, but the product continued to sell abroad for $20, a rate of 400 to 1 resulted. The compulsion of a single exchange rate to hold costs down, to force rationalization to meet world market prices, was lacking.

> Thus, by subsidies and a multiple exchange rate system, the Japanese producer was insulated from world market realities, and his mounting costs merely resulted in bigger government budget deficit. . . . By the 1949–50 fiscal year, price subsidies had surpassed Occupation costs to become the largest single item of expenditure in the Japanese budget, totaling 202 billion yen out of a general account total of 704 billion yen, or 28.7 percent [10, p. 86].

Public Finance.   Besides controls, another way to help check inflation would be a pay-as-you-go public budget, or even a "super-balanced" budget to generate a surplus and reduce the public debt. Under Occupation prodding, taxes were increased and made more progressive in a number of steps starting in early 1946, but the Japanese budget remained in the red. Not only was inflation pushing up the normal costs of government, but also state outlays had to cover such extraordinary charges as the Occupation costs, repatriation of colonials, price subsidies, and government-supported investment in rebuilding. Reflecting the failure of state income to cover all these charges, Japan's national debt almost doubled from ¥265 billion at the end of fiscal 1946 to ¥524 billion at the end of fiscal 1948.

Formation of the Reconstruction Finance Bank. Turning to rehabilitation, the Occupation found great needs and little capacity on the part of business to generate the funds required even for working capital, let alone investment. In view of fast-rising costs and low-level operations, such an incapacity was inevitable, but it was aggravated by artificial factors arising out of Occupation actions. Thus, when the Occupation canceled the government's debt to producers of war material but not these producers' debts to their suppliers, some firms—typically large zaibatsu firms—would have gone bankrupt if not reorganized [16, p. 19]. And when, early on, the Occupation ordered a freeze on the valuation of assets, firms found that their allowable depreciation charges were reduced to "utterly meaningless" levels in relation to replacement costs [9, p. 45]. At the same time, profits (if any) appeared so high in relation to investment that they became subject to the excess profit tax. This tax was at a rate of 20 percent; added to other taxes on profits, it drove the total up to 60 to 65 percent [10, p. 85].

With neither profits nor depreciation generating adequate funds for the internal financing of investment, business had to borrow. But from where? In view of the obvious need, the Occupation acquiesced in a new agency, the Reconstruction Finance Bank (RFB), which was to raise money for loans by selling its debentures to the Bank of Japan. Once the new bank

was under way in January 1947, its debentures rose quickly. They were ¥4 billion at the end of one month and ¥131 billion by March 1949 [10, p. 85]. According to a Japanese source, "The total loans made by the bank amounted to 74.1% of the total investment in all industries" [42, p. 28].

However helpful to investment, RFB operations proved detrimental to another main Occupation objective, i.e., that of controlling inflation.

> Since ever increasing costs prevented firms from repaying most of their loans from the RFB, and since the RFB could not therefore repurchase its debentures from the Bank of Japan, the loans caused by the inflationary costs were continually monetized by the central bank and more and more money was thereby drawn into circulation and never returned. Thus inflation begot inflation [10, p. 85].

Planning Agency. Besides money, rehabilitation required agreement at the highest levels on which reconstruction needs should have priority for Japan's limited resources. Yet in early 1946 the Occupation found that major Japanese cabinet ministries—such as those for finance, commerce and industry,[8] and agriculture—were pushing for competing claims. Under these circumstances, what the Occupation wanted was a central planning agency, something like the agencies that had worked during the war to match scarce resources to top needs.[9] Accordingly, in May 1948 the prime minister was directed to create an organization for this purpose and to give it cabinet rank.

Set up in August, the new national planning agency encountered numerous problems: the Ministry of Commerce and Industry insisted on "lending" it its initial

---

[8] Precursor to the far-famed Ministry of International Trade and Industry (MITI).

[9] In the United States, the agency the Occupation had in mind was the War Production Board (WPB).

staff; unforeseen Occupation decisions obsoleted the agency's work on more than one occasion; and in 1949 long-term conservative Premier S. Yoshida told the Diet, "Long-range planning is no good." Despite this lack of support, planning in the early years was credited with positive if limited results. It not only helped to set priorities by pinpointing certain bottlenecks (coal in 1947, electricity in 1951), but it also possibly helped to convince the Occupation that reparations had been set too high in relation to the target for revival [5, pp. 192, 193; 15, pp. 29, 30; 18, pp. 121–127, 129, 132]. In any event, between the fall of 1945 and April 1948, the value of facilities to be removed for purposes of reparations was scaled down from ¥2466 million to ¥666 million (both in 1939 prices). Of the latter figure only ¥102 million represented industrial facilities rather than primary war facilities [17, p. 146].

Moreover, whether due to planning or not, priorities for reconstruction were established. Thus, of all RFB loans, 84 percent were allocated to only six key industries. These six fields and the proportion of their investment supplied by the RFB were as follows: coal, 98 percent; electricity, 93 percent; shipbuilding, 84 percent; iron and steel, 73 percent; fertilizer, 64 percent; and textiles, 45 percent [42, p.28].

Allocation of Materials. Besides requiring that funds be allocated, postwar shortages also required the allocation of scarce materials. These were assigned, first to industries and then to companies, just as they had been during the war. The Japanese machinery for this purpose was still in place when the Occupation landed. It consisted of industry trade or "control" associations and commodity "control companies," both of which were under the direction of the Ministry of Commerce and Industry.

Seeing allocation as a public function from which private influence ought to be excluded, the Occupation planned to dismantle this system and to replace it with something else. As time passed, however, pressure to alter this machinery abated. The two chief changes made were to give a role to the Planning Board "in cooperation with the particular ministries concerned" and to replace some former control companies with new state-owned, public corporations (*kodan*). Yet, as agencies of public control the kodan did not prove entirely satisfactory, "in part because they were crowded with personnel from the former control companies, and in part because of the expenditure or even the misappropriation of large funds" [5, p. 196].

"REVERSE COURSE?"

The Occupation had announced in 1945 that its chief focus would be on reform rather than on rehabilitation, but by 1948 (if not before) the Japanese saw signs of a "reverse course" [29, p. 106]. The chief impetus for change came from the emerging Cold War and from the increasing probability that China would go communist.

> Prior to 1948, high policy had been to build up China at Japan's expense. This meant, for Japan, holding down heavy industry to the amount required for her 1934–36 living standard, and the dismantling of a constantly re-estimated number of plants which had produced war materials. . . . It also meant a punitive policy toward traditionalist Japanese and toleration if not support for the Japanese Left. In and after 1948, policy changed to the restoration of Japan's pre-war position as the "workshop of Asia" and to the preservation of her economy as far as possible from Socialist encroachments [16, p. 23].

Other motives for a change in US policy included the threat of crippling strikes under the leadership of leftist Sanbetsu, conservative US criticism of some of SCAP's on-going reforms, and US hopes to cut the cost of aid by getting Japan back on her feet.

Unions Curbed

One of the earliest signals of a shift in Occupation thinking on reform came in early 1947 and had to do with placing curbs on unions. Hitherto, the Occupation had been "neutral" as Japan's new national unions turned left and opted for political tactics. A "sudden reversal" came in January 1947, provoked by the announced intention of the unions to mount a general strike—partly to harass the government in power. At the last moment, General MacArthur intervened to forbid the strike and it did not take place [16, p. 23; 29, pp. 162–167].

Another curb on unions came in mid-1948. This time, unions of state employees were demanding substantial wage increases which the government did not want to pay. Before a showdown could occur, MacArthur published a letter stating that state employees, including even workers in state-owned businesses like the railroads, had no right to strike. It was even doubtful, he added, if they had a right to collective bargaining [29, p. 169]. Since some of Japan's strongest unions were those made up of state employees, a curb on them was especially meaningful.

Radicalism in the union movement received another setback in 1950, when, at the start of the Korean War, SCAP initiated a "Red Purge" which destroyed the power of the Communist Party by removing all known communists from positions of authority. At this time, with the gleeful assistance of management, 2546 union officials were dismissed from their jobs and from their union positions as well, since current legislation demanded that union officials be employed at firms which bargained with the union [20, pp. 68, 69].

Relaxed Curbs on Business

Other signals of a reverse course followed passage of the Law for the Elimination of Excessive Economic Power. Besides antagonizing the Japanese, this law attracted critical US attention. Under the heading, "Far to the Left of Anything Now Tolerated in America," *Newsweek* opened the attack in December 1947. Blame was placed on the absence of businessmen in SCAP at the policy-making level and on SCAP's "economic advisors" who were "for the most part either former instructors at universities who have also served some years in one of the many bureaus in Washington, or recent college graduates" [27, p. 36].

After *Newsweek*, the attack was taken up in Congress by Senator William Knowland (R., Calif.), who found himself "dismayed" and "shocked" by sundry US measures in Japan and more particularly by a US policy statement only recently "leaked" to the press [17, p. 137; 29, p. 113]. "It seems to me," he said, "that in both Germany and Japan our policy should be to eliminate trusts and cartels, but not to promote socialism or a controlled economy" [17, p. 140].

Still snother attack on SCAP's policies came in January 1948 from Secretary of the Army Kenneth Royall:

> . . . for political stability to continue and for free government to succeed in the future, there must be a sound and self-supporting economy. . . .
>
> We also realize that the United States cannot forever continue to pour hundreds of millions of dollars annually into relief funds for occupied areas. . . . Earlier programs are being re-examined. . . .
>
> We are not averse to modifying programs in the interests of our broad objectives . . . [17, pp. 138, 139].

Next, to acclaim in the Japanese press, a US "economic mission" was sent on a two-week tour of Japan, after which it publicly reported in April 1948 that, in effect, a "new lenient recovery program" should be substituted for a "reform-punishment program" [5, pp. 142–144; 42, p. 22].

Following these and other signals of changing US attitudes, plans for breaking up Japanese big business were cut back. Of the 83 companies on the designated holding company list, only 16 were eliminated; 37 were reorganized; and the remaining 30 were untouched. Of the 325 companies to be reviewed for "excessive concentration," only 19 were split up [17, p. 443]. Thus, "the most drastic action taken in the whole deconcentration program" [17, p. 147] turned out to be the July 1947 dissolution of Japan's most powerful trading companies, Mitsui Busan and Mitsubishi Busan. These were not only abolished, but abolished under conditions that "fragmented" their successors [17, p. 148]. Inasmuch as Mitsui and Mitsubishi busan had been key factors in Japan's prewar international trade, the extreme treatment accorded to them tended to strengthen Japanese suspicion that the Occupation was engaged in "some vast conspiracy to drive Japanese industry from international competition . . ." [16, p. 20]. Over all, however, concentration in major fields was not much, if any, less after the Occupation's reforms than it had been in 1937 (see Exhibit 3).

ECONOMIC RESULTS THROUGH 1948

In spite of the stratagems to which the Occupation and Japan's conservative leaders had resorted, recovery was slow through 1947 and remained below target through 1948, with real GNP not even back to its 1931 level. (Data on gross national expenditure, employment and output by sector, fiscal and monetary factors, comparative wages and prices, the balance of payments, and the composition of trade are given in Exhibits 4 through 16.) How the Japanese felt about this record was subject to dispute by US analysts, some of whom believed that the old power structure—far from having been effectively dismantled—actually wanted things that way.

> The fact was that real control of the Japanese economy did not rest with the occupation authorities. It rested with the old Japanese business leaders, working through the government and its semiofficial "control" agencies and associations. These men favored a laissez-faire policy that permitted, or even encouraged, the development of inflation. They were prepared to hoard their materials, operate in the black market, let the economy stagnate, and wait for the end of the occupation. Unless the occupation authorities could place new men in control of government and industry, they faced a hopeless task in seeking to reverse this economic trend [29, p. 97].

Exhibit 3

Proportion of Total Output Provided by the Five Largest Firms in 1937 and 1949 (in percent)

Year	Coal Mining	Rolled Steel	Elec Copper	Ship-bldg	Alumi-num	Super-phosphate	Plate Glass	Cement	Cotton Yarns	Rayon Yarns	Staple Fiber	Cotton Fabrics
1937	44.4	66.4	98.2	86.8	100.0	59.5	100.0	54.3	42.8	53.4	53.8	22.8
1949	43.7	68.3	92.8	56.5	100.0	61.7	100.0	70.7	57.2	94.1	59.0	31.0

SOURCE: S. Tsuru [38(Nov. 1955), p. 91]. Reprinted with permission.

Exhibit 4

Gross National Expenditure (Product) in Current Prices (millions of yen 1931–44; billions of yen 1946–52, and percentage breakdown)

Year	Private Cnsmptn Expndtr ¥	%	Gnrl Govt Cnsmptn Expndtr ¥	%	Gross Dmstc Fxd Capital Formation ¥	%	Increase in Stocks ¥	%	Expts of Goods & Srvcs and Factor Income Rcvd fr Abroad ¥	%	Less Impts of Goods & Srvcs and Factor Income Paid Abroad ¥	%	GNE at Market Prices ¥	GNE Implicit Price Deflator
1931	9,926	74.0	1,684	12.6	1,946	14.5	—		1,895	14.1	−2,047	15.3	13,404	95.2 (1934–36 = 100)
1932	9,945	72.6	1,839	13.4	2,030	14.8	—		2,294	16.7	−2,412	17.6	13,696	93.6
1933	11,000	71.8	2,046	13.4	2,466	16.1	—		2,845	18.6	−3,042	19.9	15,315	95.5
1934	12,257	71.9	2,005	11.8	2,923	17.1	—		3,424	20.1	−3,563	20.9	17,046	97.3
1935	12,825	69.8	2,117	11.5	3,346	18.2	—		3,985	21.7	−3,911	21.3	18,362	99.6
1936	13,505	69.6	2,184	11.3	3,622	18.7	—		4,382	22.6	−4,291	22.1	19,402	103.0
1944	26,554	35.6	27,672	37.1	17,390	23.3	3,265	4.4	3,950	5.3	−4,328	5.8	74,503	370.0
1945	(not available)													
1946[a]	333	70.1	55	11.6	78	16.4	28	5.9	5	1.1	−24	5.1	475	43.6 (1934–36 = 1)
1947	915	69.9	102	7.8	263	20.1	83	6.3	28	2.1	−82	6.3	1,309	109.4
1948	1,741	65.3	282	10.6	516	19.4	236	8.9	81	3.0	−191	7.2	2,665	191.4
1949	2,261	67.0	394	11.7	623	18.5	208	6.2	217	6.4	−327	9.7	3,376	233.3
1950	2,397	60.7	437	11.1	639	16.2	368	9.3	469	11.9	−364	9.2	3,946	243.0
1951	3,018	55.5	552	10.1	1,093	20.1	570	10.5	908	16.7	−699	12.8	5,442	295.4
1952	3,861	61.7	668	10.7	1,277	20.4	385	6.2	788	12.6	−720	11.5	6,259	307.6

SOURCE: K. Ohkawa and H. Rosovsky [32, pp. 286, 287, 306, 308]. Reprinted with permission.
[a] Figures for 1946 and later are for fiscal years (April 1 to March 31 of the following year).

Exhibit 5

Gross National Expenditures in Constant 1934–36 Prices (millions of yen and percentage breakdown)

Year	Private Cnsmptn Expndtr ¥	%	Gnrl Govt Cnsmptn Expndtr ¥	%	Gross Dmstc Fxd Capital Formation ¥	%	Increase in Stocks ¥	%	Expts of Goods and Services and Factor Income Rcvd from Abroad ¥	%	Less Impts of Goods and Services and Factor Income Paid Abroad ¥	%	GNE at Market Prices ¥	Year-to-Year Change %
1931	11,425	81.2	1,841	13.1	2,197	15.6	—		2,091	14.9	−3,487	24.8	14,067	1.0
1932	11,232	76.9	1,981	13.6	2,302	15.8	—		2,488	17.0	−3,393	23.2	14,610	3.9
1933	11,999	74.9	2,173	13.6	2,565	16.0	—		2,606	16.3	−3,317	20.7	16,026	9.7
1934	12,757	72.9	2,061	11.8	2,955	16.9	—		3,483	19.9	−3,746	21.4	17,510	9.3
1935	12,747	69.1	2,108	11.4	3,355	18.2	—		4,096	22.2	−3,869	21.0	18,437	5.3
1936	13,082	69.4	2,135	11.3	3,559	18.9			4,197	22.3	−4,134	21.9	18,839	2.2
1944	7,006	34.8	7,301	36.3	4,723	23.5	1,218	6.1	2,310	11.5	−2,445	12.2	20,113	—
1945	(not available)													
1946[a]	6,826	62.8	1,123	10.3	2,545	23.4	812	7.5	102	0.9	−534	4.9	10,874	—
1947	7,410	61.9	828	6.9	2,965	24.8	1,273	10.6	247	2.1	−757	6.3	11,966	10.0
1948	8,391	60.3	1,360	9.8	2,973	21.3	1,734	12.5	352	2.5	−889	6.2	13,921	16.3
1949	9,297	64.3	1,619	11.2	2,756	19.0	1,230	8.5	753	5.2	−1,186	8.2	14,469	3.9
1950	10,077	62.1	1,838	11.3	2,741	16.9	1,277	7.9	1,614	9.9	−1,307	8.0	16,240	12.2
1951	11,040	59.9	2,022	11.0	2,929	15.9	2,009	10.9	2,187	11.9	−1,757	9.5	18,430	13.5
1952	12,927	63.5	2,395	11.8	3,581	17.6	1,365	6.7	2,354	11.6	−2,262	11.1	20,360	10.5

SOURCE: K. Ohkawa and H. Rosovsky [32, pp. 288, 289]. Reprinted with permission.

[a] Figures for 1946 and later are for fiscal years (April 1 to March 31 of the following year).

Exhibit 6

Sectoral Distribution of the Workforce (population in thousands and percentage breakdown)

Year	Agriculture (incldg Forestry & Fishing)	%	Mining & Mfg	%	Facilitating Industry[a]	%	Construction	%	Services	%	Total Gainfully Occupied	Private Nonagriculture	%	Total Population
1931	14,865	49.6	5,785	19.3	1,156	3.9	836	2.8	7,295	24.4	29,937	13,169	44.0	65,457
1932	15,014	49.7	5,659	18.7	1,107	3.7	834	2.8	7,610	25.2	30,224	13,081	43.2	66,433
1933	14,891	48.8	5,835	19.1	1,060	3.5	860	2.8	7,896	25.9	30,542	13,296	43.5	67,431
1934	14,752	47.9	6,137	19.9	1,091	3.5	818	2.7	8,030	26.0	30,828	13,629	44.2	68,309
1935	14,571	46.7	6,461	20.7	1,121	3.6	833	2.7	8,228	26.4	31,214	14,176	45.4	69,254
1936	14,609	46.2	6,708	21.2	1,137	3.6	846	2.7	8,308	26.3	31,608	14,472	45.8	70,133
1944	12,074	40.4	9,421	31.5	1,897	6.3	1,101	3.7	5,384	18.0	29,877	—	48.4	74,433
1945	(not available)		—	—	—	—	—	—	—	—	—	—	—	72,147
1946	17,446	53.2	5,480	17.0	1,687	5.1	1,242	3.8	6,969	21.2	32,824	—	—	75,750
1947	17,811	53.4	6,107	18.3	1,709	5.1	1,320	4.0	6,382	19.1	33,329	—	—	78,101
1948	17,610	51.6	6,165	18.1	1,743	5.1	1,390	4.1	7,187	21.1	34,095	—	—	80,002
1949	17,409	49.9	6,222	17.8	1,777	5.1	1,461	4.2	7,991	22.9	34,860	—	—	81,773
1950	17,208	48.3	6,280	17.6	1,811	5.1	1,531	4.3	8,796	24.7	35,626	—	—	83,200
1951	16,989	46.7	6,511	17.9	1,858	5.1	1,581	4.3	9,413	25.9	36,352	—	—	85,541
1952	16,769	45.2	6,743	18.2	1,906	5.1	1,631	4.4	10,031	27.1	37,080	17,305	46.7	85,808

SOURCE: K. Okhawa and H. Rosovsky [32, pp. 310, 311]. Reprinted with permission.

NOTE: Data on NDP by sector are not available in constant values for 1941–52.

[a] Facilitating industry comprises transportation, communications, and public utilities.

Exhibit 7

Selected Indices of Output and Employment

A. INDICES OF INDUSTRIAL AND AGRICULTURAL PRODUCTION

	1944	1945	1946	1947	1948	1949	1950	1951	1952
Industry (1934–36 = 100) (mining & mfg)	178.8	60.2	30.7	37.4	54.6	71.0	83.6	114.4	126.4
Agriculture (1933–35 = 100) (incldg forestry & fisheries)	84.1	65.5	78.2	80.1	92.1	93.2	100.4	106.0	122.2

B. INDICES OF EMPLOYMENT AND OUTPUT IN MANUFACTURING (1934–36 = 100)

	1946	1947	1948	1949	1950	1951	1952
Employment	—	137.8	139.3	140.7	133.9	144.0	148.5
Production	28.9	35.1	52.5	68.9	82.0	115.1	128.2

SOURCES: Part A from Bank of Japan [4, p. 197: table 96, p. 199: table 97]; Part B from J. B. Cohen [10, pp. 15, 101], reprinted with permission.

Exhibit 8

Revenues and Expenditures on the General Account of the National Government, the National Debt, and Changes in the Net Financial Position of the National Government, 1944-52 (billions of yen)

(1) Year Begin 4/1	(2) Expn-dtrs	(3) Rvns (Non-brrwd)	(4) Srpls (+) or Dfct (−)	(5) Loans Fltd for the GA	(6) Accmltd GA Srpls	(7) Change in Accmltd GA Srpls	(8) Natl Debt	(9) Change in the Natl Debt	(10) Net Change in the Gvt's Fincl Position
1943	12.6	11.2	−1.4	1.9	1.4[a]	0.5	85.1	28.0	−27.5
1944	19.9	14.2	−5.7	5.4	1.1	−0.3	152.0	66.8	−71.1
1945	21.5	13.3	−8.2	9.0	1.9	0.8	199.5	47.5	−46.7
1946	115.2	72.4	−42.8	44.5	3.6	1.7	265.3	65.8	−64.1
1947	205.8	210.8	5.0	—	8.6	5.0	360.6	95.3	−90.3
1948	462.0	499.4	37.4	—	46.0	37.4	524.4	163.8	−126.4
1949	699.5	712.6	13.1	—	59.1	13.1	637.3	112.9	−99.8
1950	633.3	657.6	24.3	—	83.4	24.3	554.0	−83.4	107.7
1951	749.8	812.0	62.2	—	145.6	62.2	645.5	91.5	−29.3

SOURCES: H. G. Moulton [31, pp. 207–209] [for method]; Bank of Japan [3, pp. 132, 133, 159: tables 39 and 49]; Japan Ministry of Finance, *Quarterly Bulletin of Financial Statistics* [25(first quarter) p. 24: table A 1-1].

NOTE: As indicated by the fact that the national debt continued to rise (columns 8 and 9) even when the General Account showed a surplus (column 3), the General Account does not include all national government revenues and expenditures. For example, war expenditures of ¥153.7 billion did not appear on the General Account for 1940–45. Various other income and outlay not regarded as part of "normal" government expenditure are also carried in "special accounts" not shown in the table.

[a] In the previous year, accumulated GA surplus was ¥0.9 billion.

Exhibit 9

Fiscal and Monetary Data

A. NATIONAL INCOME AND TAX BURDEN, 1930–52

	1930	1935	1940	1946	1947	1948	1949	1950	1951	1952
National income (¥ billion)	11.7	14.4	30.9	386.7	968.5	1962.2	2737.8	3363.2	4537.8	5206.4
Taxes, total (¥ billion)	1.7	1.8	5.0	41.2	209.8	525.5	778.8	759.1	995.4	1150.8
Taxes/natl income (%)	14.5	12.7	16.1	10.6	21.7	26.8	28.5	22.6	21.9	22.2
Of which, natl (%)	9.4	8.3	13.6	9.7	19.6	22.8	23.2	17.0	15.9	16.2
local (%)	5.1	4.4	2.5	0.9	2.1	4.0	5.3	5.6	6.0	5.9

B. FACTORS IN THE MONEY SUPPLY, 1937–52 (BILLIONS OF YEN)

	1937	1944	1945	1946	1947	1948	1949	1950	1951	1952
Currency in circulation	2.5	18.0	54.8	90.0[b]	210.1	338.1	336.0	408.7	492.0	554.3
Deposits[a]	3.7	—	36.0	73.8[b]	132.4	280.3	342.3	380.3	556.0	710.4
Total	6.2	—	90.8	163.8	342.5	618.4	678.3	789.0	1048.0	1264.7

SOURCES: Part A from Japan Ministry of Finance [25(first quarter), p. 25: table A-2]; Part B from United Nations [40, p. 486: table 166].

[a] In commercial banks only.
[b] Notes partly exchanged. Balance placed in blocked accounts.

Exhibit 10

Comparative Wholesale Price Indices (1929 = 1)

Year	Japan	US	Great Britain	Germany	France
1931	0.70	0.77	0.77	0.81	0.80
1932	0.77	0.68	0.75	0.70	0.68
1933	0.88	0.69	0.75	0.68	0.64
1934	0.90	0.79	0.77	0.72	0.60
1935	0.92	0.84	0.78	0.74	0.54
1936	0.96	0.85	0.83	0.76	0.66
1944	2.16	1.10	1.45	0.86	2.74
1945	3.26	1.12	1.47	—	3.88
1946	15.13	1.27	1.53	—	6.70
1947	44.79	1.60	1.67	—	10.23
1948	119.00	1.74	1.92	4.06	17.70
1949	194.20	1.64	2.01	4.10	19.67
1950	229.60	1.69	2.39	4.00	21.31
1951	318.60	1.90	2.80	4.73	27.22
1952	324.80	1.86	2.83	4.88	28.53

SOURCE: Bank of Japan [3, p. 395: table 139].

Exhibit 11

Comparative Cash Earnings of Employees

Year	Japan Monthly Avg [a] (¥)			US per Year ($)
	All Industries	Mfg		Mfg
1947 (avg)	1,950	1,756	No	2,793
1948	5,324	4,869	US $	3,038
1949	8,810	8,416	equivalent	3,095
1950	(series revised)			3,302
1951	12,200	11,708		3,608
1952	14,103	13,516		3,832

SOURCES: Bank of Japan [3, pp. 70, 71: table 15]; U.S., Bureau of the Census [41, p. 166].

[a] Regular full-time employees only. No US dollar equivalent for the yen in early years. In 1951 and 1952, Japanese average monthly earnings in manufacturing were equivalent to $32.52 and $37.54 per month or approximately $390 and $450 per year.

Exhibit 12

Indices of Wages and Consumer Prices, Japan (1934–36 = 1)

Year	Consumer Prices (Tokyo)	Wages in Mfg
1947	109	33
1948	189	92
1949	237	157
1950	220	188
1951	225	235
1952	266	272

SOURCE: J. B. Cohen [9, pp. 100, 101]. Reprinted with permission.

Exhibit 13

Indices of Export and Import Prices, All Commodities, Japan (July 1949–June 1950 = 100)

Year	Export Prices	Import Prices
1949	106.5	100.6
1950	115.6	107.8
1951	165.5	136.3
1952	134.9	122.1

SOURCE: Bank of Japan [4, pp. 315, 316: table 117].

Whether or not Japan's condition in 1948 resulted from "Japanese ineptness or skill" [17, p. 134], it was unsatisfactory to the United States. By mid-1948, the latter wanted at least a self-supporting Japan. But, in view of all that had been tried, what sort of program would accomplish this objective?

Exhibit 14

Index of Labor Productivity in Manufacturing in Japan (1934–36 = 100)

Year	Index [a]
1947	25.5
1948	37.7
1949	50.0
1950	61.2
1951	79.9
1952	86.3

SOURCE: Exhibit 7, Part B.

[a] Production index divided by employment index.

ALTERNATIVES FOR RECOVERY: THE "ISHIBASHI LINE"

Among right-wing spokesmen for Japan, one at least had a prescription for recovery. This was Tanzan Ishibashi, Japan's Minister of Finance from May 1946 to May 1947, when he was removed at the Occupation's request. Despite the personal eclipse of its author, his point of view remained "influential," the *Oriental Economist*[10] being "the most effective English language proponent of his view" [7(Aug. 1950), p. 285]. In 1950 Martin Bronfenbrenner described the Ishibashi Line as follows:

> Mr. Ishibashi calls himself a Keynesian. His Keynesianism, however, is of a fundamentalist variety which takes literally the view that *no* monetary expansion should be considered inflationary so long as production and employment are increasing along with prices. . . .

[10] Mr. Ishibashi was the editor of this magazine.

Exhibit 15

Annual Balance of Payments Data 1945–46 through 1952 (millions of US $)

Item	1945–46	1947	1948	1949	1950	1951	1952
Merchandise trade							
Exports	129.9	180.1	343.7	534.7	772.8	1297.3	1289.2
Imports	−134.7	−163.8	−244.5	−422.0	−645.5	−1725.1	−1718.4
Balance of							
merchandise trade	−4.8	16.3	99.2	112.7	127.3	−427.8	−429.2
Aid imports	−247.1	−476.5	−473.8	−494.3	−361.2	−180.3	−5.4
Balance of aid &							
merchandise trade	−251.9	−460.2	−374.6	−381.5	−233.9	−608.1	−434.6
Invisible trade							
Receipts							
Special procurement	—	—	—	—	148.9	591.7	824.2
Other	2.5	8.0	35.9	91.0	86.6	351.6	125.8
Total	2.5	8.0	35.9	91.0	235.5	943.3	950.0
Payments	—	—	—	—	−31.7	−146.9	−138.1
Balance of							
invisible trade	2.5	8.0	35.9	91.0	203.8	796.4	811.9
Gold movements	—	—	—	—	—	—	—

Balance of all current items	−249.4	−452.2	−338.7	−290.5	−30.1	188.3	377.3
Capital movements							
Receipts	126.5	59.5	36.1	54.4	—	56.5	19.2
Payments	−23.0	−92.5	−77.9	−64.5	—	−37.3	−68.4
Balance of capital movements	103.5	−33.0	−41.8	−10.1	—	19.2	−49.2
Adjustment items	−40.1	−11.8	−5.9	−43.4	—	—	—
Totals							
Receipts	258.9	247.6	415.7	680.1	1008.3	2297.1	2258.4
Payments							
Including aid[a]	−444.9	−744.6	−802.1	−1024.2	−1038.4	−2089.6	−1930.3
Excluding aid	−197.8	−268.1	−328.3	−529.9	−677.2	−1909.3	−1924.8
Errors & omissions, etc.							
Including aid[a]	186.0	497.0	386.4	344.1	30.1	−207.5	−328.1
Excluding aid	−61.1	20.5	87.4	−150.2	−331.1	−387.8	−333.6

SOURCE: Japan Ministry of Finance [23: table 1]. Figures for 1947, 1949, 1950, 1951, and 1952 adjusted to exclude arithmetic errors.

NOTE (1): Fiscal years through 1949; calendar years thereafter. Japan's fiscal year ends March 31 of the following calendar year.
NOTE (2): In the absence of a single exchange rate for the yen until April 1949, the value of Japan's foreign transactions was commonly reported in US dollars. After April 1949, the yen exchange rate was set at ¥360 = US $1.

[a] If aid imports were paid in foreign currency.

Exhibit 16

Analysis of Foreign Trade

A. EXPORTS AND IMPORTS (BILLIONS OF YEN)

Year	Exports	Imports
1936	2.7	2.8
1946	2.3	4.1
1947	10.0	20.3
1948	52.0	60.3
1949	169.8	284.4
1950	298.0	348.2
1951	488.8	737.2
1952	458.3	730.4

B. PERCENTAGE BREAKDOWN OF VALUE OF EXPORTS AND IMPORTS BY MAIN COMMODITY GROUP

	Exports					Imports				
Year	Food-stuffs	Crude Materials	Fabricated Materials	End Products	Other	Food-stuffs	Crude Materials	Fabricated Materials	End Products	Other
1936	7.6	4.7	26.6	58.0	3.1	8.4	62.9	17.2	10.6	0.9
1946	9.3	15.5	61.9	13.2	0.1	40.8	49.5	4.9	4.6	0.2
1947	6.9	16.7	21.2	54.9	0.3	52.7	19.7	10.3	16.8	0.5
1948	5.4	7.9	28.1	58.6	0.0	47.9	24.3	8.1	18.7	1.0
1949	4.5	3.3	23.8	68.1	0.3	43.1	34.0	11.7	10.0	1.2
1950	6.3	2.9	25.7	64.4	0.7	33.5	42.0	6.3	18.1	0.1
1951	5.1	2.8	29.4	60.8	1.9	27.7	58.4	7.3	6.5	0.1
1952	7.8	3.0	35.0	52.6	1.6	32.2	52.1	6.6	9.1	0.1

C. PERCENTAGE BREAKDOWN OF VALUE OF EXPORTS BY PRINCIPAL COMMODITY

Commodity	1936	1946	1950	1951	1952
Shellfish	2.8	0.3	3.5	2.6	3.6
Tea	0.4	8.3	0.6	0.4	0.6
Textiles	43.3	40.6	35.1	38.8	29.3
Iron & steel products	2.8	—	8.7	15.1	20.6
Nonferrous metals	3.7	11.9	7.0	3.3	1.6
Fish oil	0.3	0.2	0.8	0.6	0.6
Cement	0.3	0.3	0.7	1.1	1.4
Machinery					
Spinning, sewing	0.6	0.1	2.4	2.8	3.3
Rolling stock, ships	2.7	5.4	4.9	2.4	2.4
Other	3.5	2.3	2.7	2.6	2.9
Clothes	5.5	0.1	2.8	2.5	3.0
Chemicals	3.2	1.7	1.9	2.7	3.1
Wood	0.5	9.1	0.6	0.8	1.0
Paper products	1.4	0.7	0.6	1.2	0.6
Chinaware	1.4	—	2.1	2.5	2.3
Other	27.6	19.0	25.6	20.6	23.7
Total	100.0	100.0	100.0	100.0	100.0

Exhibit 16 (continued)

D. PERCENTAGE BREAKDOWN OF VALUE OF EXPORTS BY AREA OR COUNTRY

Area/Country	1936	1946	1950	1951	1952
Asia	51.1[a]	33.1	46.3	51.5	51.6
China	24.4	9.8	2.4	0.4	—
Hong Kong	2.2	2.1	6.4	7.4	6.3
India, Pakistan	9.6	0.0	9.2	12.4	12.1
Korea, Formosa	—	19.4	6.8	4.8	8.4
Europe	11.3	1.2	12.0	10.7	14.0
N and S America	26.7	65.1	29.1	21.6	23.5
US	22.1	65.1	21.7	13.6	17.2
Africa	7.4	0.0	8.9	8.2	7.4
Australia, Oceania	3.6	0.6	3.6	7.9	3.5
Total (¥ millions)	2,693	2,260	298,033	488,777	458,253

E. PERCENTAGE BREAKDOWN OF VALUE OF IMPORTS BY AREA OR COUNTRY

Area/Country	1936	1946	1950	1951	1952
Asia	38.5[a]	8.8	32.6	28.9	31.2
China	14.3	6.7	4.1	1.1	0.7
India, Pakistan	13.5	0.0	4.2	7.6	7.7
Korea, Formosa	—	—	5.3	2.9	4.1
Europe	11.8	1.2	4.0	7.8	6.9
N and S America	38.2	86.4	52.0	51.5	51.7
US	30.6	86.4	43.2	33.9	37.9
Africa	3.9	2.9	2.7	3.9	2.6
Australia, Oceania	7.6	0.6	8.7	7.8	7.6
Total (¥ millions)	2,764	4,069	348,196	737,241	730,354

SOURCE: Bank of Japan [4(1952), p. 269: table 106; pp. 271, 272: table 109; pp. 273–280: table 110; pp. 281–284: table 111].

[a] Except Korea and Formosa, which were in the Japanese empire.

To supporters of the Ishibashi Line, recovery depends upon increased production. This depends, in turn, upon capital accumulation, which can be encouraged by high rates of profit even when basic raw materials are physically short. In financing capital accumulation, taxes are to be kept low while easy credit is made available from a Reconstruction Finance Bank. The budget is to be unbalanced deliberately. Foreign exchange is to be secured by yen devaluation . . . to whatever extent is necessary. Full employment is to be assured by monetary expansion and curbs on trade-union wage-raising activity. Official prices, if they cannot be eliminated altogether, are to be fixed at premium rates high enough above production cost to encourage increased output. Far from opposing price increases, the Ishibashi Line rather welcomes their effect on production, denies their long-run inflationary character, and tries to close its eyes to the resulting concentration of the cost of reconstruction upon consumers and upon labor . . . [7, pp. 285, 286]. Reprinted by permission of the University of Chicago Press.

THE "DODGE LINE"

In contrast to the Ishibashi Line, which put growth before stability, a new US economic mission concluded by mid-1948 that Japan must stabilize her economy before she could become self-supporting. A multi-point program for this purpose was urged upon Japan in July and ordered in December. Then, in February 1949, Joseph M. Dodge, the conservative ("some said ante-diluvian") president of the Detroit Bank [29, p. 135], arrived in Japan "with the rank of Minister to bring economic order out of monetary and fiscal chaos" [10, p. 86]. Although some steps toward stabilization antedated Mr. Dodge's arrival,[11] the program came to be known as his "line."

In discussing what he planned to do, Mr. Dodge acknowledged that "a rough and rocky road" lay ahead. Japan so far was a "rigged economy," resting on the "stilts" of US aid and government subsidies, and "continuously living beyond its means." "It is the height of folly," Dodge added, "to point with pride at an increasing production index or increasing exports which may actually represent only increased US aid, increased subsidies, and increased deficits. . . . Too little attention is being given to the need for creating the greatest possible net production and using imported raw materials so as to create the greatest possible amount of net exports" [14, pp. 131, 132].

Steps in the Dodge Line comprised a rapid-fire series of measures, mostly in April 1949:

1. The exchange value of the yen was stabilized at ¥360 to the dollar—not only to bring pressure on Japanese producers to

meet the world price for their products, but also to "attract foreign investment, which was critically needed to alleviate the capital shortage . . . in Japan" [42, p. 29].

2. The Japanese budget was brought into balance for the first time in eighteen years, and debt retirement was initiated from revenues collected in excess of outlays.

3. Future US aid was made conditional on payment by Japan of the yen-cost of the goods she received into a new Counterpart Fund. This fund was to be used under SCAP supervision for debt retirement and investment.

4. The RFB was prohibited from making any further loans except out of repayments made to it on current loans outstanding. All its debentures were to be retired. In short, the RFB's "diminished activities could no longer result in the monetization of inflation-created debt" [10, pp. 88].

5. Subsidies were eliminated in some areas and reduced gradually in others.

6. Stock markets—closed since the end of the war—were reopened to stimulate the flow of capital to industry and to help dispose of formerly zaibatsu-held securities.

7. A Credit Control Board was established. Modeled on the US Board of Governors of the Federal Reserve System, it was to provide "a sort of directorate for . . . monetary policy" [10, p. 88].

8. The "abolition of officially controlled prices on 7,500 commodities" was announced by SCAP headquarters in August 1949 [30, p. 642].

Like the deflations of 1882 and 1929, the Dodge Line was "hard medicine," particularly for Japan's civil servants, 25 percent of whom lost their jobs in the interest of balancing the budget. Some acts of sabotage against the state-owned railroads fol-

---

[11] The chief deflationary step before Dodge arrived was a November directive stating that wage increases could not be granted if they required higher official prices or larger government subsidies or loans.

lowed, and a railroad director was murdered "under mysterious circumstances." "But," in the words of Edwin Reischauer, "the Communists had overplayed their hand. Popular support for them declined, and resistance to the dismissals subsided. The Occupation had won a second head-on clash with the labor movement which it created" [34, p. 279]. Communist-dominated Sanbetsu, already weakened by earlier Occupation moves against strikes, was further weakened by selective Dodge Line firings in state and private firms and by the Communist purge that accompanied the Korean War. It all but disappeared at this time, and unions of various stripes joined a new, less radical confederation, called *Sohyo*, which remained the leading body of its kind even after numerous defections. Meanwhile, the labor movement as a whole shrank in size: from 1949 to 1950 the number of unions fell from 34,688 to 29,144; union membership fell from 6.7 million to 5.8 million; and the percentage of the workforce that was organized fell from 55.7 to 45.9 [10, pp. 204–206; 19, pp. 217–220].

Still another factor helpful to the Dodge Line was the support, however grudging, of conservative Premier S. Yoshida, now in power with a majority. According to one analyst, "It can only be surmised that he recognized at last that Japan's problems could be met only by strong government action, and that the positive hard-hitting and authoritarian character of the program appealed to him. The public directive from General MacArthur . . . largely relieved him of responsibility for the unpopular actions demanded . . ." [14, p. 128].

Judged in relation to its goal of checking inflation, the Dodge program was a success, although "the Japanese complained of tight money, stagnant output, rising unemployment and an increase in small business failures" [10, p. 89]. Most of the major economic outcomes of the Dodge Line show up in parts of Exhibits 4 through 15,

when trends in 1949 and 1950 are compared with trends in the earlier postwar years.

ROUNDING OUT THE DODGE LINE WITH LONGER-RANGE MEASURES

As a crash program for ending inflation, the Dodge Line needed rounding out by longer-range measures to build a stable future. Work started on these when a mission headed by Carl S. Schoup, a professor from Columbia University, arrived in Japan on the heels of Mr. Dodge to work on tax reform.

Shoup Tax Proposals

Prior to the Shoup mission of June–September 1949, the Japanese tax structure had been characterized by "extremely high" rates, accompanied by such "wholesale evasion" that the Occupation had to use troops to help with tax collection [14, pp. 151, 152]. "Anti-tax sentiment of the public was strong." In addition, the corporate sector was pleading "more and more vocally for tax laws that would help the re-establishment of Japanese industry" [42, p. 31].

Professor Shoup's proposals went part way to satisfy these demands. His report emphasized that a prime objective would be "a tax cut for every Japanese" [42, p. 32]. He had, however, virtually "no control" over state expenditures and no control "over the basic policy of budgetary overbalance" [8(Dec. 1957), p. 349]. Thus, except insofar as the Dodge Line resulted in economies, the Shoup program would have to find new taxes to compensate for any tax cuts recommended. Besides helping to keep the budget balanced, Shoup's mandate also included making provisions for the tax support of local government. Despite the "allocation of a great volume of public functions" to the local level by the Occupation, "local autonomy was foundering . . . because of the dependence of the local units upon variable and capricious grants from Tokyo" [8(Sept. 1957), p. 238].

Against this background, the Shoup mission proposed tax changes "along lines generally familiar to Americans, adding, however, a number of novel features designed to give Japan 'the best tax system in the world'" [8(Sept. 1957), pp. 238, 239]. Thus, a "progressive and broad-based personal income tax" was its "mainstay"—the first time anything of the kind had been attempted in the Orient" [8(Sept. 1957), pp. 238, 239]. Other major revenue sources were to be corporate taxes, indirect taxes, and a new local tax on "value added" (VAT).[12] This tax was to replace the current local "enterprise tax" on business income. Along with relatively nondiscretionary, formula-based grants-in-aid from the central government, VAT was to become a chief means for providing local financial independence.

Compared with the existing postwar setup, the main proposed changes in the personal income tax called for larger exemptions and a decrease in the "paper" ceiling rate from 80 to 55 percent. To make up for this loss in progressivity as well as to compensate for any revenue lost to the state, differential rates were no longer to be assigned to a person's income from various sources (e.g., personal employment or capital gains); rather, his or her income from all sources would in effect be totaled before the applicable tax rate was applied. In addition, gifts and inheritances were to be cumulated over time and taxed on a progressive basis. Moreover, a progressive tax was to be lev-

ied on personal wealth, ranging from 0.5 to 3 percent, with a large exemption. The chief proposed change in indirect taxes, apart from a decline in their relative importance, called for their elimination on essentials (e.g., textiles), the loss to be offset by a higher rate on luxuries (e.g., liquor and tobacco). The chief proposed changes in the corporation tax would at last permit asset revaluation in line with current price levels and would also do away with the excess profits tax. In addition, revaluation would be subject to a 6 percent charge; a small tax on surplus would be levied; and, most important, the value of depreciable tools and machines would become subject to the local property tax along with land and plant.

The purpose of the Shoup mission "was to recommend a tax system that would require no changes for several years to come" [42, p. 32]. In 1949 the Japanese adopted most of the national tax proposals (which were tax-reduction proposals) almost without change. The local tax proposals, which would increase local taxes by ¥40 billion, had rougher going and could not be put through until 1950. Even then, the proposed shift to VAT was rejected [8(Sept. 1957), p. 241; 14, p. 197]. Although it was anticipated that some aspects of the Shoup tax program might be changed in every future budget, no further major overhaul occurred for the remainder of the Occupation.

Control of Foreign Trade and Investment

Besides the Shoup tax program, a second set of longer-term, Dodge-era measures aimed at reviving foreign trade and foreign investment. In December 1949 nearly all controls on exports were removed, and the power of deciding just what imports Japan would buy out of her limited foreign exchange was turned over to the Japanese.

---

[12] Still untried when proposed for Japan, VAT is a tax on producers' gross income less payments to outside suppliers.

Control was to begin with the drawing up of an annual foreign-exchange budget and with the listing of all commodities for which foreign exchange might be released. Some types of goods were to go onto a list for which import permits were to be automatic up to a specified aggregate expenditure; other types were to go onto a list for which certificates-to-import were needed. Several ministries were involved in making up the budget and drawing up the lists, with the Ministry of Commerce and Industry—now renamed the Ministry of International Trade and Industry (MITI)—having an important voice. In addition, MITI was put in charge of granting certificates-to-import. Elaborating on this arrangement, one analyst noted, ''A high degree of discrimination is practiced by MITI in the selection of applicants to whom these certificates are granted'' [21, pp. 225-227].

The Foreign Exchange and Foreign Trade Control Law passed in December 1949. Six months later a law concerning foreign investment followed. This law had two objectives: to prevent the ''carpet-bagging'' of existing Japanese assets by foreigners at prices reflecting the low exchange value of the yen [16, pp. 16, 17], and to pave the way for foreign investment that would be helpful to Japan in her condition of capital shortage. Foreign investment was made controllable by making it subject to permits. Without a permit, the ''fruits'' of investment (interest, dividends, or royalties) could not be ''repatriated'' by their recipients in foreign currencies, nor would payment be made by Japan in foreign currency for any foreign asset that might be nationalized [21, pp. 225-227].

To be permissible, a foreign investment must meet certain criteria. ''The investment must 'contribute to the self-support and sound development of the Japanese economy and to the improvement of the international balance of payments' '' [17, p. 401; 24, sec. 0-17]. Such an investment could take any of several forms: equity, debt, or

technological assistance which was to be paid for via royalties. There were limits, however, on equity investment. Repatriation was not to be allowed for the fruits of a new wholly-owned subsidiary, although a company already in Japan might apply to add a branch and any foreign firm might apply to participate in a joint venture. So far as industrial investment was concerned, the granting of permits would be up to MITI, and MITI might amplify the existing law by more detailed regulations [21, pp. 225-227].

Modification of the Anti-Monopoly Law

According to the Japanese, a chance to repatriate the fruits of investment would not suffice, alone, to attract foreign investors who would still be ''put off'' by Japan's Anti-Monopoly Law. According to the chairman of Japan's FTC, ''It is going a little too far when all provisions of the law are written for the sole purpose of enabling the strictest enforcement'' [17, p. 198]. Encouraged by signs of the Occupation's ''reverse course'' at the end of 1948, the Japanese started to agitate for amendment of the Anti-Monopoly Law shortly after it was enacted. Their campaign bore fruit during the Dodge era in June 1949. The new amendments, however, ''did much more than soften provisions that had barred close relations between foreign and Japanese companies'' [5, p. 188]. These amendments also relaxed prohibitions or near-prohibitions on all intercorporate stockholding, multiple directorates, and mergers. Henceforth, such ties would be permitted if not obtained by ''unfair methods,'' if not tending ''to lessen competition,'' or if not resulting in ''disparities of bargaining power.'' FTC ''permission'' for such moves need not be obtained, although they must be ''registered'' with the FTC, which had 30 days to object [17, pp. 198, 199].

THE POSTWAR TAKEOFF: THE IMPACT OF THE WAR IN KOREA ON JAPAN

What the long-run outcome of the Dodge-era measures might have been was destined to remain undiscovered. Events in the form of the Korean War (which started in June 1950 and ended in July 1953) soon established new priorities. Japan's proximity to the conflict meant she could be used for staging and sourcing. Orders poured in, production expanded, and even foreign exchange grew plentiful as US "off-shore" procurement in Japan added its impact to that of US aid.[13]

The price for these favorable outcomes, however, was another attack of inflation. This was most severe in the early months of the conflict, but even after the initial war boom ebbed—which it did around April 1951—Japanese prices continued to rise, in contrast to US and some other prices. The differing impacts of the Dodge line and the conflict in Korea can be traced in Exhibits 4 through 16.

POST-KOREAN LEGISLATION

With the Occupation intent on the war, most of the measures it initiated during the last two years of its stay were designed to help its military cause. These measures included a "purge" of Communist Party leaders, a "depurging" of nearly all the businessmen and politicians who had been purged after World War II, encouragement of increased expenditures by Japan on

---

[13] On a prorated basis, aid and special procurement combined from June 1950 through June 1952 were approximately $1.5 billion, or almost as much as total aid receipts during the previous years of Occupation.

"military" outlays to provide at least her own internal security, and an interdiction on further trade with China. Within two years Japan's exports to China fell from 2.4 percent of her total to only 0.01 percent and her imports from 4.1 percent to 0.7 percent [10, p. 172].

Japan's most important initiatives came after the war boom faltered, starting in April 1951. Finding some of her industries beset not only by high costs but also by acute excess capacity, Japan sought to provide financial help. To assist high-cost exporters, a new Export-Import Bank was created. To assist high-cost industries to engage in "rationalization," public investment was increased and a new bank was set up in place of the postwar RFB, which the Dodge Line had curtailed. This was the Japan Development Bank which obtained all its financing from the state. In the event, however, these financial measures helped to fuel the problem they were designed to solve. In the words of Jerome Cohen (who had been a member of the Shoup tax mission), "These events, when coupled with the expansion of bank loans to the (still) prosperous capital goods industries, had the total effect of increasing the money supply and thus maintaining inflationary pressures" [10, pp. 89, 90].

In still other efforts to help industries that were plagued by high costs and excess capacity as the war boom faltered in 1951, MITI took the lead in devising arrangements to temper the severe effects of competition. Thus, in April 1951 MITI recommended "less than full capacity operation (*so-tan*) to the three industries most affected by the sudden curtailment" of special procurement. Later in the year, as a part of its so-called "save-the-bankruptcies" policy, MITI designed and the Diet rushed through a Stabilization Act for Medium-Small Industries. This in effect "required adjustment . . . of production, investment, and shipment but not price-fixing which would have been impossible in any case" [42, pp. 44–46]. As pointed out by one analyst, MITI's so-called "recommendation" really had the force of an order. Since all three of the industries affected relied on imported raw materials, and since MITI controlled all access to foreign currency, it could cut off essential supplies "to disobedient firms" [42, pp. 44–46].

In the face of such departures from Occupation-sponsored antitrust measures, "the attitude of SCAP was one of apparent inconsistency" [42, p. 49]. Thus, SCAP accepted MITI's so-tan recommendations and the Medium-Small Industries Act, but it "refused" a proposed amendment to the Export-Trade Act that would have permitted cartels in the domestic market, and it "sternly rejected" the suggestion for a "large-scale amendment" to the Anti-Monopoly Law. Meanwhile, Japan's FTC had begun to play its appointed role as the champion of competition. Thus, the FTC challenged two of MITI's three so-tan orders in 1951. In the same year it also issued orders to the iron and steel and ammonium sulphate industries to stop alleged price fixing. Both industries acceded without plea. The FTC also reportedly believed that several other industries might be guilty "of some type of underground collusions. . . . However, no action was taken, based on its finding that 'activities were not collusive, even though they appeared to be collusive'" [42, pp. 44–46].

LOOKING AHEAD TO INDEPENDENCE

In preparation for independence, which came on April 28, 1952, Japan was invited by SCAP to set up an Occupation Legislation Screening Committee "to review all the laws and orders promulgated since the be-

ginning of the Occupation" [42, p. 43]. Besides considering what Occupation measures she might reasonably hope to change, Japan faced a major problem of deciding her industrial strategy. Once the Korean War was over and aid—already much reduced—was finally ended, Japan would again be dependent on world trade. But with what areas and in what products? Even during Japan's China conquests, light industries, particularly textiles, had provided most of her exports. Since that time, other product categories had risen, but without excluding textiles from first place (*see* Exhibit 16).

In order to direct future investment, it was important to decide ahead of time where the export emphasis should be. Arguments advanced against the old light industry focus included speculation that demand for such products would decline as the Third World started to industrialize. Also, it was known that heavy industry contributed more to Japan by way of "value added" than did light, and it was on value added that Japan would have to survive. On the other hand, labor-intensive light industries seemed to be where Japan had her only "natural advantage," given her large supply of high-grade labor and her lack of natural resources.

Before making up their minds what to do, the Japanese carefully studied the prices quoted by their own light and heavy industries versus the prices of foreign competitors. As reported by the Ministry of Finance, some findings for September 1951 and June 1952 are shown in Exhibit 17.

Japanese Prospects: Outside Assessments

Six months before independence, Joseph Dodge wound up a trip to Japan with an

Exhibit 17

International Price Comparisons (Japan's Price = 100)

Item[a]	Date	US	UK	West Germany	Other
Raw silk	9/51	100	—	—	—
	6/52	118	—	—	—
Cotton yarn	9/51	78	80	—	—
	6/52	102	142	—	29 (Italy)
Cotton fabric	9/51	75	124	—	113
	6/52	86	107	—	87 (Hong Kong)
Rayon yarn	9/51	—	—	—	—
	6/52	—	—	—	—
Pig iron	9/51	65	41	—	109
	6/52	63	43	—	109 (Belgium)
Steel bar	9/51	60	57	52	62
	6/52	60	65	67	62 (Belgium)
Sheet steel	9/51	38	47	44	58
	6/52	45	65	65	69 (Belgium)
Electrolytic copper	9/51	105	93	—	—
	6/52	88	89	—	—
Zinc	9/51	55	108	—	—
	6/52	72	—	—	—
Tin	9/51	63	75	—	103 (Hong Kong)
	6/52	96	96	—	—
Ammonium sulphate	9/51	109	—	—	—
	6/52	84	68	—	—
Crude rubber	9/51	101	104	—	94
	6/52	98	97	—	81 (Hong Kong)
Coking coal	9/51	—	—	—	—
	6/52	43	—	—	—

SOURCE: Japan Ministry of Finance [23(1955): table 23].

[a] Detailed specifications omitted.

"open letter" giving his opinion of her current course and its prospects:

> At present, Japan is suffering from a plague of false legends, which include some dangerous delusions. A few of these are:
>
> That a nation that must export to live can afford to price itself out of its export markets with a domestic inflation.
>
> That there is anything but trouble ahead in an attempt to chase inflationary price increases with stop-gap measures which merely feed the fires of inflation.
>
> That every difficulty caused by excessive debt, speculative purchasing and similar acts of bad management always is the fault of others, it is not the inevitable result of the previous mistakes of the individuals concerned, and should be borne by the government or the consumers.

The progress and the present favorable status of Japan has been the result of a series of extremely fortunate external circumstances, which cannot be expected to be repeated and continued indefinitely [10, pp. 90, 91].

More sympathetic but not more optimistic was the assessment of Edwin Reischauer at about the same point in time:

First of all, there is the problem of whether or not Japan, regardless of the political and economic system she eventually chooses, can maintain any satisfactory standard of living in the future. She cannot grow enough food to feed all her people. She cannot produce the greater part of the fibers from which she must spin clothes for her millions. She has very little oil or iron and is lacking in adequate quantities of most of the other minerals and raw materials needed to maintain a modern industrial economy. Nylon and other synthetic fibers have destroyed most of the demand for silk, the one major export item she produced entirely within her boundaries. All she has to offer on the world market is her own energy—manpower and the energy of coal and water. With these she can transform imported raw materials into goods for re-export. The slim margin of profit from this re-export trade must be sufficient to pay for all the imports Japan must have to support her own people. To do this, Japan's export trade must be huge. But where is she to find her markets in a divided world and in a Far East disrupted by revolutions and bitterly determined not to trade with her? Japan's situation is basically similar to England's but infinitely worse. She is far less richly endowed with the vital resources of coal and iron than are the British Isles. She is less highly industrialized. She has no overseas empire to aid her but instead an international legacy of distrust and hate. And she has almost twice the population of Great Britain to support on her more meager resources [34, pp. 50, 51]. Reprinted by permission of Harvard University Press.

REFERENCES

In English

1. Acino, Hirosi. "Control of Restrictive Trade Practices in Japan," in *Restrictive Business Practices*, the proceedings of a conference sponsored by the Graduate School of Business of the University of Chicago. Glencoe, Ill.: Free Press of Glencoe, 1960.

2. Allen, George C. *Japan's Economic Recovery*. London: Oxford University Press, 1958.

3. Bank of Japan. *Hundred-Year Statistics of the Japanese Economy*. Tokyo, 1966.

4. ————. *Economic Statistics of Japan* (later *Economic Statistics Annual*). Tokyo, annual.

5. Bisson, T. A. *Zaibatsu Dissolution in Japan*. Berkeley, Calif.: University of California Press, 1954.

6. Borton, Hugh. *Japan's Modern Century*. New York: Ronald Press, 1955.

7. Bronfenbrenner, Martin. "Four Positions on Japanese Finance," *Journal of Political Economy*. (August 1950), pp. 281–288.

8. ————, and K. Kogiku. "The Aftermath of the Shoup Tax Reforms," *National Tax Journal* (September 1957), pp. 236–254; (December 1957), pp. 345–360.

9. Cohen, Jerome B. *Economic Problems of Free Japan*. Princeton, N.J.: Center for International Studies, 1952.

10. ————. *Japan's Postwar Economy*. Bloomington, Indiana: Indiana University Press, 1958.

11. Cole, Robert E. *Japanese Blue Collar: The Changing Tradition*. Berkeley, Calif.: University of California Press, 1971.

12. Cook, Alice H. *Japanese Trade Unionism*. Ithaca, N.Y.: Cornell University Press, 1966.

13. Dore, R. P. *Land Reform in Japan*. London: Oxford University Press, 1959.

14. Fearey, Robert A. *The Occupation of Japan, Second Phase: 1948–50*. New York: Macmillan (Institute of Pacific Relations), 1950.

15. Fine, Sherwood M. *Japan's Postwar Industrial Recovery*. Tokyo: Foreign Affairs Association of Japan, 1953.

16. Goodman, G. K. (compiler). *The American Occupation of Japan: A Retrospective View*. Topeka: University of Kansas (Center of East Asian Studies), 1968.

17. Hadley, Eleanor M. *Antitrust in Japan*. Princeton, N.J.: Princeton University Press, 1970.

18. Hagan, Everett E. (ed.). *Planning Economic Development*. Homewood, Ill.: Richard D. Irwin, 1963.

19. Halliday, Jon. *A Political History of Japanese Capitalism*. New York: Pantheon Books, 1975.

20. Harari, Ehud. *The Politics of Labor Legislation in Japan: National–International Interaction*. Berkeley, Calif.: University of California Press, 1973.

21. Hollerman, Leon. *Japan's Dependence on the World Economy*. Princeton, N.J.: Princeton University, 1967.

22. Japan Economic Planning Board (formerly Japan Stabilization Board). *Economic Survey of Japan*. Tokyo, annual.

23. Japan Ministry of Finance. *General Survey of the Japanese Economy*. Tokyo, annual.

24. ————. *Japan Laws, Ordinances and Other Regulations Concerning Foreign Exchange and Foreign Trade* (March 1, 1954). Tokyo: Foreign Exchange Study Association, 1954.

25. ————. *Quarterly Bulletin of Financial Statistics*. Tokyo.

26. Komiya, R. (ed.). *Postwar Economic Growth in Japan*. Berkeley, Calif.: University of California Press, 1966.

27. "A Lawyer's Report on Japan Attacks Plan to Run Occupation . . . Far to the Left of Anything Now Tolerated in America," *Newsweek* (Dec. 4, 1947), pp. 36–38.

28. Levine, Soloman B. *Industrial Relations in Postwar Japan.* Urbana: University of Illinois Press, 1958.

29. Livingston, Jon, *et al.* (eds.). *Postwar Japan, 1945 to the Present,* vol. 2 of *The Japan Reader.* New York: Pantheon Books, division of Random House, 1973.

30. Matsumura, Yutaka. *Japan's Economic Growth, 1945–60.* Tokyo: Tokyo News Service, 1961.

31. Moulton, Harold G. *Japan: An Economic and Financial Appraisal.* Washington: Brookings Institution, 1931.

32. Ohkawa, Kazushi and Henry Rosovsky. *Japanese Economic Growth: Trend Acceleration in the Twentieth Century.* Stanford: Stanford University Press, 1973.

33. Patrick, Hugh T. (ed.). *Japanese Industrialization and Its Social Consequences.* Berkeley, Calif.: University of California Press, 1976.

34. Reischauer, Edwin O. *The United States and Japan* (3d. ed.). New York: Viking, 1964. (Original edition, Cambridge, Mass.: Harvard University Press, 1950.)

35. Sakurabayashi, Makoto and Robert J. Ballon. "Labor-Management Relations in Modern Japan: A Historical Survey of Personnel Administration." Tokyo: Sophia University, 1962, pamphlet.

36. Scalapino, Robert A. and J. Masumi. *Parties and Politics in Contemporary Japan.* Berkeley, Calif.: University of California Press, 1962.

37. Shiomi, Saburo. *Japan's Finance and Taxation, 1940–1956,* translated by S. Hasegawa. New York: Columbia University Press, 1957.

38. Tsuru, Shigeto. "Internal Industrial and Business Trends," *Japan Since Recovery of Independence, The Annals of the American Academy of Political and Social Science* (November 1955).

39. —————. *Japan's Economy—Present and Future.* Tokyo: Japan Institute of Foreign Relations, 1950.

40. United Nations. *Statistical Yearbook,* 1956.

41. United States, Bureau of the Census. *Historical Statistics of the United States,* vol. 1, series D, 1949.

42. Yamamura, Kozo. *Economic Policy in Postwar Japan: Growth Versus Economic Democracy.* Berkeley, Calif.: University of California Press, 1967.

In Japanese

43. Suehiro, Izutaro. *Nihon Rodo Kumiai Undo Shi* (The History of the Japanese Trade Union Movement). Tokyo: Chuo Koron Sha, 1954.

Japan D1: A Strategy for Economic Growth

In 1952 as the Occupation made ready to depart, it suggested that Japan review the institutional and other changes of the past seven years with an eye to deciding what to keep and what to drop. Regardless of what political and economic system Japan might choose, however, analysts wondered whether she would be able to maintain "any satisfactory standard of living in the future." Despite the infusion of $2.1 billion in US aid and $1.5 billion in US offshore procurement for the prosecution of the war in Korea, Japan's real GNP had only recently recovered the level attained in 1936. To keep on growing as offshore procurement declined, Japan would need a "huge" export trade. But where was she "to find her markets in a divided world and in a Far East disrupted by revolutions and bitterly determined not to trade with her?" [36, pp. 50, 51].

Despite this gloomy outlook, within a few years Japan's economy was growing at a rate "without precedent or parallel elsewhere." By 1970 she had pulled ahead of Britain, France, and West Germany in terms of total GNP (*see* Exhibit 1), and some were predicting that by the year 2000 she would have pulled ahead of Russia and the United States as well [1, pp. 1, 25, 179, and *passim*].

Such performance and such prospects roused worldwide interest. How had such a record been achieved? What if any threats seemed to darken the future?

Exhibit 1

Trend of Gross National Product in Constant 1972 Prices, 1952–1971 (in billions of US dollar equivalents)

	Japan	US	France	West Germany	UK
1952	53.9	577.2	78.1	94.7	85.7
1971	306.9	1089.0	206.7	277.6	148.3
Growth (in %)	469.4	88.7	164.7	193.1	73.0

SOURCE: U.S., Agency for International Development [38, p. 7: table 4c and p. 17: table 8c].

REVIEWING THE INSTITUTIONAL FRAMEWORK

Although the Occupation had invited Japan to review the changes of the past seven years, both countries knew that her freedom of decision was subject to certain constraints. Thus, Japan depended on the United States for a large share of her trade, for her defense umbrella, and for sponsorship of her pending application to become a member of the Organization for Economic Cooperation and Development (OECD) as well as a signator to the General Agreement on Tariffs and Trade (GATT). By the late 1960s Japan would also look to the United States for the return of Okinawa, an island she had lost after World War II.

Political Institutions

Constitutional Developments.   Concern with US reactions did not prevent some Japanese from wanting to revise their new constitution—especially the controversial provisions that made the people, not the emperor, sovereign and that denied Japan the right to wage war. In the event, however, the constitution survived unchanged, its renunciation of war proving to be particularly popular.

Along with war the Japanese continued to reject a military establishment other than a small internal self-defense force. One result of this decision was a substantial budgetary saving compared to that of other countries (*see* Exhibit 2)

Parties.   Besides a new constitution, the Occupation era left Japan with a spectrum of political parties. This spectrum survived after 1952, as did the dominance of conservatism. Under the guidance of big business, the conservatives not only managed to enlist the support of farmers and small business, they also managed in 1953 to merge their two major parties into one, the Liberal Democratic Party (LDP). In contrast, the left never managed to extend its power base beyond labor and intellectuals or to heal the rifts that divided its supporters into at least two parties if not three: a very small (but growing) Communist Party, plus left- and right-wing socialist factions.

Exhibit 2

Military Expenditures as a Share of GNP, 1970 (in percent)[a]

Japan	Italy	West Germany	France	UK	US	USSR (est.)
0.8	2.6	2.9	3.8	5.6	7.8	8.0

SOURCE: P. Peterson [35, chart 6].

[a] Excludes nonmilitary space and atomic energy.

Although the LDP remained dominant, its strength in the Diet showed a slow decline (*see* Exhibit 3). Thus, observers believed that the political prospects of the left could not be written off as hopeless. Combined, its several factions usually won from 35 to 40 percent of the Diet. A minority of this size might be converted into a majority by any of a number of factors—among them a decision by the socialists themselves to become less rigidly doctrinaire and Marxist ("dottily Maoist" as some saw it) [28, p. XXIX]. As William W. Lockwood put it, "Untested as yet is the success that the Socialist Party might achieve if it should move decisively away from its narrow orientation as a party of the 'working class' and make a broad appeal to the masses in the middle" [27, p. 519].

Education

Like the constitution and multiparty politics, the Occupation-fostered education system proved destined to survive in Japan. Such was the case especially with the thrust toward wider access to higher education. Compared with Great Britain, for example, the Japanese system was particularly open, as attested by the following account by Norman Macrae in *The Economist* in 1967.

> Seventy per cent of Japanese children (versus under 40 per cent of British ones) now stay on at school to around or past the age of eighteen; some 16 per cent (versus under 10 per cent in Britain) go on to college or university, and the number is rising fast. In about five year's time, aided admittedly by the huge drop in the birth rate after 1950 which will temporarily reduce the proportion of teenagers to early twenty-year-olds, some 30 per cent of Japan's new young entrants to the labour market will have college or university degrees [28, p. XI].

According to Macrae, Japan's widespread education was "one of the main motive

Exhibit 3

Percentage of Votes in Diet House of Representatives Elections

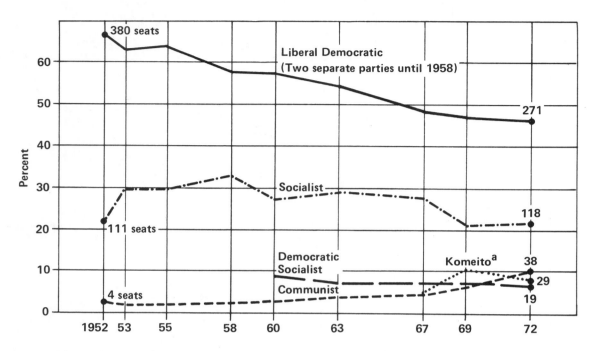

SOURCE: *The Economist* [16(March 31, 1973), p. 27]. Reprinted with permission.
[a] Clean government party.

forces" behind her "miracle" growth in GNP. Growth in turn helped to provide the improved standard of living that permitted more people to stay in school longer, even though higher education was expensive except at the elitist state-supported schools.

For the individual, motivation to continue his studies was mainly the prospect of improved job status. It was also that of higher pay (*see* Exhibit 4).

Agriculture

Of all the Occupation's reforms, the most secure was the one that virtually ended tenant farming. Farms remained uneconomically small, however. Despite the spread of small power tools, Japan's farm workforce was still 16 percent of the total in 1970, compared with only 4 percent for the US. Although most food was imported, farmers needed—and received—tariff protection. Rice, the chief crop, was further protected by a floor on prices and a government purchase-and-distribution program. This made rice relatively so profitable that it was in glut by 1970. The government hoped to end this problem by providing incentives for diversification and by forcing at least part of the rice crop into private distribution channels.

Labor

As one of its reforms, the Occupation had revived trade unions in Japan, but later it had moved to temper militancy and scotch

Exhibit 4

Position, Education and Compensation, Twenty-Five Large Japanese Companies, 1966

Position	Average Education (in percent)				Average Annual Compensation (in dollar equivalent)		
	College or University	Higher School	Middle School	Total	Salary or Wages	Bonus	Total
Top mgt	94	5	1	100	11,496	6,994	18,490
Middle mgt	74	23	3	100	3,408	2,466	5,874
Employees							
Male	10	37	53	100	1,524	646	2,170
Female	2	57	41	100	840	320	1,160
Temporary workers	0	1	99	100	756	262	1,018

SOURCE: J. Abegglen (ed.) [1, pp. 44, 45]. Reprinted with permission.

the threat of communist control. Political restraints plus purges and hard times brought a 25 percent decline in union membership between 1949 and 1951. The same adverse factors destroyed Sanbetsu, the unions' large, radical postwar confederation and also ended any challenge labor had made to the traditional ideology of "familial" labor-management relations.

Such a labor movement was another legacy of the Occupation era with which a free Japan was willing to live. The familial stance of Japanese labor differed widely from the western stance of confrontation.

Instead of seeking strength from nation-wide craft or industrial unions, Japanese labor entrusted its interests to unions organized at the enterprise level. Instead of excluding all white-collar workers, these unions were willing to enroll lower supervisors and often even to elect them to office. Instead of demanding equal pay for equal work, these unions accepted a pay package of wages, bonuses and allowances (see Exhibit 5) that varied with the size of the firm as well as with such personal factors as the employee's age, seniority, sex, education, and status as a regular or temporary worker (see Exhibits 6 and 7). Instead of proseletiz-

Exhibit 5

Breakdown of Labor Costs per Regular Employee in Industry, 1971 (in percent)

	Regular Pay	Bonuses	Over-time	Welfare Costs		Payments in Kind	Severance Fund	Recruitment Training, Other
				Compulsory	Voluntary			
Industrial average	58.8	20.8	6.8	5.1	4.1	0.5	2.8	1.1
Firms with 5000 or more employees	54.6	22.6	7.4	4.9	5.1	0.6	3.5	1.3

SOURCE: Japan Ministry of Labour [23(1971), pp. 203, 208, 210, 211: tables 87, 89, 90].
NOTE: Monthly labor costs per worker in 1971 averaged ¥91,886 for all industrial firms with 30+ employees, ¥116, 793 for firms with 5,000+ employees.

Exhibit 6

**Selected Data on Wage Differentials
(in percent)**

Year	Female/Male Office Workers in Manufacturing	Small Firm/ Large Firm Employee[a]	Large Firm/ Small Firm Starting Wage (Males)[a]
1956	40.5	56.1	133.8
1971	47.8	69.9	99.3

SOURCE: H. Patrick and H. Rosovsky [34, pp. 603, 606]. Reprinted with permission.

[a] Firms with 30 to 99 employees versus firms with more than 500 employees.

ing or insisting on the union shop, these unions tended to ignore their employer's low-paid casual and female workers and the low-paid workers of his subcontractors, preferring to maximize gains for present members. Instead of backing their demands with long strikes, the unions appeared to have regard for their firm's competitive position [3, p. 72; 7, pp. 136, 226–229, 172; 11, pp. 218, 219; 34, pp. 634–639, 866–871]. Thus, of 6082 labor disputes in 1971, 4653 were strikes that lasted less than four hours [24(1972), p. 79: table 46]. Such behavior was seen as implying an almost "ceremonial" quality to many Japanese labor protests.

The system could be seen as one involving tradeoffs: young workers, commonly recruited right out of school, accepted low entry-level pay; in return they could look forward to remuneration rising as their family needs increased and to relatively secure employment. If recruited into the public service or into large private enterprises, a young male worker could even look forward to "permanent" employment until he retired (normally at age 55). This high level of job security was the most distinctive feature of the Japanese labor system, but no one knew exactly how widespread it was. One guesstimate was as follows:

About 51 percent of all male employees . . . in . . . the nonagricultural private sector . . . in 1972 were in firms employing fewer than 100 employees, which are not likely to practice permanent commitment. Another 21 percent were in firms employing between 100 and 1,000 employees, where there is only partial use of the system. It is primarily in the remaining 28 percent that permanency of employment would be the rule. . . .

. . . Female employees are generally excluded . . . [34, pp. 614, 615].

Over time, the system changed little. From 1950 through 1970 union membership increased from 5.8 to 11.8 million, but union penetration of the workforce fell from 45.9 to 34.9 percent [6, p. 206; 29(1973), p. 53]. Under the impact of high growth and nearly full employment (*see* Exhibits 8 and 9), wage differentials moderated (Exhibit 6), temporary workers declined as a percent of the total,[1] and permanent employment spread. Real wages advanced rapidly, while nominal wages rose somewhat faster than productivity (Exhibit 7). Perhaps the biggest changes occurred at the union confederation level. The chief activity here was politics, and it was in the political arena, rather than in the plant, that Japanese labor showed aggressiveness. Thus, Sanbetsu had been radical, a fact that contributed to its demise. Sanbetsu's successor, the more "cautious" Sohyo [11, p. 220], also moved toward the left; in 1970 it supported Japan's more radical socialist party. Another confederation, Domei, formed by schism within Sohyo, supported the moderate socialists. A third confederation, Churitsuroren, tried to avoid internal division by leaving members free to support whatever political party they chose. About one-third

---

[1] Official statistics for 1972 show temporary workers as 5.3 percent of the workforce and day workers as another 2 percent, but this was "undoubtedly an underestimate," since a special study of 1961 showed "the ratio of temporary to regular workers was almost two and a half times the official estimate" [34, p. 619].

of all union members belonged to no confederation [34, p. 630].

The union confederations were aware of the disadvantages inherent in a purely political role, and, starting in 1955, Sohyo managed to extend their sphere. It made them a role in collective bargaining by leading what it hoped would be a pattern-setting "spring wage offensive" (*shunto*). At this time the unions as a group, under the leadership of Sohyo, selected "top batters," or strong unions, to negotiate initial wage agreements which set a pattern for the rest of the contracts in the country. Several shunto were directed against state-owned enterprise, where the negotiators on the management side were members of special state commissions. The selection of such targets "is predicated on the expectation that these industries may seriously affect the daily life of the nation" [3, pp. 247, 248; 34, p. 643].

Assessment.   Given Japan's industrial success, analysts took a lively interest in labor's possible contribution to it. Did the system work productively? If so, why?

Based on studies of work days lost through strikes, relative turnover[2] and absenteeism,[3] labor itself found the system satisfac-

[2] Based on a limited study for 1965–1966, Robert Cole reported in his *Japanese Blue Collar* that "the ratio of U.S. males changing jobs (9.9%) was more than twice as high as that for Japanese males (4.7%)." Cole added, however, that "U.S. females enjoyed only a small advantage (6.9%) over their Japanese counterparts (6.5%)." Moreover, "if we compare the labor turnover rates of Japan, England and Germany, it appears that the Japanese rate is only slightly below the latter two" [7, pp. 116, 117].

[3] Based on a special year-long study of absenteeism in Tokyo starting in August 1970, the researchers reported that man-days lost from this cause was 1.72 percent for factories with a 40- to 42-hour work week [15(July 1973), pp. 82, 83]. In contrast, the authors of an official US study stated that "a rate of 3% of available work time has often been considered a 'reasonable level,' with the 'attainable minimum' at 2% or below" [41(Oct. 1977), p. 16].

tory. Perhaps more to the point, based on trends in relative labor productivity and to some extent in labor costs per unit of output (Exhibit 7B), the system worked well for the growth of GNP.

Even so, critics raised questions. Was not permanent employment a source of risk to business? Did not Japan's rapid growth rest almost entirely on low wages? Addressing themselves to the first of these questions, analyst S. B. Levine and other observers argued that the "cost rigidity" implicit in the system had been exaggerated. For one thing, firms had temporary workers who could be let go in hard times; for another, the large bonus element in pay might help labor costs to vary in the same direction as profits. The early retirement age was another cost-reducing factor, while the extensive use of subcontractors also gave some element of flexibility [27, pp. 660–663; 34, p. 618ff.]. Going further, analyst James Abegglen argued that permanent employment benefited the whole economy: "The system . . . puts brakes on the extremes of labor unrest." "The economic costs of bidding competitively for personnel are avoided," and "the costs of recruiting are much reduced." In addition—given a fast-expanding economy—"efficient allocation of the work force" is assisted in three ways: "the rapidly growing company is able to recruit the largest numbers," is "likely to attract the best recruits," and is able to benefit both from low entry-level wages and the tendency of young management talent "to be the more aggressive and risk-taking leaders" [1, pp. 55, 56].

Addressing himself in 1971 to the claim that low wages were the chief cause of Japan's success, US Presidential Assistant Peter Peterson referred to this view as a "persistent myth."

> Japan's labor rates have, of course, been low compared with those of some western countries. However, in the sophisticated sectors of the economy—those like steel

Exhibit 7

Wage and Comparative Labor Cost Data

A. WAGE DIFFERENCES IN MANUFACTURING FOR REGULAR EMPLOYEES: BY AGE, SENIORITY, HOURS WORKED, SEX, EDUCATION, AND SIZE OF ENTERPRISE, JUNE 1971

All Manufacturing Enterprises with 30 or More Employees

	Average Age	Years of Service	Monthly Hours Worked		Monthly Contractual Earnings (¥1,000)		Annual Special Earnings (¥1,000)	Estimated Employees
			Total	Regular	Total	Regular		
All employees	33.4	7.5	201	184	64.9	57.8	205.0	880,193
Male	34.5	8.8	205	183	77.7	67.8	253.9	595,428
Production worker: total male	33.9	7.7	207	183	70.0	59.6	195.2	384,004
Lower secondary school	36.3	8.6	208	185	71.2	60.7	196.6	258,018
Upper secondary school & over	28.8	5.7	204	181	67.5	57.3	192.5	125,987
Salaried employee: total male	35.7	10.9	201	183	91.7	82.7	360.4	211,424
Lower secondary school	42.0	15.2	207	184	94.9	82.3	332.9	50,493
Upper secondary school	33.3	10.0	202	184	83.7	75.4	314.4	94,709
Junior college	40.5	12.6	196	184	112.0	106.5	518.8	10,618
College/university	33.3	8.1	196	180	98.6	91.1	433.7	55,604
Female	31.0	4.6	193	187	38.2	36.8	102.9	284,764
Production worker: total female	32.3	4.6	193	188	35.8	34.5	89.4	206,076
Lower secondary school	33.3	4.9	194	188	35.3	34.0	87.8	167,160
Upper secondary school & over	28.4	3.5	191	186	37.8	36.4	96.4	38,916
Salaried employee: total female	27.4	4.7	191	185	44.6	42.7	138.1	78,688
Lower secondary school	34.7	7.4	194	188	45.4	43.5	148.2	15,000
Upper secondary school & over	25.7	4.0	190	184	44.4	42.6	135.7	63,689

Manufacturing Enterprises with 1,000 or More Employees

	Average Age	Years of Service	Monthly Hours Worked		Monthly Contractual Earnings (¥1,000)		Annual Special Earnings (¥1,000)	Estimated Employees
			Total	Regular	Total	Regular		
All employees	31.2	9.3	191	172	74.8	65.0	277.2	332,651
Male	33.2	10.7	194	171	85.6	73.1	321.8	248,683
Production worker: total male	31.7	9.2	194	170	76.1	63.0	242.2	144,896
Lower secondary school	34.9	11.3	194	169	80.7	66.8	262.3	85,768
Upper secondary school & over	27.0	6.1	194	170	69.4	57.6	213.1	59,128
Salaried employee: total male	35.3	12.8	193	173	98.8	87.2	432.9	103,786
Lower secondary school	42.5	19.0	199	172	106.8	89.6	408.2	24,283
Upper secondary school	32.3	11.6	194	172	87.4	76.5	366.8	43,938
Junior college	39.6	16.0	186	174	125.7	119.0	683.7	4,754
College/university	33.3	9.1	190	173	104.7	95.8	508.1	30,811
Female	25.2	5.0	183	177	42.8	40.8	145.0	83,968
Production worker: total female	24.9	4.8	184	179	39.9	38.2	128.6	52,859
Lower secondary school	25.4	5.3	185	180	39.3	37.7	127.8	40,101
Upper secondary school & over	23.4	3.3	182	176	41.7	39.8	131.4	12,759
Salaried employee: total female	25.5	5.3	180	173	47.8	45.3	172.7	31,109
Lower secondary school	33.4	10.5	181	174	53.0	50.1	214.4	5,048
Upper secondary school & over	24.0	4.3	180	173	46.7	44.4	164.6	26,061

Exhibit 7 (continued)

B. COMPARATIVE TRENDS IN WORKER COMPENSATION, PRODUCTIVITY, AND UNIT LABOR COSTS IN MANUFACTURING

	US	Canada	France	Italy	Japan	UK	West Germany
Hourly compensation ($)							
1960	2.66	2.13	0.83	0.63	0.26	0.82	0.83
1970	4.20	3.46	1.74[a]	1.75	0.99	1.46[a]	2.32

Average Annual Rate of Change in Manufacturing (%)

	US	Canada	France	Italy	Japan	UK	West Germany
Hourly compensation (own currency)							
1960-65	3.4	3.6	9.2	12.4	13.5	6.8	9.8
1965-70	6.0	7.6	9.2	9.7	15.2	8.2	8.9
Productivity							
1960-65	4.5	4.6	5.2	7.1	8.5	3.8	6.4
1965-70	1.3	4.1	6.5	5.2	13.1	3.4	5.2
1970-71	5.6	6.7	5.2	4.8	3.5	4.8	5.1
Unit labor costs (own currency)							
1960-65	−1.1	−0.9	3.8	5.0	4.5	2.9	3.2
1965-70	4.7	3.4	2.6	4.3	1.8	4.6	3.5
Unit labor costs (US $)							
1960-65	−1.1	−3.0	3.8	4.9	4.4	2.9	4.1
1965-70	4.7	4.1	0.1	4.2	2.0	1.4	5.4
1970-71	1.0	3.7	6.7	13.8	15.3	11.2	13.8

SOURCES: Part A: Japan Ministry of Labour [23(1972), p. 139: table 66]. Part B: United States, Council on International Economic Policy [40(1977), pp. 98–105 *passim*].

[a] Figure affected by devaluation.

and machinery that are growing fastest and are the most competitive in world trade—direct labor rates are at European levels [35, pp. 60, 61].

Contributing Factors. Looking beyond Japan's labor system to discover why it worked as well as it did, analysts pointed to various potential causes. Fast-rising wages and nearly full employment were two obvious factors (Exhibits 7B and 9B). Another feature that made the Japanese workplace attractive was its egalitarianism. This showed up in dress codes, dining facilities, hours of work, and even in wage and salary differentials (Exhibits 4 and 7A) [33, p. 45; 34, pp. 887–889].

Still another reason for workers to place a high value on their jobs was the under-developed state of Japan's social security system (*see* Exhibit 10). Social Security old-age pensions were a special case in point. Whereas Japan's health and unemployment insurance aimed at replacing 60 percent of earnings up to a certain ceiling [22, pp. 28–32; 30, p. 464], both the eligibility for old-age pensions and the size of the pension benefits were restricted because the postwar plan required accumulation of "vast reserves" [30, p. 470]. Thus, in March 1965, when persons aged 65 and over numbered 6.2 million, old-age pensions paid out numbered only 133,032, and when monthly earnings averaged ¥39,360, benefits averaged only ¥3,586, or 9 percent. This sum was actually "far below the average level of public welfare payments [7, p. 28]. The next five years brought little

Exhibit 8

Gross National Expenditures in Current and Constant 1965 Prices, 1956–71

A. GROSS NATIONAL EXPENDITURE (PRODUCT) IN CURRENT PRICES (BILLIONS OF YEN[a] AND PERCENTAGE BREAKDOWN)

Year	Private Cnsmptn Expndtr ¥	%	Gnrl Govt Cnsmptn Expndtr ¥	%	Gross Dmstc Fxd Capital Formation ¥	%	Increase in Stocks ¥	%	Expts of Goods & Srvcs & Factor Income Rcvd fr Abroad ¥	%	Less Impts of Goods & Srvcs & Factor Income Paid Abroad ¥	%	GNE at Market Prices ¥
1952	3,837	63.4	629	10.4	1,286	21.3	231	3.8	789	13.0	720	11.9	6,051
1953	4,604	66.1	747	10.7	1,559	23.4	137	2.0	789	11.3	870	12.5	6,965
1954	5,162	65.9	860	11.0	1,698	21.7	140	1.8	854	10.9	882	11.3	7,831
1955	5,529	64.1	894	10.4	1,705	19.8	421	4.9	979	11.4	904	10.5	8,624
1956	6,012	61.8	936	9.6	2,290	23.5	507	5.2	1,189	12.2	-1,208	12.4	9,726
1957	6,597	59.5	1,009	9.1	2,946	26.6	740	6.7	1,338	12.1	-1,549	14.0	11,080
1958	7,057	61.2	1,104	9.6	2,941	25.5	252	2.2	1,318	11.4	-1,150	10.0	11,522
1959	7,722	59.7	1,209	9.4	3,435	26.6	418	3.2	1,531	11.8	-1,390	10.8	12,926
1960	8,823	56.9	1,382	8.9	4,682	30.2	551	3.6	1,774	11.4	-1,713	11.1	15,499
1961	10,106	52.8	1,607	8.4	6,370	33.3	1,382	7.2	1,860	9.7	-2,199	11.5	19,126
1962	11,747	55.4	1,864	8.8	7,136	33.7	459	2.2	2,142	10.1	-2,148	10.1	21,199
1963	13,769	56.3	2,200	9.0	7,875	32.2	884	3.6	2,349	9.6	-2,613	10.7	24,464
1964	16,027	55.4	2,554	8.8	9,404	32.5	1,083	3.7	2,889	10.0	-3,036	10.5	28,921
1965	18,105	56.7	2,949	9.2	9,767	30.6	776	2.4	3,563	11.1	-3,197	10.0	31,962
1966	20,620	56.0	3,329	9.0	11,344	30.8	1,038	2.8	4,165	11.3	-3,666	10.0	36,829
1967	23,594	54.1	3,734	8.6	13,965	32.0	2,296	5.3	4,468	10.3	-4,473	10.3	43,585
1968	27,266	52.8	4,277	8.3	17,328	33.5	2,366	4.6	5,528	10.7	-5,088	9.8	51,677
1969	31,382	52.0	4,925	8.2	20,939	34.7	2,229	3.7	6,819	11.3	-5,990	9.9	60,304
1970	36,341	51.2	5,827	8.2	24,843	35.0	3,213	4.5	8,273	11.7	-7,489	10.5	71,008
1971	41,239	52.0	6,865	8.7	27,208	34.3	1,906	2.4	9,896	12.5	-7,807	9.8	79,307

B. GROSS NATIONAL EXPENDITURE (PRODUCT) IN CONSTANT 1965 PRICES (BILLIONS OF YEN[a] AND PERCENTAGE BREAKDOWN)

Year													
1954	7,435	63.1	1,848	15.7	2,255	18.9	153	1.3	855	7.3	781	6.6	11,783
1955	8,041	62.5	1,840	14.3	2,291	17.8	499	3.9	977	7.6	790	6.1	12,859
1956	8,672	62.5	1,832	13.2	2,798	20.1	474	3.4	1,150	8.3	1,037	7.5	13,889
1957	9,217	61.4	1,822	12.1	3,323	22.1	658	4.4	1,304	8.7	1,326	8.8	14,997
1958	9,885	62.5	1,905	12.0	3,462	21.9	273	1.7	1,389	8.8	1,113	7.0	15,801
1959	10,660	61.7	2,004	11.6	3,968	23.0	443	2.5	1,564	9.1	1,381	8.0	17,258
1960	11,743	59.7	2,094	10.6	5,225	26.5	559	2.8	1,799	9.1	1,720	8.7	19,699
1961	12,753	56.0	2,222	9.7	6,700	29.4	1,359	5.9	1,924	8.4	2,193	9.6	22,766
1962	13,972	57.6	2,409	9.9	7,422	30.6	380	1.5	2,244	9.2	2,199	9.1	24,228
1963	15,342	57.3	2,610	9.7	8,159	30.4	856	3.2	2,410	9.0	2,601	9.7	26,776
1964	17,137	56.3	2,775	9.1	9,551	31.4	1,062	3.5	2,908	9.5	2,981	9.8	30,453
1965	18,112	56.8	2,943	9.2	9,766	30.6	705	2.2	3,563	11.2	3,198	10.0	31,892
1966	19,629	55.9	3,104	8.8	10,920	31.1	949	2.7	4,114	11.7	3,582	10.2	35,133
1967	21,629	54.2	3,273	8.2	12,895	32.3	2,090	5.2	4,374	10.9	4,383	11.0	39,878
1968	23,717	52.0	3,499	7.7	15,751	34.6	2,181	4.8	5,357	11.7	4,946	10.8	45,558
1969	26,016	50.9	3,722	7.3	18,437	36.1	2,110	4.1	6,430	12.6	5,656	11.1	51,059
1970	27,966	49.6	3,957	7.0	20,895	37.1	2,897	5.1	7,453	13.2	6,832	12.1	56,337
1971	29,926	49.7	4,262	7.1	22,537	37.4	1,733	2.9	8,788	14.6	7,061	11.7	60,187

SOURCE: Bank of Japan [4(1969)], pp. 298, 303: table 176, pp. 284, 289: table 166; 4(1971), p. 284: table 166; p. 289: table 167; 4(1973), pp. 293, 303: table 169].

NOTE: Minor discrepancies in the above two sets of 1965 figures appeared in the original.

[a] Through August 1971 the exchange rate of the yen was 360 to $1 US.

Exhibit 9

Sectoral Distribution of Current Value Net Domestic Product and Workforce

A. DOMESTIC PRODUCT BY SECTOR IN CURRENT PRICES (BILLIONS OF YEN AND PERCENTAGE BREAKDOWN)

Year	Agri-culture[a] ¥	%	Manu-facturing ¥	%	Mining ¥	%	Con-struction ¥	%	Trade, Finance, Rl Est, Insrnce ¥	%
1954	1,460	22.3	1,552	23.8	144	2.2	278	4.3	1,462	22.4
1960	1,906	14.9	3,743	29.2	210	1.6	701	5.5	3,218	25.1
1965	2,881	11.2	7,166	27.9	220	0.9	1,807	7.0	7,042	27.4
1966	3,250	11.0	8,236	27.9	233	0.8	2,105	7.1	8,096	27.5
1967	3,994	11.4	10,072	28.7	253	0.7	2,487	7.1	9,567	27.3
1968	4,187	10.0	12,345	29.6	303	0.7	2,969	7.1	11,768	28.2
1969	4,220	8.7	14,578	30.2	339	0.7	3,480	7.2	13,763	28.5
1970	4,431	7.7	17,373	30.2	348	0.6	4,324	7.5	16,599	28.8
1971	4,254	6.6	18,985	29.5	381	0.6	5,091	7.9	18,804	29.2

B. POPULATION AND WORKFORCE BY SECTOR (IN THOUSANDS AND PERCENTAGE BREAKDOWN)

Year	Agri-culture[a]	%	Manu-facturing	%	Mining	%	Con-struction	%	Trade, Finance, Rl Est, Insrnce	%
1954 (Dec)	14,150	36.1	7,640	19.5	710	1.8	1,680	4.3	7,510	19.2
1960 (Dec)	12,530	28.5	9,560	21.7	500	1.1	2,750	6.3	9,000	20.5
1965 (Avg)	11,130	23.5	11,500	24.3	290	0.6	3,280	6.9	10,080	21.3
1966 (Avg)	10,720	22.2	11,780	24.4	260	0.5	3,500	7.3	10,530	21.8
1967 (Avg)	10,360	21.1	12,520	25.4	260	0.5	3,690	7.3	10,850	22.1
1968 (Avg)	9,880	19.8	13,050	26.1	270	0.5	3,700	7.4	11,110	22.2
1969 (Avg)	9,460	18.8	13,450	26.7	240	0.5	3,710	7.4	11,330	22.5
1970 (Avg)	8,860	17.4	13,770	27.0	200	0.4	3,940	7.7	11,440	22.5
1971 (Avg)	8,140	15.9	13,810	27.0	190	0.4	4,130	8.1	11,780	23.0

SOURCE: Bank of Japan [4(1962), pp. 291–292: table 151; 4(1969), p. 286: table 166; 4(1972), pp. 255–256: table

a Includes forestry and fishing.

b Transportation, communications, utilities.

change; thus, in FY 1970 Japan's average old-age annuity was only 13.7 percent of her average per capita income. This compared with roughly 35 percent in the US, Britain, and France (as of seven or eight years earlier) [17(1970–71), p. 88]. These low benefits made retirees dependent on savings, on finding new jobs, and on company retirement benefits. Many employers—or at least large employers—had stepped into the broad breach left by the state. The typical private benefit was a lump-sum payment: perhaps four years' pay for an employee of a large firm with 30 years' experience, perhaps two years' pay in a smaller firm [34, p. 661]. As one observer put it:

The widespread existence of company-paid lump-sum retirement allowances outside the social security system is a reflection of the underdeveloped state of the statutory

Exhibit 9 (continued)

Facilitating Industry[b] ¥	%	Srvcs, Other ¥	%	Government ¥	%	Total NDP ¥
581	8.9	723	16.1	334	5.1	6,534
1,184	9.2	1,380	10.8	490	3.8	12,833
2,203	8.6	3,286	12.8	1,052	4.1	25,656
2,570	8.7	3,814	12.9	1,178	4.0	29,482
2,906	8.3	4,433	12.6	1,379	3.9	35,090
3,294	7.9	5,331	12.8	1,567	3.8	41,765
3,826	7.9	6,230	12.9	1,829	3.8	48,265
4,599	8.0	7,674	13.3	2,196	3.8	57,543
5,190	8.1	8,989	14.0	2,599	4.0	64,293

Facilitating Industry[b]	%	Srvcs, Other	%	Government	%	Total Emplyd	Unemplyd	Total Popltn	Popltn Age 15+ Yrs
1,860	4.7	4,310	11.0	1,280	3.3	39,170	690	88,239	58,540
2,370	5.4	5,970	13.6	1,280	2.9	43,990	400	93,419	65,200
2,940	6.2	6,490	13.7	1,580	3.3	47,300	570	98,275	72,870
3,110	6.4	6,820	14.1	1,550	3.2	48,270	650	99,036	74,320
3,160	6.4	6,890	14.0	1,570	3.2	49,200	630	100,196	75,570
3,290	6.6	7,130	14.3	1,540	3.1	50,000	590	101,331	76,780
3,380	6.7	7,220	14.3	1,560	3.1	50,400	570	102,536	77,820
3,530	6.9	7,510	14.7	1,610	3.2	50,940	590	103,720	78,850
3,610	7.1	7,740	15.1	1,670	3.3	51,140	640	105,014	79,700

144, p. 288: table 166, p. 292: table 168].

pension in Japan. This system, to a great extent, has taken the place of social security as a means of guaranteeing the livelihood of the retired [7, p. 29].

Still another reason for the success of Japan's labor system was the cultural heritage. From early times a high value was placed on loyalty; consensus was much preferred to conflict; the work ethic was strong as was pride in national achievement. "Growth rates," wrote Herman Kahn, are watched "with sports-like devotion" [25, p. 217]. Although continuing urbanization, westernization, and arrival at the workplace of a younger generation were seen by some as likely to bring a decline in traditional values [2, p. 165 *passim*; 33, pp. 46–49; 34, p. 889ff.], old values still appeared to dominate. Writing in 1970, Kahn, like other observers, was impressed to see Japanese workers ending their day

Exhibit 10

Social Security Benefits as a Percentage of GDP

Year	Japan	US	France[a]	West Germany[a]	Italy[a]	UK
1959–60	4.5	6.3	12.5	14.6	11.0	10.2
1970–71	5.0	9.8	13.9	16.3	16.9	13.2

SOURCE: International Labour Office [14, pp. 92–96: table 2].
[a] Years 1960 and 1971.

in unpaid overtime and starting it by singing a company song.

Matsushita Workers' Song

For the building of a new Japan,
Let's put our strength and mind together,
Doing our best to promote production,
Sending our goods to the people of the
  world,
Endlessly and continuously,
Like water gushing from a fountain,
Grow, industry, grow, grow, grow!
Harmony and sincerity!
Matsushita Electric! [25, p. 217]

A Japanese worker does not rush out of the factory, and an employee from his office, when the time is out. They often finish the job begun, sit around for a while and review some of the problems, clean up together and give thus the feeling that they are personally committed to their work. They do not separate their work time from their leisure as sharply as the Western worker tends to do [25, p. 212].

Industry Structure

Of all the Occupation's institutional changes, one of the least welcome was one that sought to substitute active competition for big-business combines. Even before the Occupation left, it had allowed the Japanese to modify their Anti-Monopoly Law. After freedom, further amendment became a lively issue at once.

As had been the case for some years, the chief driving force for relaxing the Anti-Monopoly Law was the Ministry of International Trade and Industry (MITI). MITI's proposal did not have plain sailing, however, since competition had won supporters among the socialists in the Diet, as well as among farmers and small businessmen, who made up the largest blocs in the ruling LDP. The cause of amendment was, however, helped by an economic slump which followed the close of the Korean War [43, pp. 54, 55]. In this slump of 1953, Japan's industries found themselves beset with costs that were still relatively high and with substantial excess capacity (*see* Exhibit 11).

The cure for high costs lay in investment for modernization, but investors were hardly willing to come forward if old and inefficient plants were pouring products onto the market on a contribution-to-overhead basis. Under these circumstances, the proposal for cartels to control production became politically viable again, and MITI's long-sought further revision of the Anti-Monopoly Law went through in September 1953.

Cartels. The new law of 1953 had a number of provisions, but the "most significant" of

Exhibit 11

Trends in Operating Rates and Productive Capacity, June 1953

	Metals	Machinery	Ceramics	Textiles	Chemicals	Rubber	Average
Operating rate (in %)	70.4	62.1	71.5	75.8	73.8	47.7	68.3
Capacity (1950 = 100)	130.9	141.3	169.3	163.2	188.5	139.7	157.9

SOURCE: Japan Ministry of Finance [19(1956): tables 29 and 32].

its changes was the "legalization" of cartels when "deemed . . . necessary on the grounds of averting a recession or for the purpose of rationalization" [43, pp. 56, 57]. Such cartels could be initiated by a "competent" government ministry or by an industry group with the concurrence of such a ministry. In either case, however, the consent of Japan's Federal Trade Commission (JFTC) was required [43, p. 56].

The new Anti-Monopoly Law was soon supplemented by other measures to pave the way for additional cartels. Some of these pertained to groups of industries. Thus, an Export and Import Trading Act of 1953 and some 1955 amendments to the Medium–Small Enterprise Stabilization Act of 1951 both spawned numerous cartels. These acts reportedly reflected "MITI's contention that the export sector must be protected if Japan was 'to survive and grow,'" as well as MITI's "ostensible belief that if small firms were left alone they would repeat the cycle of overinvestment, cut-throat competition, and quality degradation" [43, pp. 63, 64]. Still other measures authorized cartels in single industries, often for purposes of export promotion. Individual cartels came and went, but the total number expanded rapidly. Counting multiple arrangements in single industries, one analyst said he found 150 cartels in July 1957, 448 in March 1960, and 836 eleven years later [9, pp. 76, 77; 43, p. 63]. (See Exhibits 12 through 14 for selected data on Japanese business.)

As for the substance of the cartel agreements, they generally covered quantity and price. Some also covered quality, market share, sales or buying methods, reduction of capacity, areas of product specialization, or reorganization of inefficient producing units [43, pp. 64–66]. As for administration, several of the laws gave MITI a very strong hand. Thus in 1955, MITI was able to end the need for getting JFTC approval of export and medium–small enterprise cartels [43, pp. 61, 62]. In some cases MITI also won the power to force compliance by nonmember firms in cartel decisions for certain industries [9, pp. 78, 79; 43, pp. 64, 65].

New provisions on cartels were not the only changes made by the Japanese in their 1953 revision of the Occupation's Anti-Monopoly Law. In addition, companies were no longer forbidden to place restrictions on new facilities, technologies, and methods. Although holding companies were still prohibited, controls on mergers, overlapping directorates, and inter-company stock ownership were relaxed. For example, companies and banks could now own at least 10 percent of another corporation's stock instead of only 5 percent [43, pp. 10, 11, 55–57].

Concentration and Scale. Although the Occupation had been concerned with concentration in single industries as well as with Japan's big conglomerate combines (zaibatsu), its Law Concerning Excessive Concentrations had in effect become a dead let-

Exhibit 12

Selected Data on Japanese Industry

A. ANALYSIS OF CORPORATE SALES GROWTH AND PROFITS, ALL INDUSTRIES (IN PERCENT)

	1966	1967[a]	1968	1969	1970	1971	1972
Sales increase (%)	—	+30.1	+17.3	+22.8	+16.2	+7.8	+15.2
Net worth/assets	18.4	17.2	16.8	16.8	16.1	15.8	15.3
Pretax profit ratios:							
Ordinary profit/assets	3.8	4.3	4.4	4.9	4.4	3.4	3.7
Ordinary profit/sales	2.7	2.9	3.0	3.3	3.1	2.4	2.8
Total profit/assets	3.8	4.0	4.2	4.6	4.2	3.3	3.6
Total profit/sales	2.7	4.0	4.2	3.1	4.2	3.3	3.6
Post-tax profit/net worth	12.3	13.7	14.7	16.3	15.0	11.5	13.0
Profit distribution (%)							
Taxes	40.1	41.4	40.7	40.3	42.5	44.7	44.4
Officers' bonus	3.8	3.7	3.8	3.5	3.7	4.2	3.9
Dividends	25.6	23.0	21.3	19.2	19.5	22.9	19.0
Retained earnings	30.6	31.8	34.1	36.9	34.2	28.2	32.7

B. SCALE OF ESTABLISHMENTS IN MANUFACTURING [a]

Percentage Breakdown of Japanese Manufacturing Establishments by Employee Size-Class

Comparative Factory Scale: Percentage Breakdown of Factories by Employee Size-Class

Employees	Establish-ments 1955	Establish-ments 1971	Persons Engaged 1955	Persons Engaged 1970	Shipments 1955	Shipments 1970	Country/Year	Persons Employed 1–99	Persons Employed 100–499	Persons Employed 500–999	Persons Employed 1000 & up
1–99	98.6	97.6	60.7	51.8	39.2	32.1	Japan 1971	97.6	2.1	0.2	0.1
100–299	1.0	1.8	12.9	16.1	16.9	17.1	US 1967	89.2	6.5	3.6	0.7
300–999	0.3	0.5	11.8	14.9	20.4	21.7	W Ger 1972	85.1	12.0	1.7	1.2
1000 & up	0.1	0.1	14.6	17.2	23.5	29.1					
	100.0	100.0	100.0	100.0	100.0	100.0					

SOURCES: Part A: Japan Ministry of Finance [20(1976), p. 41 ff]. Part B: *Nippon, A Charted Survey of Japan* [29(1975–76 edition), pp. 147, 149], reprinted with permission.

[a] Earlier figures not wholly comparable. In terms of current value yen, between 1966 and 1972 sales increased from ¥98,240 billion to ¥456,562 billion; assets from ¥69,179 billion to ¥319,890 billion; net worth from ¥12,711 billion to ¥44,616 billion; and pretax profits from ¥2,617 billion to ¥6,709 billion.

ter when "recovery" replaced "reform" as the chief US goal for Japan. The Japanese themselves were more concerned with the problems of inadequate scale than with those of undue concentration. Thus, encouragement of cartels was supplemented by encouragement of mergers, a wave of which was set off by a short recession in 1965. According to MITI, "The creation of Mitsubishi Heavy Industries, the merger of Nissan and Prince Motor Companies, the merger of Toyoba and Goba in textiles, trading company mergers and cooperative investments in some industries were all evidence of movements to solve the problems which had been created by excessive competition and investment" [21, p. 27].

In line with this industrial philosophy major modern industries in Japan remained

Exhibit 13

Laws Authorizing Cartels and Number of Cartels Authorized under Each, March 1971

Law	Number of Cartels	Comment
Rationalization cartels, authorized under Anti-Monopoly Act	13	Includes 9 cartels in the iron & steel industry, to set conditions, quantities, and prices of scrap. Includes 4 cartels in the textile industry to control quality of product.
Emergency Act for the Promotion of the Machine-Tool Industry	17	Two of 41 emergency laws enacted since the end of the Korean War for the promotion of particular industries (usually the promotion of exports). Permits cartels for the purpose of maintaining agreements on types and specifications of products, on methods of buying raw materials & parts, on limitation of production capacities, and on areas of specialization by cartel members if the absence of cartels would "materially hamper national economic progress."
Emergency Act for the Promotion of the Electronics Industry	2	
Emergency Act for Price Stabilization, in the Fertilizer Industry	4	Permits fixing prices and quantities exported.
Law Concerning Tax Collection & Trade Organization in the Sake & Related Industries	7	Of purely domestic interest.
Law Concerning the Promotion of Exports by the Marine Products Industries	8	Authorizes agreements on prices, quantities exported, productive capacity, and the time and method of sale. Products covered include major ones exported.
Trade Association Act for the Adjustment of Marine Products	7	Of purely domestic interest.
Law Concerning the Optimization of Activities in the Service Industries Relating to Sanitation	123	Of purely domestic interest.
Trade Association Act Pertaining to Domestic Sea Transportation	21	Of purely domestic interest.
Export-Import Trading Act	195	Includes 124 cartels among exporters, 60 exporters' cartels in domestic markets, 3 import cartels, and 8 export trade associations. Industries covered are mainly in textiles, heavy industry, chemicals, agriculture, and marine products and sundry. Agreements most commonly allowed pertain to price, quality, market share, or sales methods.
Law Concerning the Organization of Trade Associations of Small-Medium Enterprises	439	The number is large owing to inclusion of multiple regional cartels. Only 42 industries affected.

SOURCE: I. Frank [9, pp. 77-79]. Reprinted with permission of the Committee for Economic Development.

Exhibit 14

Production, Production Capacity, and the Excess Capacity Ratio
(manufacturing industries, seasonally adjusted)

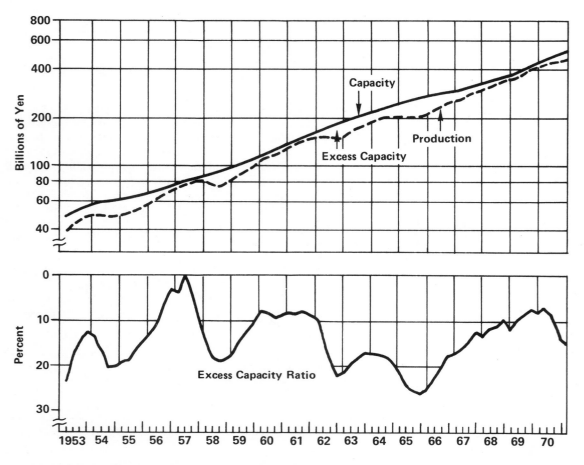

SOURCE: Japan Economic Planning Agency [17(1970–71), p. 27].

concentrated. For example, in 1971 the three largest companies produced all the sheet glass, the four largest all the beer, and the five largest all the aluminum bullion. The top five also produced over 90 percent of pig iron, passenger cars, electrolytic copper, nylon, and polyacrylic fiber, and they produced over 70 percent of polyester fiber, ammonium sulphate, crude steel, and trucks [29(1973), p. 248: chart 16–4].

All this was not to say that Japan had completed her transition from a "dual" to an advanced economy. In 1971 more than half her manufacturing workforce was still employed in establishments with fewer than 100 employees (versus fewer than 25 percent in the US in 1967). (*See* Exhibit 12B.)

Zaibatsu Revival? Even before the Occupation left, some observers were charging that its intended breakup of zaibatsu had failed. That is, while the few owning families and their holding companies were gone, former operating companies continued to be members of an effective combine. Proponents of this view emphasized the role of banks as the chief but not the only new locus of control. The following account appeared in *The Economist* in 1962:

> . . . After the war the Americans, with reforming zeal, split up the firms in these mass [*zaibatsu*] empires into individual entities; but this was like grappling with a jellyfish, for the habit of cohesion has remained. It is secured now by interlocking directorships and high-level executive consultation among the firms that used to belong to the old groups; by inter-company shareholdings among group members; and by the fact that one of the big city banks— several of which are successors of the old zaibatsu banks—is likely to hold a central position in each group. This last point is important because of the major role which the banks still play in financing new fixed investment in Japan . . . [8, p. 807].

Business Associations and Politics. Like business in the West, business in Japan organized to support its interest vis-à-vis the state and other pressure groups. Of four major business associations, Keidanren was said to be "the most powerful and prestigious."[4] It was also said to be "much more vital a meeting ground for Japanese business than . . . either the National Association of Manufacturers or the Chamber of Commerce for American Businessmen" [42, pp. 54, 59].

> Keidanren strives to mobilize consensus within the business community and influence the government to adopt policies that are responsive to industry's wishes. . . .
>
> Keidanren's thirty-seven committees cover the entire span of economic issues, both domestic and foreign, and are chaired by leading businessmen. . . . There is constant communication, exchange of documents, and meetings between Keidanren staff members and MITI bureaucrats. There are also regular meetings of Keidanren's leadership with top-level bureaucrats and cabinet ministers. . . .
>
> Keidanren regularly issues various proposals, 'requests' and 'demands' to the government. . . .
>
> Keidanren is an important source of funds for the [ruling] LDP. It assesses each constituent trade or industrial association a defined amount [for this purpose] [42, pp. 55, 56, 59].

In addition to working with one another, Keidanren's leaders also sometimes worked with the leaders of the other main business associations. This mixed group was known as the *zaikai* (literally, "financial circle"), and it was seen by some as wielding extraordinary political power [34, p. 770; 42, pp. 36–38]. Other observers believed, however, that the power of zaikai and Keidanren was declining. For one thing, individual companies had grown along with Japan's prosperity, and thus they had become less dependent on mutual help through associations. For another, business interests had diverged, and associations had found that the consensus they could represent was shrinking. As one observer put it in 1973, "If anything, many businesses are now more concerned with guarding their independence from encroachments by MITI than with seeking government support" [42, pp. 59–63].

So far as the LDP was concerned, its financial dependence on business did not guarantee its subservience to this group. For one thing, party leaders knew that business had no alternative party to which it might turn. For another, business contributions went to party factions as well as to the party itself, "thereby diffusing the impact of money among the chronic contenders for

---

[4] Besides Keidanren, whose members represented more than 100 commercial, industrial, and financial associations and more than 700 leading corporations, these groups were Keizai Doyukai, Nikkeiren, and Nissho. The first three were big-business groups; the last spoke for small and medium-size business. Nikkeiren was the most specialized, since it spoke for business vis-à-vis labor.

power." In the third place, the LDP had to be broad-based to succeed: "The argument that the LDP is the party of big business in Japan, although valid enough, cannot be taken to mean that it is less the party of other interest groups, some of which indeed have, along with votes, points of view and economic demands contrary to the interests of big business" [34, pp. 771, 772].

Business Policy

Although observers tended to focus on industry structure, those who also looked at policy noted that Japanese business characteristically put more stress on growth and market share than on profit and return on investment. This emphasis had a variety of causes. The semi-fixed nature of labor costs was one. A highly leveraged capital structure was another, since it tended to make managers satisfied with any rate of return on investment that exceeded the after-tax cost of borrowed funds. And, so long as the banks were willing to lend, Japanese firms were less constrained by the need to build equity than were their foreign counterparts. Still another factor was the knowledge that MITI would favor a cartel if recession was brought on by excess output, plus the knowledge that output quotas would be assigned to firms in the cartel mainly on the basis of relative capacity.

Subordinating profit to growth might well initiate a virtuous circle if, as some analysts claimed, costs could be reduced as production experience increased, thereby permitting prices to be cut and market penetration to be pushed still further. Seeking to quantify what might be achieved in this way, the Boston Consulting Group conducted some research on US industries. It concluded that "each time cumulative experience doubles, costs fall to 70%–85% of their starting level" [1, p. 67].

Banking and Financial Institutions

When the Occupation arrived in Japan, a chief objective in the financial area was to split up Japan's "Big Five" commercial banks, four of which were zaibatsu-owned. Reorganization of Japan's financial structure had "barely begun," however, when the Occupation shifted its goal from reform to recovery. Thus, big commercial "city" banks survived and continued to dominate their field. For example, in 1970 only 20 percent of all commercial banks (15 out of 76) accounted for roughly 65 percent of all commercial banks' assets, loans and advances, discounts and deposits [4(1972), pp. 65–70: table 28; 5, p. XVI].

Besides planning to break up big banks, the Occupation also planned to promote widespread stock ownership by reviving and reforming Japan's stock market. Starting from a very small base, stocks in fact gained rapidly; even so, they remained unimportant relative to other sources of financing. The reason did not lie in popular reluctance to save, for personal savings were relatively high (Exhibit 15), owing to the large bonus element in pay and the low level of pensions, etc. [5, pp. 68–70]. Personal savings flowed, however, not into equities but into banks and other financial institutions. It was these institutions that in turn supplied most of industry's needs for substantial outside financing.

Although banks purchased some industrial stocks and debentures, most of their financing took the form of loans, so that loans from banks and other financial intermediaries made up a very high, if declining, share of the yearly net supply of industrial funds (*see* Exhibit 16). Looking at such figures, western observers were for the most part highly critical. With debt playing so large a role, industry would face largely fixed financing charges and banks would face impaired liquidity, inasmuch as business was known to be using short-term loans to finance long-term needs. Banker Joseph Dodge (the author of the "Dodge Line" for Japanese recovery in 1949) expressed his disapproval in 1951: "Japan is suffering a plague of false legends," he said, among them the belief that "granting progressively larger amounts of commercial bank credit for capital purposes can be substituted for the normal process of capital accumulation" [5, p. 165].

In contrast, some analysts argued that using so much debt worked well for Japan— or at least worked well for the big, efficient companies that government was seen as wanting to develop. According to this view (as expressed in Abegglen's 1970 study [1]), both big banks and big business had ways to cut risks and thus to warrant extensive use of debt, especially since use of stock would be still more expensive.[5] For example, big companies could cut their risks by diversifying and using subcontractors whom they could quickly drop in hard times. Big banks could cut their risks by sharing big loans with one another and by placing their own personnel into advisory positions with their clients. In addition, big banks could restore liquidity by borrowing from the Bank of Japan (except in times of credit stringency) or even by refusing to renew credit granted to their smaller customers [1, pp. 56–64]. Both sides allegedly knew, moreover, that government would not permit major banks and companies to fail, although it might be more than willing to see a shake-out of small competitors:

> How is it that Japanese companies can assume the level of risk associated with such heavy debt? . . . In brief answer . . . the government of Japan stands behind the debt position of major Japanese companies, thus making possible both the financing necessary for rapid growth and ensuring that the government through the power of the purse will play a central role in determining the nature and direction of that growth. And since these guarantees of debt do not apply to smaller and less efficient companies, the system ensures a rapid move toward concentration of production in the hands of the more efficient producers [1, p. 4].

If industry's dependence on outside financing enhanced the power of the banks, the latter's dependence on the Bank of Japan enhanced the power of that institution. Whereas before the war the ordinary banks sought to borrow from the central bank only in periods of crisis, after the war they sought to borrow even in normal times, the reason being that they were in a so-called "over-loaned" condition. That is, they were making more loans to clients than their own resources would permit. Since overloans were viewed as "one of the most distinctive features of Japan's financial structure" [1, p. 63], official statistics kept track of their volume (*see* Exhibit 17).

Business–Government Relations

"Administrative Guidance." Still another Occupation legacy—one that was probably unintended—included some specific contributions to the distinctive Japanese practice known as "administrative guidance" of business. This was described as follows for the US businessmen in a 1972 Department of Commerce publication:

> . . . Japan's economic destiny has not been left to the free play of market forces. The government has undertaken from the beginning . . . to identify objectives and priorities for the Japanese economy. The gov-

---

[5] Although Japanese interest rates were commonly judged to be relatively high [5, p. 57], interest costs— but not dividends—could be written off as an expense prior to the corporate income tax which was at a rate of 48 percent. In addition, companies were required by practice to let existing stockholders buy common stock at par, which might be substantially lower than market. The median yield on stocks was 10 percent, also calculated on par value [5, p. 129].

Exhibit 15

Comparative Savings and Investment

A. TOTAL SAVINGS AS A PERCENT OF TOTAL DISPOSABLE NATIONAL INCOME

Year	Japan	Canada	US	France	West Ger	Italy	UK
1960	27.7	8	9	16	22.0	—	11
1961	—	7	8	16	—	19	10
1962	—	10	9	16	—	19	9
1963	26.6	10	9	16	18.9	16	10
1964	—	12	10	17	—	16	11
1965	24.4	13	11	17	19.5	16	12
1966	24.8	14	11	18	18.4	15	12
1967	27.6	13	9	18	15.9	16	11
1968	29.5	12	9	17	18.8	17	11
1969	29.9	13	9	20	19.7	17	13
1970	31.4	11	8	17	20.5	16	13
1971	34.0	12	8	17	18.6	15	11

B. HOUSEHOLD OR PERSONAL SAVINGS AS A PERCENT OF DISPOSABLE HOUSEHOLD OR PERSONAL INCOME[a]

Year	Japan[b]	Canada	US	France	West Ger	Italy	UK
1960	17.4	4	5	10		—	5
1961	19.2	3	6	9		16	6
1962	18.6	6	6	11		16	5
1963	18.0	6	5	11		15	5
1964	16.4	5	6	11		15	5
1965	17.4	6	6	11		17	6
1966	17.4	8	6	11	n.a.	16	6
1967	19.0	7	8	12		14	6
1968	19.5	6	8	11		15	5
1969	19.2	6	7	10		17	5
1970	20.0	6	9	13		16	6
1971	20.7	8	9	13		19	6

C. HOUSEHOLD OR PERSONAL SAVINGS AS A PROPORTION OF TOTAL SAVINGS[c]

Year	Japan	Canada	US	France	West Ger	Italy	UK
1960	48	39	39	47	27	—	32
1961	48	37	53	47	28	66	44
1962	50	48	47	56	31	71	38
1963	52	47	41	54	37	74	37
1964	50	32	47	47	38	72	35
1965	57	35	42	50	45	85	37
1966	55	39	45	47	44	83	41
1967	53	38	69	51	51	74	41
1968	51	33	61	50	46	75	32
1969	48	31	54	39	46	80	28
1970	47	38	90	58	49	81	32
1971	51	48	91	59	53	106	35

Exhibit 15 (continued)

D. COMPARATIVE ANALYSIS OF GROSS FIXED CAPITAL FORMATION AS A PERCENTAGE OF GNP OR GDP EXPRESSED IN CONSTANT PRICES[d]

Japan (at 1965 prices)

	1960	1965	1968	1969	1970	1971
Private sector	19.5	21.6	24.1	26.0	26.8	26.1
Dwellings	4.1	5.7	6.3	6.6	6.7	6.5
Machinery & equipment	15.4	16.0	17.8	19.4	20.1	19.6
Public sector	7.0	9.0	8.4	8.3	8.2	9.6
Dwellings	0.3	0.4	0.4	0.5	0.5	0.6
Other	6.6	8.6	7.9	7.8	7.7	9.0
Total/GNP	26.5	30.6	32.5	34.3	35.1	35.7

United States (at 1970 prices)

	1960	1965	1968	1969	1970	1971
Housing	4.6	4.4	3.9	3.9	3.6	4.6
Other construction	7.0	7.7	7.3	7.1	6.8	6.4
Transport equipment	1.4	1.8	2.0	2.1	1.7	1.8
Machinery & other equipment	4.1	5.1	5.0	5.2	5.3	4.9
Total/GDP	17.2	19.1	18.2	18.2	17.3	17.7

France (at 1963 prices)

	1960	1965	1968	1969	1970	1971
Housing	5.2	6.7	6.4	6.5	6.6	6.4
Other construction	5.8	7.3	7.8	7.8	7.9	7.8
Transport equipment	2.1	2.0	2.3	2.4	2.3	2.5
Machinery & other equipment	6.8	8.2	8.9	9.5	9.7	9.9
Total/GDP	20.0	24.4	25.4	26.1	26.5	26.6

West Germany (at 1963 prices)

	1960	1965	1968	1969	1970	1971
Housing	6.2	6.2	5.6	5.0	4.8	5.1
Other construction	8.1	9.0	8.5	8.3	8.5	8.4
Transport equipment	2.2	2.4	2.3	2.6	3.0	3.2
Machinery & other equipment	8.5	9.3	8.5	9.5	10.3	10.4
Discrepancies	−0.3	−0.2	−0.2	−0.3	−0.3	−0.3
Total/GDP	24.7	26.7	24.7	25.1	26.4	26.8

United Kingdom (at 1970 prices)

	1960	1965	1968	1969	1970	1971
Housing		3.5	3.8	3.6	3.2	3.4
Other construc & land devel	n.a.	5.7	6.2	6.2	6.3	6.4
Transport equipment		1.7	1.9	1.8	1.9	1.9
Machinery & other equipment		6.7	6.9	7.0	7.2	6.9
Total/GDP	15.0	17.5	18.8	18.6	18.7	18.7

SOURCES: Part A: United Nations [37(1975), vol. I: tables 2 and 3; vol. III: table 10]. Part B: Bank of Japan [4(1971), p. 285: table 167; (1976), p. 315: table 175]; United Nations [37(1975), vol. III: table 10]. Part C: United Nations, *ibid.* Part D: Bank of Japan [4(1973), p. 295: table 168; (1975), p. 303: table 168]; United Nations [37(1976), vol. I: tables 1b and 9b]. Reprinted with permission.

[a] Includes private nonprofit institutions.

[b] Personal savings data for Japan; household data for the other countries.

[c] Besides households, other saving (or dissaving) sectors were corporate and quasi-corporate enterprise and general government.

[d] Besides savings, depreciation also played a major role in gross accumulation. Another contributing factor might be capital transfers from abroad, but this was unimportant to the listed countries during the periods covered.

Exhibit 16

Percentage Distribution of Net Supply of Industrial Funds by Source

Year	Total (¥100 million)	Own Capital[a]	Foreign Investment	Stocks	Bonds	Total Loans	Private Loans Bank	Private Loans Other	Govt Loans
1952	14,834	31.1	—	8.2	2.5	58.0	39.3	14.3	4.4
1960	51,279	42.9	—	9.2	3.0	44.9	25.9	14.8	4.3
1970	246,695	48.5	0.3	4.1	1.5	45.7	26.9	14.6	4.1

SOURCE: Bank of Japan [4(1973), p. 39: table 17].

[a] Profit and depreciation.

ernment has also sought to facilitate the achievement of these goals. It has, in any case, tried to assure that the private sector does not lack the wherewithal for this purpose.

Yet, put all this together and one does not come out with a totally planned economy of the Russian type—far from it. The essential characteristic of the Japanese government-business relationship is that the business community and the various government departments have been in close communication with each other from the days of the Meiji Restoration. The result is a style of industrial development which has allowed Japanese business considerable initiative and independence even when subject to administrative guidance facilitated by a variety of government aids and incentives. The acceptance, to a greater or less degree, by Japanese business men of the government's goals and priorities is based on two all important factors:

- a reluctance on the part of both business and government to unilaterally adopt policies or undertake major moves in the high priority sectors of the economy without consulting each other;
- a propensity, which all Japanese share, for a consensual approach to harmonizing differences that may exist within as well as between each group [26, p. 10].

The Occupation made at least four decisions that facilitated administrative guidance.

1. It failed to change Japan's central banking system, where the policies of an increasingly important central bank were controlled by the Ministry of Finance.

2. It permitted Japan to set up government banks to make public loans to key industries, namely, the inflationary postwar Reconstruction Finance Bank and its successor, the Japan Development Bank.

3. It demanded that Japan create a National Planning Agency to set priorities for postwar reconstruction.

4. It decided in 1949 and 1950 that the Japanese government should, at least for the time being, control business access to imports of goods, foreign capital, and technology. Implicit in the power to control such imports was the power to determine which industries or even companies would get essential products from abroad, as well as the further power to shield certain industries from foreign competition, or conversely, to expose them to it.

MITI. The power to sanction the import of goods (under the Foreign Exchange and Foreign Trade Control Law of 1949) as well as the import of foreign technologies (under the 1950 Law Concerning Foreign Investment) came to be largely concentrated in one government ministry—that for Inter-

Exhibit 17

Selected Indices of Overloans: Lending Ratios and Ratio of Borrowing from the Bank of Japan for City Banks at Year's End

Ratios	1953	1954	1955	1956	1957	1958	1959	1960	1961	1962	1963	1964	1965	1966	1967	1968	1969	1970
Lending[a]	111	106	91	94	107	101	98	98	103	105	102	104	99	97	99	96	97	99
Borrowing from Bank of Japan[b]	14	11	1	4	15	9	7	8	18	16	12	9	9	10	8	8	8	8

SOURCE: Bank of Japan [5, p. 134]. Reprinted with permission of St. Martin's Press, Inc.

a Lending ratio = $\dfrac{\text{Lending}}{\text{Real deposits + debentures issued}} \times 100$

b Ratio of borrowing from Bank of Japan = $\dfrac{\text{Borrowing from Bank of Japan}}{\text{Real deposits + debentures issued + borrowing from the Bank of Japan}} \times 100$

national Trade and Industry (MITI). These were both critical powers in the context of a capital-poor nation anxious to modernize after a long lag. In addition, as previously noted, MITI pushed itself to the fore as the spearhead of the Japanese drive to revise the Occupation's controversial Anti-Monopoly Law. As if this were not enough, MITI also made itself Japan's decision center on what industrial policy to follow, that is, on what industries to build up as a basis for the export drive that would become vital for Japan with the end of US aid and offshore procurement. Furthermore, inasmuch as MITI influenced industrial policy, it also came to have a strong informal influence on Japan's banks. That is, the banks looked to MITI for leads on what investments to make, knowing that the suggested investments would enjoy state protection and support [31, p. 16].

With so much territory in its power base, MITI came to be identified as the hand in the glove of government guidance. Its fame spread abroad, where attitudes turned hostile and remained suspicious even after foreign pressure had forced Japan to start to "liberalize" her imports, thus blunting one of MITI's most effective weapons. Even so, a spokesman for Japan felt it necessary to de-emphasize MITI in a book published in 1972 whose purpose was to explain Japan's industrial policy to concerned parties in the western world:

> . . . First of all, we would like to say that the relationship between MITI and industry is not one in which MITI wields vast authority to dictate to industry. Even nowadays, other ministries in charge of economic affairs, including those dealing with Finance, Agriculture, Construction, Transportation, Postal Service and Welfare, still maintain direct controls on private business as a main tool for their policy implementation, while MITI's direct control has been drastically reduced during the past twenty years. It is not true that MITI encourages industry by means of vast subsidies. MITI's budget comprises a mere 1% of the entire national budget, and of that less than one-

half is used for subsidies. Furthermore, in this connection, some people have recently expressed the opinion in relation to Japan's industrial policy that Japan in its entirety is like a corporation ("Japan, Inc."), that the Japanese Government, particularly MITI, is the corporate headquarters, and that each enterprise is a branch or division of the corporation. Some view the relationship between the government and industry as being that of "hand in glove." But whatever the postwar recovery period may have been, today there is no such thing as unilateral MITI direction of business activity of individual enterprise or passive acceptance by businesses of government judgment.

> Businesses introduce products and develop export markets on their own initiative. The main role of MITI is to arrive at a vision that may serve as a policy target and to persuade and guide industry towards that vision. Furthermore, in creating this vision, MITI seeks the opinion of business, consumers, and men of learning and experience within various councils and other frameworks, in respect to both industrial policy as a whole and policies concerning specific categories. In this way considerable effort is exerted to arrive at mutual understanding between business and government [31, p. 30].

Economic Planning Agency. Besides MITI, another agency with a role in economic guidance was the Economic Planning Agency (EPA), which had been set up in 1946 at the Occupation's request. Unlike MITI, the planners were not credited with wielding any power but rather with performing services. One of their functions was to draw up five-year plans covering at least the broad components of GNP and GNE, although through 1970 these plans had not succeeded in proposing a growth rate as rapid as the actual figure.[6] Another

---

[6] For example, the five-year plan for 1955–1960 set a target of 5.5 percent average annual growth in GNP; actual was 7.1 percent; the target for 1958–1962 was 6.5 percent; actual was 10.7 percent; the target for 1966–1971 was 8.5 percent; actual was 12.9 percent through 1969 [32(July 1964), p. 21; 32(July 1970), pp. 9–11].

contribution of the EPA was to help assemble and interpret some of the facts and figures that were one essential basis for political decisions on economic policy. The following comment on Japanese planning comes from the previously cited article in *The Economist* for May 1967:

> . . . The great differences between so-called western planning and the Japanese EPA's planning stick up like banners in the sky. The Japanese government publishes and keeps amending a running estimate of what it at present expects to be the movement in the country's main economic indicators during the twelve months ahead. . . . It keeps tabs on what is happening to the structure of the economy by a census of manufacturing every year, and of commerce every other year; more important, it stands ready to undertake sample surveys of almost any problem, not necessarily in depth but with sufficient quality to serve as a guide for indicative planning, apparently almost at a drop of a hat.

In what might be called the more static part of governmental analysis and planning, the Japanese are mainly concerned to find out what is the trend of the productivity of capital and labour both in the economy as a whole and within particular industries; when there are clear signs that this productivity is declining in some fields, it becomes deliberate government policy to encourage new resources to move into newer fields instead. When the calculations show that a particular industry has reached this stage, one can almost hear the relevant civil service official leap up from his adding machine with a hiss. True, some protective cushions will be left or put in place to enable the resources still in these industries to stay there and improve their productivity—in the case of anti-import protectionism, frankly internationally immoral cushions. . . . But the determination to get newer resources into more profitable lines for the future is specific and immense.

Even before these trends begin to show, however, what might be called the dynamic part of Japan's planning is based on a very careful analysis of production trends abroad. The object is to see what are the production patterns in countries richer than Japan. Then, since it is a datum assumption that Japan is going to get richer fast, the planners can tell from that what Japan's likely growth industries and likely declining industries will be. Moreover, marvellously weird calculations of entities like Japan's "structural change coefficient" are made and published, in constant survey of whether Japan's economic structure is in fact changing in this right direction [28, pp. XXIII, XXIV].

DESIGNING A NEW STRATEGY FOR GROWTH

As the Japanese looked ahead after independence to revitalizing their economy, they concluded that most policies would have to be framed with one key consideration in mind: what impact they would have on the balance of payments. The Ministry of Finance put this point as follows in its *General Survey of the Japanese Economy*, which appeared in 1955:

> The position of Japan in the world economy has been completely changed by the defeat, and Japan is becoming even more dependent upon the international economy than she was before the war. The future of Japan's economy, therefore, depends largely upon the course of balance of payments [18(1955), p. 5].

Given the overriding importance attached to the payments picture, Japan would clearly need to develop exports. As a corollary, she would need an industrial policy to select potential export industries, to channel investment capital their way, and to make export industries competitive with their international rivals. Until exports could be built up, moreover, scarce supplies of foreign exchange would have to be conserved by import controls (unless they were to be augmented by permitting foreign investment).

Framing Industrial Policy

Product Emphasis. Even before freedom, one of the basic policy issues to receive attention at the highest levels was that of what industries should provide the basis of Japan's coming export drive. As most observers saw it, Japan's only plentiful resource was her abundant supply of cheap labor, an advantage which implied that she should continue her prewar emphasis on labor-intensive export products (what a MITI official later called "low-quality textiles" and "masses of gadgets") [31, p. 15]. But the Japanese saw risks in this approach, including the risk that export opportunities for light manufactures were bound to decline as the Third World started to industrialize.

In this dilemma, what was actually decided and why was described by a high official from MITI in an account for the OECD entitled, "Basic Philosophy and Objectives of Japanese Industrial Policy":

> Should Japan have entrusted its future, according to the theory of comparative advantage, to these industries characterized by intensive use of labour? That would perhaps be a rational choice for a country with a small population of 5 or 10 million. But Japan has a large population. If the Japanese economy had adopted the simple doctrine of free trade and had chosen to specialize in this kind of industry, it would almost permanently have been unable to break away from the Asian pattern of stagnation and poverty, and would have remained the weakest link in the free world, thereby becoming a problem area in the Far East.

> The Ministry of International Trade and Industry decided to establish in Japan industries which require intensive employment of capital and technology, industries that in consideration of comparative cost of production should be the most inappropriate for Japan, industries such as steel, oil refining, petro-chemicals, automobiles, aircraft, industrial machinery of all sorts, and later

electronics, including electronic computers. From a short-run, static viewpoint, encouragement of such industries would seem to conflict with economic rationalism. But, from a long-range point of view, these are precisely the industries where income elasticity of demand is high, technological progress is rapid, and labour productivity rises fast. It was clear that without these industries it would be difficult to employ a population of 100 million and raise their standard of living to that of Europe and America with light industries alone; whether right or wrong, Japan had to have these heavy and chemical industries [31, p. 15].

Not indicated in this account is the difficulty of some of the decisions. For example, going into the auto industry was an idea championed by MITI, but "The Ministry of Finance (MOF), the Ministry of Transportation (MOT) and the Bank of Japan (BOJ) initially opposed its development as being high-cost and contrary to the international division of labor" [9, p. 39]. Also omitted in the above account was the long time span involved. Most of the industries listed by MITI were in their infancy during the fifties and "came of age" only in the late sixties. Furthermore, they were preceded by still other export industries in the period just after freedom. Still another account by MITI provided some of these additional facts which, as MITI pointed out, helped to explain Japan's reluctance to open her markets to foreign competition:

> During this period [of booming world trade and growth that followed the aftermath of the Korean War] there were significant changes in the industrial and trade structure of the [Japanese] economy and numerous legislative measures were taken to encourage the development of key industries. For example, light machinery such as sewing machines, cameras and binoculars became important export items to the United States. . . .

By 1955 technology had been introduced and the automobile industry was in its beginning stages of development. Legislation was passed in the same year to encourage the development of the petrochemical industry. In 1956 a law on Extraordinary Measures to encourage the development of the machinery industry was enacted, and a similar law was passed for the electronics industry in 1957.

In 1958 legislation was passed which established the Japan Aircraft Manufacturing Corporation . . . [21, pp. 23, 24].

How rapidly Japan moved forward in the sixties to implement the industry strategy chosen shows up in part in Exhibit 18, which indicates her rising share of world motor vehicle and steel production.

Concentrating Financial Resources on Strategic Industries. Although market prospects and value added[7] might have looked most favorable for the products of heavy industry, studies of comparative prices in 1951 and 1952 quickly revealed to the Japanese that the prices charged by their heavy industries (metals, chemicals, coal) might be more than half again as high as those of rival export nations.[8] In order to price competitively, it was imperative for Japan to cut costs, and cutting costs required investment.

Funneling investment into one industry rather than another was not, however, beyond the power of government, given companies' dependence on the banks for capital and given the ability of major ministries to influence both companies and banks. The routing of investment to strategic uses was described by a Japanese official in a publication by the OECD:

> According to Napoleon and Clausewitz, the secret of successful strategy is the concentration of fighting power on the main

battle grounds; fortunately, owing to good luck and wisdom spawned by necessity, Japan has been able to concentrate its scant capital in strategic industries.

The Ministry of International Trade and Industry (MITI) and the Ministry of Finance have played an essential part in this operation. The Ministry of Finance put the banking industry under its strict control after the depression of the 1930s and tacitly established the principle that banks will not and shall not fail. At the same time banks received strict control from the Ministry of Finance over loan interest rates, deposit interest rates, dividend rates, opening of branch offices, etc. With the dividend rate held down to under 10%, bank competition came to center on competing for larger shares of deposits and loans. In a fast-growing economy, banks find it essential to select growth industries and businesses to finance if they want to maintain and expand their share of business. In judging what makes a growth industry, banks relied on the judgment of MITI as one of their chief criteria. While affording protection to those industries and enterprises that were considered worthy of encouragement by means of the system of quantitative restrictions on imports and controls on introduction of foreign technology, MITI also devised policies of encouragement, such as financial measures through the Japan Development Bank and implementation of various types of tax incentives. It also exercised, from time to time, administrative leadership in order to prevent temporary excesses in equipment investment and production [31, pp. 15, 16].

Making Strategic Industries Competitive. The Japanese government was anxious to see that Japan's strategic industries were not held back by foreign competition in the domestic market, cutthroat domestic competition in periods of oversupply, inadequate scale, or inferior technology. To prevent or mitigate such problems, the state intervened in various ways. For example, in order to expand an "infant" industry, tariffs and quotas on competing imports could be used, in addition to loans. If expansion

[7] Value added: roughly the difference between the cost of outside purchases and the value of shipments to outsiders.

[8] See "Japan C," Exhibit 17 for details as of June 1952.

Exhibit 18

World Production of Motor Vehicles and Steel (percent of world total)

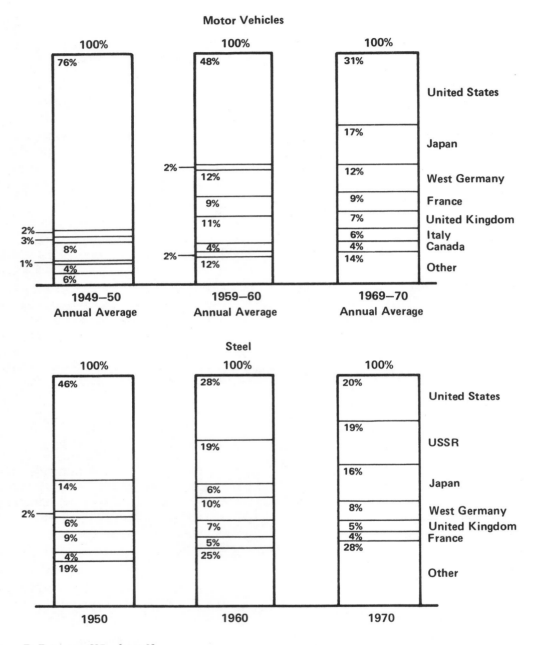

Motor Vehicles

	1949–50 Annual Average	1959–60 Annual Average	1969–70 Annual Average	
	76%	48%	31%	United States
			17%	Japan
	2%	2% / 12%	12%	West Germany
	3%	12%	9%	France
	8%	9%	7%	United Kingdom
	1%	11%	6%	Italy
	4%	4% / 2%	4%	Canada
	6%	12%	14%	Other

Steel

	1950	1960	1970	
	46%	28%	20%	United States
			19%	USSR
	14%	19%	16%	Japan
	2%	6%	8%	West Germany
	6%	10%	5%	United Kingdom
	9%	7%	4%	France
	4%	5%	28%	Other
	19%	25%		

SOURCE: P. Peterson [35, chart 9].

went too far and the industry was troubled by oversupply, MITI might take the lead in forming cartels to control the operating rate of existing plants and the addition of new facilities. If, as was often the case, a strategic industry needed new technology from abroad, MITI might participate in selecting the best foreign technology available, and it would then provide the several permits needed to license the use of the technology and to make payments for it. Conversely, if the optimal size for plants in an industry was very large, MITI might withhold the various permits required to build a new facility unless it was planned to the necessary size. If firms in an industry were deemed too small to finance new investments and too prone to excessive competition, MITI might initiate a cartel. Or, MITI might mobilize support for a merger and then help to design an agreement that would survive scrutiny by the Federal Trade Commission. Going further, MITI might initiate the merger itself. If firms were reluctant to comply, and they sometimes were, MITI might engage in a "persuasive" dialogue. So long as MITI could control a firm's access to imported raw materials and technologies or a firm's exposure to foreign competition, MITI was in a strong position. In addition, it had the power to say which firms would share in subsidies granted to an industry under a particular law. Three industries in which MITI used one or another of its powers to "facilitate" a merger were steel, motor vehicles, and, later on, computers.[9]

Conserving Foreign Exchange via Import Controls

To protect the current balance as much as possible, Japan sought to limit imports to only the most essential products. The case for controls had been recognized by the Occupation itself, and in 1949 it had passed a Foreign Exchange and Foreign Trade Control Act which a free Japan was to use as the basis for her system of import controls.

Besides tariffs (which were the most common way to impose selective restrictions on imports) Japan used a number of additional, more effective—but more controversial—methods. These included quantitative

controls on how much foreign exchange it would pay out (exchange budgets) or how much foreign goods it would let in (import quotas). Japan started out with an exchange budget; when this came under criticism by international bodies (1964), she switched to quotas.

A continuing feature of Japan's control system was the practice of dividing imports into three groups for differential treatment. In the case of the most restricted group (which included food, some raw materials, and other essentials), MITI drew up a separate budget or quota for each commodity, and no one was allowed a license to import any commodity in this group without first obtaining an "allocation certificate" from MITI. In commenting on this group, Leon Hollerman notes, "Originally the government designated the countries of origin from which imports of [these] items would be permitted. Also, a high degree of discrimination was practiced by MITI in the selection of applicants to whom allocation certificates were granted." In the case of the second most restricted group (which included items for which it was difficult to estimate import demand, mainly machinery and consumers' goods), MITI drew up a joint or commingled budget that could not be exceeded by imports for the category as a whole. Again, no importer could get a license to import goods in this category unless an "allocation certificate" from MITI was obtained first. In the case of the least restricted group of imports, MITI drew up still another joint or commingled budget, and anyone could get a license to import so long as the budget for the group was not exceeded [12, pp. 226, 227, 232].

Policy on Foreign Investment

When Japan was at her nadir after World War II, the Occupation saw that foreign capital could enter the country and acquire assets at a fraction of their worth. To pre-

---

[9] MITI's intervention in computers, motor vehicles, and steel has been described in a book published in 1972 by the US Department of Commerce and titled *Japan: The Government-Business Relationship—A Guide for the American Businessman* [26, see esp. pp. 41-54 and appendices A, B, and C].

vent such an outcome, in May 1950 the Occupation passed a Law Concerning Foreign Investment. This made foreign investment subject to official approval, and it established criteria according to which approval might be granted. Like the earlier Foreign Exchange and Foreign Trade Control Act, the Law Concerning Foreign Investment laid the basis for policies pursued by Japan when the Occupation left. Under this law, Japan need not accept foreign investments. Rather, these investments were to be accepted only if they contributed to (1) the improvement of the international balance of payments; (2) the development of essential industries or public enterprises; or (3) the continuation or revival of needed technological assistance contracts [12, p. 270]. To implement this policy, the law stated that if the foreign investor wanted to get foreign exchange in order to "repatriate" either the "fruits" or the principal of his investment, then the investment must be licensed or validated. Licensing applied to short-term capital and was handled by the Ministry of Finance; validation applied to long-term investment and was handled by the "appropriate ministry." In practice, this provision came to mean that decisions were made by a Foreign Investment Deliberation Council on which several ministries were represented. MITI was only one of these, but a negative MITI vote was said to be decisive.

Partly because Japan was capital-poor and partly because foreign investment should, at least initially, constitute a contribution to, rather than a drain upon, her slender resources of foreign exchange, Japan was expected to welcome investments meeting her criteria. Foreigners soon found, however, that all investment was screened and that some types were much more welcome than others. Thus, loans and investment in debt were the easiest types to get validated; licensed technology was also relatively easy to arrange. Among the factors MITI might check in the validation process, however, were the relative merits of the technology

compared with competing types available; "excessive competition" of Japanese firms for duplicative technology that might lead to overcapacity in an industry; the amount and kind of payment the licensor was asking and the restrictions he was imposing on the export of products made under his patents. Foreigners also discovered that MITI might try to better the terms they had tentatively worked out with the private company seeking the license [12, pp. 268, 272, 273; 31, p. 85].

Foreign purchases of existing shares on the stock exchange, without participation in management, were still another form of foreign investment that the Japanese were ready to accept, although they set strict limits on it: 5 percent for an individual, 15 percent for foreigners as a group in most industries, and only 10 percent for particularly sensitive industries (i.e., utilities, shipbuilding, banking, mining, and fisheries) [12, pp. 262, 263].

An investment designed to be accompanied by control was the most difficult to get validated. Thus, foreign companies not already established in Japan usually found it quite impossible to create a wholly owned Japanese branch. (The few exceptions to this rule were foreign companies with essential products, materials, or technologies that Japan could not otherwise obtain: IBM, Mobil, Shell, and Exxon are examples) [26, p. 84]. For most foreign companies, the most that could be hoped for was a joint venture with a Japanese firm, and ownership on a 50–50 basis or even a 40–60 basis proved very difficult to get approved. Even at this level, the acquiring foreigner had to bring technology into the bargain, not simply cash [12, p. 267].

After several years, the application of these policies showed up clearly in statistics for different forms of investment. Of some $4 billion foreign investments between the spring of 1949 and the end of 1962, 66.3 percent was in loans and only 5.7 percent

Exhibit 19

Japan: Direct Investment vs Technology Purchases

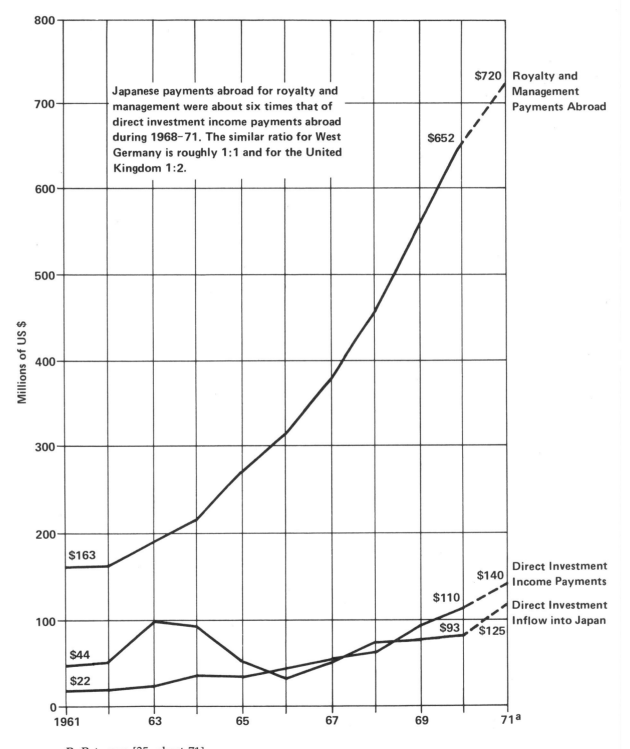

Japanese payments abroad for royalty and management were about six times that of direct investment income payments abroad during 1968–71. The similar ratio for West Germany is roughly 1:1 and for the United Kingdom 1:2.

$720 Royalty and Management Payments Abroad

$652

$163

$140 Direct Investment Income Payments

$110

$93 $125 Direct Investment Inflow into Japan

$44

$22

Millions of US $

800

700

600

500

400

300

200

100

0

1961   63   65   67   69   71[a]

SOURCE: P. Peterson [35, chart 71].
[a] 1971 cumulative direct foreign investment in Japan excluding reinvestment earnings, $900 million.

Exhibit 20

Balance of Payments (millions of US dollars)

A. DEVELOPMENT OF THE BALANCE OF PAYMENTS IN FOUR POSTWAR PERIODS (ANNUAL AVERAGE)

	Postwar Rehabilitation 1946-52	Attaining Economic Independence 1953-57	Transition to High-Rate Growth & Open Economic Structure 1958-64	Latest Years 1965-70
Trade balance	−233	−360	151	2,588
(Exports)	(661)	(2,041)	(4,480)	(12,601)
(Imports)[a]	(894)	(2,401)	(4,329)	(10,013)
Services	100	211	−304	−1,239
Transfers	316	12	−64	−160
Current balance	183	−137	−217	1,189
Long-term capital	−8	23	116	−670
Basic balance	175	−114	−101	519
Short-term capital, errors & omissions	17	33	85	303
Over-all balance	192	−81	−16	822
Change in official reserves	143	−58	211	400
Others in balance of monetary movements	49	−23	−227	443

B. YEAR-TO-YEAR DEVELOPMENTS, 1960–71

Year	Current Balance	Trade Balance	Exports	Imports (Payments Value)[a]	Net Services	Net Transfers	Long-term Capital[a]	Balance of Monetary Movements						
								Assets	Liabilities	Short-term Capital[b,c]	Errors & Omissions	Over-all Balance	Gold & Foreign Exchange Reserves	Others
C.Y.1960	143.0	268.0	3,979.0	-3,711.0	Δ100.0	Δ25.0	Δ55.0	Δ172.0	117.0	Δ16.0	33.0	105.0	502.0	Δ397.0
1961	Δ982.4	Δ557.9	4,149.2	-4,707.1	Δ382.7	Δ41.8	Δ10.0	Δ312.0	302.0	21.0	19.0	Δ952.4	Δ338.0	Δ614.4
1962	Δ48.7	402.2	4,860.9	-4,458.7	Δ420.5	Δ30.4	171.7	Δ310.0	481.7	107.7	5.7	236.4	355.0	Δ118.6
1963	Δ780	Δ166	5,391	-5,557	Δ569	Δ45	467	Δ298	765	107	45	Δ161	37	Δ198
1964	Δ480	377	6,704	-6,327	Δ784	Δ73	107	Δ451	558	234	10	Δ129	121	Δ70
1965	932	1,901	8,332	-6,431	Δ884	Δ85	Δ415	Δ446	31	Δ61	Δ51	405	108	297
1966	1,254	2,275	9,641	-7,366	Δ886	Δ135	Δ808	Δ706	Δ102	Δ64	Δ45	337	Δ33	370
1967	Δ190	1,160	10,231	-9,071	Δ1,172	Δ178	Δ812	Δ875	63	506	Δ75	Δ571	Δ69	Δ502
1968	1,048	2,529	12,751	-10,222	Δ1,306	Δ175	Δ239	Δ1,096	857	209	84	1,102	886	216
1969	2,119	3,699	15,679	-11,980	Δ1,399	Δ181	Δ155	Δ1,508	1,353	178	141	2,283	605	1,678
1970	1,970	3,963	18,969	-15,006	Δ1,785	Δ208	Δ1,591	Δ2,031	440	724	271	1,374	903	593
1971	5,797	7,787	23,566	-15,779	Δ1,738	Δ252	Δ1,082	Δ2,231	1,149	2,435	527	7,677	10,836	Δ3,031

SOURCES: Part A: Japan Economic Planning Agency [17(1970-71), p. 78]. Part B: Bank of Japan [4(1968), pp. 245, 246: table 141; 4(1972), pp. 209, 210: table 121].

NOTE: The basic balance (not shown in the 1960-71 array) was the sum of entries prior to short-term capital. The basic balance became a significant measure during the mid-1960s because it excluded flows of "hot money" that showed up in short-term capital movements.

[a] Payments value imports (adjusted fob basis).

[b] Δ (deficit) shows outflows of capital (an increase of assets or a decrease in liabilities).

[c] Excluding transactions that belong to monetary movements.

Exhibit 21

Analysis of Trade

A. EXPORTS AND IMPORTS BY PRINCIPAL COMMODITIES (MILLIONS OF DOLLARS)

Exports by Commodities

Year	Total	Food-stuffs	Textiles	Iron & Steel Products	TV Receivers	Radio Receivers	Tape Recorders	Motor Vehicles	Vessels	Scientific & Optical Equipment
1964	6,673.2	323.0	1,426.5	909.5	57.9	213.7	69.9	180.7	490.5	171.7
1965	8,451.7	343.8	1,581.7	1,290.4	84.9	216.5	79.5	237.3	747.9	216.7
1966	9,776.4	382.6	1,762.4	1,293.1	146.5	278.2	120.8	305.9	823.8	271.6
1967	10,441.6	372.4	1,703.7	1,272.4	164.6	333.7	195.1	434.1	982.5	314.5
1968	12,971.7	431.8	1,977.3	1,712.5	266.4	421.3	271.8	712.9	1,084.1	372.0
1969	15,990.0	571.6	2,270.6	2,164.8	353.5	579.7	400.0	983.6	1,137.2	439.0
1970	19,317.7	647.7	2,407.3	2,843.7	383.8	694.9	450.8	1,337.4	1,409.6	498.5
1971	24,018.9	678.7	2,772.1	3,541.8	498.8	790.8	490.3	2,372.5	1,848.9	573.6

Imports by Commodities[a]

Year	Total	Food-stuffs & Feeds	Wool	Raw Cotton	Iron & Steel Scrap	Soya Beans	Wood	Coal	Crude Oil	Machin-ery
1964	7,937.5	1,386.5	367.3	439.4	235.2	184.5	438.2	211.2	982.9	881.9
1965	8,169.0	1,470.0	342.6	441.8	153.1	225.8	492.5	270.3	1,047.3	760.1
1966	9,522.7	1,676.3	420.1	423.9	145.1	272.0	676.6	302.6	1,200.4	820.1
1967	11,663.1	1,804.7	364.8	442.8	311.7	272.0	934.4	400.8	1,457.1	1,053.4
1968	12,987.2	1,878.7	363.0	510.7	158.4	274.1	1,160.9	518.3	1,685.3	1,326.9
1969	15,023.5	2,141.2	392.0	424.2	208.6	281.0	1,274.9	674.8	1,906.9	1,634.7
1970	18,881.2	2,574.1	348.3	470.7	431.1	365.8	1,572.1	1,010.1	2,235.0	2,297.7
1971	19,711.7	2,917.2	276.0	515.7	123.4	421.5	1,459.0	1,004.7	3,047.6	2,408.9

B. EXPORTS IN RELATION TO PRODUCTION INCLUDING AGRICULTURE, FORESTRY, FISHING, MINING, QUARRYING, AND MANUFACTURING (IN PERCENT)

Year	Japan	US	Canada	West Ger	UK	EEC
1950	18.3	9.1	42.5	17.3	42.8	17.7
1960	24.9	11.6	44.7	22.4	37.8	22.4
1969	30.1	12.8	62.6	21.8	47.9	21.8

SOURCES: Part A: Japan Ministry of Finance figures cited in *Fuji Bank Bulletin* [10(May 1975), p. 171]. Part B: P. Peterson [35, vol. 2, chart 15].

[a] Customs value imports (cif).

was in stocks with participation in control. Of some $1.33 billion in compensation paid on foreign investment, 47 percent was for technology and 41 percent was for loans [13(1966), p. 20]. This story is carried through 1971 and is contrasted with that of other countries in Exhibit 19.

SELECTED RESULTS THROUGH 1971

Japan's strategy was not without its problems, but it achieved positive results in varied areas.[10] These can best be traced, not in words but in figures. Exhibit 7 gives details on Japanese wages as well as on comparative labor costs, etc. Exhibit 8 provides information on the growth and allocation of GNE. Exhibit 9 shows trends in output and employment by sector. Exhibits 12–14 provide other data on the structure and performance of Japanese businesses. Exhibit 15 shows comparative savings and investment. Exhibit 20 gives a balance of payments and Exhibit 21 an analysis of trade.

---

[10] The reader is referred to "Japan D2."

REFERENCES

1. Abegglen, James C. (ed.). *Business Strategies for Japan*. Tokyo: Sophia University Press for the Boston Consulting Group, 1970.

2. Austin, Lewis. (ed.). *Japan: The Paradox of Progress*. New Haven, Conn.: Yale University Press, 1976.

3. Ballon, Robert J. (ed.). *The Japanese Employee*. Tokyo: Charles E. Tuttle, 1969.

4. Bank of Japan. *Economic Statistics Annual*. Tokyo.

5. —————. *Money and Banking in Japan*, translated by S. Nishemura. New York: St. Martin's, 1973.

6. Cohen, Jerome B. *Japan's Postwar Economy*. Bloomington, Ind.: Indiana University Press, 1958.

7. Cole, Robert E. *Japanese Blue Collar: The Changing Tradition*. Berkeley, Calif.: University of California Press, 1971.

8. "Consider Japan," *The Economist* (September 1 and 8, 1962), unsigned surveys.

9. Frank, Isaiah (ed.). *The Japanese Economy in International Perspective*. Baltimore: Johns Hopkins, 1975. (A supplementary paper of the Committee for Economic Development.)

10. *Fuji Bank Bulletin* (May 1975), p. 175.

11. Halliday, Jon. *A Political History of Japanese Capitalism*. New York: Random House, Pantheon Books, 1975.

12. Hollerman, Leon. *Japan's Dependence on the World Economy: The Approach Toward Economic Liberalization*. Princeton, N.J.: Princeton University Press, 1967.

13. *Industrial Review of Japan*, editors of the Nihon Keizai Shimbun (Japan Economic Journal). Tokyo, annual.

14. International Labour Office. *The Cost of Social Security, Eighth International Enquiry, 1967–1971*. Geneva, 1976.

15. International Labour Organization. *International Labour Review*. Geneva, monthly.

16. "Japan: A Special Strength," *The Economist* (March 31, 1973), survey.

17. Japan Economic Planning Agency. *Economic Survey of Japan*. Tokyo, annual.

18. Japan Ministry of Finance. *General Survey of the Japanese Economy*. Tokyo, 1955.

19. —————. *General Survey of the Japanese Economy*. Tokyo, 1956.

20. —————. *Quarterly Bulletin of Financial Statistics* (1976).

21. Japan Ministry of International Trade and Industry. *The Industry of Japan*. Japan External Trade Organization. Tokyo, 1974.

22. Japan Ministry of Labour. *Labour Administration in Japan*. Tokyo, 1973.

23. —————. *Year Book of Labour Statistics*. Tokyo, 1971.

24. Japan Office of the Prime Minister. *Japan Statistical Yearbook*. Tokyo, annual.

25. Kahn, Herman. *The Emerging Japanese Superstate: Challenge and Response*. Englewood Cliffs, N.J.: Prentice-Hall, 1970.

26. Kaplan, Eugene J. *Japan: The Government–Business Relationship*. Washington: U.S. Department of Commerce, 1972.

27. Lockwood, William W. (ed.). *The State and Economic Enterprise in Japan: Essays in the Political Economy of Growth*. Princeton, N.J.: Princeton University Press, 1965.

28. Macrae, Norman. "The Risen Sun," *The Economist* (May 27, 1967), pp. XI, XXIII, XXIV, surveys; (June 3, 1967), p. XXIX, survey.

29. *Nippon. A Chartered Survey of Japan*, edited by the Tsuneta Yano Memorial Society, annual.

30. Okochi, Kazuo, B. Karsh, and S. B. Levine (eds.). *Workers and Employees in Ja-*

pan. Princeton, N.J.: Princeton University Press, 1974.

31. Organization for Economic Cooperation and Development. *The Industrial Policy of Japan*. Paris, 1972.

32. —————. *OECD Economic Surveys: Japan*. Paris, annual.

33. Patrick, Hugh (ed.). *Japanese Industrialization and Its Social Consequences*. Berkeley, Calif.: University of California Press, 1976.

34. ————— and H. Rosovsky (eds.). *Asia's New Giant: How the Japanese Economy Works*. Washington: The Brookings Institution, 1976.

35. Peterson, Peter G. *The United States in the Changing World Economy*, vol. 2. Washington: U.S. Government Printing Office, 1971.

36. Reischauer, Edwin O. *The United States and Japan*. Cambridge, Mass.: Harvard University Press, 1954.

37. United Nations. *Yearbook of National Accounts Statistics*. New York, annual.

38. United States, Agency for International Development. *Gross National Product, Growth Rate and Trend Data*. Washington: U.S. Government Printing Office, 1974.

39. —————, Council on International Economic Policy. *International Economic Report of the President and Annual Report of the Council*. Washington: U.S. Government Printing Office, 1974.

40. —————. *International Economic Report of the President and Annual Report of the Council*. Washington: U.S. Government Printing Office, 1977.

41. —————, Department of Labor. *Monthly Labor Review*. Washington: Bureau of Labor Statistics.

42. Vogel, Ezra F. (ed.). *Modern Japanese Organization and Decision Making*. Berkeley, Calif.: University of California Press, 1975.

43. Yamamura, Kozo. *Economic Policy in Postwar Japan: Growth versus Economic Democracy*. Berkeley, Calif.: University of California Press, 1967.

Japan D2: A Strategy for Meeting the Problems of Growth

Welcome as it was, Japan's unprecedented growth from independence through 1971 was not devoid of problems. These included concern about inflation and protests from trade partners. The latter were resentful of high-volume imports from Japan, especially in certain product categories. They were also increasingly resentful of the barriers Japan had erected to protect her own domestic markets. During the decade of the sixties, Japan found need to take remedial action in both of these problem areas.

COMBINING GROWTH WITH STABILITY

Extra high investment and industrial activity, as achieved by Japan after freedom, was apt to be accompanied by rising consumption, rising imports, rising wholesale and export prices, slowing exports, and a crisis in the balance of payments. When this train of events was set in motion, Japan's economy was diagnosed as "superheated" and remedial action was begun.

Analysts agreed that control of superheating relied far more on a restrictive monetary policy than on a restrictive fiscal policy (see Exhibit 1). Restrictive monetary policy, moreover, meant more than just arranging for interest rates to rise to the point where they would bring supply and demand for funds into balance at a lower level of investment. Rather, when the Japanese government wanted to cool the economy, it informed the Bank of Japan to initiate a period of "window guidance," or credit rationing.

How effectively tight money worked to cool superheating in 1957–1958, 1961–1962, and 1963–1964 shows up in graphs from the Bank of Japan which are reproduced as Exhibits 2 and 3. How often superheating occurred shows up in Exhibit 4, which records six periods of upswing from 1951 through 1971, some of them lasting longer than 10 quarters. Of these, the last was atypical in that the balance of payments remained strong during this time. Even so, tight money was imposed owing to domestic inflation (see Exhibit 5).

The following account of Japan's policy for the "management" of superheating is excerpted from "Consider Japan," which appeared in The Economist in 1962. The author several times pauses to contrast Japanese and orthodox western practice, particularly Japanese and British practice.

Easy Budgets

"Japan's system of managing its economy has been to run what would be regarded in Britain as very expansionary budget policies, with large planned increases in government expenditure and sizeable reductions in personal taxation a regular feature of most recent years (see adjoining table), and to use monetary policy and rises in interest rates as the main restraining weapons, when and if any restraints are needed. This pattern has been widely misunderstood abroad, because of the barriers which economists (particularly government economists) raise in the way of understanding each other's language.

"Most Japanese economists will worthily insist—and American economic commentators will generally approvingly report—that Japan has constantly balanced its annual estimates of budget expenditure and revenue ever since Mr. Dodge laid down that balanced budget estimates were the right thing to have. But the balancing act is done in a very peculiar way.

"Around the turn of every calendar year (and thus three or four months before the fiscal year begins on April 1) everybody in Japan seems to enter into an annual guessing game to recommend what the target rate for growth in next year's gross national product should be. The ruling Liberal Democratic party, in solemn convention assembled, recommends that gross national product should grow at one rate; the Ministry of Finance recommends that it would be safer to aim to grow at a slightly lower rate; the Economic Planning Agency makes a final calculation, and the Cabinet splits the

Japan's Decade of Tax Reliefs
(billions of yen, which virtually equal millions of pounds)

| | Current Balance of Payments | Value of Tax Relief in that Year's Budget | | |
Fiscal Year	Deficit (−) or Surplus (+)	On Personal Income Tax	On All Taxes	Growth in Real GNP (%)
1951	+118	61	113	+13.5
1952	+112	113	90	+10.5
1953	−69	77	124	+6.7
1954	+36	31	17	+3.9
1955	+177	53	66	+10.1
1956	+104	23	2	+8.2
1957	−137	110	62	+7.1
1958	+183	6	37	+3.7
1959	+121	23	10	+17.7
1960	+39	nil	−7	+13.2
1961	−388	56	75	+15.2

This table can be extended through 1968 as follows:

Selected Data on Fiscal Policy and Its Environment, 1963–1968

| | Current Balance of Payments (¥ billion) | Tax Relief | |
Fiscal Year[a]		Personal Income (¥ billion)	Total (¥ billion)
1962	−17	47	116
1963	−280	67	68
1964	−173	74	168
1965	+336	65	120
1966	+451	158	358
1967	−68	92	112
1968	+377	125	89

SOURCES: First half of data presented here is from *The Economist* [4]; latter half from the Bank of Japan [2(1969): table 140; 2(1972): table 121]; *The Economist* [4]; and OECD [16(June 1968), p. 25]. Reprinted with permission.

[a] Starts on April 1.

differences. Thus one reads in the newspapers that the Cabinet after a long session decided that the rate of growth should be 9.2 per cent in fiscal 1961 or 5.4 per cent in fiscal 1962.

"This apparently absurd guessing game, expressed to a precise point of decimals, has a genuine economic importance. For every 0.1 per cent of the agreed target rate for growth in

national income the Japanese reckon that they can expect a stated amount of extra tax revenue on the basis of existing tax rates. Thus with a target growth rate of 5.4 per cent this fiscal year, they reckoned on nearly £500 million of extra revenue; and by the rules of the budget balancing act precisely that sum—together with the surplus of tax revenue carried over from the previous year—is then assumed to be available for deliberate increases in government expenditure or for new tax reliefs. The remarkable feature of the game, from the reflationist's point of view, is that the larger the target figure for growth which the planners-cum-bargainers eventually decide upon—and the bigger the growth in production in the preceding year (i.e., the nearer the economy has been running to capacity)—the bigger the tax reliefs and deliberate increases in government expenditure which this system tells them it is orthodox for them to give away.

"These reliefs, be it noted, are regarded as 'orthodox' even in years when the balance of payments has run into large deficit. Indeed, if the gross national product has been rising particularly swiftly during a year of balance of payments crisis—which will usually be the case since Japanese balance of payments troubles are generally of the import *boomu* (Japanese-English for boom) type—it is practically certain that the uncovenanted surplus of tax revenue to be carried over into the next year, and probable that the rise in national income to be counted on for the next year as a whole, will be correspondingly high also. Under the rule of the game, this makes it 'orthodox' to make the new year's tax relief or deliberate increase in government expenditure particularly large. Thus in the middle of the balance of payments crisis of 1957 (while Japan's international exchange reserves were dropping sharply) the income tax levied on the average lower middle class and upper working class salary was literally cut in half. During this last year's balance of payments cri-

sis, Japanese taxes were reduced by about £116 million (at a time when Mr. Selwyn Lloyd, in his July and April budgets combined, was raising British taxes by over £200 million); and this Japanese cut of £116 million, reported the *Oriental Economist* truthfully, aroused 'general public complaint of a conservative tax relief.'

"In these circumstances it may seem a bit odd that the Japanese economy ever slows down at all, at any point short of raging inflation. But—at least until this last year, when living costs in the cities have suddenly bounded by 10 per cent—the policy has not in fact proved very inflationary. . . . Moreover—again until last year—Japan has managed to escape out of its balance of payments crises and periods of 'overheating,' back on to expansion again, much more quickly than Britain. The weapon used to counter periods of overheating has never been fiscal, but always monetary, policy.

"The way in which a restrictive monetary policy is worked in Japan at times of balance of payments difficulty—once again, to the foreigner it seems a very peculiar way—will be discussed below. But it is worth pausing here to consider the rationale of their system. It is customary in Britain to say that monetary policy cannot work as a restrictive device in times of balance of payments crisis if budgetary policy is pulling the opposite way. Experience in Japan goes a long way towards casting doubt on this belief—because their experience is that the two weapons work with quite different time intervals of effectiveness. Monetary policy works much the more quickly and much the more directly upon the balance of payments,

both on capital account (by drawing in loanable funds, such as Euro-dollars, from abroad) and on current account (by cutting down imports). By contrast, restriction of demand by higher tax rates works on the balance of payments only after a time lag; and the Japanese say that at times of balance of payments trouble the restriction of demand and imports after a time lag is likely to be the precise reverse of what they want.

. . . But Tight Money

". . . Because the commercial bankers have to come begging to [the Bank of Japan] when they want new funds to increase their lending further, the entire credit structure of Japan now seems to the visiting foreigner to lie snugly under the Bank of Japan's control.

"The Bank itself would deny this; its position of absolute power, as lender of last resort, over the credit situation does sometimes mean that it cannot use that power to quite the extent that its exasperation with some aspects of the *boomu* might make it wish to do. It cannot very well turn away big banks who ask it for funds if the result would be to cause a massive financial crash of Overend Gurney proportions.[a] But in banking, as in international diplomacy, an authority that possesses an unusable thermonuclear deterrent does not necessarily thereby become less able than an unarmed country to make its wishes felt.

"The control by the Bank of Japan is exercised in various ways. The one 'orthodox' weapon is Bank rate, this summer at 7.3 per cent, which it is

---

[a] A British bank that failed.

certainly able to make effective; most of Japan's other (very high) interest rates are tied to it, and Japanese businesses' heavy dependence on borrowing means that they are very susceptible to changes in borrowing rates. A second and more controversial weapon is the so-called 'window operation'. The Bank of Japan holds regular consultations with the commercial banks, reviews the likely trend of advances of each bank for perhaps a month ahead, and warns individual banks (or; at times of balance of payments crises, warns all big city banks) that they should please start to restrain their advances; if necessary it will even suggest an 'overall loan level' for the big banks as a whole. Finally, although the Bank will not generally in the last resort refuse to lend to any big banks, it does levy penalty rates on what it regards as its ultimate margin of less desirable loans to the commercial banks. As part of the same process the Bank of Japan will offer favourable discount rates on particular types of lending paper—especially, to the annoyance of competing British exporters, it will help indirectly to subsidise Japanese exports in this way.

"The commercial banks in turn also have a schedule of penalty rates which they levy on those who borrow from them, according to the status of the borrower concerned. And when they have to cut back lending, they have no hesitation about putting pressure on borrowers whose position they regard as unsound. The small local banks, who lend mostly to smaller local firms, will do the same thing when a credit squeeze makes it more profitable for them to use some of their funds in other ways (per-

haps, for example, to lend call money to the big city banks at very high interest rates). The consequence is that tight money during credit squeezes can lead to bankruptcies of small firms in Japan.

". . . The more closely one studies the history of the Japanese economy in the last decade, the more one becomes convinced that success in economic policy nowadays springs from a policy of favouring the forward-looking and most prospering and efficient firms, and beating the less efficient ones into the ground. The fact that control through monetary policy in Japan has—until this last year—generally worked in this direction may not be a sign of great social and humanitarian virtue; but it has been of enormous economic utility. Your correspondent became convinced that there are two important lessons for Britain here.

"First, the general British method, during the crises of the last decade, of restraining demand by tough budgets and tax regulators has automatically laid its main restraining power on the growth industries, while the opposite Japanese method has worked the other way round. Growth industries by definition are those that will be given the biggest impetus to expand their production when the next few hundred million pounds' worth of marginal demand is pumped into the economy; so, of course, they are also those that suffer most severely when the next few hundred million pounds' worth of marginal demand is siphoned out of the economy by means of a restrictive budget. By contrast, the Japanese method of pumping in extra demand through stimulatory budgets, and then using mon-

etary policy and high interest rates as a rationing device, has caused restrictions to impinge mainly on those whom the banks regard as the worst business risks. The rationed capital has become available only to those who can use it most profitably—except when political considerations intervene and gum the process up.

"Secondly, the British have got used to saying that a policy of expansionary budgets and high interest rates will penalise investment at the expense of stimulating consumption. Japanese experience surely proves this to be nonsense. Japan (where industrial borrowing in recent years has cost about 10 per cent) has recently been devoting nearly 40 per cent of its gross national product to total investment. Britain, on the same basis of comparison, has devoted less than 20 per cent. The truth is that it is a spirit of dynamism among thrusting growth industries that nowadays serves to impel an economy along the high road of expanding investment. A policy of stimulatory budgets provides the oats that beckon the horse forward, while a policy of high interest rates provides the reins to guide the horse and also (at least in Japan) helps to provide the high savings (and, sometimes, at appropriate moments of the trade cycle, also the temporary increase of borrowing from abroad) which makes the continuance of heavy investment possible. A policy of low interest rates relaxes the reins so that the horse will find it easier to rush forward faster if it wishes, but this is not much use when, because of lack of expansion of marginal demand, the horse itself is standing still" [4(Sep. 1, 1962), pp. 793–819]. Reprinted with permission.

Exhibit 1

Fiscal and Monetary Data

A. CENTRAL GOVERNMENT REVENUE, EXPENDITURES, AND NATIONAL DEBT (BILLIONS OF YEN)

FY (Apr 1– Mar 31)	General Account			Net Totals for General and Special Accounts[b]		Net Rev Less Expendtr[c]	Government Affiliated Organizations			Natl Debt[d] (end of FY)
	Reptrd Rev	Adj Rev[a]	Expndtr	Revs	Expndtrs		Rev	Expendtr	Net	
1954	1,185	983	1,041	2,088	2,009	79	844	712	132	933
1955	1,126	982	1,018	2,284	2,169	115	878	747	131	1,057
1956	1,232	1,137	1,069	2,562	2,284	278	978	837	141	1,000
1957	1,400	1,237	1,188	2,745	2,463	282	1,143	1,004	139	970
1958	1,454	1,242	1,332	2,800	2,636	163	1,232	1,065	167	1,075
1959	1,597	1,475	1,495	3,208	2,916	292	1,377	1,207	170	1,253
1960	1,961	1,859	1,743	3,764	3,269	495	1,634	1,425	209	1,340
1961	2,516	2,298	2,063	4,441	3,740	701	2,049	1,847	202	1,230
1962	2,948	2,496	2,557	4,826	4,374	452	2,369	2,175	194	1,281
1963	3,231	2,840	3,044	5,446	5,059	387	2,671	2,472	200	1,185
1964	3,447	3,261	3,311	6,338	5,800	538	2,829	2,695	134	1,349
1965	3,773	3,440	3,723	7,109	6,586	523	3,303	3,135	268	1,767
1966	4,552	3,836	4,459	7,896	7,621	275	3,866	3,612	254	2,662
1967	5,299	4,497	5,113	9,519	8,969	550	4,219	4,039	180	3,818
1968	6,060	5,412	5,937	11,415	10,415	1,000	4,788	4,545	243	4,786
1969	7,109	6,573	6,918	13,451	12,086	1,365	5,542	5,213	329	5,479
1970	8,459	7,921	8,188	15,608	13,727	1,881	6,253	5,871	382	6,226
1971	9,971	8,513	9,561	17,228	15,524	1,704	7,152	6,775	377	7,605[e]

B. NATIONAL INCOME AND TAX BURDEN (BILLIONS OF YEN AND PERCENTAGE BREAKDOWN)

Fiscal Year	(A) Natl Inc by Distrbtve Shares ¥	Tax Amount			Tax Burden		
		(B) Natl Tax ¥	(C) Local Tax ¥	(D) Total ¥	(B)/(A) %	(C)/(A) %	(D)/(A) %
1958	9,616.1	1,190.8	544.0	1,734.8	12.4	5.6	18.0
1959	11,023.3	1,372.4	610.9	1,983.3	12.4	5.6	18.0
1960	13,269.1	1,801.5	744.2	2,545.7	13.6	5.6	19.2
1961	15,755.1	2,227.7	906.5	3,134.2	14.1	5.8	19.9
1962	17,729.8	2,390.7	1,056.7	3,447.4	13.5	5.9	19.4
1963	20,607.2	2,731.7	1,212.9	3,944.6	13.3	5.8	19.1
1964	23,329.3	3,159.2	1,399.6	4,558.8	13.5	6.0	19.5
1965	25,977.4	3,279.7	1,549.4	4,829.1	12.6	6.0	18.6
1966	30,326.4	3,663.0	1,768.6	5,431.6	12.1	5.8	17.9
1967	35,913.9	4,396.8	2,149.5	6,546.3	12.2	6.0	18.2
1968	42,467.0	5,323.8	2,580.1	7,903.9	12.5	6.1	18.6
1969	49,319.3	6,455.4	3,090.2	9,545.6	13.1	6.3	19.4
1970	58,340.0	7,707.7	3,539.8	11,247.5	13.2	6.1	19.3
1971	66,950.0	8,827.5	4,074.8	12,902.3	13.2	6.1	19.3

Exhibit 1 (continued)

C. YEAR-TO-YEAR CHANGES IN THE MONEY SUPPLY (YEN IN 100 MILLION)

FY (Apr 1– Mar 31)	Currency and Deposits (M1)			Time and Savings Deposits			M2 Total	Change	Change %
	Outstanding	Change	Change %	Outstanding	Change	Change %			
1952	15,861	3,240	—						
1953	18,381	2,520	15.9						
1954	18,936	555	3.0						
1955	21,487	2,551	13.5						
1956	25,731	4,244	19,8						
1957	26,787	1,056	4.1						
1958	30,000	3,213	12.0						
1959	34,971	4,971	16.6						
1960	41,460	6,489	18.6	61,783	—	—	103,243	—	—
1961	49,094	7,634	18.4	73,654	11,871	19.2	122,748	19,505	18.9
1962	57,252	8,158	16.6	89,686	16,032	21.8	146,938	24,190	19.7
1963	77,029	19,777	34.5	109,650	19,964	22.3	186,679	39,741	27.0
1964	87,044	10,015	13.0	128,181	18,531	16.9	215,225	28,546	15.3
1965	102,874	15,830	18.2	151,070	22,889	17.9	253,944	38,719	18.0
1966	117,162	14,288	13.9	178,065	26,995	17.9	295,227	41,283	16.3
1967	133,688	16,526	14.1	207,289	29,224	16.4	340,977	45,750	15.5
1968	151,550	17,862	13.4	239,988	32,699	15.8	391,538	50,561	14.8
1969	182,825	31,275	20.6	281,173	41,185	17.2	463,998	72,460	18.5
1970	213,595	30,770	16.8	328,778	47,605	16.9	542,373	78,375	17.0
1971	276,931	63,336	29.7	397,051	68,273	20.8	673,982	131,609	24.3

SOURCES: Part A: Bank of Japan [2(1972), p. 178: table 102] and OECD [16(July 1964), p. 35]. Part B: Japan Ministry of Finance [8(1971), qus. 3 and 4, p. 9: table A2]. Part C: Bank of Japan [2(1966), p. 11: table 7; (1968), p. 11: table 7 and (1973), p. 11: table 7].

a Includes revenue from taxes and stamps, government monopoly and other. Borrowings and surplus from the preceding year, as included in the officially reported figures, have been deducted from columns 2 and 4.

b After deductions for overlap between the general and special accounts. The latter numbered about 40, of which the most important were the foodstuff control program, various insurance and trust funds, and the transfer account for national taxes shared with local governments.

c In commenting on this surplus, the OECD stated, "It should be borne in mind . . . that for a substantial part this surplus corresponds to the accumulation of assets by typical savings institutions (like the Welfare Insurance, the [government-operated] Post Office Life Insurance, etc.)" [16].

d Following the "Dodge Line," the national budget was substantially balanced up to the "depression" year of 1965, but not thereafter.

e Of which ¥47,452 million, or 0.6 percent, was foreign-held.

As shown by the figures in Exhibit 4, the application of tight money might be followed more or less promptly by a period in which growth dropped so low as to constitute recession by Japanese standards. Of these downswings, that of 1965 was especially notable because of the remedial action it evoked: "For the first time in the postwar period, fiscal policy (rather than monetary policy) was resorted to as the prime component of economic administration" [9, p. 13]. Thus, the Dodge-given precept of balancing the budget was formally abandoned at this time. Thereafter, the national debt rose each year, with the biggest jump coming in 1971—another year of recession.

Exhibit 2

Changes in the Official Discount Rate and Other Major Short-term Interest Rates, 1955–1971

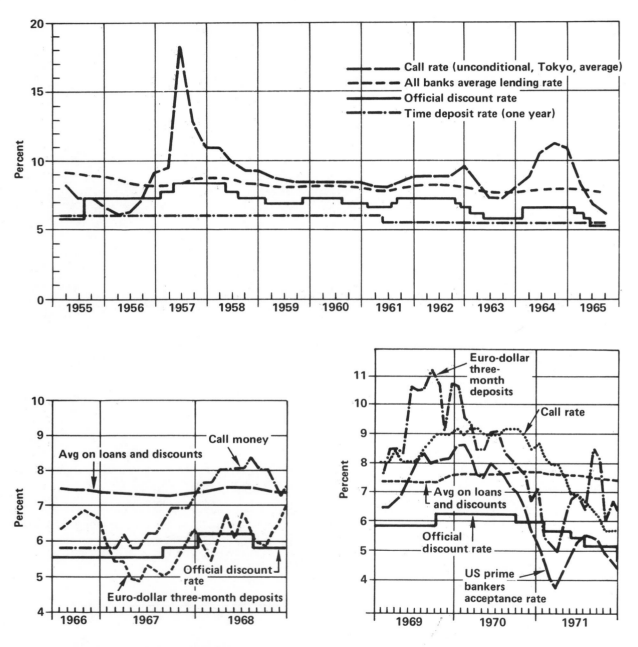

SOURCE: Bank of Japan data, cited OECD [16(Dec. 1965), p. 27; 16(Aug. 1969), p. 36; 16(June 1972), p. 24].
Reprinted with permission.

Exhibit 3

Tight Money Policy and Key Statistics

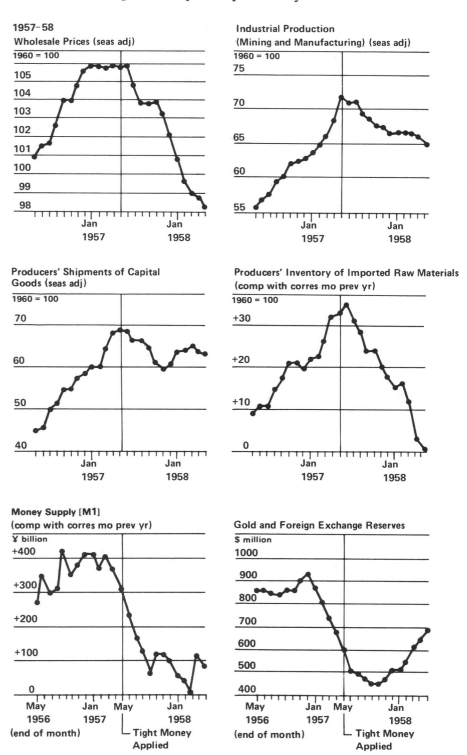

Exhibit 3 (continued)

1961–62
Wholesale Prices (seas adj)

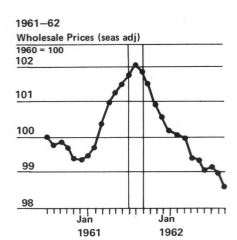

Industrial Production
(Mining and Manufacturing) (seas adj)

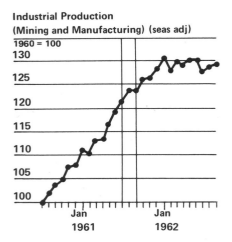

Producers' Shipments of Capital
Goods (seas adj)

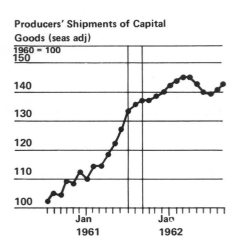

Producers' Inventory of Imported Raw Materials
(comp with corres mo prev yr)

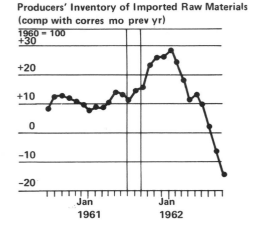

Money Supply [M1]
(comp with corres mo prev yr)

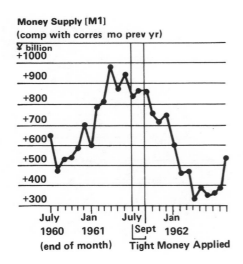

Gold and Foreign Exchange Reserves

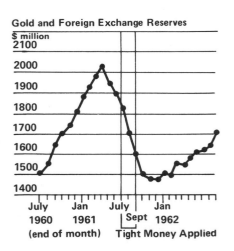

Exhibit 3 (continued)

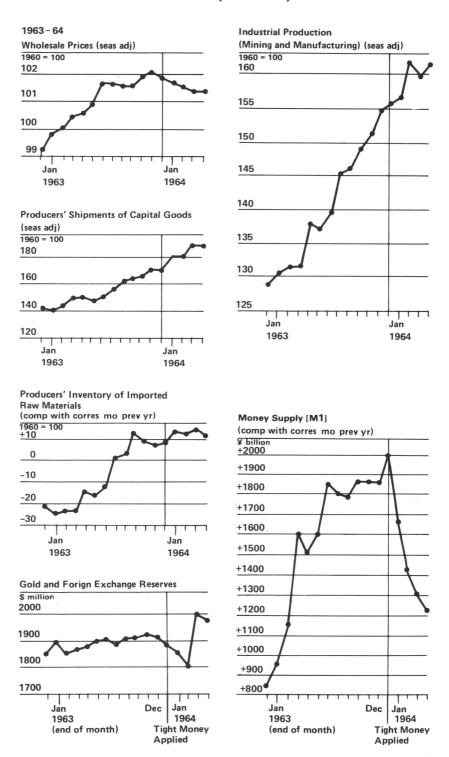

SOURCE: Bank of Japan [3, pp. 65, 67, 69].

Exhibit 4

Upswings and Downswings in GNP, 1952–1971

Cycles	Movement	Dates	Quarters	Annualized Change Ratios
1	Upswing	1951 IV–1954 II	10	+12.4[a]
	Downswing	1954 II–1954 III	1	−8.0
2	Upswing	1954 III–1957 II	11	+13.5[a]
	Downswing	1957 II–1958 II	4	[b]
3	Upswing	1958 II–1961 IV	14	+17.1[a]
	Downswing	1961 IV–1962 IV	4	+2.5
4	Upswing	1962 IV–1963 II	2	+13.5
	Upswing	1963 II–1963 IV	2	+18.3
	....			
	Downswing	1964 IV–1965 IV	4	+3.7
5	Upswing	1965 IV–1966 II	2	+13.9
	Upswing	1966 II–1966 IV	2	+11.4
	....			
	Upswing	1969 III–1970 III	4	+12.7
	Downswing	1970 III–1971 IV	5	+3.9

SOURCES: From "A Century of Japanese Growth" by K. Ohkawa and H. Rosovsky, Tables 1 and 2, pp. 89, 90, and adapted from Table 1 of H. T. Patrick, "Cyclical Instability and Fiscal-Monetary Policy in Postwar Japan" in W. Lockwood (ed.) [13, p. 572] (copyright © 1965 by Princeton University Press). Reprinted by permission of Princeton University Press. OECD [16(June 1972), p. 7; 16(July 1973), p. 8], reprinted by permission.

NOTE: Based on constant prices.

[a] Total percentage change for the period divided by the number of years. The quarterly figures have been seasonally adjusted.

[b] Computed by one source as −4.0, by another as +4.4.

PLACATING TRADE PARTNERS

Besides "superheating," a second major problem that resulted from Japan's unparalleled growth was confrontation with trade partners. So long as Japan was a small factor in world trade and one beset with chronic balance-of-payments problems, trade partners and world international organizations did not challenge her practice of supplementing tariffs with quantitative controls on imports and restricting foreign investment. By the later 1950s, however, Japan's share of world trade was going up and her over-all balance was often in the black. Under these conditions, trade partners were demanding that Japan "liberalize" her administrative restraints.

By 1960 this pressure had become so strong that Japan decided to comply. This was not an easy choice to make, however, and MITI decided that something should be done at the same time to strengthen the position of home industry. Japanese fears and responses—including a new supportive program that MITI attempted to push through—were described by the Ministry itself in a 1974 publication, *The Industry of Japan*:

The year 1960 was filled with upheavals and important changes in policy direction.

The general plan for liberalization was announced, and Prime Minister Ikeda published his Income Doubling Plan which proposed a policy of very rapid economic expansion. The threat of liberalization acted to encourage heavy investments to improve productivity and modernize sectors likely to be affected by gradual reduction of import protection provisions. Clear evidence of this can be seen in the rapid increase in imports of foreign technology after 1960. The psychology of maintaining and increasing market share at all costs was brought to a feverish pitch. The ratio of producers' durable goods to the Gross National Product rose in the years following 1960, particularly rapidly in 1961. This boom in investment, amid mixed feelings of prosperity and imminent external threat, resulted in [a general economic] boom. Japan's rate of improvement in capital equipment, improvement in labor productivity and improvement in relative export price position proceeded at a rapid pace. During this period new entrants in many industrial fields appeared and rates of industrial concentration in synthetic fibers, chemicals, automobiles and steel declined in consequence. The ratios of debt to equity increased during this period of rapid investment.

The events of this period acted to deepen the sense of urgency which was felt within the Ministry of International Trade and Industry, which had the responsibility for administering the liberalization policy. At about the same time the European Economic Community was formed and showed evidence of success. This drew the attention of [the] world, but created a sense of isolation and uneasiness in Japan. The strong competitive instinct for competing economically with Europe and the United States resulted in soul-searching inquiries into exactly how and why Japan differed from those countries. The inquiry ranged widely, from specific products, to examination of the structure of industries and the economy itself. . . .

As a result of this inquiry, which involved businessmen, academicians, government officials and others, a policy of government business cooperation was developed. The legal expression of this was to be the Temporary Measures Law for the Encouragement of Selected Industries. This legislation accepted the principle of competition within a capitalist society as basic, but also recognized the fact that there are many industries and sets of circumstances where competition must be limited. In these cases it is appropriate to provide a meeting ground for government, business and financial institutions where the proper direction of the economy can be discussed and a consensus reached. The function of this consensus is to supplement the shortcomings of the principle of free competition. Due to problems of misunderstanding, sectionalism and political bargaining, this legislation was never passed [11, pp. 25, 26].

MITI's failure to win passage of its Law for the Encouragement of Selected Industries had a number of effects. One was on the ministry itself, which thereby lost its bid to perpetuate the power it would be losing when liberalization undermined its earlier legal right to determine which industries—and even firms—would be granted access to controlled foreign imports. Another result was that alternative means would be devised to protect Japan's industries from the full effect of liberalization. One analyst of these events (Leon Hollerman) coined the term "countermeasures" to apply to Japan's varied moves in this direction.

Trade Liberalization and Countermeasures

Despite the loss of MITI's bid to provide "encouragement" to chosen industries, import liberalization moved forward. In fact, according to MITI, between 1960 and 1963 it proceeded faster than at first intended. But the move stopped short of being complete, and countermeasures helped to cut its impact.

Japan's method of trade liberalization involved the progressive transfer of more and more products from her most restricted im-

Exhibit 5

Japanese and Comparative Prices

A. INDEX OF SELECTED JAPANESE WHOLESALE PRICES FOR ALL COMMODITIES AND BASIC COMMODITY GROUPS (1965 = 100)

Year	All Commod	Chng fr Prev Year (%)	Non-Mfg Prods	Food-stuffs	*Products of Manufacturing*					
					Larger Enter-prises	Smaller Enter-prises	Combined	Textiles	Mach & Equip	Chemcls, Etc
1956	99.6	+4.4	84.7	86.3	—	—	105.4	113.1	104.1	116.7
1957	102.6	+3.0	89.9	88.8	—	—	107.0	105.5	111.2	116.6
1958	95.9	−6.5	85.8	88.1	—	—	98.9	96.4	107.1	108.5
1959	96.9	+1.0	86.1	88.6	—	—	100.4	98.5	105.9	105.7
1960	97.9	+1.0	88.0	90.4	—	—	100.9	98.5	105.5	105.7
1961	98.9	+1.0	92.3	91.2	—	—	100.9	99.3	103.9	103.1
1962	97.3	−1.6	92.0	91.3	—	—	98.9	96.9	102.4	99.6
1963	99.0	+1.7	95.9	97.1	—	—	100.0	105.9	101.1	98.1
1964	99.2	+0.2	96.8	96.6	—	—	100.0	102.9	100.1	99.4
1965	100.0	+0.8	100.0	100.0	100.0	100.0	100.0	100.0	100.0	100.0
1966	102.4	+2.4	105.7	103.6	101.0	103.9	101.7	101.3	100.4	97.1
1967	104.3	+1.9	110.3	105.4	101.1	108.3	102.9	107.3	100.9	95.7
1968	105.1	+0.8	114.1	110.9	100.5	111.0	103.2	108.3	101.1	93.8
1969	107.4	+2.2	117.5	116.0	101.6	114.7	105.2	106.7	101.0	92.7
1970	111.3	+3.6	119.1	118.4	104.6	122.9	109.6	112.9	102.5	93.3
1971	110.5	−0.7	118.4	123.0	103.0	124.2	108.8	111.7	102.7	93.3

B. INDEX OF COMPARATIVE WHOLESALE PRICES (1963 = 100)

Year	Japan	US	France[a]	W Ger	Italy	UK[b]
1966	103	106	107	105	107	108
1967	105	106	105	104	106	107
1968	106	108	101	99	107	117
1969	109	113	113	101	111	121
1970	112	117	129	107	119	126
1971	112	121	129	112	123	132

Exhibit 5 (continued)

C. PERCENTAGE CHANGE, CONSUMER, EXPORT, AND IMPORT PRICES

Period	Japan	US	France	W Ger	Italy	UK
			Consumer Prices			
1960–72						
Annual Avg	5.8	2.9	4.3	3.1	4.2	4.7
1970	7.7	5.9	5.2	3.4	4.9	6.4
1971	6.3	4.3	5.5	5.3	4.8	9.4
			Export Prices (US $ basis)			
1960–72						
Annual Avg	0.8	2.2	2.5	3.6	1.8	2.5
1970	5.6	5.7	3.2	10.6	3.8	7.5
1971	3.1	3.2	6.0	7.5	6.3	7.2
			Import Prices (US $ basis)			
1960–72						
Annual Avg	1.3	2.3	1.6	2.1	2.1	1.8
1970	2.9	7.1	3.6	7.8	3.3	4.3
1971	2.8	5.2	3.8	3.8	6.4	6.2

SOURCES: Part A: Bank of Japan [2(1971), p. 249: table 142(2)]. Part B: Japan Ministry of Foreign Affairs [10(1972), p. 63]. Part C: U.S., Council on International Economic Policy [21(1977), p. 140: table 4].

[a] Domestic goods.

[b] Basic materials.

port category to one of her two less restricted categories. Under this definition of liberalization (which the OECD agreed to accept), Japan claimed that by September 1963 imports were already "92%" liberalized. This, however, was deemed an overstatement. The OECD formula by which this ratio was computed ignored products not traded in 1959; on the more "reasonable" basis of dividing liberalized imports by total imports, Professor Hollerman recomputed the ratio in 1964 as closer to 85 percent than 93 percent [6, pp. 226–239 *passim*].

Besides stopping short of a full liberalization of imports, Japan also took countermeasures to mitigate the impact of such moves as she made. MITI's proposed law

may have failed, but sundry other *ad hoc* arrangements were used to cut the risks of liberalization. These countermeasures included (1) at least temporary tariff increases on products whose liberalization was being most urgently demanded; (2) provisions for an "emergency tariff which could be invoked when 'increased imports of foreign goods injure or are seriously likely to injure' domestic industries"; (3) occasional provisions for paying over import duties as a subsidy to domestic producers; (4) the practice of rebating to domestic manufacturers any tariffs paid on imported raw materials used in the production of exports; and (5) the practice of demanding that importers make an "advance deposit" on the value of any goods to be brought in at the time of applying for the import license. Since this deposit, which varied selectively by type of product, could run as high as 35 percent, this device was seen as "particularly effective in Japan's chronically 'tight-money' circumstances" [6, pp. 234, 235, 244–249].

In addition to these general countermeasures, industries threatened by liberalization might be given a form of protection more specific to their needs. For example, when foreign movies were liberalized, the movie houses specializing in such films were asked to show domestic films for a certain portion of the year. When auto imports were considered for liberalization, "MITI decided to forestall 'excessive sales competition' by limiting the amount of funds that could be brought into Japan for the financing of installment automobile sales" [6, pp. 258, 259].

A program thus conducted did not appease trade partners. One way to push Japan to move faster was to question the method she was using to hold down the imports of products that were still subject to controls. This became feasible when, in 1963, Japan was pressed to accept the full obligations associated with her membership in the International Monetary Fund (IMF). At year's end the IMF informed her that, "as an Article 8 member she could no longer justify on grounds of defending the balance of payments . . . the maintenance of exchange controls on current transactions" [6, p. 238].

This ploy produced few substantive results. Japan responded to the letter of the IMF complaint by switching her method of import control from import "budgets" (which imposed restrictions on "payments") to import "quotas" (which ended the need to restrict payments by restricting transactions instead) [18(1971), pp. 76, 77]. In any event, by 1970 Japan's "liberalization ratio" for imports had not yet risen to 95 percent—or by two percentage points since 1964 [6, pp. 228–234].

Capital Liberalization and Countermeasures

Prevailing on Japan to become a full member of the IMF in 1963 enabled trade partners to bring still another type of pressure upon her—this time to liberalize the restraints imposed upon the movement of short-term capital for dividend payments abroad, etc. Henceforth, if a foreign company had ventured to invest on a "yen basis" (that is, without the validation or licensing that would permit it to repatriate its profits in its own currency), Japan now had to agree to furnish foreign exchange for this purpose. At the same time, however, Japan brought all future foreign investment—yen-based as well as other—under her system of investment controls. As the minister of finance put it, "Although Japan may be forced to open the front door, she cannot be prevented from closing the back door" [6, p. 276].

Another loophole closed at the time of the 1963 liberalization was one by which companies already established in Japan could open additional wholly-owned branches simply by sending a "notice" to the government stating that the branch had been established. Henceforth such companies were to file a report regarding their intentions, and firms discovered that they were well advised to take no further action until this report had been formally accepted; otherwise, they might find that the Ministry of Finance would not let the overseas head office send its Japanese branches any funds or even any free technology, both being actions that from now on would require a license [6, pp. 277, 278].

After these adjustments of 1963, no important liberalization of investment took place until 1967, when—under increasing foreign pressure—Japan announced a four-step program to be carried out in the next few years. The main thrust of the change was to ease foreign investment in new firms in an expanding list of industries: when an industry was placed in "Category A," foreign ownership would receive "automatic" sanction up to a level of 50 percent; when in "Category B," up to 100 percent. At the same time, foreign firms got a new list of guidelines. For example, "Avoid concentration . . . in specific industries; avoid suppressing small enterprises when entering into industries characterized by small firms; avoid entering into unduly restrictive arrangements with parent companies abroad and do not resort to unreasonable restrictions concerning transactions or to unfair competition; take positive steps toward developing Japanese technology . . .; appoint Japanese to the board of directors and to management . . . ; avoid closures of plants or mass dismissal . . . ; conform to government economic policy" [5, p. 279].

The first step in the new liberalization program was to list 33 industries in Category A (up to 50 percent foreign ownership of new firms) and 17 industries in Category B (up to 100 percent foreign ownership). Foreigners were not impressed: three months after this initial step was taken, foreigners had made "not a single application" to enter any of the designated fields. As the English-language *Industrial Review of Japan* put it, "The reason for this is simple. The fifty categories liberalized are those in which domestic enterprises are firmly in control of the market" [7(1968), p. 13]. Similarly, after the second round of liberalization, which occurred in March 1969, only nine industries had attracted entrants after sixteen months [5, p. 285].

Under increasing pressure from abroad and with much debate at home, the third liberalization of investment, which took place in September 1970, was more generous. It increased the number of industries in Category A to 447 and those in Category B to 77 for a total of 524 (compared with 154 in round two) [15, p. 141]. In addition, limits on foreign stockholding in existing firms were raised, the new ceilings being 7 per-

cent for an individual, 15 percent for all foreigners in "restricted" industries and "under 25% in other industries" [15, p. 142].

Foreigners remained dissatisfied, however, with both the general scope of the program and the exclusion of certain industries, including computers, automobiles, and distribution [5, p. 285]. In this last area, foreign complaints went beyond demands for freer entry, and foreigners increasingly pointed out that it was hard to sell through Japanese channels because of such factors as multiple layers of wholesalers, resultant high mark-ups, the large number of sometimes weak retailers, and the close and varied ties binding the domestic links of the production-distribution chain.

Market Share and Trade Balances

Regardless of Japan's concessions to trade partners, her share of their imports rose substantially in the 1960s. By the turn of the decade, moreover, her trade balance had become strongly and persistently favorable, with a great leap forward in 1971. Exhibits 6 and 7 show Japan's trade relationships with the United States, her chief trade partner, and also with the European Economic Community (EEC).

More comprehensively, Japan's over-all balance of payments was jumping to its highest recorded figure, and foreign exchange reserves were piling up to record levels. Again, the trend was in sharp contrast to what was happening to the United States (*see* Exhibit 8).

Partners' Retaliatory Measures

The United States had not sat idly by while this imbalance developed. Thus, from 1965

Exhibit 6

Japanese Trade Relations 1960–1971 with the US ($ millions)

	1960	1961	1962	1963	1964	1965	1966	1967	1968	1969	1970	1971
Total Japan exports (A)	4,055	4,236	4,916	5,452	6,673	8,452	9,776	10,442	12,972	15,990	19,318	24,019
Japan US exports (B)	1,102	1,067	1,400	1,507	1,842	2,479	2,969	3,012	4,086	4,958	5,940	7,495
Total US imports (C)	15,073	14,761	16,464	17,072	18,749	21,427	25,618	26,889	33,226	36,043	39,952	45,563
B/A (in percent)	27.2	25.2	28.5	27.6	27.6	29.3	30.4	28.8	31.5	31.0	30.7	31.2
B/C (in percent)	7.3	7.2	8.5	8.8	9.8	11.6	11.6	11.2	12.3	13.8	14.9	16.4
Trade balance of Japan with US	−452	−1,028	−408	−570	−494	+113	+311	−200	+559	+868	+38	+2,517

SOURCES: Bank of Japan [2(1972), pp. 191–193: table 112]; United Nations [20(1972), pp. 398–400: table 146].

Exhibit 7

Japanese Trade Relations 1960–1971 with the EEC ($ millions)

	1960	1961	1962	1963	1964	1965	1966	1967	1968	1969	1970	1971
Total Japan exports (A)	4,055	4,236	4,916	5,452	6,673	8,452	9,776	10,442	12,972	15,990	19,318	24,018
Japan EC exports (B)	175	215	275	330	365	485	600	550	687	968	1,303	1,635
Total EC imports (C)	29,610	32,180	35,790	40,430	44,920	49,150	53,650	55,070	61,990	75,580	88,270	99,070
B/A (in percent)	4.3	5.1	5.6	6.1	5.5	5.7	6.1	5.3	5.3	6.1	6.7	6.8
B/C (in percent)	0.6	0.7	0.8	0.8	0.8	1.0	1.1	1.0	1.1	1.3	1.5	1.7
Trade balance of Japan with EEC	−355	−101	−70	−63	−79	+93	+149	−109	−50	+148	+186	+497

SOURCES: Bank of Japan [2(1972), pp. 191–193: table 112]; United Nations [20(1972), pp. 398–400: table 146].

Exhibit 8

Over-all Balance of Payments and International Reserves of Japan and the US, 1967–1971 (US $ billions)

	1967	1968	1969	1970	1971
Over-all balance					
Japan	−0.6	+0.9	+0.8	+1.0	+7.7
US	−3.6	+1.7	+2.7	−10.7	−22.7
Reserves (year-end)[a]					
Japan	2.0	2.9	3.7	4.8	15.4
US	14.8	15.7	17.0	14.5	13.2

SOURCES: Bank for International Settlements [1(1969), p. 80; 1(1971), p. 92; 1(1972), p. 86]; United Nations [20(1972), pp. 643–646: table 191].

[a] Gold, foreign exchange, SDRs, etc.

through 1969 as many as 15 Japanese commodities had been "slapped with dumping charges" [18(1971), pp. 75, 76], while by 1967 Japan had been prevailed on to adopt so-called "orderly marketing" arrangements whereby she voluntarily limited her exports to the US of some 70 or more products [6, pp. 207–218].

Meanwhile, the US also became increasingly critical of Japan's failure to move toward fuller liberalization of both goods and capital imports. It showed "deepest concern" about automobiles and distribution in 1970 and computers in 1971 [5, pp. 285, 287], but also showed concern about certain agricultural products (beef, fruit juice, oranges, and miscellaneous beans [7(1972), p. 13]. Conflicts over such areas ran deep. The US depended heavily on agriculture and high-technology products for exports, but Japan regarded agriculture as a "weak" sector that had to be protected—especially inasmuch as she was asking farmers to diversify away from rice, which was in surplus, into new products. She regarded computers as an especially valuable "infant" industry, one that would help her to progress from her postwar emphasis on heavy industries to some even more desirable fields that she referred to as "knowl-

edge-intensive." These fields appealed to Japan not only as the most advanced but also as the least dependent on imported raw materials [5, pp. 174, 184, 189; 7(1972), pp. 11, 13, 14].

Besides the US, other trade partners were also irate with Japan, particularly the developing nations. As exporters, these countries had suffered from a long cyclical movement toward low prices for raw materials, which had been especially helpful to Japan. As candidates for aid from more advanced nations, they had received little from Japan compared to what they saw as her capacity to give. (Aid averaged only about 0.70 percent of her GNP for 1967–1969.) Moreover, Japan's aid had been accompanied by relatively "severe" conditions, as the Japanese themselves admitted [18(1971), pp. 79, 81]. As for trading partners in Europe, these had long taken measures to control imports from Japan, and for this and other reasons took a relatively small share of her exports [5, pp. 174, 175, 186–188]. Even so, European countries joined in the general alarm as the EFTA-EEC trade deficit with Japan rose from about $0.25 billion in 1969 to almost $1.0 billion in 1971 [5 pp. 164, 175, 186; 7(1972), p. 7].

Three US Demands

Against this backdrop of wide-ranging criticism, between 1968 and 1971 the United States made three specific remedial proposals. One was that Japan limit textile exports to the US market; another was that Japan revalue the yen; and the third was that Japan adopt a new growth strategy—one focused elsewhere than on export industries.

Textiles—and Okinawa. By January 1969, President Richard M. Nixon and Premier Eisaku Sato had both made pledges to the electorate that neither could fulfill without the other's help. In his recent election campaign, Nixon had promised to secure a reduction of Japan's textile exports to the United States; Sato had promised to secure the return of the Ryukyu Islands to Japan, especially the principal island, Okinawa. So long as this remained under US occupation, it was a constant source of embarrassment to Sato, for socialists and radical students might mount a riot whenever they heard of a crime committed by an Occupation soldier, of US stockpiling of poison gas, or other similar incidents. Neither government, of course, spoke of a "deal" involving textiles and Okinawa, but journalists noted that the two were "intertwined."

Hoping to make good on his promise about textiles, President Nixon dispatched three high-level economic missions to Japan between May and October 1969, two of them headed by Secretary of Commerce Maurice Stans. Each of them returned with no success on textiles, after publicly voicing "disappointment" [14(May 11, 1969); (May 13, 1969); (July 29, 1969); (July 31, 1969); (Oct. 7, 1969); and (Oct. 8, 1969)].

At this point, Nixon took over. Sato was invited to Washington, where he conferred with Nixon for two days. A later account of this meeting was reported in the *New York Times*.

On the first day, according to authoritative Japanese sources, the President conceded to Mr. Sato all the points he desired. The next day, however, the President took up economic problems, specifically that of textiles. . . .

A grateful Mr. Sato apparently replied that he would do his best to solve this problem, an undertaking that the President accepted as a commitment to restrict textile shipments to the U.S. by a government-to-government agreement [14(Aug. 4, 1971)]. © 1971 by The New York Times Company. Reprinted by permission.

When it soon emerged that Sato did not view his statement in this light, Nixon was reportedly much angered [14(Aug. 4, 1971)], with results that later helped to cause Sato's downfall. Meanwhile, the textile issue remained. Nixon next tried new trade legislation, but Congress wanted to extend import quotas in a manner he felt to be unwarranted, so this effort was abandoned. Eventually, it was the US Senate that resolved the textile issue. It refused to ratify the treaty for the return of Okinawa until US officials became convinced that the Sato government had "finally lived up to an informal understanding" to limit textile imports in exchange [14(Oct. 16, 1971)]. Once this happened, the treaty was ratified by 84 to 6 in less than a month, on November 5, 1971 [14(Nov. 6, 1971)].

Revaluation. While the issue of textile exports hung fire in 1970 and 1971, the United States and other trading partners began to press for a more far-reaching solution to the problem of Japan's trade imbalance. This was revaluation of the yen.

Since having an undervalued currency "has been compared to being downwind in a sailing ship race" [19, p. 69], Japan was determined not to yield this advantage. Rather, she sought alternative approaches. Thus, in June 1971 an eight-point program was adopted, entitled "Eight Items of Urgent Policy Measures to Avoid Yen Revaluation." In line with this goal, Japan had taken a number of steps toward implementation by August:

1. She had promised to institute "Kennedy-Round" tariff reductions on 1923 items, with lower rates on 105 items than the Kennedy Round had proposed.

2. She had promised to conform to a 1970 UN decision calling for favorable treatment for developing nations.

3. She had promised to increase aid to a level of one percent of GNP.

4. She had moved to facilitate an ongoing trend toward Japanese investment abroad.

5. She had liberalized imports of goods to the point where only 60 items remained on the "Residual Import Restriction List" compared with 118 items at the end of 1969.

6. She had liberalized foreign investment in existing firms to the extent of permitting foreign individuals to hold 10 percent of a company's shares instead of 7 percent as before.

7. She had liberalized foreign investment in new firms to the point where over 500 industries were in Category A (for 50 percent foreign control) and 228 in Category B (for 100 percent foreign control), compared with the previous figures of 447 and 77 [5, pp. 8, 287; 7(1972), p. 13; 15, p. 41].

At the same time, a "negative list" approach to total investment exclusion was adopted, and only seven industries were placed on this negative list. Although the list was controversial in that it included computer manufacture, sales, and leasing, Japan soon sought to meet US objections by a cabinet-level decision.[1] Overriding industry objections, the cabinet stated that computer hardware was to be 50 percent

---

liberalized three years hence; software would be "allowed to come under individual screening"; and products such as semiconductors would be immediately decontrolled [7(1972), p. 13].

Further indication of Japan's interest in restoring balance without revaluing the yen was a MITI-sponsored proposal for an "orderly exports" program along the lines of that rejected for textiles. Being readied for completion in June 1971, this program was running into flack at home for reasons identified as follows by the *Oriental Economist* in their *Japan Economic Yearbook*:

> Some, however, are strongly opposed to the theory of "orderly marketing." One of the most important reasons for the opposition is the belief that the frictions . . . Japanese commodities are now causing in the U.S. markets are as much due to the relative decline of international competitiveness of U.S. industries involved as to the sharp increase of the export power of Japanese commodities. They maintain that the problem should be solved by the Americans themselves.
>
> The second reason is that the annual export growth levels which the Americans are likely to consider "orderly" are extremely low. To accept such low-level annual export growth ratios is to virtually stifle the economic growth of Japan.
>
> The third reason is that, once Japan accepts voluntary export controls for some commodities, they are bound to continue forever and, at the same time, have serious effects on other export commodities [18(1971), p. 75].

US Proposals for a New Strategy. In addition to all their other demands, by 1970–1971 US negotiators were using their annual trade talks with Japan to press for a still more radical solution to Japan's mounting payments surplus. This was a new industrial strategy. Specifically, the Americans urged Japan to adopt a domestically oriented growth strategy, one focused on such "nonproductive" investments as housing,

---

[1] Other industries on the list were agriculture-forestry-marine; oil refining and sales; hides and leather and their products; data processing; real estate; and chain stores in groups of more than eleven.

urban facilities, etc. Revaluation, it was pointed out, would assist rather than impede such a domestic orientation, since it would make needed imports cheaper.

Partly in response to US pressure, but partly also to appease domestic critics, various bodies in Japan began advancing somewhat similar ideas. For example, in mid-1971 the Industrial Structure Council (an advisory organ to MITI) brought out a publication titled *Trade and Industry Policies for the 1970's* in which it was proposed that Japan abandon the "'growth-for-growth' principle" in favor of seeking improvement in the quality of life. Among other changes related to this goal, government expenditures on such life-related projects as urban decongestion and environmental cleanup should go as high as $60 billion over the next decade, and R&D expenditures should expand six-fold over the same time span from $2.5 billion to $25 billion a year, as Japan prepared to shift to new, cleaner "knowledge-intensive" industries [5, pp. 52, 54].

In summing up the rationale for the proposed industrial strategy, its authors indicated that continued emphasis on "growth-for-growth's sake" not only constituted a "sacrificing of livelihood" for the people of Japan, but also might be "liable to force a similar sacrificing of livelihood of peoples of the advanced countries through international competitiveness." Thus, one objective of the plan was "promotion of harmony between Japan's economy and international economic society" [17(1972), p. 11].

The "Nixon Shocks"

As Japan pondered her strategy for appeasing both domestic and foreign critics,

time ran out on her effort to achieve these goals on her own terms. Two "shocks" hit her in July and August 1971, both occurring without prior warning.

On July 15, 1971, President Nixon announced that he would visit Communist China. This signaled a rapprochement between Japan's chief trading partner and her nearest, largest neighbor. Coming without prior consultation, this move was seen as a significant change in US–Japanese relations. Aside from the embarrassment caused to the Japanese government, the announcement was bound to be upsetting, given the fact that Japan, out of consideration for recent US efforts to isolate China, had no diplomatic relations with the mainland and did more business with the Island of Taiwan (Nationalist China) than with the much more populous Peoples' Republic.

Trade of Japan with the Two Chinas, 1971 ($ millions)

	Taiwan	Peoples' Republic of China
Exports	923.3	578.2
Imports	286.0	323.2

SOURCE: Bank of Japan [2(1972), p. 191: table 112].

Just one month later, on August 15, President Nixon announced an eight-point "dollar defense" program which suspended the convertibility of the dollar and imposed a 10 percent import surcharge on imports. While affecting US relations with all trading partners, these moves were interpreted as aimed primarily at Japan, and as aimed particularly at forcing a revaluation of the yen.

In the face of this intensified move by the United States to force revaluation, Japan first resisted by having her central bank continue to buy dollars at their existing rate of ¥360 to US $1. In spite of a deluge of dollars, this policy was continued until the ten-day cost hit about $4 billion. To avoid a continuation of this drain, the yen was allowed to start floating upward on August 28. Six weeks later, in the course of a general currency realignment (in return for which the US import surcharge was abandoned), the yen was revalued to ¥308 to the dollar. This was an increase of 16.88 percent—a margin that was "unexpectedly wide," and one that was considerably higher than the next highest increase (13.57 percent for West Germany and Switzerland) [17(Jan. 1972), p. 2].

Uncertain Outlook

Two weeks after this blow, the Japanese government announced its economic forecast for 1972: the anticipated real growth rate was put at 7.7 percent. Many observers, however, saw this forecast as "excessively optimistic." The *Oriental Economist*, for example, wrote that, "Economic circles as a whole are feeling greatly concerned over the impact of the sharp upward revaluation of the Yen rate, the first experienced in history, which has made the business outlook completely uncertain" [17(Jan. 1972), p. 3].

REFERENCES

1. Bank for International Settlements. *Annual Reports*. Basle, Switzerland.

2. Bank of Japan. *Economic Statistics Annual*. Tokyo.

3. —————. *Outline of Japanese Economy and Finance*. Tokyo, 1964.

4. "Consider Japan," *The Economist* (September 1 and 8, 1962), unsigned surveys.

5. Frank, Isaiah (ed.). *The Japanese Economy in International Perspective*. Baltimore: Johns Hopkins University Press, 1975. (A supplementary paper of the Committee for Economic Development.)

6. Hollerman, Leon. *Japan's Dependence on the World Economy: The Approach Toward Economic Liberalization*. Princeton, N.J.: Princeton University Press, 1967.

7. *Industrial Review of Japan*, editors of the Nihon Keizai Shimbun (Japan economic journal), annual.

8. Japan Ministry of Finance. *Quarterly Bulletin of Financial Statistics*. Tokyo.

9. Japan Ministry of Foreign Affairs. *Japan's Economy at the Crossroads—Thirty Years of Transition*. Tokyo, 1976.

10. —————. *Statistical Survey of the Economy of Japan*, Tokyo, annual.

11. Japan Ministry of International Trade and Industry. *The Industry of Japan*. Japan External Trade Organization. Tokyo, 1974.

12. Japan Office of the Prime Minister. *Japan Statistical Yearbook*. Tokyo, annual.

13. Lockwood, William W. (ed.). *The State and Economic Enterprise in Japan: Essays in the Political Economy of Growth*. Princeton, N.J.: Princeton University Press, 1965.

14. *New York Times*.

15. Organization for Economic Cooperation and Development. *The Industrial Policy of Japan*. Paris, 1972.

16. —————. *OECD Economic Surveys, Japan*. Paris, annual.

17. *Oriental Economist*. Tokyo, monthly.

18. Oriental Economist, *Japan Economic Yearbook*. Tokyo, annual.

19. Rolfe, Sidney E. and James L. Burtle. *The Great Wheel: The World Monetary System*. New York: McGraw-Hill, 1973.

20. United Nations. *U.N. Statistical Yearbook*, annual.

21. United States, Council on International Economic Policy. *International Economic Report of the President and Annual Report of the Council*. Washington: Government Printing Office, annual.

Japan E1: 1972–1977, Recurring Trade Imbalance and Trouble with Trade Partners

Although the 17 percent revaluation forced on Japan late in 1971 led to fears of an export downturn, these fears turned out to be groundless. In fact, an overfavorable trade balance and resulting trouble with trade partners remained a dominant problem until 1973, when it was temporarily put to rest by a domestic boom, a second forced revaluation, rising import costs and deteriorating terms of trade, a relatively vigorous bout of inflation, and—most serious of all—the oil crisis that dominated the last months of the year. After the oil cutoff of August and the fourfold oil price hike announced in December, oil-hungry Japan expected no further problems from an overfavorable balance. On the contrary, "Most of the early forecasts . . . spoke of a 'total economic collapse,' a cut in industrial output of up to 30%, runaway inflation, unemployment on an unprecedented scale, a cut in real GNP of about 10% and a spectacular increase in the external payments deficit." (The money market to some extent agreed, for the yen–dollar rate went down 6 percent in November and another 4.6 percent in January) [9(I 1974), pp. 4, 6, 7].

Before the end of 1975, however, Japan's trade surplus was on the rise again—at least with the industrial world. Along with the surplus came the familiar problems of trade partners' resentment, their demands for remedial action, and their threats of retaliation. As suggested by Japan's trade statistics, this issue was as critical in 1976 and after as it was in 1971–1972, particularly vis-à-vis the United States (see Exhibits 1–5).

Meanwhile, the trade surplus problem was not the only problem confronting Japan as the 1970s advanced (see Japan E2). Thus, inflation in 1973 was followed by stagflation in 1974, in the wake of the oil crisis. Moreover, domestic demand did not bounce back even after inflation had been licked. This meant that exports were the only buoyant sector, which, in turn, meant trouble on the home front as well as continued trouble with trade partners. Japan's response was an increasing effort to reflate, but over-all growth continued to miss target. It was slow compared with past performance and sometimes even slower than that of the West (see Exhibit 6).

Finding solutions for Japan's varied problems was the responsibility of the Liberal Democratic Party (LDP). This remained the largest single party in the Diet and it still controlled the premiership, although a long, slow decline had culminated in the loss of its lower house majority in elections held December 5, 1976. With only 249 out

Exhibit 1

Japan's Trade Balance, 1969–1977 ($ billions)

Basis[a]	1969	1970	1971	1972	1973	1974	1975	1976	1977
Payments value	3.7	4.0	7.8	8.9	3.7	1.5	5.0	9.9	17.3
Customs value	1.0	0.4	4.3	5.1	−1.4	−2.6	−2.1	2.4	9.7

SOURCE: U.S., Department of Commerce [24(Sept. 1978), p. 46: table 25].

[a] Japanese trade balances are available on two bases, both using exports fob, but using different import figures. The use of imports fob constitutes the "payments value" basis; the use of imports cif constitutes the "customs value" basis.

Exhibit 2

Japan's Foreign Trade, 1970–1974

SOURCE: OECD [17(June 1975), p. 28]. Reprinted with permission.

Exhibit 3

Japan's Foreign Trade, 1974–1978

SOURCE: OECD [17(Aug. 1978), p. 28]. Reprinted with permission.

Exhibit 4

US Trade Balance and Balance with Japan, 1971–1977 ($ billions)

US Balance[a]	1971	1972	1973	1974	1975	1976	1977
Total	−2,014	−6,384	+1,347	−2,343	+11,014	−5,875	−26,715
Balance with Japan	−3,204	−4,101	−1,363	−1,659	−1,705	−5,359	−8,101

SOURCE: U.S., Bureau of International Commerce [22(1978, no. 21), p. 5: table 2].

[a] FAS (free alongside ship) transaction value.

Exhibit 5

US Share of Japan's Exports and Imports, 1971–1977 (in percent)

US Share	1971	1972	1973	1974	1975	1976	1977
Japan's exports	31	31	26	23	20	24	24
Japan's imports							
Total imports	25	25	24	20	20	18	18
Manufactured imports	41.1	39.2	31.7	33.2	34.9	33.6	—

SOURCE: U.S., Bureau of International Commerce [22(1978, no. 21), pp. 31, 32: table 13].

Exhibit 6

Comparative Growth Rates of Real GDP or GNP (percent change)

Period	Japan	US	France[a]	Italy[a]	W Ger	UK[a]	Canada
1972–71	8.9	5.7	6.1	3.2	3.5	3.2	6.0
1973–72	10.5	5.3	5.7	5.9	5.3	5.4	6.9
1974–73	−1.3	−1.4	2.9	3.9	0.4	0.1	3.7
1975–74	1.4	−1.3	0.1	−3.5	−2.5	1.7	1.3
1976–75	6.5	5.7	5.2	5.7	5.7	3.7	5.5
1977–76	5.4	4.9	3.0[b]	1.7	2.4	1.2	2.7

SOURCE: U.S., Department of Commerce [24(Sep. 1978), p. 11 and earlier issues].
[a] GDP.
[b] IV 1977–IV 1976.

of 511 seats, the LDP was forced to depend on other conservative and center parties—including perhaps a party as far left as the Democratic Socialists. According to the Economist Intelligence Unit (EIU), the "selective support" of these parties could be expected only at the price of "substantial concessions by the government" [9(IV 1976), p. 17; 9(I 1977), pp. 7, 8].

The new premier, chosen in January 1976, would be Takeo Fukuda. Fukuda had been Eisaku Sato's "crown prince" when Sato stepped down in mid-1972, but the Nixon shocks had so far undermined Sato's influence that the LDP had rejected his nominee at that time [9(III 1972), p. 2]. Fukuda had, however, served as minister of finance or deputy premier under two immediate predecessors, Kakui Tanaka (July 1972–November 1974) and Takeo Miki (December 1974–January 1976). In describing his qualifications to shape policy for this period, Fukuda had proclaimed, "I'm not a finance man but a fireman who attacks inflation" [14(1976), p. 7].

CONTINUED EXPORT SURPLUSES, 1972

By forcing the yen up almost 17 percent at the end of 1971, US President Richard M. Nixon had hoped to put an end to the big export surplus Japan had been running with the United States. This "Nixon shock" proved unsuccessful, however. The Organization for Economic Cooperation and Development (OECD) later explained why. The first of several reasons cited was Japan's underlying relative strength: i.e., "the rapid technological progress and expansion of capacity associated with the very high rates of investment in recent years, notably in export-oriented industries" had not been fully offset in the currency upheaval of 1971 [18(1972), p. 31; (1973), pp. 25, 26]. In addition, at least in the first part of the year, some export prices did not rise in line with the higher value of the yen, either because they were denominated in dollars or because "exporters initially absorbed part of the revaluation so as to avoid large market-share losses" [18(1973), p. 32]. By the time this policy was dropped, prices had gone up elsewhere, too.

As the OECD put it, "In the second half of 1972 Japanese export prices in dollars were about 20% above their 1970 level, thereby fully reflecting the revaluation, but in terms of relative prices the deterioration was only on the order of 2%, as competitor's prices had also risen in the meantime by over 17%" [18(1973), p. 32].

US RESPONSES

The drawback to a large trade surplus was, again, trouble with trade partners, especially the United States. "What the Americans wanted," wrote the EIU in July 1972, was "a reduction in their trade deficit—currently running at an annual rate of $3.5 billion—by a cut in Japan's exports of sensitive products as well as a rapid increase in its purchases of agricultural commodities, most of which are subject to severe quota restraints" [9(III 1972), p. 9]. Besides many lower level talks about the problem, President Nixon discussed the trade imbalance with the Japanese premier in January and August, while Secretary of State Henry Kissinger brought it up in June during talks

on other matters [16(Jan. 8, 1972, June 11, 1972); 26(Jan. 7, 1972, June 12, 1972, Aug. 31, 1972)].

Apart from talking, the United States underscored its concern with Japan's trade surplus by investigating numerous charges that Japan was "dumping" some of her exports or supporting others by state subsidies (*see* Exhibit 7). While dumping would incur penalties only if US producers were found to be substantially "injured," a subsidy had to be offset with a countervailing increase in the tariff. Under these circumstances, Japan was especially upset by a mid-May announcement that the US Treasury was making a major investigation of alleged Japanese government subsidies to producers of consumer electronic products sold on the American market. According to the *Wall Street Journal*, this step was the "biggest ever taken in the 75-year history of the law on duties." It was credited with getting Japan to promise a package of concessions just a few days later [26(May 19, 1972 and May 22, 1972)].

JAPAN'S REMEDIAL MEASURES, 1972

In trying to pacify angry trade partners, Japan took a variety of steps. One was to reiterate that national priority would henceforth be assigned, not to expanding the industrial base, but to improving the quality of life. Thus, when Sato stepped down in July, the LDP passed over the conservative Fukuda (who had been Sato's "crown prince") [9(III 1972), p. 2], and gave the premiership to a colorful politician who had managed to identify himself with the quality-of-life movement in a recently published best seller. This new leader was Kakui Tanaka, a former minister of finance and former head of the powerful Ministry of International Trade and Industry (MITI); his book was *Building a New Japan, A Plan for Remodeling the Archipelago.* According to Tanaka's proposals, Japan must attack urban congestion and pollution by moving people and industries to new, decentralized, more livable cities of about 250,000 persons each, and by shifting the productive "center of gravity" from heavy, energy-consuming industries to cleaner "knowledge-intensive" types. To serve the new cities, the transportation network would have to be "revamped" and the communication network expanded. "Good housing for all" was to be provided, as well as better social services. Even rural life was to be "revitalized" pending further shrinkage of the primary sector [21, pp. 66, 67, 81–104, 180, 200, 201]. In short, Japan's growth would not be stopped, but would be redirected toward new goals that would not threaten her trade partners.

Besides these promised changes—some of which were soon reflected in a revised national plan and to some extent in the budget—a more immediate way to cut the trade surplus was to spur domestic growth, thus increasing domestic consumption of both home output and imported goods [18(1973), pp. 71–73]. In line with this thinking, monetary and fiscal policy was made increasingly expansionary during 1972, and it remained expansionary even though wholesale prices started moving up at an ever-quickening rate.[1] The EIU explained:

> . . . there is no doubt that some government circles regard an acceleration in inflation as desirable, in spite of its harmful domestic economic and social consequences. In fact, in a recent speech the Minister of International Trade and Industry went so far as to imply that a policy of "adjustment inflation" may be one of the best ways of re-

ducing the country's balance of payments surplus [9(IV 1972), p. 8].

A third approach to the trade surplus problem was to try to bring the basic balance, if not the current balance, into equilibrium. That is, Japan hoped to mollify her critics by offsetting her current surplus with a deficit in her long-term capital account. To this end, the government took a number of steps to increase capital outflows and reduce capital inflows:

> . . . Various measures were taken in 1972 to bring about a [high net capital outflow.] Firstly, the already tight capital controls on inward movements were reinforced . . . by restricting nonresident purchases of Japanese securities. Second, and more importantly, outward movements were liberalized and net bank lending abroad encouraged. Thus, between February and June, restrictions on purchases of foreign securities by banks, institutional investors and private individuals were lifted. Moreover, restrictions on the purchases of real estate abroad and foreign capital investments by Japanese companies were suppressed in June. Swap operations were concluded with the authorized foreign exchange banks and funds in foreign exchange were also deposited with them to discourage the banks from borrowing overseas. Finally, in September, government institutions and foreign exchange banks were authorized to extend foreign currency loans to Japanese investors for up to 70% of the value of their overseas direct investment. As a result, securities investment abroad and loans (largely extended by banks) rose from less than U.S. $0.8 billion in 1971 to more than U.S. $2.9 billion in 1972. . . . Private direct investment also rose sharply . . . [18(July 1973), p. 42].

Besides these measures, Japan increased her capital outflow by increasing aid to developing countries. During 1972 her total aid rose to 1.44 percent of GNP, which was well above the level reached by other countries that had joined together for this purpose as the Development Assistance Com-

---

[1] Wholesale prices were up 0.2 percent in July 1972, 0.7 percent in August, 0.9 percent in September, 1.0 percent in October, 2.3 percent in November ("the largest monthly increase in over 20 years") and about 2.0 percent in December [9(I 1973), p. 5].

Exhibit 7

Proceedings against Japan under Anti-dumping and Compensatory Duties Acts

Product or Product Group[a]	Charge	Outcome[b]
TV sets	Subsidies	Charge made (3/22/72). Charge denied (3/24/72). Orderly marketing agreement announced (4/19/72).
Heavy electrical transformers	Dumping	Injury found (4/21/72).
Steel	—	Steelmakers in Europe and Japan agree to tighten restrictions on exports (5/9/72).
Electronics products, including TV parts	Subsidy	Investigation started (5/9/72). "Step biggest in 75-year history . . . ." Inquiry broadened (6/7/72).
Miscellaneous	—	Japan maps broad plan to curb exports as foreign pressure rises (5/22/72).
Steel (stainless sheet)	Dumping	Investigation discontinued (5/30/72).
TV picture tubes	Dumping	Investigation started (6/29/72). Dumping confirmed (9/27/72). No injury found (12/27/72).
Steel (welded stainless pipe and tubing)	Dumping	Investigation started (6/29/72). Investigation dropped (8/4/72). Japan agrees to limit export rise to 18.5 percent a year (11/8/72).
Wool and polyester wool worsted fabrics	Dumping	Dumping confirmed (8/14/72). No injury found (11/27/72).
Microwave ovens	Dumping	Investigation started (9/21/72). No dumping found (4/3/73).
Steel (roller chain)	Dumping	Dumping confirmed (12/1/72). Injury found (3/2/73). Penalties assessed.
Miscellaneous	—	Japan moves to curtail consumer goods exports (1/12/73).
Electronic ceramic parts	Dumping	Investigation ended when Japanese supplier promises to charge fair value (1/31/73).
Ball bearings	—	Investigation started (2/1/73). Nixon boosts duty on about half the ball bearings US imports from Japan (4/1/74).
Plastic resin	Dumping	Investigation started (2/7/73). Dumping confirmed (10/8/73). No injury found (1/7/74).
A food additive	Dumping	Dumping confirmed (2/15/73).
Steel (wire rope)	Dumping	Dumping suspected (3/9/73). Dumping confirmed (6/7/73). Injury found (9/10/73).
Zippers	Dumping	No injury found (4/12/73).
Steel (upholstery wire)	Dumping	Investigation started (4/12/73). Investigation discontinued (8/10/73).
Synthetic rubber	Dumping	Investigation started (6/14/73). Injury found and duties imposed (11/2/73).
Miscellaneous	—	Japan allowing curbs on exports of 20 major products to expire (8/21/73).
Unpowered hand tools	Dumping	Investigation started (9/25/73). Dumping confirmed on some (6/21/74 and 9/5/75). Denied (6/24/74). No injury found on some (10/23/74 and 12/4/75). Precision types found not dumped (6/5/75).
TV sets	Dumping	Duties previously imposed under anti-dumping act are upheld in court (10/10/74). Sony wins exemption (8/5/74).
Portable electric typewriters	Dumping	Investigation started (3/20/74). Dumping confirmed (3/20/75). No injury found (6/23/75).

Exhibit 7 (continued)

Product or Product Group[a]	Charge	Outcome[b]
Roller bearings	Dumping	Investigation under way (6/5/74). Dumping confirmed (9/6/74). Injury found likely (1/27/75).
TV sets and consumer electronic products	Subsidies and violations of antitrust laws	Suits filed by Magnavox (8/10/74), Zenith (9/23/74), and others. Treasury finds compensating duties not due (2/5/75 and 1/6/76). ITC investigates charges of unfair competition (3/30/76). Suspends two of three investigations (12/14/76). Customs Court reverses Treasury and orders countervailing duties (4/13/77), but US will appeal ruling (4/13/77). Ruling reversed (7/29/77).
Ball bearings (radial)	Dumping	Investigation started (12/20/74). Major Japanese producer promised 10 percent price increase (2/27/75). No extra duty to be levied (6/23/75).
Wooden door parts	Dumping	Investigation started (1/13/75). Dumping and injury found. Penalties ordered (1/4/76).
Rechargeable batteries	Dumping	Investigation started (1/24/75).
Alternating current adapter	Dumping	Investigation started (10/7/75).
Steel (stainless flatware)	Dumping	Injury found and penalties imposed (3/3/76).
Synthetic rubber	Dumping	Injury not found (3/30/76).
Above-ground pools	Dumping	Dumping charged (4/21/76). Investigation dropped (12/28/76).
Steel	—	US President Ford approves three-year import quotas on specialty steels (6/8/76).
Nuts, bolts, screws	Subsidies	Investigation started (6/11/76). "Tentative" finding (10/27/76). Extra duties imposed (5/6/77).
Acrylic sheet	Dumping	Injury found (7/28/76).
Steel (stainless pipe and tube)	Unfair competition	Curb sought by eight US makers (10/27/76). Investigation ordered (2/2/77).
Bicycles	Subsidies	Subsidies confirmed (10/27/76).
Saccharin	Dumping	Investigation started (12/2/76). Dumping found in some cases, not others (9/15/77).
Steel	—	Japanese steel makers urge voluntary curbs (2/28/77, 4/18/77, 5/27/77).
TV sets	—	Japan offers orderly marketing agreement on TV (4/8/77). Accord delayed (4/11/77). Accord reached (5/23/77).
Motorcycles	Dumping	Charge made (6/8/77). Investigation started (7/15/77).
Nuts, bolts, screws	Dumping	Investigation of injury started (6/23/77).
Certain chemical products	Dumping	Charge brought (8/18/77).
Steel	Subsidy	Case pending in Customs Court (7/29/77).
Steel (wide range of products)	Dumping	Charge made by US Steel (9/21/77).
Steel (plate)	Dumping	Dumping confirmed for five Japanese producers (10/4/77).
Steel (carbon)	Dumping	Investigation started (10/20/77).
Steel (wire strand)	Dumping	Investigation started (11/23/77).
Steel	—	Reference price system announced (see text).

SOURCE: *Wall Street Journal Index* [27(1972–77)].

[a] Not a complete report. These entries are limited to those reported in the *Wall Street Journal Index*.

[b] Under the Anti-dumping Act, no penalty could be imposed without a finding of injury. Under the Compensatory Duties Act, however, penalties had to be imposed if the Treasury found that subsidies had been paid to the exporter. Following strengthening of this Act in 1974, the number of cases brought under it greatly increased.

mittee (DAC) of the OECD (*see* Exhibit 8). In commenting on Japanese aid, however, one observer noted that quantitatively it had "caught up" but "its quality [was] still very poor," with little being given in the form of grants, interest rates on loans being relatively high, and a "large proportion" taking the form of export credits tied to purchases of Japanese goods [14(1977), p. 18].

A fourth approach to the trade surplus problem was to take direct measures to expand imports. The OECD summarized as follows:

> The growth of imports in 1972 has been stimulated by a series of import liberalization measures taken by the government in both 1971 and 1972. The number of items subject to residual import restrictions was reduced from 90 at the end of 1970 to 40 in

Exhibit 8

Japan's Aid Performance

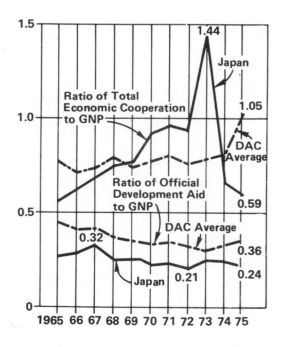

SOURCE: *Industrial Review of Japan* [14(1977), p. 42]. Reprinted with permission.

1971,[2] and to 33 in May 1972, of which 9 are manufactured goods and 24 agricultural and fishery products. . . . Moreover, in November 1972, existing quotas were increased by 30%, with quotas smaller than the equivalent of 7% of domestic consumption being enlarged to the 7% level. Tariff cuts on 238 items were implemented in April 1972[3] and in November an across-the-board 20% cut was decided for 1,865 items.[4] However, seasonal tariffs were imposed or tariff rates increased on certain commodities that were freed from quantitative restrictions. Other measures included the abolition of the import deposit system, improved conditions for import financing (including a reduction of the interest rate), and a simplification of importing procedures. Action was also taken to investigate imports under the sole agent system, with a view to restrain monopoly practices and to pass on to consumers the lower yen costs of imported goods. The prices of wheat, barley and cigarettes, which are imported exclusively by the government, were also reduced [18(1973), p. 40].

Still another move to increase imports was a September 1972 promise to purchase $1.1 billion of "emergency" supplies from the US:

> Following President Nixon's talks with Mr. Tanaka in September, Japan agreed to

---

[2] Products on which import quotas were removed in 1971 included light aircraft, certain computer and radio equipment, light and heavy oil, and sulphur. The value of these imports in 1970 was about $90 million [26(Feb. 10, 1972 and May 22, 1972)].

[3] The April 1972 tariff cuts were 5 to 10 percent. The principal imports affected were soybean products ($330 million in 1970) and computers, computer equipment, machine tools and film ($215 million in 1970) [26(Feb. 10, 1972 and May 22, 1972)].

[4] The items affected by the November 1972 tariff cuts were industrial, mining, and processed agricultural products, not the raw materials that accounted for the bulk of Japan's imports [26(Oct. 23, 1972)]. The cuts were predicted to reduce the trade surplus by $500 to $600 million, but this estimate was widely regarded as "unduly optimistic" [9(I 1973), p. 8].

make emergency imports of around $1.1 billion, made up of about $450 million worth of farm products, $320 million worth of aeroplanes, helicopters and related equipment, and purchases of enriched uranium valued at $320 million. The original American request was for an increase . . . of about $2 billion [9(IV 1972), p. 11].

A fifth approach to cutting the trade surplus was to reduce Japanese exports. Moves in this direction generally took the form of offering orderly marketing agreements. The most important of such agreements to emerge in the first three quarters of 1972 were summarized as follows by the EIU:

> Considerable attention has . . . been given to limiting the growth of exports of certain products to the U.S. and Western Europe. In April, the Minister of International Trade and Industry announced a new scheme of self-restraint, based on quotas and price increases, on exports of some electronic products to Western Europe. At the same time, the steel makers decided to extend their voluntary restrictions on exports to the U.S. for another three years, on terms that provide for a significantly slower growth in shipments than hitherto, while the chemical industry and MITI have been trying to hammer out a similar scheme for a number of chemical products. MITI also appears to have been putting some pressure on the car makers for more "orderly" marketing, but—emphasizing that Japanese cars are exported at fair prices—manufacturers have decided not to take any concrete steps at the moment [9(II 1972), p. 11].

> During the last three months two new voluntary export-restraint schemes have been announced; one limits the growth of electronic desk-top calculator sales to Europe and the U.S. to 20% and 40% of their level in fiscal 1971, while the other, which has been formulated after extensive talks with European shipbuilders, pledges restraint in the export of large oil tankers from 1975 onwards. . . . A number of other similar schemes are under consideration; these include an export cartel for TV sets, tape re-

corders, and some other electronic goods that was originally planned to come into effect last month . . . but is not now likely to see the light of day until the autumn, as well as some restrictions on overseas sales of cars and synthetic fibres.

> . . . Efforts are also being made to settle the ball-bearing dispute; in June representatives of the Japanese manufacturers held extensive talks with their UK and other European counterparts in order to work out a mutually acceptable scheme for exports. In spite of the fact that the Japanese have recently raised their export prices by about 10% (and have promised another 5% increase in August), they agreed to submit proposals for voluntary restraints before September. Whether these will satisfy the powerful European ball-bearing lobby remains to be seen; certainly, judging by their shrill complaints of the "disastrous" effects of "unfair" Japanese competition, UK producers are likely to take a pretty tough line [9(III 1972), pp. 10, 11].

In the following month, October 1972, further major marketing agreements were promised as part of a larger program to deal with Japan's mounting surpluses. Following up on this promise in November, MITI "unveiled" a "tentative list of 18 product categories on which it planned to impose controls" [26(Nov. 8, 1972)]. Over the next few months, some of these plans were given final form and their possible effect could be evaluated. The EIU made the following appraisal:

> Following the original [October 1972] announcement, the government introduced controls in respect of cars, trucks, buses, motorcycles, radios, tape recorders, stereo equipment, home electric appliances, etc., and drew up a list of another ten to twelve products where exports need to be curbed.

> At the time of writing, little is known about the restrictions on exports of electronic items, although it seems that—as in the case of the four automotive products referred to above—they will be administered by the government itself. The intention seems to be that most other items will be

controlled by voluntary cartels but the effectiveness of these is open to question. Furthermore, the curbs so far announced are extremely generous and will still allow a rapid expansion in exports. In the case of passenger cars, for example, the aim is to cut back growth from an estimated 37% to 27% in the September 1972/August 1973 period, while for motorcycles, trucks, and seamless tubes the ceiling is reported to be 23%, 28% and 19%, respectively [9(I 1973), p. 8].

Twice during 1972—in May and October—Japan sought to show her concern about imbalance by packaging several remedies together in multipart programs to trim her surpluses. Both programs included stimulus to the economy, tariff and quota liberalization, promises of orderly marketing agreements, more aid or trade concessions for developing countries, and further stimulus to overseas investment.

Two other remedial measures often discussed but rejected were the imposition of export tariffs and another increase in the value of the yen. In fact, the multipart programs of May and October came to be known as "yen-defense programs" because they were designed to preclude revaluation.

CRITICAL ASSESSMENTS

Like the yen-defense program of 1971, those of 1972 were seen by some as holding little prospect for success. Thus, some analysts referred to the October program as "just another example of too little and too late" [26(Oct. 23, 1972)]. The EIU was even more critical:

> [The October yen-defense program] is vague, it makes few specific suggestions of real importance and, in view of the way in which the two previous yen-defense programs have been chopped about, watered down and finally aborted, it is not surpris-

ing that it has failed to impress overseas and domestic opinion [9(IV 1972), p. 8].

Speculators, too, doubted the efficacy of these programs. As the 1972 trade balance headed toward $9 billion on a "payments value" basis, more and more "hot money" poured into Japan. "Even right after the October program, the Central Bank was forced to mop up large amounts of dollars for several days . . . and speculation on an early revaluation continue[d] as strong as ever" [9(IV 1972), p. 9].

As Japan bought dollars to keep the yen down, her holdings of foreign exchange rose even higher than they would have otherwise. Acknowledged reserves hit $16.5 billion in October, and analysts claimed that reserves were really $5.2 billion higher, counting another $0.9 billion the authorities had put into foreign bonds and $4.3 billion they had deposited in foreign and domestic commercial banks [9(IV 1972), p. 9]. (The charge that Japan was "hiding" reserves was to surface again in 1977 [19, p. 194].)

SECOND FORCED REVALUATION OF THE YEN

Early in 1973, just as in late 1971, initiative for controlling trade imbalance passed from Japan to the United States. On February 12, the latter announced a 10 percent devaluation of the dollar. Japan and other countries responded by allowing their currencies to float and the yen quickly moved up from ¥308 to ¥265 to US $1, for an appreciation of 16 percent, or almost 36 percent since 1970 [18(1973), p. 26].

In explaining why Japan accepted this outcome without mounting more of a fight, analysts noted that by early 1973 the government was increasingly concerned about inflation, and it hoped to check price increases by raising interest rates. Unless the yen was up and floating, however, the benefits expected from higher interest rates would be at least partially offset by an increased inflow of foreign capital.

TEMPORARY DISAPPEARANCE OF THE TRADE SURPLUS PROBLEM

Whereas the 1971 revaluation had produced little effect, that of 1973 was one of several factors that served to interrupt Japan's trade surplus problem. Others were domestic boom and inflation and the rising price of raw materials imports. High world demand also led to scarcities. For example, the US embargoed shipments of lumber and soybeans needed by Japan in order to protect domestic supplies. Thus, the oil crisis at year's end was only a part, though a dramatic part, of the over-all raw materials picture. Since Japan depended on foreign imports for 98 percent of her oil and for at least three-quarters of her energy supplies, the effect was expected to be devastating [8(1978), p. 8; 10(1974, no. 4), p. 9].

With memories of a big trade surplus now effaced by fears of a bigger deficit, Japan moved quickly to undo measures taken in 1972 to cut export growth and to produce a negative capital balance. The EIU and the OECD summarize these shifts in policy:

> With effect from the beginning of September [1973], MITI rescinded the [export] restrictions on eleven items which were imposed last September. . . . The newly freed items include automobiles, radios, stereo sets, cameras and movie cameras (although some restraints will remain on shipments bound for Canada, the U.S.A. and Hong Kong), tape recorders (except for cassettes) and home electric appliances. It has also been decided to do away with the more flexible administrative guidance and voluntary restraint agreements on nine other items, including internal combustion engines and seamless tubes [9(IV 1973), p. 9].

After the outbreak of the oil crisis, the government in November reversed some of the policy measures adopted in 1972 to encourage capital outflows and to discourage capital inflows. Controls on nonresidents' purchases of Japanese stocks and bonds were abolished and purchases by residents of short-term foreign securities restricted. These measures were followed by others in December. . . . Travel allowances in excess of $3,000 were made subject to verification by the Bank of Japan. Overseas investments in real estate were withdrawn from the foreign currency lending programme. The ceiling on free remittances abroad was reduced from $3,000 to $1,000, and controls over the issuance abroad of securities by Japanese firms were relaxed. More importantly, the practice of depositing official foreign exchange funds with authorized banks was discontinued and banks were required to repay some of the loans received previously [18(July 1974), p. 39].

A second response was to intensify an ongoing attack on inflation, since the oil price hike had raised this already serious problem to the point of being "clearly intolerable" [18(July 1974), p. 5]. Thus, on a 1970 base the index of wholesale prices had risen from an average of 100.0 in 1972 to 148.4 by March 1974; the index of export prices had risen from 97.8 to 134.0, and the index of consumer prices from 110.9 to 146.8 [2(1973), pp. 265, 274, 275: tables 154, 157, 158; 2(1974), pp. 265, 270, 279: tables 155, 156, 159]. Moreover, after looking at these price increases, labor demanded—and won—the biggest wage gain ever: 32.9 percent in its 1974 spring wage offensive. Based on such trends, Japan's demand management policy remained restrictive in 1974, even though the year soon showed that it would be one of recession. Priorities did not really change, moreover, until the latter part of 1975, another very poor year by previous standards.

At this point domestic interest blocs as well as trade partners were clamoring for reflation in Japan. Europe, in particular, was making such demands, since Japan's current surplus had risen with Europe while such pressure had eased for the US. What motivated trade partners at this time was not just the re-emerging Japanese surplus but also their own domestic recession and their resultant wish to raise exports to Japan [3(1975), p. 30].

RECRUDESCENCE OF THE TRADE SURPLUS PROBLEM: 1976, 1977

After reappearing toward the end of 1975, Japan's trade surplus rose so rapidly as to become the nation's leading problem once again in the next two years. In explanation, the OECD noted that, owing to Japan's long deflation plus reflation elsewhere, the price competitiveness of Japanese goods improved "rapidly" in 1975 and remained "strong" in 1976 [18(July 1977), p. 28].

Thus, as western economies revived, Japan was able to increase exports to them. Meanwhile, imports continued to stagnate because of depressed domestic demand. The extreme decline from past experience and Japan's implied dependence on exports for her recovery in 1976 are illustrated in Exhibit 9.

Against this backdrop, Japan's trade gap widened. It was $9.9 billion in 1976 and $17.6 billion in 1977, despite a 4 percent rise in the dollar value of the yen in the first of these two years and an 18.2 percent rise in the second.[5]

Predictably, trade partners were angry. Thus, 1976 and 1977 were marked by a new wave of criticisms and demands and by new steps of retaliation.

---

[5] After the oil crisis the yen fell in value from ¥280 = US $1 to ¥300.95 by the end of 1974 and to ¥305.15 by the end of 1975. It advanced again in the next two years, ending at ¥292.80 in 1976 and ¥240.00 in 1977.

Exhibit 9

Trends in Domestic Demand: Percentage Changes Based on Data in 1970 Prices

	Annual Average 1963–73	1974	1975	1976	1977
Private consumption	8.7	1.5	6.2	4.4	3.3
Public consumption	5.9	4.4	7.4	3.8	3.7
Gross fixed investment	13.4	−10.2	−2.7	3.6	4.2
Private dwellings	15.1	−12.9	7.3	6.9	−0.3
Other private	14.0	−10.8	−13.1	3.4	2.7
Public	11.2	−6.7	11.5	1.7	10.2
Stockbuilding[a]	(0.6)	(0.2)	(−2.1)	(0.5)	(0.2)
Domestic demand	10.1	−2.5	0.8	4.5	3.8
Foreign balance[a]	(0.3)	(1.2)	(1.7)	(1.7)	(1.5)
Exports	15.2	21.2	4.4	16.8	10.4
Imports	13.8	12.4	−8.2	8.0	2.0
GNP	10.2	−1.3	2.5	6.0	5.1

SOURCE: OECD [18(1978), p. 6]. Reprinted with permission.

[a] Changes in percent of GNP in the preceding period.

TRADE PARTNERS' DEMANDS: 1976, 1977

In 1976 and 1977 accusations and demands from trade partners focused on the value of the yen, on Japan's slow growth, and on her export and import policies.

So far as the yen was concerned, its modest rise in 1976 led to charges of a "dirty float," and even the rapid gains of 1977 did not still all criticism. For example, on September 22, with the yen already up to ¥266.6 to US $1, Henry Reuss, chairman of the US House Banking Committee, accused Japan of acting to hold down the value of the yen, and he asked that sanctions be applied by the International Monetary Fund [26(Sep. 22, 1977)]. On November 18, with the yen up to ¥246.1 to US $1, it was reported that the United States believed Japan's exports could not be reduced "to any major extent" unless the rate went up to "200 or 210 to the dollar" [16(Nov. 18, 1977)]. According to a Japanese economist, however, a continuous range of 240 to 245 would have a "serious impact," not only on "the smaller Japanese exporting companies but also on the major exporters, such as producers of steel, autos, and electronics." In his opinion, a value of ¥270 to the dollar "might be a reasonable level at this time" [16(Nov. 18, 1977)]. At about the same date, "at least" ¥255 to US $1 was suggested as the minimum figure by half the respondents in a survey of one hundred "leading" Japanese companies [16(Nov. 25, 1977)].

Along with charges of a dirty float, there were further charges that Japan was again hiding reserves, and that these were actually higher than the high reported figure of $23.3 billion [19, p. 194].

As for complaints about Japan's slow growth, these had been made in 1975 and were reiterated in 1977 at an Economic Summit held in May. In response, Japanese Premier Takeo Fukuda promised that his country would achieve a 6.7 percent rise in real GNP during the on-going fiscal year and that Japan would also cut her current balance to minus $700 million by December.

When it later became clear that Fukuda would miss his current balance target (by around $10 billion) and would probably miss his growth target, too, the government readied a $7.5 billion reflationary "business propping" program to present to the Diet in September. This was the sixth such program introduced since 1975, but it was not expected to placate Japan's trade partners. Even Japanese economists were reported to believe that the program was inadequate to meet its goal of pushing growth up to 6.7 percent for the twelve months ending March 31, 1978 [26(Sep. 8, 1977)]. Japanese businessmen, too, were skeptical. Although "pleased" to get a program larger than expected, they remained in a "cautious mood," partly because only about half the promised outlay would be made in the current fiscal year [6(Oct. 1977), p. 122].

As for complaints about trade policies, these came to a head on November 21, 1977, when—after five days of talks—a US mission handed Japan what the latter regarded as an "ultimatum" [16(Nov. 22, 1977)]. Its exact contents were not made public, but the *New York Times* reported that the "single most important" demand was that Japan transform its current surplus (now headed toward $10 billion) into a current account deficit and that she set a target date for this change [16(Dec. 8, 1977)]. Other more specific demands were said to include:

1. Tariff reductions on a "broad" range of "significant" imports from all of Japan's trading partners;

2. An end to the quantitative restrictions which Japan still maintained on twenty-seven import categories, mostly agricultural products;

3. A "restructuring" designed to increase the proportion of manufactured imports from the current low level of 20 percent, which compared with about 50 percent in West Germany and Great Britain;

4. The re-examination of other trade policies, including restraints on government procurement abroad, obstacles to easy import financing, "aggressive" export promotion, and many nontariff barriers to trade.

The nontariff barriers to which trade partners objected included, besides quotas, a "costly" and "time-consuming" ten-step recording and inspection procedure for imports [16(Dec. 20, 1977)]; a "meticulous array of health and safety standards" which were "strictly enforced" and which frequently differed from those of other countries; a distribution system that relied on a "double or even a triple layer of wholesalers," each of which contributed a share to the often "fantastic markups" on imports; and alleged "administrative guidance" against buying foreign products [12(July 26, 1977)]. Specific examples included a requirement that each can in a shipment be marked on arrival with the name of the importer and the date of import, and the requirement (recently rescinded) that pharmaceuticals undergo retesting in Japan.

Along with these demands for policy changes, a "hope" was expressed that Japan would raise her growth target to 8 percent for the upcoming year, and a "suggestion" was made that Japan "commit" herself within three weeks. Questioned on this approach, "official American sources admitted it was 'extraordinary' for one nation to advise another on its economic policies." On the other hand, they added, "These were extraordinary times" [16(Nov. 22, 1977)].

Compared with the United States, the EEC had done little to draw up a broad program

of demands upon Japan. On December 7, however, it was reported that "Western European heads of government" would make "a concerted attempt of their own to persuade Japan to bring its trade with Europe into balance." Japan would be threatened with "protectionist action" if she did not make "voluntary export cuts" or "open her market to European goods." Behind the new attack, officials said, was the belief that the US was "being more successful" than Europe "in persuading the Japanese government to balance its trade on a bilateral basis" [16(Dec. 7, 1977)].

WESTERN RETALIATION

In addition to making demands on Japan, trade partners started to retaliate. They felt that one possible approach was to toughen up the way in which alleged dumping would be handled, and late in 1977 this was tried by both the US and Europe. Another possible approach, at least in the opinion of US industry—was to broaden the definition of a "subsidy" so that it would include the remission of the value-added tax (VAT) that foreign governments commonly made in the case of exported goods. Should industry succeed in an on-going effort to get the courts to redefine "subsidies" in this way, then the effect would be dramatic: whereas under US law dumping brought no penalty unless US industry was injured, an export subsidy had to be offset by imposing a countervailing duty.

Dumping and "Reference Prices"

The new and tougher method of handling dumping charges that was planned for 1978 involved the use of so-called "reference prices." The essence of this scheme was spelled out in a *Newsweek* article on November 21, 1977, the same day that Japan received the so-called US ultimatum:

> As of now, it may take a year to reach a [dumping] judgment, during which the dumping continues. What's proposed is a system of "reference prices" below which penalties would automatically be assessed and held in escrow while the case is being investigated [7, p. 75]. © 1977 by Newsweek, Inc. All Rights Reserved. Reprinted by Permission.

The first US industry to be promised a set of reference prices was steel. This choice reflected the recent filing of 19 steel dumping charges, a strong congressional steel lobby, the rising market share of steel imports (which appeared would grow from 13 to 20 percent of the market during 1977), and the loss of perhaps 60,000 jobs [16(Dec. 11, 1977)].[6]

As news of the upcoming plan emerged, it became clear that steel's reference prices would reflect the costs of the most efficient producer—Japan—so that any imports coming in below these prices could be presumed to be dumped.[7] Although no immediate charge would be levied on such imports, they would trigger an automatic investigation that would be completed in 60 to 90 days, or "several months faster" than had so far been the case. Once dumping had been established (and while the FTC was investigating its impact on the US in-

dustry), importers would have to post a bond equal to the difference between the actual price and the "fair" price. The effect would be to notify importers and buyers that any "bargain" prices might prove "illusory" since extra duties might be imposed "months" after a shipment had arrived [16(Dec. 11, 1977 and Jan. 4, 1978); 26(Jan. 4, 1976)].

From industry's point of view, the exact level of the reference prices would be the "critical" factor. When announced for the first group of products to be covered, this averaged 5.7 percent below domestic prices. The industry was "relieved," however, since it believed that many buyers would not use foreign steel unless they could get it at 10 percent or more below domestic prices. On the other hand, the US industry planned to raise prices by about 5.7 percent early in 1978 [11, p. 30; 16(Dec. 7, 1977 and Jan. 4, 1978); 26(Jan. 4, 1978)].

A more decisive negative note came from the Federal Trade Commission. This agency claimed that "the system would create an expensive new Federal bureaucracy and cost American taxpayers more than $1 billion a year." If protectionism was "inevitable," the commission reportedly believed that tariffs would be "less harmful than either reference prices or quotas" [16(Jan. 5, 1978); 28, p. 26].

Despite all the doubts that could be raised about the use of reference prices, the idea caught fire in the EEC as well as in the US. In Europe, too, it was first applied to steel, an industry that was especially hard pressed. Over the longer run, however, the EEC looked forward to setting minimum prices for steel whether sold by domestic *or* foreign suppliers. This plan emerged in response to three years of losses for the EEC's steel industry and after France had threatened to act on her own if the Community refused to take joint action [11, pp. 29, 30; 16(Nov. 30, 1977)].

[6] This was the highest of several figures mentioned. The *Wall Street Journal* gave 35,000 and a later *New York Times* article 20,000 [16(Jan. 8, 1978); 26(Dec. 7, 1977)].

[7] Besides the producer's average costs, the reference price would cover a producer's profit allowance, freight to the East or West Coast, and US tariffs. Lest US guesstimates of Japanese costs be too low (as suggested by a decision on the Gilmore Steel Company's dumping charges), MITI and six major Japanese steel companies had agreed to supply the cost data needed to develop the US reference prices [12(Jan. 4, 1978); 16(Jan. 10, 1978)].

VAT Remission as a Subsidy

Although the remission of VAT on exports was permitted under the rules of the General Agreement on Tariffs and Trade (GATT) to which the United States was a party, and although such remissions were widespread and long-standing, the hard-pressed US electronics industry decided to challenge this prevailing legal doctrine. Zenith Corporation brought suit, and in April 1977 a US Customs Court ruled in favor of the company.

If this ruling were upheld and used as a precedent, the US Treasury estimated that it could potentially affect 60 to 70 percent of US imports. Thus, the Treasury felt it had gone too far and consequently planned to challenge it in a higher court [26(Apr. 14, 1977)]. In addition, GATT warned the US on letting this decision stand [26(June 6, 1977 and June 17, 1977)].

JAPANESE RESPONSES TO US PRESSURE

US demands on Japan were accompanied by repeated warnings that failure to make a positive response would lead to protectionist measures by Congress, and US labor did its best to make this threat convincing. Thus, the long-term president of the American Federation of Labor, George Meany, castigated free trade at a national union convention in California on December 8, 1977:

> Foreign trade is the guerrilla warfare of economics—and right now the United States economy is being ambushed. Free trade is a joke and a myth. And a government trade policy predicated on old ideas of free trade is worse than a joke—it is a prescription for disaster. The answer is fair trade, do unto others as they do to us—barrier for barrier—closed door for closed door [16(Dec. 9, 1977)]. © 1977 by The New York Times Company. Reprinted by permission.

Responding to such pressures, Japan permitted a moderate yen advance, and Premier Fukuda urged business leaders to enter into US joint ventures, to curb the growth of exports, and to avoid concentrating a narrow range of products on a single export market [26(Mar. 25, and May 24, 1977)]. Negotiations began with Europe over curbing exports of ships [26(Feb. 8, and Feb. 11, 1977)], and a pact was signed with the United States to curb exports of televisions [26(Apr. 8, May 16, and May 23, 1977)]. Major steel company executives also urged the signing of a pact on steel [26(Feb. 28, and Apr. 18, 1977)].

On the other hand, Japan was reported to believe that US threats were exaggerated. "Japan's Exporters Doubt Real Curbs Loom" was a headline in the *Wall Street Journal* on May 20, 1977. "Japanese officials . . . say privately they believe the American line is . . . merely posturing for the benefit of protectionist forces in the Congress and in industry and labor," reported the *New York Times* on January 2, 1978.

The Japanese, moreover, defended their own trade record and criticized the export performance of the West. Thus, they often pointed out that Japan had only 27 products still protected by an import quota, or fewer than several European countries. And, since her 20 percent tariff cut late in 1972, Japan's duties on industrial products were "slightly below" the average for industrial countries as a group [12(July 26, 1977) (Part 3)].

The Japanese also pointed out that their success in selling abroad derived not only from low prices but also from growing acceptance of their goods—based on design, quality, and service. In addition, the Japanese said that the West did not try hard enough to penetrate their markets; for example, western companies set relatively high profit targets and dropped out of competition if these were not met relatively soon. Also, the Japanese asserted that the West had done little to solve the structural problems that beset some of its own industries. Western steel, for example, had been allowed to fall behind Japanese steel in efficiency. Whereas Japanese output in 1975 was 327 metric tons per employee, the US figure was about 25 percent less and the European figure about 50 percent less [20, p. 49]. The United States was seen as underrating all Japan had done to limit exports and was further accused of "looking for a scapegoat to deflect attention from its own inability to control energy imports." These formed the "largest component" in the roughly $26 billion US trade deficit that was foreseen for 1977 [16(Dec. 14, 1977)].

In any event, Japan's response to the US demands of November 21, 1977, was a cabinet shakeup which brought an expansionist critic of Fukuda into control of MITI and N. Ushiba, former ambassador to the United States, into the newly created post of Minister of External Economic Affairs [5 (Dec. 12, 1977)]. Acting as his nation's spokesman on December 8, 1978, Ushiba indicated that some of the recent US demands were simply impossible to meet. Of the US proposal that Japan commit herself to a deficit in the current account by a specified date, he asked, "Who can do that? No country in the world. You know exporting and importing are done by private companies." Of the US proposal that Japan increase the share of manufactures in her imports, he asked, "How can we force our people to buy foreign manufactured goods if there's no demand?" Ushiba urged the US not to expect anything "dramatic" from Japan's upcoming specific proposals, and he said that his presentation would largely consist of outlining the economic and political constraints operating on Japan's policy. "I must tell [the Americans] again and again. Maybe they don't understand," he said [16(Dec. 9, 1977)].

A few days after making these remarks, Ushiba came to Washington with Japan's specific reply to the so-called US "ultimatum." Not all details were made public, but the main concessions were the liberalization of some quotas (but not the elimination of these) and tariff reductions averaging about 23 percent on 318 specific items. These were mostly industrial products, but not all of them were important and not all of those that were important (e.g., autos) were products on which Japan feared the competition of western imports [16(Dec. 14, and Dec. 16, 1977)].

In assessing these measures, analysts agreed that their impact would not be great. According to a press report in Japan, these measures might cut the national current account surplus to $5 billion by early 1979, an outcome clearly falling far short of what the US had demanded [5(Dec. 12, 1977)]. According to the *New York Times*, "The actual import impact . . . is expected to be minimal. . . . The total import value of the items on which tariffs are to be reduced is just $2.2 billion a year [16(Dec. 15, 1977)]. According to one US negotiator, the effect of the plan would be "very modest," perhaps increasing annual US exports to Japan by about $735 million [26(Dec. 15, 1977)].

Although the Japanese argued that these measures were the "maximum possible now" because of "fierce domestic opposition" (especially among farmers, who were traditionally the backbone of the tottering Liberal Democratic Party) [16(Dec. 14, 1977)], US opinion was strongly critical. Mike Mansfield, then the US ambassador to Japan, termed the concessions "insufficient"; Richard Strauss, the chief US trade negotiator, said they fell "considerably short" of what was necessary. Commerce Secretary Juanita Krebs echoed this view, adding that a Japanese trade surplus with this country in the neighborhood of $8 billion was "simply unacceptable, politically and economically." "Key members" of the House Ways and Means Committee told

Ushiba bluntly that the measures "would not quell mounting pressures in Congress to pass protectionist legislation." The ambassador of another major trading nation called Japan's package "typically cosmetic" [5(Dec. 13, 1977); 16(Dec. 15, 1977); 26(Dec. 14, 1977)].

Faced with all this "heat," Ushiba announced another key concession before he left for home; Japan would set her target growth rate at 7 percent for 1978, up from the previously favored level but still a percentage point lower than the US had proposed [16(Dec. 16, 1977)]. Negotiator Strauss found this move "very positive," but with the two nations "still far apart,"

he planned to visit Japan and see what other concessions he could get. Meanwhile, Senator Edward M. Kennedy, who was in Japan at the time, reminded his hosts that the "important factor" would be the "reaction in Congress" [16(Dec. 13, 1977)].

COMPARATIVE TRENDS IN PRICES AND COSTS

Comparative trends in prices and costs, a summary of Japanese balance of payments, and an analysis of Japanese trade are given in Exhibits 10–24.

Exhibit 10

Trends in Comparative Wholesale Prices (1967 = 100)

A. WHOLESALE PRICES, ALL COMMODITIES—ANNUAL AND QUARTERLY

Period	US	France	W Ger	Italy	Neth	UK	Japan	Canada
1970	110.4	118.1	102.0	111.9	107.5	n.a.	106.9	108.4
1971	113.9	122.6	104.9	115.7	108.5	n.a.	106.0	109.8
1972	119.1	129.7	108.5	120.4	112.4	n.a.	106.9	117.5
1973	134.7	146.2	119.2	141.9	126.6	n.a.	123.8	142.7
1974	160.1	180.7	134.7	199.8	144.3	n.a.	162.6	174.7
1975	174.9	182.6	139.3	216.9	154.2	n.a.	167.5	186.1
1976	183.0	201.4	147.3	266.5	178.5	n.a.	175.9	194.0
1977	194.2	214.9	150.0	310.7	n.a.	n.a.	179.2	211.7

B. WHOLESALE PRICES, MANUFACTURED GOODS—ANNUAL AND QUARTERLY

Period	US	France[a]	W Ger	Italy	Neth	UK	Japan	Canada
1970	110.2	117.0	106.3	112.0	103.6	115.2	106.5	108.8
1971	113.8	119.5	110.7	116.0	108.3	125.6	105.3	112.8
1972	117.9	125.0	113.3	119.5	113.9	132.3	106.2	121.0
1973	129.2	143.4	121.0	137.6	121.6	141.9	122.3	139.4
1974	154.1	185.2	137.2	200.2	133.5	175.1	156.9	166.8
1975	171.1	174.6	141.7	216.6	142.5	217.4	159.3	183.7
1976	179.0	187.5	146.7	265.8	152.3	253.0	166.3	193.9
1977	190.1	198.0	150.7	311.7	160.5	301.5	169.2	210.8

SOURCE: U.S., Department of Commerce [25(Sep. 1978), pp. 64, 66: tables 63, 64].

[a] Industrial products only, and excludes machinery, transport equipment, consumer goods, food products, and processed foods.

Exhibit 11

Trends in Export and Import Prices (1967 = 100)[a]

A. EXPORT PRICES

Period	US	Canada	Japan	European Community	UK	France	W Ger	Italy
1970	111	111	110	108	104	105	115	108
1971	114	115	113	114	111	111	123	115
1972	118	121	126	125	121	123	136	126
1973	137	137	155	152	134	153	168	147
1974	174	186	200	184	166	179	199	187
1975	195	198	200	212	191	212	225	211
1976[a]	205	211	200	205	187	199	225	192

B. IMPORT PRICES

Period	US	Canada	Japan	European Community	UK	France	W Ger	Italy
1970	112	110	104	105	105	102	110	105
1971	117	116	109	112	112	106	114	111
1972	126	121	115	120	120	117	121	122
1973	148	129	146	151	150	142	154	156
1974	223	163	243	209	223	193	199	242
1975	241	181	260	225	240	213	210	256
1976[b]	258	189	261	222	240	204	214	242

SOURCE: U.S., Council on International Economic Policy [23(Jan. 1977), p. 143: tables 9 and 10].

[a] US dollar basis.

[b] Estimate.

Exhibit 12

Terms of Trade, Selected Countries (1970 = 100)

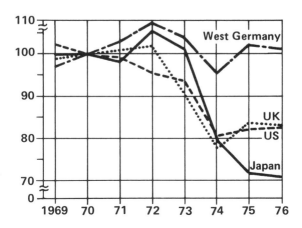

SOURCE: Japan Ministry of Foreign Affairs [15(1977), p. 52].

Exhibit 13

Japanese Export and Import Price Indices, Major Commodity Groups (1975 = 100)

A. EXPORT PRICES

| | All Commodities | | | | | | | | | |
		Chng fr Prev Yr (month)	Except Ships	Textiles	Metals & Related Prods	Elec Mchnry	Transport Equip	General Mchnry & Precision Instrmnts	Chemicals	Misc Prods
Number of items	214		213	22	53	32	9	37	26	35
Weight	1000.0		899.0	68.1	235.6	123.1	259.1	159.3	79.9	74.9
Calendar year										
1969 avg	68.9	+2.5	71.0	85.1	61.8	86.3	61.7	78.2	57.9	63.3
1970	72.3	+4.9	74.1	85.8	67.9	87.6	65.0	80.0	57.3	67.8
1971	72.7	+0.6	73.0	82.6	65.5	87.4	73.3	79.4	54.2	68.9
1972	70.6	−2.9	70.7	78.3	64.3	85.6	73.1	75.4	49.4	67.4
1973	77.0	+9.1	77.9	96.7	73.3	86.1	73.2	78.1	59.7	75.1
1974	102.9	+33.6	104.2	107.5	118.3	99.2	91.3	94.9	103.2	100.6
1975	100.0	−2.8	100.0	100.0	100.0	100.0	100.0	100.0	100.0	100.0
1976	98.4	−1.6	99.3	103.5	97.2	97.4	97.9	98.7	93.3	105.1
1977	93.5	−5.0	94.7	93.6	91.8	91.4	93.4	97.3	80.5	107.8

B. IMPORT PRICES

| | All Commodities | | | | | | | | |
		Chng fr Prev Yr (month)	Foodstuffs & Feed	Textiles	Metals	Mchnry & Equip	Petroleum, Coal & Related Prods	Wood, Lumber & Related Prods	Misc Prods
Number of items	139		41	13	21	13	8	16	27
Weight	1000.0		180.5	49.2	114.0	74.7	434.0	55.4	92.2
Calendar year									
1969 avg	46.7	+2.2	43.6	68.9	78.0	88.6	23.4	65.5	61.4
1970	48.3	+3.4	47.8	68.4	81.4	89.0	23.7	66.4	61.0
1971	48.3	0.0	48.2	68.9	71.1	87.0	27.4	65.3	59.9
1972	46.2	−4.3	46.6	73.4	62.6	83.1	26.6	63.9	58.0
1973	55.9	+21.0	63.1	116.1	74.0	83.4	28.6	92.9	62.8
1974	92.9	+66.2	93.6	113.4	109.3	92.8	83.9	105.9	89.1
1975	100.0	+7.6	100.0	100.0	100.0	100.0	100.0	100.0	100.0
1976	106.0	+6.0	99.3	120.9	103.0	105.8	107.5	112.4	104.1
1977	101.5	−4.2	95.1	112.4	97.7	101.9	103.3	110.7	98.3

SOURCE: Bank of Japan [2(1977), p. 290: table 163].

Exhibit 14

Recent Changes in Japanese Labor Costs and Productivity

	1974	1975	1976	1977
Total cash earnings				
Establishments with 30 regular employees and more[a]	27.2	14.8	12.8	9.2
(in real terms)[b]	(2.2)	(2.7)	(3.2)	(1.1)
Contractual[c]	27.6	19.6	11.7	9.8
Overtime	4.4	1.1	23.9	13.5
Special (bonus)[d]	32.8	6.6	13.1	7.1
Establishments with 5 to 29 employees	26.0	15.8	9.0	10.2
Productivity				
Whole economy[e]	−0.8	2.8	5.0	3.7
Manufacturing	−0.5	−3.9	12.3	5.1
Unit labor costs				
Whole economy[f]	26.5	14.5	6.6	7.0
Manufacturing	26.8	16.0	0.3	4.2

SOURCE: OECD [18(July 1978), p. 20]. Reprinted with permission.

[a] The shares of components in total cash earnings are 67.5 percent for contractual, 6.2 percent for overtime, and 26.2 percent for "special" (in 1977).

[b] Deflated by consumer price index.

[c] Excluding overtime pay.

[d] The figure for Q2 refers to the average of June to August (summer bonus), and that for Q4 to the November–December period (year-end bonus).

[e] GNP at constant prices divided by total employment.

[f] Compensation of employee divided by GNP at constant prices.

Exhibit 15

Comparative Trends in Unit Labor Costs, Output per Man Hour, and Hourly Compensation (1967 = 100)

A. UNIT LABOR COSTS AND PRODUCTIVITY IN MANUFACTURING—ANNUAL

Period	US[a]	France	W Ger	Italy	Neth	UK	Japan	Canada
				Unit Labor Costs in US Dollars				
1970	116.5	98.9	125.7	119.2	108.7	106.0	113.4	111.8
1971	117.6	104.7	142.8	135.6	120.6	118.1	131.3	116.1
1972	118.1	120.0	164.3	152.2	139.2	126.6	161.6	122.4
1973	123.2	147.9	211.7	172.5	174.0	132.8	197.3	127.9
1974	143.1	158.7	236.3	183.1	198.3	160.3	237.9	148.7
1975	152.4	206.4	270.0	246.2	247.5	199.2	285.6	166.5
1976	158.3	195.0	258.1	213.2	240.1	184.7	275.2	187.4
1977	168.3	205.6	293.4	244.6		199.7	314.7	184.1
				Unit Labor Costs in National Currencies				
1970	116.5	111.1	115.0	119.8	109.1	121.7	112.2	108.1
1971	117.6	117.3	124.5	134.3	116.9	132.9	126.0	108.7
1972	118.1	123.1	131.4	142.4	124.1	139.2	135.3	112.4
1973	123.2	133.4	140.7	160.8	134.2	149.1	147.6	118.6
1974	143.1	155.0	153.1	190.8	147.7	188.4	191.5	134.8
1975	152.4	179.6	166.3	257.4	173.3	246.6	233.9	157.0
1976	158.3	189.2	162.9	283.6	176.1	281.5	225.2	171.3
1977	168.3	205.4	170.8	345.9		314.8	232.7	181.3
				Output per Man Hour				
1970	104.5	121.2	116.1	117.8	134.0	108.6	146.5	114.7
1971	110.3	128.5	121.4	123.5	143.0	112.9	150.5	122.8
1972	116.0	136.8	128.7	132.9	154.4	121.2	161.0	128.1
1973	119.4	143.7	136.6	147.8	170.2	126.3	179.0	133.4
1974	112.8	147.8	145.0	155.9	184.3	127.6	180.3	135.6
1975	117.9	151.1	150.4	150.2	181.0	124.4	172.4	133.4
1976	123.5	165.3	162.8	161.5	198.9	128.7	194.8	137.8
1977	126.7	171.6	169.6	162.3		126.6	206.6	143.3

Exhibit 15 (continued)

B. HOURLY COMPENSATION—ANNUAL

Period	US[a]	France	W Ger	Italy	Neth	UK	Japan	Canada
				In US Dollars				
1970	121.7	119.9	145.9	140.4	145.6	115.1	166.2	128.2
1971	129.8	134.5	173.4	167.5	172.5	133.4	197.7	142.6
1972	137.0	164.3	211.4	202.3	215.0	153.3	260.3	156.8
1973	147.0	212.6	289.3	255.0	296.1	167.7	353.2	170.6
1974	161.4	234.5	342.5	285.4	365.4	204.5	428.8	201.7
1975	179.7	311.9	406.2	370.0	448.0	247.8	492.3	222.1
1976	195.6	322.4	420.1	344.2	477.6	237.8	536.0	258.2
1977	213.2	352.7	497.5	396.8		252.9	650.2	263.8
				In National Currencies				
1970	121.7	134.7	133.5	141.1	146.2	132.1	164.3	124.0
1971	129.8	150.6	151.2	165.9	167.1	150.1	189.6	133.5
1972	137.0	168.4	169.1	189.2	191.5	168.6	217.8	144.0
1973	147.0	191.7	192.2	237.6	228.4	188.2	264.2	158.2
1974	161.4	229.1	221.9	297.4	272.2	240.4	345.2	182.9
1975	179.7	271.4	250.2	386.7	313.8	306.8	403.3	209.4
1976	195.6	312.9	265.2	457.9	350.3	362.4	438.7	236.0
1977	213.2	352.4	289.7	561.3		398.6	480.8	259.8

SOURCE: U.S., Department of Commerce [24(Sep. 1978), pp. 86, 87: tables 112–116].

NOTE: Indices of unit labor costs and hourly compensation are adjusted for changes of exchange rates in order to express them in US dollars.

[a] Revised series.

Exhibit 16

Shares of World Exports, Ratios of Exports to Production, and Current Account Balances

A. SHARES OF TOTAL WORLD EXPORTS (IN PERCENT)[a]

Period	US (Excl Exports to US)	US	France	W Ger	Italy	Neth	UK	Japan	Canada
1960	21.0	18.2	6.0	10.1	3.2	3.6	9.4	3.6	5.1
1969	18.3	15.6	6.2	11.8	4.8	4.1	7.2	6.6	5.9
1970	18.0	15.4	6.5	12.2	4.7	4.2	6.9	6.9	6.0
1971	16.4	14.0	6.6	12.4	4.8	4.4	7.1	7.6	5.8
1972	15.6	13.3	7.1	12.5	5.0	4.5	6.5	7.6	5.7
1973	15.8	13.7	7.0	13.0	4.3	4.6	5.9	7.1	5.1
1974	14.7	12.8	6.0	11.6	3.9	4.3	5.1	7.2	4.5
1975	15.5	13.6	6.7	11.4	4.4	4.4	5.6	7.1	4.3
1976	14.8	12.8	6.4	11.4	4.1	4.5	5.2	7.5	4.5
1977	13.8	11.8	6.4	11.6	4.4	4.3	5.7	8.0	4.2

B. SHARES OF WORLD EXPORTS OF MANUFACTURES (IN PERCENT)[a]

Period	US (Excl Exports to US)	US	France	W Ger	Italy	Neth	UK	Japan	Canada
1960	25.3	22.8	9.1	18.2	4.8	3.8	15.3	6.5	4.5
1969	22.5	19.3	7.8	18.7	7.0	4.2	10.7	10.7	6.0
1970	21.3	18.4	8.3	19.0	6.9	4.2	10.1	11.2	6.0
1971	20.1	17.2	8.3	19.3	6.9	4.0	10.5	12.7	5.8
1972	19.1	16.3	8.7	19.3	7.1	4.0	9.7	13.5	5.7
1973	19.5	16.7	8.7	20.3	6.2	4.5	9.0	13.3	5.3
1974	20.2	17.7	8.2	20.2	6.2	4.7	8.2	14.8	4.7
1975	21.2	18.9	9.0	18.6	6.6	4.3	9.0	14.2	4.5
1976	20.5	18.3	8.9	19.1	6.3	4.5	8.4	14.8	4.7
1977	19.8	17.6	8.9	19.2	6.6	4.1	9.1	15.5	4.5

Exhibit 16 (continued)

C. RATIO OF EXPORTS TO PRODUCTION OF GOODS[b]

Period	US Final Sales and Changes in Inventories[c]	US Prodn of All Gds	France	W Ger	Italy	Neth	UK	Japan[d]	Canada
1970	9.3	14.4	30.6	40.5	41.8	n.a.	47.3	23.7	70.5
1971	9.1	14.1	37.3	41.0	44.6	n.a.	50.0	26.7	70.2
1972	9.3	14.3	38.4	42.3	47.6	n.a.	48.3	25.8	71.2
1973	11.7	17.7	41.0	45.7	44.3	n.a.	52.1	25.1	71.4
1974	15.2	23.2	50.7	55.3	53.9	n.a.	56.4	33.1	75.6
1975	15.6	24.3	48.0	52.9	55.0	n.a.	57.5	32.1	72.6
1976	14.9	22.8	49.9	55.4	58.4	n.a.	62.5		76.0
1977	14.3								

D. BALANCE ON CURRENT ACCOUNT (BILLIONS OF DOLLARS)

Period	US	France	W Ger	Italy	Neth	UK	Japan	Canada
1970	2.4	0.1	0.9	0.9	−0.5	1.7	2.0	1.1
1971	−1.4	0.5	0.9	2.0	−2.0	2.6	5.8	0.4
1972	−6.0	0.3	0.8	2.3	1.3	0.3	6.6	−0.4
1973	6.9	−0.7	4.3	−2.2	2.3	−2.2	−0.1	0.1
1974	1.7	−6.0	9.8	−8.0	2.1	−8.3	−4.7	−1.5
1975	18.4	−0.1	4.0	−0.6	2.0	−3.7	−0.7	−4.7
1976	4.3	−6.1	3.8	−2.9	2.7	−1.6	3.7	−3.8
1977	−15.2	−3.2	3.8	2.3	0.3	0.3	11.0	−3.9

SOURCE: U.S., Department of Commerce [24(Sep. 1978), pp. 58–60, 75: tables 49, 51, 55].

[a] "World exports" are defined as the sum of the exports of the fourteen major industrial countries.

[b] Exports fob and imports cif, except as noted.

[c] Series preferred for US ratios. Comparable series not available for foreign countries.

[d] Prior to 1974 customs values are shown.

Exhibit 17

Japan Balance of Payments (millions of US dollars)

A. SUMMARY DATA

Year	Balances on Current Transactions	Current Transactions					Balances on Capital Transactions[a]		Errors and Omissions	Over-all Balances	Settlement of Balances[c]	
		Visible Trade			Services	Transfer Payments	Long-term	Short-term[b]			Changes in Gold & Foreign Currency	Changes in Other Assets
		Balances	Exports	Imports								
1971	5,797	7,787	23,566	15,779	-1,738	-252	-1,082	2,435	527	7,677	10,836	-3,031
1972	6,624	8,971	28,032	19,061	-1,883	-464	-4,487	1,966	638	4,741	3,130	1,771
1973	-136	3,688	36,264	32,576	-3,510	-314	-9,750	2,047	-2,595	-10,074	-6,119	-3,955
1974	-4,693	1,436	54,480	53,044	-5,842	-287	-3,881	1,778	-43	-6,839	1,272	-8,111
1975	-682	5,028	54,734	49,706	-5,354	-356	-272	-1,138	-584	-2,676	-703	-1,973
1976	3,680	9,887	66,026	56,139	-5,867	-340	-984	111	117	2,924	3,789	-865
1977	10,918	17,311	79,333	62,022	-6,004	-389	-3,187	-648	657	7,743	6,244	1,499
Fiscal year												
1971	6,321	8,420	24,653	16,233	-1,778	-321	-1,647	3,131	238	8,043	11,205	-3,002
1972	6,160	8,333	29,437	21,104	-1,836	-337	-5,959	2,135	626	2,962	1,462	1,500
1973	-3,918	789	38,943	38,154	-4,370	-337	-9,110	2,283	-2,662	-13,407	-5,699	-7,708
1974	-2,330	3,940	57,266	53,326	-5,960	-310	-2,083	901	120	-3,392	1,726	-5,118
1975	134	5,843	56,004	50,161	-5,364	-345	-260	-1,376	-270	-1,772	30	-1,802
1976	4,682	11,148	69,394	58,246	-6,096	-370	-1,606	402	-226	3,252	2,815	437
1977 (P)	14,030	20,423	83,280	62,857	-5,974	-419	-2,457	-483	1,055	12,145	12,211	-66

B. LONG-TERM CAPITAL MOVEMENTS[d]

	1973	1974	1975	1976	1977	Outstanding at End of 1977
Foreign capital	−1,282	182	3,120	3,575	2,063	19,575
Direct investments	−42	202	226	113	21	2,229
Security investments	−591	−865	1,518	1,595	1,256	14,094
Import credits	−12	−6	−26	−5	−13	80
Loans	−313	−232	166	326	−324	2,099
Bonds	−198	80	1,235	1,509	1,099	n.a.
Others	−126	1,003	1	37	24	1,073
Japanese capital	−8,468	−4,063	−3,392	−4,559	−5,247	42,085
Direct investments	−1,904	−2,012	−1,763	−1,991	−1,645	11,958
Security investments	−1,787	−141	−24	−146	−1,718	5,595
Export credits	−1,048	−672	−29	−571	−1,388	9,121
Loans	−3,038	−1,136	−1,295	−1,525	−472	12,344
Others	−691	−102	−281	−326	−24	3,067
Net	−9,750	−3,881	−272	−984	−3,184	22,510
Private	−8,359	−4,010	828	−591	n.a.	15,129
Official	−1,391	129	−1,100	−393	n.a.	7,381

SOURCES: Summary data from *Fuji Bank Bulletin* [13(Aug. 1978), p. 163: table 12]. Remaining information from OECD [18(July 1978), p. 28]. Reprinted with permission.

NOTE: Over the period covered in these tables, the yen-dollar exchange rate moved as follows (year-end values):

	1971	1972	1973	1974	1975	1976	1977
Yen per US $1	315.7	302.5	281.0	301.6	306.2	293.7	241.1

NOTE: Failure of data to add for CY 1971–1973 and FY 1971 is in original. Sign has been changed in final entry for CY 1971.

[a] Minus sign indicates outflow of capital (increase in Japanese assets held abroad or decrease in foreign currency claims).

[b] Transactions for the settlement of balances are not included.

[c] Minus sign indicates decrease in assets or increase in liabilities.

[d] Minus sign indicates capital outflow.

Exhibit 18

Analysis of Japanese Trade

A. TRENDS IN EXTERNAL TRADE[a]

	1974	1975	1976	1977
Exports				
Value in dollar terms	50.4	0.4	20.6	19.7
Value in yen terms	61.6	2.1	20.4	8.6
Volume	17.1	2.0	23.3	3.0
Unit value	38.0	0.1	−2.3	5.4
Imports				
Value in dollar terms	62.1	−6.8	12.0	9.3
Value in yen terms	73.7	−5.0	11.4	−0.6
Volume	−2.3	−12.5	10.4	3.4
Unit value	77.8	8.6	1.0	−3.8

B. JAPAN'S EXTERNAL TRADE BY AREAS AND PRINCIPAL COUNTRIES

	1970		1975		1976	
	Exports	Imports	Exports	Imports	Exports	Imports
Total (millions of $)	19,318	18,881	55,753	57,863	67,225	64,799
Total (in percent)	100.00	100.00	100.00	100.00	100.00	100.00
North America	33.66	34.36	22.06	24.38	25.6	22.4
US	30.74	29.44	20.00	20.06	23.3	18.2
Western Europe	15.01	10.24	14.33	7.53	16.3	7.7
EEC[b]	6.75	5.92	10.18	5.83	10.8	5.6
Other	8.26	4.32	4.14	1.70	4.9	1.8
Australia, New Zealand, & South Africa	5.34	10.48	5.39	9.32	5.1	10.1
Latin America	6.15	7.27	8.54	4.36	7.5	3.8
Southeast Asia	25.27	15.96	22.37	18.29	20.9	20.7
Hong Kong	3.63	0.49	2.47	0.42	2.7	0.5
Indonesia	1.63	3.37	3.32	5.93	2.4	6.3
South Korea	4.24	1.21	4.03	2.26	4.2	3.0
Taiwan	3.63	1.33	3.27	1.40	3.4	1.8
Middle East	3.41	13.41	11.71	28.65	10.8	28.8
Iran	0.93	5.27	3.33	8.60	2.5	6.9
Saudi Arabia	0.43	2.30	2.42	10.60	2.8	12.1
Africa (excl South Africa)	5.21	3.60	6.88	1.84	6.5	1.5
Liberia	3.04	0.17	4.64	0.03	4.2	0.1
Communist bloc	5.41	4.70	8.40	5.19	6.9	4.4
China	2.94	1.34	4.05	2.65	2.5	2.1
USSR	1.76	2.55	2.92	2.02	3.3	1.8

SOURCES: Part A: OECD [18(July 1978), p. 23]. Reprinted with permission. Part B: Japan Ministry of Foreign Affairs [15(1977), p. 34ff.: table 37].

[a] Percent change at a seasonally adjusted annual rate, customs clearance basis.

[b] EEC—six countries in 1970, nine in 1975. For eight countries of the latter EEC (excluding Ireland), the 1970 figures were exports 8.56 percent, imports 8.17 percent.

Exhibit 19

Analysis of Trade: Japan's Current Balance by Region

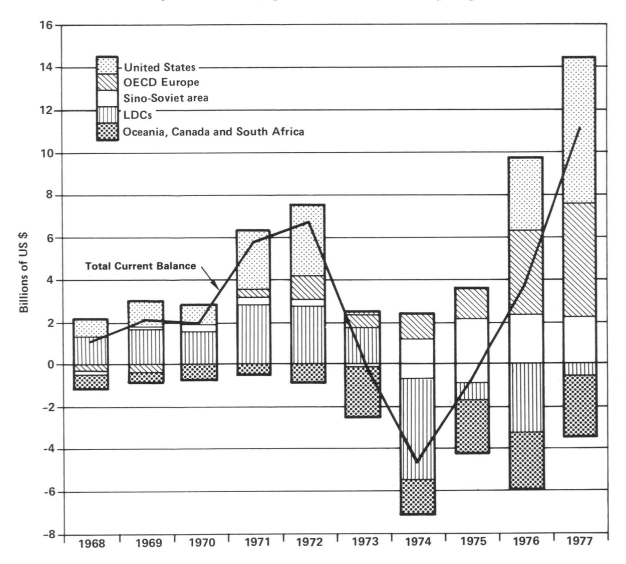

SOURCE: OECD [18(July 1978), p. 38]. Reprinted with permission.

Exhibit 20

Analysis of Japanese Trade: Value of Exports and Imports by Principal Commodity Groups (1970–1976)

Exports (1970 = 100)

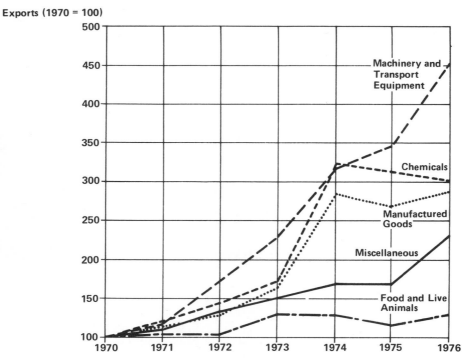

Imports (1970 = 100)

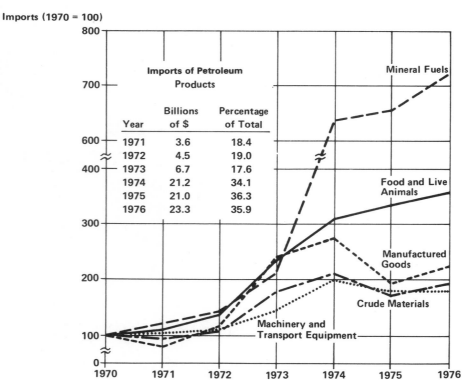

SOURCE: Japan Ministry of Foreign Affairs [15(1977), pp. 48, 50].

Exhibit 21

Percent Share of Export Structure by Major Commodity and Product (in US dollar terms)

Year	Textiles	Chemicals	Iron and Steel	Machinery		
				Total	TV Sets	Automobiles
1960	30.1	4.5	9.6	25.5	0.0	2.0
1965	18.7	6.5	15.3	35.2	1.0	2.8
1970	12.5	6.4	14.7	46.3	2.0	6.9
1975	6.7	7.0	18.3	53.8	1.4	10.7
1977	5.8	5.3	13.1	61.8	1.7	14.4

SOURCE: OECD [18(July 1978), p. 34]. Reprinted with permission.

Exhibit 22

Shares of Japan's Manufactured Imports: Annual Average, 1968–1970 and 1976–1977

Product Category/Source	Total 1977 Japan Imports (billions US $)	1968–1970 Share (%)	1976–1977 Share (%)	Share Change (%)
Capital equipment	4.4			
US		61.0	51.3	(9.7)
Western Europe		35.2	34.0	(1.2)
Developing Asia		1.0	10.7	9.7
Chemicals	2.9			
US		41.2	39.6	(1.6)
Western Europe		42.3	37.3	(5.0)
Developing Asia		2.1	8.3	6.2
Finished metals	2.0			
US		8.6	6.3	(2.3)
Western Europe		8.1	8.9	0.8
Developing Asia		17.4	19.1	6.7
Consumer nondurables	1.5			
US		32.4	12.6	(19.8)
Western Europe		31.8	25.6	(6.2)
Developing Asia		23.0	53.1	30.1
Consumer durables	1.3			
US		39.5	27.2	(12.4)
Western Europe		51.8	42.4	(9.4)
Developing Asia		4.4	25.1	20.7
Textiles	0.7			
US		8.7	5.6	(3.1)
Western Europe		46.0	29.1	(16.9)
Developing Asia		38.0	48.6	10.6

SOURCES: Boston Consulting Group [4]. Cf. J. C. Abegglen and T. M. Hout [1, p. 146ff.]. Excerpted by permission from *Foreign Affairs* (Fall 1978). Copyright 1978 by Council on Foreign Relations, Inc.

NOTES: Western Europe includes EEC, EFTA and others. Developing Asia includes South Korea, Taiwan, Singapore, Hong Kong, Indonesia, Malaysia, Thailand, Philippines; excludes People's Republic of China. Clothing classified under consumer nondurables.

Exhibit 23

Market-size Data (Production Less Exports Plus Imports) in 1975 and 1977, and Export Share of Japanese Production and Import Share of Japanese Market in 1977

Product Group, Products	1975				1977 (estimated)				1977 Imports/Market (%)	1977 Exports/Prdctn (%)
	Domestic Production	Imports	Exports	Market	Domestic Production	Imports	Exports	Market		
	(millions of dollars)				(millions of dollars)					
Agricultural machinery										
Total	1,829	89	86	1,833	2,683	91	185	2,588	3.5	6.9
Harvesting equip	679	27	14	691	1,081	31	21	1,091	2.8	1.9
Tractors	576	43	41	577	895	38	115	818	4.6	12.8
Business equip, systems & supplies										
Total	3,442	537	1,015	2,964	4,799	604	1,620	3,783	16.0	33.8
Computers	1,824	441	130	2,135	2,359	498	191	2,666	18.7	8.0
Chemical processing equip, controls										
Total	594	48	162	480	618	46	260	404	11.4	42.1
Construc equip, bldg matls										
Total	30,840	627	1,504	29,963	41,618	1,018	2,767	39,869	2.6	6.6
Construction tractors	1,102	12	542	572	1,031	9	572	468	1.4	55.5
Hand tools	368	22	90	299	602	45	224	422	10.7	37.2
Electric power equip										
Total	2,786	147	770	2,163	3,780	91	1,272	2,599	3.5	33.7
Generators	908	108	363	653	1,237	56	626	668	8.3	50.6
Transmission equip	1,878	38	407	1,510	2,542	35	647	1,931	1.8	25.5

Food processing & pkging equip										
Total	545	76	42	579	712	73	59	726	10.0	8.3
Machine tools, metal working equip										
Total	1,643	173	504	1,312	2,364	144	840	1,667	8.6	35.5
Cutting tools	766	73	208	631	1,056	65	346	775	8.4	32.8
Metal forming, shaping	685	83	217	551	1,001	61	366	696	8.8	36.6
Medical, dental equip, supplies										
Total	704	115	159	660	1,037	194	217	1,014	19.1	20.9
Metallurgical & primary metals production equip										
Total	1,542	42	214	1,370	1,432	30	230	1,233	2.4	16.1
Printing, publishing equip										
Total	204	59	36	227	264	76	52	288	26.4	19.7
Telecommunications equip										
Total	5,160	72	1,818	3,414	6,245	106	2,408	3,944	2.7	38.6
Consumer radio, TV equip	2,995	26	1,205	1,815	3,455	32	1,565	1,923	1.7	45.3
Electronic components & production equip										
Total	2,298	332	748	1,882	3,908	537	1,229	3,216	16.7	31.4
Textile & apparel mfg equip										
Total	606	89	615	80	716	101	607	210	48.1	84.8
Motor vehicles, transport equip										
Total	34,878	1,057	13,913	22,022	48,048	1,194	20,139	29,103	4.1	41.9
Automobiles	10,767	237	4,029	6,975	14,682	299	7,215	7,766	3.8	49.1
Rail transport equip	777	10	213	575	1,086	9	253	842	1.1	23.3
Marine transport equip	6,717	121	4,791	2,047	7,890	323	5,475	2,737	11.8	69.4
Air transport equip	765	556	26	1,294	610	467	21	1,057	44.2	3.4

SOURCE: U.S., Department of Commerce [25, pp. 27, 45, 76, 102, 129, 154, 186].

Exhibit 24

Analysis of Exports to the US and Western Europe (in US dollar terms)

	Level in Millions of Dollars				Annual Rate of Change (in percent)				Percentage of Total			
	1974	1975	1976	1977	1973-74	1974-75	1975-76	1976-77	1974	1975	1976	1977
Exports to US	12,779	11,149	15,690	19,717	35.2	-12.8	40.7	25.7	100.0	100.0	100.0	100.0
Foodstuff	242	165	236	200	-4.7	-31.8	43.0	-15.3	1.9	1.5	1.5	1.0
Textiles	489	432	576	669	-6.5	-11.7	33.3	16.2	3.8	3.9	3.7	3.4
Chemicals	574	345	413	488	140.2	-39.9	19.7	18.2	4.5	3.1	2.6	2.5
Non-metallic mineral manufactures	202	180	257	337	-2.0	-10.9	42.8	31.1	1.6	1.6	1.6	1.7
Metal products	3,240	2,499	2,900	3,305	106.1	-22.9	16.0	14.0	25.4	22.4	18.5	16.8
Machinery and equipment	7,084	6,664	10,211	13,353	22.7	-5.9	53.2	30.8	55.4	59.8	65.1	67.7
(Television and radio receivers)	733	615	1,317	1,326	-12.9	-16.1	114.1	0.7	5.7	5.8	8.4	6.7
(Motor vehicles)	3,015	2,281	3,529	4,926	42.9	-24.3	54.7	39.6	23.6	20.5	22.5	25.0
(Vessels)	21	46	68	169	-4.5	119.0	47.8	148.5	0.2	0.4	0.4	0.9
Other	948	864	1,097	1,365	7.6	-8.9	27.0	24.4	7.4	7.7	7.0	6.9
Exports to Western Europe	8,593	8,130	10,946	13,044	31.3	-5.4	34.6	19.2	100.0	100.0	100.0	100.0
Foodstuff	136	166	158	102	-8.1	22.1	-4.8	-35.4	1.6	2.0	1.4	0.8
Textiles	299	229	259	301	46.6	-23.4	13.1	16.2	3.5	2.8	2.4	2.3
Chemicals	613	393	451	503	94.0	-35.9	14.8	11.5	7.1	4.8	4.1	3.9
Non-metallic mineral	108	97	123	117	-10.7	-10.2	26.8	-4.9	1.3	1.2	1.1	0.9
Metal products	1,453	1,326	1,539	1,190	84.9	-8.7	16.1	-22.7	16.9	16.3	14.1	9.1
Machinery and equipment	4,987	5,099	7,513	9,655	16.2	2.2	47.3	28.5	58.0	62.7	68.6	74.0
(Television and radio)	482	496	751	839	7.6	2.9	51.4	11.7	5.6	6.1	6.9	6.4
(Motor vehicles)	583	917	1,358	1,692	2.5	57.3	48.1	24.6	6.8	11.3	12.4	13.0
(Vessels)	1,376	953	1,780	2,526	15.5	-30.7	86.8	41.9	16.0	11.7	16.3	19.4
Other	997	820	903	1,176	47.1	-17.8	10.1	30.2	11.6	10.1	8.2	9.0

SOURCE: OECD [18(July 1978), p. 67]. Reprinted with permission.

NOTE: Western Europe consists of EEC, EFTA and other ten western European countries.

REFERENCES

1. Abegglen, J. C. and T. M. Hout. "Facing Up to the Trade Gap with Japan," *Foreign Affairs* (Fall 1978), p. 146ff.

2. Bank of Japan. *Economic Statistics Annual*. Tokyo.

3. ——————. *The Japanese Economy in . . .* Tokyo, annual.

4. Boston Consulting Group. "Competing in Japan," *Perspectives*, no. 216. Boston, occasional.

5. *Boston Globe.*

6. *Business Japan.* Tokyo, monthly.

7. "Cracking Down on Japan," *Newsweek* (Nov. 21, 1977), pp. 75–77.

8. Economist Intelligence Unit. *Annual Economic Review, Japan, South Korea.* London.

9. ——————. *Quarterly Economic Review, Japan, South Korea.* London.

10. ——————. *Quarterly Economic Review, Oil in the Far East and Australia.* London.

11. "European Steelmen Try U.S.-Style Protection," *Business Week* (Jan. 16, 1978), pp. 29, 30.

12. *Financial Times.* London.

13. *Fuji Bank Bulletin.* Tokyo, monthly.

14. *Industrial Review of Japan.* Tokyo, annual.

15. Japan Ministry of Foreign Affairs. *Statistical Survey of Japan's Economy.* Tokyo, annual.

16. *New York Times.*

17. Organization for Economic Cooperation and Development. *Main Economic Indicators.* Paris, monthly.

18. ——————. *OECD Economic Surveys, Japan.* Paris, occasional annual.

19. "The $6 Billion that Japan Is Squirreling Away," *Business Week* (Nov. 14, 1977), p. 194.

20. "Special Report, Japan's Economy in Transition," *Business Week* (July 7, 1975), pp. 44–50.

21. Tanaka, Kakui. *Building A New Japan, A Plan for Remodeling the Japanese Archipelago*, first English ed. Tokyo: Simul Press, 1973.

22. United States, Bureau of International Commerce. *Overseas Business Reports.* Washington: Government Printing Office, occasional.

23. United States, Council on International Economic Policy. *International Economic Report of the President.* Washington: Government Printing Office, annual.

24. United States, Department of Commerce. *International Economic Indicators.* Washington: Government Printing Office, quarterly.

25. ——————. *U.S. Export Opportunities to Japan.* Washington: Government Printing Office, 1978.

26. *Wall Street Journal.*

27. *Wall Street Journal Index,* annual.

28. "What the FTC Dislikes about Reference Prices," *Business Week* (Jan. 23, 1978), p. 26.

Japan E2: The End of "Miracle" Growth?

Besides endemic problems with trade partners (see "Japan E1"), Japan faced other problems as the seventies advanced. Some of these were practical and immediate—e.g., how to "manage" demand when inflation started in 1972, soared in the next year with the oil crisis, and then hung on into 1974 to become part of a puzzling new worldwide phenomenon, stagflation. Other problems were strategic and long range—e.g., what aims to set for the direction and pace of future growth. Again, the focus changed with changes in the economic context. Thus, before the oil crisis and against a backdrop of rising GNP and high trade surpluses, Japan promised critics at home and abroad to switch her emphasis from "growth for growth's sake" to improving the "quality of life." After the crisis—and now against an anticipated backdrop of continuing shortages, deficits, and inflation—Japan laid plans for reducing future growth from the "miracle" pace of the past two decades to an average of only 6.25 percent a year.

Hardly had this target been announced, however, when the stated goal changed from holding growth down to pushing it ahead. In the background of this about-face was a spotty recovery from the recession of 1974, in which exports soared but home demand stagnated (see Exhibit 1).

From both a foreign and domestic point of view this situation was unsatisfactory. In a context once more marked by threats from trade partners as well as by unemployment,

production cutbacks (see Exhibits 2 and 3) and election losses for the ruling Liberal Democratic Party (LDP), a new premier, Takeo Fukuda, promised to take remedial action by getting Japan growing again. At an Economic Summit in April 1977, Fukuda told the world that Japan would grow at 6.7 percent during the current fiscal year (ending March 31, 1978). Although it was evident before year's end that growth would fall well short of this target, on December 22 Fukuda pledged Japan to an even higher growth rate of 7 percent for upcoming FY 1978.

As 1977 drew to a close, Premier Fukuda's program drew many questions: Could growth be increased to the level he had promised? Were the government's pump-priming efforts sufficient to implement this objective? Did the costs of such pump priming outweigh any probable gains? Even if Japan could grow as fast as Fukuda had pledged, could the angry West be placated? What other solutions might be forced upon Japan, and what other initiatives might offer some hope of solving her related trade and growth-rate problems?

Looking beyond these policy issues, analysts pointed to still other problems outside the political arena. Many of Japan's most entrenched practices (such as "permanent" employment and age-related pay) had served well during an era marked by rapid growth and a large supply of young workers, but they were proving costly as growth slowed down and the average age of the workforce increased. What were the implications of current social and demographic trends for industry? For policy makers?

THE CHALLENGE TO "GROWTH FOR GROWTH'S SAKE," 1972

Of the several growth-related issues that succeeded one another in the 1970s, the first was the challenge to "growth for growth's sake"—as some described the strategy Japan had followed so far. The idea that Japan should switch resources from enlarging the industrial base to improving the quality of life was advocated not only by trade partners but also by many circles in Japan. Significantly, when Eisaku Sato stepped down as premier in mid-1972, the winner in the battle to succeed him was a politician who had managed to identify himself with the quality-of-life movement. This was Kakui Tanaka, who had recently published a best seller titled, *Building a New Japan: A Plan for Remodeling the Japanese Archipelago.*

Some proposals for building a "new Japan" involved improvements in the social infrastructure (housing, sewers, water, etc.). Others called for reducing pollution and congestion by dispersing people and plants to new towns, as well as by shifting resources out of heavy industries into clean, "knowledge-intensive" lines such as electronics (including computers) [27, *passim*]. This last prescription was advanced for economic as well as social reasons. Besides reducing pollution, etc., such a shift should increase value added. It should also enable Japan to moderate her need for raw materials imports before her rapidly rising share of these developed into another trade problem.

Although plans to build a new Japan emerged at a time of rising growth and high trade surpluses, the much-changed context after the oil crisis did not cause these plans to be forgotten. Thus, in 1974, an advisory Industrial Structure Council, recently created by the Ministry of International Trade and Industry (MITI), prepared a report (*Japan's Industrial Structure—A Long-Range Vision*) that endorsed such goals as "the growth of national welfare" and "qualitative improvements in the people's life," while it also advocated that Japan become "a healthy informationalized society with computerization as its axis [29, p. 8]. According to the Organization for Economic Cooperation and Development (OECD), similar proposals could be found in successive national economic plans, starting with the one developed for FY 1970–75 [24(July 1976), p. 39]. The actual progress of high technology versus heavy industry in 1970–1977 can to some extent be traced in Exhibit 3; the actual shift of public emphasis toward the social end of the spectrum can to some extent be traced in expenditure data for the national General Account and the Fiscal Investment and Loan Program (FILP) (*see* Exhibits 4, 5, and 6). Further information on changing national aims and the budget is given in the following run-down by the OECD, covering the postwar era as a whole.

> During the reconstruction period (from 1945 to around 1952–1953) economic policies aimed primarily at recovering from the damages of the war and restoring price stability. Subsequently, and until the end of the sixties, policies were essentially directed at achieving a high rate of economic growth, mainly through a high rate of private investment; various tax relief measures, such as: accelerated depreciation of particular types of investment, favourable tax treatment for constitution of special reserves, refunding of customs duties, extraordinary deductions for income from exports, etc., were granted on a highly selective basis to particular industries or investment projects. Public funds under the Fiscal Investment and Loan Programmes [FILP] also contributed importantly to the

Exhibit 1

Gross National Expenditure in Current and Constant Prices, 1970–1977

A. GNE IN CURRENT PRICES (BILLIONS OF YEN)

	1970	1971	1972	1973	1974	1975	1976	1977
Consumers' expndtr	36,286	41,232	47,209	56,727	69,975	82,486	93,449	103,891
Govt current expndtr	5,827	6,865	8,156	10,055	13,198	16,150	17,945	20,244
Gross fixed asset formation	24,771	27,214	31,298	40,658	45,236	44,870	48,755	53,038
Change in stocks	3,041	1,873	1,848	3,600	5,201	2,242	3,093	3,491
National expenditure	69,925	77,184	88,511	111,040	133,610	145,748	163,242	180,664
Exprts of gds and srvcs	8,273	9,896	10,377	12,126	19,453	20,255	23,836	25,541
Less: imprts of gds and srvcs	7,489	7,807	8,236	12,076	20,700	20,350	22,657	22,585
GNP at mkt prices	70,709	79,273	90,652	111,090	132,363	145,653	164,420	183,620
Less: net indirect taxes	4,546	4,965	5,700	6,964	7,398	7,718	9,082	
GNP at factory cost	66,163	74,308	84,952	104,126	124,965	137,935	155,338	183,620

B. GNE IN CONSTANT 1970 PRICES (BILLIONS OF YEN)

	1970	1971	1972	1973	1974	1975	1976	1977
Consumers' expndtr	36,251	38,893	42,492	46,013	46,706	49,593	51,789	53,503
Govt current expndtr	5,796	6,211	6,696	7,188	7,503	8,055	8,357	8,666
Gross fixed asset formation	24,746	27,064	30,942	33,814	30,381	29,558	30,633	31,924
Residential construc	4,761	4,938	5,825	6,738	5,873	6,299	6,733	6,709
Nonresidential construc	14,195	14,835	16,670	18,566	16,565	14,399	14,893	15,294
Government	5,790	7,291	8,447	8,510	7,944	8,860	9,007	9,921
Change in stocks	3,031	1,713	1,659	3,090	3,302	1,375	1,814	2,002
National expenditure	69,824	73,881	80,789	90,105	87,892	88,581	92,593	96,095
Exprts of gds and srvcs	8,272	9,736	10,380	11,136	13,500	14,095	16,469	18,185
Less: imprts of gds and srvcs	7,491	7,789	8,431	10,368	11,658	10,708	11,564	11,797
GNP at mkt prices	70,605	75,828	82,738	90,873	89,734	91,968	97,499	102,483

C. YEAR-TO-YEAR PERCENTAGE CHANGES IN REAL GNE

	1971 1964 Annual Average	1971	1972	1973	1974	1975	1976	1977
Consumers' expndtr	8.3	7.3	9.3	8.3	1.5	6.2	4.4	3.3
Govt current expndtr	5.5	7.2	7.8	7.3	4.4	7.4	3.8	3.7
Gross fixed investment	13.3	9.4	14.3	9.3	−10.2	−2.7	3.6	4.2
Dwellings	13.1	3.7	18.0	15.7	−12.9	7.3	6.9	−0.3
Other prvt	13.7	4.5	12.4	11.4	−10.8	−13.1	3.4	2.7
Government	12.8	25.9	15.9	0.7	−6.7	11.5	1.7	10.2
Stock bldg	—	−43.5	−3.0	86.0	7.0	−58.0	32.0	10.0
Domestic demand	9.6	5.8	9.4	11.5	−2.5	0.8	4.5	3.8
Foreign bal	—	200.5	0.0	−60.6	240.0	183.9	144.8	130.2
Exports (gds and srvcs)	16.9	17.7	6.6	7.3	21.2	4.4	16.8	10.4
Imports (gds and srvcs)	13.2	4.0	8.2	23.0	12.4	−8.2	8.0	2.0
GNP	10.0	7.4	9.1	9.8	−1.3	2.5	6.0	5.1

Exhibit 1 (continued)

D. PERCENTAGE BREAKDOWN OF REAL GNE

	1970	1971	1972	1973	1974	1975	1976	1977
Consumers' expndtr	51.3	51.3	51.4	50.6	52.0	53.9	53.1	52.2
Govt current expndtr	8.2	8.2	8.1	7.9	8.4	8.8	8.6	8.5
Gross fixed asset formation	35.0	35.7	37.4	37.2	33.8	32.1	31.4	31.2
Residential construc	6.7	6.5	7.0	7.4	6.5	6.8	6.9	6.5
Nonresidential construc	20.1	19.6	20.1	20.4	18.5	15.6	15.3	14.9
Government	8.2	9.6	10.2	9.4	8.9	9.6	9.2	9.7
Change in stocks	4.3	2.2	2.0	3.4	3.7	1.5	1.9	2.0
National expenditure	98.9	97.4	97.6	99.2	97.9	96.3	95.0	93.8
Exprts of gds and srvcs	11.7	12.8	12.5	12.3	15.0	15.3	16.9	17.7
Less: imprts of gds and srvcs	−10.6	−10.3	−10.2	−11.4	−13.0	−11.6	−11.9	−11.5
GNP at market prices	100.0	100.0	100.0	100.0	100.0	100.0	100.0	100.0

SOURCE: *OECD Economic Surveys, Japan* [24(July 1975), p. 10; 24(July 1978), pp. 6, 60-62]. Reprinted with permission.

financing of private investment through the various government sponsored financial institutions.[1] It should, furthermore, be noted that public expenditure was largely concentrated on capital projects aimed at fostering the development of private investment, e.g., harbours, roads, railways, preparation of industrial sites, etc.

However, as a result of the growing awareness on the part of the public and government circles of certain undesirable developments accompanying the rate and pattern of growth experienced in the sixties a reorientation of policy took place in the early seventies. A reallocation of resources was generally felt to be needed, away from business investment, and in favour of social overhead capital and services and the improvement of the quality of life . . . [24(July 1976), p. 39].

FIGHTING INFLATION, 1973, 1974

While devising schemes for a "new Japan," the Tanaka government also had to face a

[1] For the nature and scope of FILP's activities, *see* Exhibit 5, Part B.

mounting problem of inflation. Prices started rising in 1972, and in the next two years Japan experienced the greatest price explosion she had known for more than two decades.

Causes and Progress of Inflation

Factors contributing to inflation included not only Japan's domestic boom but also rising prices for raw materials imports under conditions of high world demand; physical shortage of some key imports (as when the United States embargoed shipments of soybeans and lumber in order to protect domestic supplies); bottlenecks and shortages at home, including even shortages of labor as demand outpaced capacity; and, most serious of all, the oil crisis. By its cutoff of supplies in August and its fourfold price hike at year's end, the oil crisis fed inflationary fears and expectations. Hoarding, profiteering, and price-gouging followed. Angered workers then resolved to protect their own interests. In the spring wage offensive of 1974, Japan's unions demanded, and won, their highest increase ever—almost 33 percent.

Exhibit 2

Employment, Unemployment and Net Domestic Product by Sector

A. POPULATION AGED 15 YEARS AND OVER, LABOR FORCE AND UNEMPLOYMENT

	1970	1971	1972	1973	1974	1975	1976	1977 [a]
Population age 15 years and over (000)	78,850	79,790	80,720	82,410	83,440	84,470	85,430	86,310
Labor force (000)	51,530	51,860	51,990	53,260	53,100	53,230	53,780	54,420
Unemployed (000)	590	640	730	680	730	1,000	1,080	1,100
Unemployed /labor force (%)	1.14	1.23	1.40	1.28	1.37	1.88	2.01	2.02

B. EMPLOYMENT AND NET DOMESTIC PRODUCT BY SECTOR (IN PERCENT)

Sector	Employment		Net Domestic Product	
	1970	1976	1970	1976
Primary sector	17.4	12.2	7.8	6.2
Mining	0.4	0.3	0.6	0.5
Manufacturing	27.0	25.5	30.2	25.7
Construction	7.7	9.3	7.3	8.8
Utilities [b]	6.9	7.1	7.9	7.9
Trade	22.5 [c]	25.2 [c]	17.8	18.3
Banking, insurance, real estate			11.3	13.4
Services	14.7	16.9	13.3	15.1
Public administration	3.2	3.3	3.8	4.1
Total (%)	100.0	100.0	100.0	100.0
Total employment (000)	50,940	52,700		
Total NDP (billions of yen)			57,298	140,405

SOURCES: Bank of Japan [1(1977), pp. 277, 317, 318: tables 152 and 175]. OECD [24(July 1978), p. 62, reprinted with permission.

[a] Preliminary.

[b] Electricity, gas, water, transportation, and communications.

[c] The figure combines trade and banking, insurance, real estate categories.

Fueled by such causes, Japan's inflation rose relatively rapidly in 1973 and 1974, as suggested in Exhibit 7.

The Stance of Policy in 1973

Not foreseeing how far inflation would progress, Japan at first did little to control it. The cue that signaled time for a change was the worldwide currency crisis of February 1973, the second such crisis in less than two years to be initiated by the United States. This episode set all currencies afloat and set the yen moving upward (temporarily at least, from ¥302 to ¥266 = US $1). Since Japan could not be sure that the increase at this time would have as little ill effect on exports as the increase of December 1971, demand management turned restrictive. It became more restrictive still after the August oil crisis. The effort to cap

Exhibit 3

Per Industry Indices: Industrial Production, Inventories, Capacity and Operating Ratios (1975 = 100)

Year	Indstry, Gnrl	Mfg Total	Iron & Steel	Non-ferrous Metals	Fabricated Metal Prods	Mchnry Total	Mchnry Excl Elec	Elec Mchnry	Transport Equip	Ceramics, Stone & Clay Prods	Chemcls	Petro & Coal Prods	Pulp, Paper, etc.	Tex-tiles	Lumber & Wood Prods	Food-stuffs & Tobacco	Other	Rubber	Leather
INDEX OF INDUSTRIAL PRODUCTION (PRODUCTION VALUE BASIS)																			
Weights	10,378.0	9,967.0	1,804.4	289.5	351.5	2,887.0	826.1	830.0	1,133.4	392.8	809.7	723.4	344.1	640.4	282.7	995.3	446.2	110.2	48.9
1970	90.2	90.6	89.7	93.5	96.0	86.0	102.8	88.5	73.3	99.5	91.4	78.4	97.7	107.6	119.0	88.8	93.1	87.5	86.7
1973	114.5	115.1	114.7	128.6	132.8	115.1	126.6	122.8	102.5	125.9	114.3	104.7	118.3	120.8	122.4	99.2	123.2	108.7	99.1
1974	110.3	110.8	113.8	112.7	122.5	112.9	124.7	117.4	101.5	117.0	112.8	103.1	113.6	107.1	109.4	99.0	108.7	103.8	97.5
1975	100.0	100.0	100.0	100.0	100.0	100.0	100.0	100.0	100.0	100.0	100.0	100.0	100.0	100.0	100.0	100.0	100.0	100.0	100.0
1976	110.1	110.2	108.0	117.4	116.5	114.4	110.1	129.5	105.3	109.9	111.1	102.4	113.2	109.3	106.8	101.7	113.6	110.2	104.8
1977	113.6	113.6	105.0	125.1	124.5	122.2	116.9	135.6	112.3	114.8	115.4	104.4	115.1	107.2	104.5	107.1	116.4	114.0	103.2
INDEX OF PRODUCERS' STOCKS																			
Weights	10,000.0	9,985.0	1,210.9	477.8	362.9	2,724.6	964.8	994.7	660.6	579.4	993.5	915.3	309.9	773.1	312.5	869.3	455.8	112.5	59.8
1970	63.5	63.6	58.4	34.6	57.0	61.0	54.2	77.9	46.2	72.3	68.9	67.1	50.0	66.2	67.8	80.1	74.8	73.0	65.7
1973	72.8	72.7	77.6	42.4	73.3	64.3	57.5	74.8	56.3	76.0	70.0	93.8	51.3	76.5	66.8	92.0	76.1	67.3	68.4
1974	93.6	93.6	82.3	58.3	97.0	94.8	84.5	98.0	104.0	90.7	88.9	111.7	84.2	105.9	97.0	100.9	98.2	92.4	104.3
1975	100.0	100.0	100.0	100.0	100.0	100.0	100.0	100.0	100.0	100.0	100.0	100.0	100.0	100.0	100.0	100.0	100.0	100.0	100.0
1976	98.5	98.5	112.0	85.2	100.6	93.2	88.6	87.8	107.5	87.6	101.3	105.4	95.4	97.8	84.5	105.5	100.1	97.2	96.0
1977	104.7	104.7	115.7	88.5	118.8	105.9	100.3	102.6	116.0	91.4	101.3	113.2	100.0	100.9	91.9	102.9	104.0	90.6	117.2
INDEX OF PRODUCTION CAPACITY IN MANUFACTURING																			
Weights	—	10,000.0	887.9	318.1	408.2	4,479.5	—	—	—	369.2	1,196.9	464.8	467.1	1,184.6	—	—	—	223.7	—
1973	—	91.7	90.2	88.4	99.1	92.1	—	—	—	90.5	91.4	90.1	89.2	93.8	—	—	—	83.2	—
1974	—	97.8	96.7	96.3	100.4	98.4	—	—	—	96.2	95.5	96.2	97.1	100.1	—	—	—	94.2	—
1975	—	100.0	100.0	100.0	100.0	100.0	—	—	—	100.0	100.0	100.0	100.0	100.0	—	—	—	100.0	—
1976	—	102.8	104.5	102.8	100.1	103.4	—	—	—	103.0	103.2	103.5	102.0	99.6	—	—	—	103.5	—
1977	—	106.4	109.1	104.6	100.3	108.9	—	—	—	103.8	107.0	104.0	102.2	99.8	—	—	—	108.0	—
INDEX OF OPERATING RATIOS IN MANUFACTURING																			
Weights	—	10,000.0	901.5	272.6	404.3	4,289.2	—	—	—	320.1	1,120.8	525.8	488.2	1,397.3	—	—	—	280.2	—
1973	—	128.1	127.5	152.4	146.3	129.5	—	—	—	132.4	130.7	119.6	129.2	115.1	—	—	—	122.2	—
1974	—	117.3	116.8	119.4	131.4	119.6	—	—	—	115.6	123.1	109.6	118.1	106.7	—	—	—	106.1	—
1975	—	100.0	100.0	100.0	100.0	100.0	—	—	—	100.0	100.0	100.0	100.0	100.0	—	—	—	100.0	—
1976	—	108.3	100.8	120.5	98.9	113.4	—	—	—	106.0	104.2	99.7	109.3	105.8	—	—	—	102.3	—
1977	—	107.7	93.9	121.3	101.4	114.0	—	—	—	109.1	102.4	100.1	110.2	103.0	—	—	—	105.6	—

SOURCE: Japan Office of the Prime Minister [20(1978)], pp. 230-233, 236: tables 158, 159, 162].

Exhibit 4

Public Revenues and Expenditures

A. REVENUES AND EXPENDITURES ON THE GENERAL ACCOUNT, FISCAL YEARS, BILLIONS OF YEN[a]

Item	1970 (Actual)	1971 (Actual)	1972 (Actual)	1973 (Actual)	1974 (Actual)	1975 (Actual)	1976 (Actual)	1977 (Revised Budget)	1978 (Original Budget)
Nonborrowed rev	7,921	8,513	10,434	14,134	16,235	14,913	17,265	18,988	23,297
Expndtrs	8,188	9,561	11,932	14,778	19,099	20,861	24,468	29,347	34,395
Deficit	267	1,048	1,498	644	2,864	5,948	7,203	10,359	10,998
Financing									
Transf fr prev yr	191	271	410	862	1,984	1,280	613	374	13
Bond issues	347	1,817	1,950	1,766	2,160	5,281	7,198	9,985	10,985
Transf to follow yr	271	410	862	1,984	1,280	613	608	0	0
Deficit/expndtrs (%)	3.3	11.0	12.6	4.4	15.0	29.6	29.4	35.3	32.1

B. CHANGES IN NOMINAL GNP, NATIONAL GENERAL ACCOUNT EXPENDITURES, LOCAL ORDINARY ACCOUNT EXPENDITURES[b] AND THE FISCAL INVESTMENT AND LOAN PROGRAM (FILP),[c] FISCAL YEARS

	1970	1971	1972	1973	1974	1975	1976	1977	1978
Billions of yen									
Nominal GNP[d]	73,050	81,596	94,765	115,675	136,422	149,632	169,209	188,000E	210,600E
Expndtrs									
Natl GA[e]	8,188	9,561	11,932	14,778	19,099	20,861	24,468	29,347	34,295
Local OA[f]	9,815	11,910	14,618	17,474	22,888	25,655	28,907	28,836	34,340
Net total, GA, OA[g]	14,126	16,910	20,746	25,193	32,746	37,260	42,795	45,054	54,174
FILP[e]	3,790	5,009	6,038	7,413	9,038	10,561	11,287	13,926	14,887
Percent changes									
Nominal GNP	17.3	11.7	16.1	22.0	17.9	9.7	13.4	11.1	12.0
Expndtrs									
Natl GA	18.4	16.8	24.8	23.9	29.2	9.2	17.3	19.9	16.9
Local OA	22.2	21.3	22.7	19.5	31.0	12.1	12.7	-0.2	19.1
Net total, GA, OA	21.0	19.7	22.7	21.4	30.0	13.8	14.9	5.3	20.2
FILP	19.4	31.8	20.5	26.1	21.9	17.5	7.2	23.4	6.9
Percentage of Nominal GNP									
Natl GA expndtrs	11.2	11.7	12.6	12.8	14.0	13.9	14.5	15.6	16.3
Local OA expndtrs	13.4	14.6	15.4	15.1	16.8	17.1	17.1	15.3	16.3
Net total, GA, OA	19.3	20.7	21.9	21.8	24.0	24.9	25.3	30.0	25.7
FILP	5.2	6.1	6.4	6.4	6.6	7.1	6.7	7.4	7.1

C. NET TOTAL OF INITIAL BUDGET EXPENDITURES ON THE GENERAL ACCOUNT, NATIONAL SPECIAL ACCOUNTS, GOVERNMENT-AFFILIATED AGENCIES AND LOCAL FINANCE PLAN, FISCAL YEARS (TRILLIONS OF YEN)

	1970	1971	1972	1973	1974	1975	1976	1977	1978
GA	7.95	9.41	11.47	14.28	17.10	21.29	24.30	28.51	34.29
Spec accts	16.99	18.25	20.51	24.38	30.08	36.41	46.23	56.36	67.79
Gvt-affil agencies	5.81	6.56	8.14	9.54	10.53	12.23	14.58	16.55	17.83
Total	30.75	34.23	40.11	48.21	57.71	69.93	85.11	101.43	119.91
Overlapping figures	12.68	13.67	15.90	19.22	22.82	26.64	31.85	39.41	47.25
Net total	18.07	20.56	24.21	28.99	34.89	43.29	53.26	62.02	72.66
Local finance plan	7.89	9.17	11.75	14.55	17.38	21.56	25.26	28.84	34.34
Grand total	25.96	30.28	35.96	43.54	52.27	64.85	78.52	90.86	107.00
Overlapping figures	4.16	5.02	6.21	7.63	8.78	10.83	12.64	14.47	17.26
Net total	21.81	25.26	29.75	35.92	43.49	54.01	65.88	76.39	89.74
Net total of above									
Percent change	17.1	15.8	17.8	20.7	21.1	24.2	22.0	16.0	17.5
Percentage of nominal GNP[h]	29.9	31.0	31.4	31.1	31.9	36.1	38.9	40.6	42.6

SOURCES: Japan Ministry of Finance [18(Sep. 1978) notes: pp. 43–47, and tables 1-1, 1-2, 1-3, 1-4]; Japan Office of the Prime Minister [20(1978), pp. 442, 443: table 321].

NOTES TO PART C: (1) Initial budgets are prepared by the government and presented to the Diet before the start of the fiscal year. A supplementary budget, introduced later, usually increases the initial outlay figure, and generally yields a planned expenditure that is slightly higher than is actually made. Since borrowings are keyed to the supplemented figure, "surplus" revenue is obtained, and this is later transferred to the following year (see A above). (2) Besides the General Account, the national government has a varying number of special accounts—39 of them in FY 1977. These cover the operation of special funds, public enterprises and government-sponsored financial institutions. (3) The local Finance Plan is not a budget but an estimate of the total revenues and expenditures of local governments. It is prepared by the national government and is submitted to the Diet as a "reference" only.

ª Fiscal years start April 1 of the calendar year; the General Account (GA) budget is the basic budget of the national government. Taxes are the main source of GA revenue (see Exhibit 5, Part A). Outlays include capital as well as current expenditures, plus substantial transfers to other accounts.

ᵇ The local Ordinary Account (OA) is analogous to the national GA account.

ᶜ The Fiscal Investment and Loan Program (FILP) is not a budget, but its function has come to be considered "as important as that of the budget." Funds entrusted to the government are the main source of FILP revenue (see Exhibit 5, Part B). Outlays are made for loans and investments. Recipients are mainly public enterprises and government-sponsored financial institutions. "It should be noted that part of the funds rechanneled by the FILP are already recorded in the central government and local government budgets."

ᵈ Actual GNP through FY 1976; estimated for FY 1977; prospective for FY 1978.

ᵉ Actual GA and FILP expenditures through FY 1976; revised budget figures for FY 1977; initial budget figures for FY 1978.

ᶠ Actual OA expenditures through FY 1976; initial budget for FY 1977 and FY 1978.

ᵍ The net totals of GA and OA were prepared from initial budget figures for both FY 1977 and FY 1978.

ʰ GNP estimated for FY 1977 and forecast for FY 1978.

Exhibit 5

Percentage Breakdown of GA Revenues, FILP Sources and Uses of Funds, and Japan's National Tax Revenue

A. PERCENTAGE BREAKDOWN OF GA REVENUES BY SOURCE AND EXPENDITURES BY PURPOSE, FISCAL YEARS

	1970 (Actual)	1974 (Actual)	1975 (Actual)	1976 (Actual)	1977 (Revised Budget)	1978 (Original Budget)
Revenues						
Total (billions of yen)	8,459	20,379	21,473	25,076	29,347	34,295
Total by source (%)						
Taxes, stamp duties	86.3	73.8	64.0	62.4	58.4	62.5
Monopoly profits	3.2	1.7	1.6	2.6	1.9	2.1
Govt enterprise	0.0	0.0	0.0	0.0	0.0	0.0
Surplus from prev FY	2.3	9.7	6.0	2.4	1.3	0.0
Miscellaneous	4.1	4.2	3.8	3.8	4.4	3.3
Bonds, borrowing	4.1	10.6	24.6	28.7	34.0	32.0
Total	100.0	100.0	100.0	100.0	100.0	100.0
Expenditures						
Total (billions of yen)	8,188	19,200	20,861	24,468	29,347	34,295
Total by purpose (%)						
Social security, etc.[a]	14.1	16.4	19.8	19.9	19.5	19.8
Culture, educ, science	11.8	12.1	13.0	12.5	11.9	11.2
National defense	7.2	6.4	6.6	6.2	5.8	5.5
Public works	17.6	16.1	16.7	16.0	17.0	15.9
Assistance to industry	1.7	0.8	0.9	0.9	0.9	0.7
Foodstuffs control prog	6.0	5.2	4.4	3.7	2.8	2.5
Distrib to localities	21.6	21.8	16.0	15.8	16.0	16.4
Debt service	3.5	4.4	5.3	7.5	7.9	9.4
Other	16.5	16.8	17.3	17.5	18.4	18.7
Total	100.0	100.0	100.0	100.0	100.0	100.0

B. PERCENTAGE BREAKDOWN OF SOURCES AND USES OF FUNDS IN THE FILP, FISCAL YEARS[b]

	1970	1974	1975	1976	1977	1978
Sources (billions of yen)	3,799	9,458	11,410	12,232	14,464	14,888
Sources (%)						
Spec acct for industrial investment	2.7	0.7	0.6	0.6	0.4	0.2
Postal savings	37.4	41.4	44.3	47.6	49.6	45.0
Welfare pensions	22.5	19.4	18.7	19.8	20.4	17.8
Other trust funds						
Bureau funds	13.6	23.9	23.4	16.0	13.0	18.0
Postal life insurance	10.7	10.4	8.9	9.4	9.4	9.8
Govt guar borrowing	13.1	4.2	4.1	6.6	7.2	9.2
Total	100.0	100.0	100.0	100.0	100.0	100.0

Exhibit 5 (continued)

B. PERCENTAGE BREAKDOWN OF SOURCES AND USES OF FUNDS IN THE FILP, FISCAL YEARS[b] (CONTINUED)

	1970	1974	1975	1976	1977	1978
Uses (billions of yen)	3,580	7,923	9,310	10,619	12,538	14,888
Uses (%)						
Housing	19.3	19.7	21.4	22.7	24.3	24.7
Water, sewers	11.6	16.4	16.7	15.9	14.7	14.9
Welfare facil	2.8	3.1	3.4	3.7	3.3	3.3
Educ, other facil	2.2	2.5	2.9	2.4	4.2	4.7
Smaller busn	15.4	15.5	15.6	16.6	16.7	16.1
Agricul, etc.	5.0	4.1	4.1	4.8	4.9	4.8
Transport, communications, regional devel, etc.	27.4	26.9	25.2	22.9	21.3	22.0
Basic industries	5.7	3.0	3.0	2.8	2.8	2.7
Trade, econ coop	10.6	8.8	7.7	8.2	7.8	6.8
Total	100.0	100.0	100.0	100.0	100.0	100.0

C. PERCENTAGE BREAKDOWN OF JAPAN'S NATIONAL TAX REVENUE BY SOURCE, FISCAL YEARS[c,d]

	1970	1974	1975	1976	1977	1978
Tax revenue						
Total (hundred billion yen)	77.8	157.5	145.1	168.1	182.5	227.3
Sources (%)						
Direct taxes, total	66.0	73.9	69.3	67.5	67.5	69.2
Prsnl inc tax	31.2	33.9	37.8	36.9	35.6	35.6
Corp tax	33.0	36.9	28.5	28.5	30.1	32.0
Misc direct taxes	1.8	3.1	3.1	2.1	1.8	1.6
Indirect taxes, total	34.0	26.1	30.7	32.5	32.5	30.8
Liquor	7.9	5.3	6.3	6.1	6.1	6.2
Gasoline	6.4	4.7	5.7	5.9	6.2	5.6
Commodity	4.4	3.9	4.7	4.3	4.5	4.0
Customs	4.9	2.3	2.6	3.0	2.8	2.4
Other	10.4	9.9	11.4	13.2	12.9	12.6
Total	100.0	100.0	100.0	100.0	100.0	100.0

SOURCES: Japan Ministry of Finance [18(Sep. 1973), p. 54: tables 1-10 and 1-11; (Sep. 1978), p. 54: tables 1-10 and 1-11]; Japan Office of the Prime Minister [20(1978), pp. 442, 443: table 321, p. 454: table 324B].

[a] Includes "livelihood protection," social welfare, health and sanitation measures, unemployment measures, and social insurance. The latter rose from 9.3 percent of total GA expenditures in 1974 to 12.1 percent in the budgeted figure for 1978. In addition, GA "other" expenditures include war-related and public servants' pensions. These came to an additional 3.1 to 3.9 percent of total GA outlays.

[b] Source data are actual figures through 1976, initial figures for 1977 and 1978; use data are all initial figures.

[c] Includes stamp duties and monopoly receipts.

[d] Actual figures through FY 1976; revised estimate for FY 1977; initial budget for FY 1978.

Exhibit 6

Tax Burden, Relative Tax Burden, and Debt

A. JAPAN'S NATIONAL AND LOCAL TAX BURDEN AS A PERCENTAGE OF NATIONAL INCOME

	1970 (Actual)	1971 (Actual)	1972 (Actual)	1973 (Actual)	1974 (Actual)	1975 (Actual)	1976 (Actual)	1977 (Rev Bdgt)	1978 (Orig Bdgt)
Natl tax (hundred billion yen)	77.8	84.4	104.0	140.5	157.5	145.1	168.1	182.5	227.3
Local tax (hundred billion yen)	37.5	42.4	50.0	64.9	82.4	81.5	95.6	108.2	118.5
Natl inc (hundred billion yen)	591.3	658.4	761.3	918.5	1,135.9	1,274.0	1,440.8	1,605.6	1,771.4
Natl tax/natl inc (%)	13.1	12.8	13.7	15.3	13.9	11.4	11.7	11.4	12.8
Local tax/natl inc (%)	6.4	6.5	6.5	7.1	7.2	6.4	6.6	6.7	6.7
Total tax/natl inc (%)	19.5	19.3	20.2	22.4	21.1	17.8	18.3	18.1	19.5

B. TAXATION AS A PERCENTAGE OF GNP IN SELECTED AREAS AND COUNTRIES—AVERAGE FOR 1971-1973

	Total Taxes	Gds & Srvcs Taxes	Prsnl Inc Taxes	Corp Inc Taxes	Other Taxes	Social Security Contribns
Japan	21.27	4.46	5.43	4.12	3.17	4.09
US	27.80	5.40	9.31	3.06	4.18	5.85
EEC avg	36.08	11.41	8.70	2.28	2.36	8.30
OECD avg	31.06	9.68	7.65	2.15	2.48	6.94

C. GROWTH IN NATIONAL GOVERNMENT DEBT, FISCAL YEARS, YEAR END[a]

	1970	1971	1972	1973	1974	1975	1976	1977
Total (billions of yen)	6,226	7,606	11,704	13,154	15,709	22,795	32,678	46,243
Percent change	13.6	22.2	53.9	12.4	19.4	44.3	43.4	4.15
Percent of nominal GNP	12.2	11.7	12.4	11.4	11.5	15.2	19.3	22.0

SOURCES: Japan Ministry of Finance [18(Sep. 1978), pp. 6, 63: tables 2-2 and A-3]; Japan Office of the Prime Minister [20(1977), p. 454: table 324A]. Part B: OECD [24(July 1976), p. 44], reprinted with permission.
[a] March 31 of the following calendar year.

Exhibit 7

Percentage Change in Wholesale Prices (all commodities), 1972–1974

	Japan	US	France	Italy	W Ger	UK
1973–72	15.9	13.1	12.7	16.9	8.1	No
1974–73	31.3	18.9	23.6	40.8	13.1	Series

Percentage Change in Wholesale Prices (manufactured goods), 1972–1974

	Japan	US	France[a]	Italy	W Ger	UK
1973–72	15.1	9.6	14.6	15.1	6.6	7.3
1974–73	28.4	19.3	29.1	45.5	13.4	23.4

SOURCE: U.S., Department of Commerce [28(Sep. 1976), p. 23; 28(Mar. 1978), p. 23].

[a] Industrial products.

prices was pursued not only through fiscal and monetary policy but also through a number of more direct measures.

As for monetary policy, the OECD noted that the discount rate was raised in several steps through 1973, reaching 9 percent on December 22, which was an "unprecedented level." Reserve requirements were increased four times; window guidance, too, was made "markedly more restrictive in each successive quarter"; credit ceilings were extended to include certain types of financial institutions that had never previously been affected, and the interest rate on savings was raised several times.[2] Selective guidance in the pattern of bank credit was introduced in December. This was to prove useful later in curbing loans for "nonurgent uses" and in cushioning the impact of recession on especially hard-hit sectors such as housing [24(July 1974), p. 33; 19(1975), p. 38].

As for fiscal policy, the OECD noted that after a decade and a half of not being used as an "active" means of managing demand, this had been put to work to fight the recessions of 1965-1966 and 1971-1972 [24(July 1976), pp. 38, 39].[3] Thus, the initial budget for 1973 had been drawn up with economic expansion in mind, and the stance of policy was difficult to change when deflation became the new objective. The shift was impeded by government's obligation to raise civil servants' pay by about 20 percent, as well as to finance a 15 percent increase in the producer price of rice under an already deficit-ridden public Foodstuffs Control Program.

---

[2] Window guidance, exercised by the Bank of Japan, constitutes a "supplementary weapon" of monetary policy, used mainly at times of "financial stringency." The central bank imposes "direct controls" on the amount (or growth) of lending by the "individual banks." The controls may vary among banks but do not necessarily do so [4, pp. 135, 158].

---

[3] The deliberate use of public finance for countercyclical purposes was not in accord with Dodge-era precepts, which made the maintenance of a balanced budget the chief objective of fiscal policy. This was not to say, however, that fiscal policy made no contribution to the rapid growth of Japan's GNP. The reader is referred to the opening section of "Japan D2: A Strategy for Meeting the Problems of Growth."

Nevertheless, the authorities did what they could, chiefly by means of delaying public works. Quantifying the results of this step, the OECD noted that ¥1290 billion of expenditures was carried over to FY 1974, or 17.9 percent of the expenditure on public works budgeted for FY [24(July 1974), pp. 30, 31; 24(July 1975), p. 44].

In addition, the fight against inflation was given "top priority" in the formulation of the initial budget for upcoming FY 1974. "Spending on public works which has the largest multiplier effects on GNP, was to stagnate in nominal terms and to decline substantially in volume" [24(July 1975), p. 44]. Although the personal income tax was to be cut for political reasons by approximately ¥1450 billion, the inflationary impact of this step was to be offset by raising the tax rate on corporate profits from 36.75 to 40 percent [7(I 1974), pp. 8, 9].

As for "other measures" to fight inflation, the OECD reported that

> since the spring of 1973, concerned with the rapid increase in prices, the government has taken [various] measures [outside the fiscal and monetary areas] aimed at containing inflation. In April import quotas were increased by about 30 percent and customs duties on certain basic commodities were reduced. Administrative surveillance over price trends was also intensified to ensure that the fall in the yen cost of imports deriving from the appreciation of the yen be passed on to consumers. In addition, under a newly approved law, speculative hoarding of certain commodities, including soya beans and raw silk [was] forbidden.

> With the outbreak of the oil crisis the scope of government direct intervention was greatly expanded. Early in December guidelines were issued to major industries to halt new investments in equipment . . . and these were later extended at least until September 1974. According to official estimates, this measure should result in a reduction of . . . about 10 percent of planned

investment expenditure during the second half of FY 1973. The government also instructed 11 industries, major consumers of oil and electricity, to reduce oil and electricity consumption and imposed restrictions to curtail nonessential uses of oil. Furthermore, the Diet approved two bills providing the government with the power to impose price controls and rationing of essential commodities, including petroleum products. Ceilings were imposed on certain products. Prices of petroleum products were temporarily frozen, and, on 16th March, were increased by 62 percent on average. In March the prices of certain basic commodities and essential consumer goods were also made subject to administrative guidance and the scheduled increases in the price of rice and railway fares was postponed until October [24(July 1974), pp. 35, 36].

Despite these varied efforts at control, inflation proved hard to slow down. Its intractable behavior inspired much analysis later. Why had demand-management policy worked so ineffectively for so long? And what had been the impact on Japan's social fabric?

Sluggish Response

One reason sometimes given for the slow response of demand to policy in 1973 was Japan's late start in imposing controls. Another was that big business was more liquid at this time than in earlier periods of tight money, so it was better able to engage in self-financing and less amenable to credit restraints (*see* Exhibit 8).

The most basic reason, however, was that the inflation of 1973 was not just another case of superheating, such as Japan had dealt with many times. On this occasion, inflationary fears, physical shortages, bottlenecks, and rising import prices played a dominant role. There were "exceptional"

Exhibit 8

Changes in Self-Financing Capacity of Corporate Enterprises

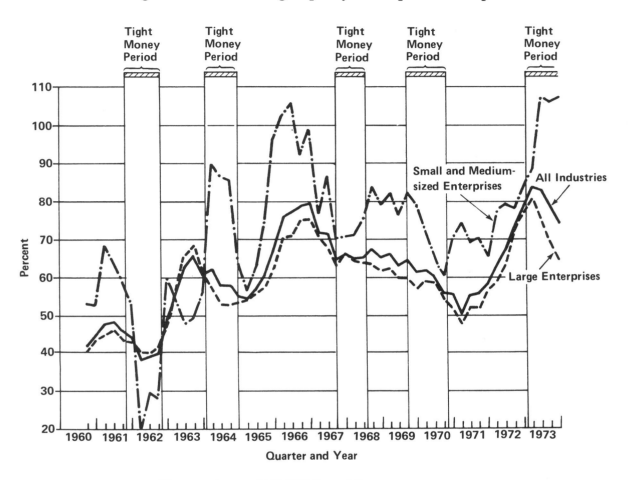

SOURCE: Japan Economic Planning Agency [14(1973/74), p. 44].

developments, and in the words of the OECD, they "could neither be prevented nor attenuated appreciably in any short period by demand-management measures" [24(July 1974), p. 56].

Social Strains

Besides defying standard methods of control, the inflation of 1973–1974 brought about social consequences that were widely viewed with concern. For example, Japan's Economic Planning Agency pointed out in

a "pessimistic" White Paper that the effort to transform Japan from the workshop of the world into a welfare society would be "severely imperilled" [22(Aug. 11, 1973)]. It also complained that hoarding and the "tight supply-demand situation" gave "unexpectedly large profit to a good number of enterprises," thereby making the distribution of the national income "considerably unfair" [14(1973), p. 4]. This maldistribution of income was dramatized when it was announced that a single real estate operator had earned $5.7 million in 1973 [22(Jan. 1, 1974)]. His reward came against a backdrop of rapidly rising prices for land. In Tokyo, for example, the rise was "astronomical":

prime office space in the city was commanding $1300 a square foot by late 1974 [31(Nov. 14, 1974)].

Class antagonism also mounted as inflation barreled ahead. Hoarding and alleged price-fixing and price-gouging became important political issues. For example, as early as April 1973, the minister of justice threatened to clamp down on speculations in and hoarding of key consumer goods by Japan's major trading houses; on the following day, the heads of six of the largest such concerns were called before the Diet to testify [22(Apr. 6, 7, 1973)]. At the same time, MITI issued "sharp warnings" to offenders and urged the public to refrain from buying certain products, such as cotton and wool, the price of which had been artificially driven up by the large trading corporations [7(II 1973), p. 6]. Such moves accelerated after the oil crisis. Thus, in January 1974 the government announced that a "nationwide search" would be made for hoarders of a number of commodities, including toilet paper, sugar, and detergents [22(Jan. 11, 1974)]. In February the Diet responded to "repeated charges from opposition parties, labor unions and consumer groups" by launching an investigation into claims that big business "had jacked up prices unnecessarily, hoarded goods, and evaded taxes." Executives of twenty trading companies, banks, oil companies, and consumer goods producers were grilled by the Diet on these charges for three days, admitting to some and denying others [22(Feb. 28, 1974)]. Just a few months later, in May, twelve oil companies and seventeen senior oil company executives were indicted on charges of conspiracy to fix prices and to control production during 1973 [22(May 29, 1974)]. Declining confidence in big business was further attested by attacks on the Keidanren—Japan's most prestigious businessmen's association—for manipulating conservative politics, failing to stop pollution, and allowing prices to "leap" [22(May 24, 1974)].

Looking back at some of the infighting over prices occurring in 1973, analysts wondered if this could be indicative of fundamental changes in the way Japanese institutions worked together. Thus, the Economic Intelligence Unit (EIU) wondered if it could be indicative of waning government influence on business [7(II 1973), p. 6]. Similarly, a US commentator suggested that "business, the consumer, unions and small enterprises are looking less and less like members of a team" [9, p. 296].

PLANNING FOR AN INDEFINITE SLOWDOWN

Inflation was only the first of several problems expected to result from the adverse trends that revealed themselves in 1973. Looking behind the price rise to its causes, Japan saw mainly the oil crisis but also the US embargoes and rising competition for raw materials. Thus, scarcities were seen as the underlying factor, and scarcities were expected to continue. In a world beset by scarcities, could Japan aspire to preserve her "miracle" rate of growth? The official answer was "no."

The belief that growth must slow showed up clearly in a forecast prepared in the aftermath of the oil crisis by the powerful and influential MITI. As presented to the OECD in November 1974, this document argued that "production growth" could probably average only 6 percent a year in 1973–1980 and only 6.5 percent in 1980–1985. Energy would be the principal constraint. Between 1970 and 1985 energy resources would probably grow by only 6 to 7 percent a year, as against 11.8 percent a year in 1960–1970. Water supply, environmental issues, and the limited supply of land and labor were listed as additional constraints, although just the last of these was quantified. Thus, the workforce was expected to increase by only 0.5 to 0.8 percent a year between 1973 and 1985, compared with 1.3 percent a year between 1965 and 1973 [24(July 1975), pp. 47-50].

Further confirmation that Japan saw future growth as having to slow down came in the next national Economic Plan, which was being readied at this time. Covering the period FY 1976-1980, it set an average real growth target of only 6.25 percent a year compared with a target of 9.1 percent set in the Economic Plan for 1973-1977 and a target of 10.6 percent set in a short-lived plan for 1970-1975 [24(July 1975), p. 48; 24(July 1976), pp. 41, 50].

As might be expected, so deep a drop in Japan's growth objective evoked both skepticism and objections. It was noted that the targets set in previous plans had always been substantially exceeded. Some economists reportedly believed that Japan's growth could still reach 7 to 9 percent [25(June 1976), pp. 6-11]. The OECD, however, found the planners' reasons for slowing growth compelling, and it saw the plan as a genuine "turning point" [24(July 1976), p. 41]. Similarly, prestigious Keidanren referred to a "growing national consensus in favor of slower growth or stable growth" [21, p. 42].

FACING STAGFLATION, 1974

Even as Japan made plans to cut growth to an average of only 6.25 percent, actual growth started to plummet well below the modest new target. It was strongly negative in the first quarter of 1974, turned down again in the fourth, and wound up in the red for the year. Yet, January's fourfold price increase for oil and April's 33 percent wage hike for labor meant that costs and prices would leap. In fact, by the end of 1974 wholesale prices were up by 31.3 per-

cent, consumer prices by 24.5 percent, and export prices by 33.7 percent [24(July 1975), p. 22]. Taken along with the drop in GNP—the first full year's downturn in more than twenty years—such trends added up to a puzzling new phenomenon, stagflation.

As these price and growth trends developed, a key issue for policy was which problem, inflation or recession, should be given top priority.

Demand Management in 1974

In point of fact, little was done by way of reflation in 1974. In its annual rundown on monetary policy, the OECD pointed out that the discount rate was kept at the previous year's high rate of 9 percent, and that the money supply "continued to decelerate sharply" until it turned up "somewhat" in the final quarter. Window guidance, too, was "progressively restrictive," until it "stabilized" late in the year [24(July 1975), p. 37].

The pattern was much the same in fiscal policy. A designedly restrictive initial budget was administered in such a way as to make it more restrictive still, and the supplementary budget was kept as small as unavoidable outlays would permit.[4] Only toward the end of the year, "when aggregate demand weakened and progress was made on the price front" did fiscal policy grow more "accommodating." Thus, additional FILP loans of ¥1.3 trillion were slated

---

[4] Some 90 percent of the supplementary budget was earmarked to cover increases in personnel pay, the producer price of rice, and revenue transfers to local government. These increases were termed "inevitable" because the government's pay scales were tied to industry's and rice prices were tied to industrial wages, while transfers to localities had to reach a fixed percentage of national tax revenue [10(1975), p. 19].

to be doled out "in several steps" over the six months starting in October. Although this policy change brought a "marked" increase of public outlays on goods and services during the period involved [10(1975), pp. 19, 20; 24(July 1975), pp. 44–46], the OECD later concluded that the impact of fiscal policy was "procyclical" in 1974 [24(July 1976), p. 40].

This was not to say, however, that no attention was paid to the recession. As the Planning Agency put it, aggregate demand was held down "firmly," but "at the same time, social unrest due to bankruptcies or unemployment was mitigated . . . in selected cases" [13(1975), p. 1].

Selective Mitigation

The groups identified as getting state help in 1974 were mainly small business, housing, industries in special difficulties, and local governments in financial straits. Several means were used to give assistance, of which public loans bulked the largest. Thus, FILP loans totaled ¥917.7 billion between April and December 1974, and these went mainly to small business (¥500 billion) and housing [10(1975), p. 20]. In addition, window guidance was used "to cushion the impact of recession on certain sectors particularly hard hit, such as residential construction [24(July 1975), p. 38]. Recession cartels were another way to help selected industries and were activated in some cases, e.g., in the spinning segment of the textiles [13(1975/76), pp. 99–101]. In addition, national purchases of local bonds were added to the ways usually used to help local governments, and these purchases were said to free up bank resources for loans to industry [10(1975), p. 20].

By year's end, two legislative bills were also being readied to help labor. As passed in early 1975, one of these extended public unemployment insurance to cover the entire workforce. (Previously, only some 45 percent were covered, the primary sector and enterprises with fewer than five employees having been exempted from the earlier law.) The second measure set up a subsidy system for companies laying off workers with part pay instead of dismissing them entirely. These subsidies covered half the companies' costs (or two-thirds in the case of smaller firms). The initial cost of this program came to ¥42.4 billion through September 1975, and the program was credited with preventing unemployment for 200,800 persons. Following these and other changes, by 1977 an unemployed regular worker would receive a "basic" daily unemployment allowance of 60 to 80 percent of his wages (or a minimum of ¥1,750 to a maximum of ¥5,460). In addition, monthly allowances for training, commuting, and lodging might total ¥24,500. The duration of these benefits would vary, being 90 days for workers under age 30 or for anyone employed less than one year, but 300 days for workers aged 55 and over. This time might be extended by 60 to 90 days under certain circumstances, or increased to a year for persons taking training of this duration [10(1976), p. 30; 13(1974/75), pp. 11, 12; 16, pp. 14–16; 24(July 1975), p. 46].

SEEKING STABILITY—PLUS RECOVERY, 1975

Early in 1975 it became clear that growth in the on-going calendar year might be little higher than in 1974, but prices appeared to be heading downward. Specifically, the first quarter showed a GNP drop of 0.3 percent while wholesale prices dropped 0.6 percent and export prices 5.4 percent against the final quarter of the preceding year [24(July 1976), pp. 6, 19]. Under these circumstances, policy had to be reassessed: How soon and how decisively should it change from deflation to reflation?

Looking ahead, the Economist Intelligence Unit (EIU) saw politics as favoring an early shift. "Most Liberal Democrats," it said, "would regard another year of recession as politically unacceptable" [7(IV, 1974), p. 10]. On the other hand, economic considerations still operated to retard a switch:

> First, deflation is seen as an effective means of eliminating the effects of the oil price increase on the balance of payments. . . . Secondly, it is argued that continuing curbs . . . are necessary . . . to prevent opportunistic price increases which would endanger the recent modest progress towards greater price stability. Thirdly, the authorities are concerned to limit the size of the forthcoming spring wage settlements, since awards on last year's scale (+32.9%) would make their aim of bringing [consumer price] inflation down to 11%–12% practically impossible [7(I 1975), p. 9].

What action to take in 1975 would be up to a new government. Before the end of 1974, Premier Tanaka had been tarred by a scandal that eventually forced him out of office. His successor was Takeo Miki, an elderly "Mr. Clean." No economist himself, Miki promised to accept the economic counsel of Takeo Fukuda, one of his chief rivals for power. Describing himself as he entered Miki's cabinet, Fukuda quipped, "I'm not a finance man but a fireman who attacks inflation" [10(1976), p. 7].

Fukuda reportedly believed that Tanaka's downfall was as much due to soaring prices as it was to his other, legal difficulties [7(I 1975), p. 9]. Thus, the new team moved with caution in changing demand-management policy from restrictive to reflationary, even though growth continued to waver. Three small cuts in the discount rate, some additional easing of credit, and three so-

called "business propping" programs were announced in the first half of the year, but only in August was Fukuda ready to put recovery on a par with price stability as one of government's "dual" objectives, to be attained "at the same time" [13(1974/75), p. i].

Just one month later, however, Fukuda announced that progress on the price front now permitted "drastic" efforts to "wipe out" the recession [31(Sep. 15, 1975)]. To implement this shift, the government made a deep cut in the discount rate (see Exhibits 9 and 10). In addition, it proposed a fourth "business propping" program that would be more vigorous than its predecessors: whereas the prior programs in February, March, and June had simply moved up the date for public works expenditures and housing loans that would have been made later anyway [21, p. 13; 24(July 1976), p. 36], September's program called for additional outlays. These were to be financed through a supplementary budget of ¥0.8 trillion. Half would be spent on public works, the rest on "additional loans to house building and small enterprises, and incentives to encourage private antipollution investments" [24(July 1976), pp. 31, 36].

Reviewing policy at year's end, analysts tended to disagree on how far it had helped to pull Japan out of the previous year's recession. According to the OECD, "Expansionary fiscal policy in 1975 contributed importantly to reflating the depressed economy, both through discretionary changes in expenditure and a marked automatic tax impact." Elaborating on the latter point, the OECD noted that economic growth and thus tax yield had been overestimated when the year's initial budget was drawn up. At this time, the planned deficit was to be only ¥2.7 trillion [24(July 1976), pp. 36, 37, 41], in contrast to the ¥5.9 trillion that was actually incurred (see Exhibit 4).

Exhibit 9

Monetary Trends: M1 and M2

A. THE MONEY SUPPLY IN BILLIONS OF YEN: M1 AND M2 (1970–1977)

	1970	1971	1972	1973	1974	1975	1976	1977
M1	21,360	27,693	34,526	40,311	44,951	49,948	56,179	60,787
M2	54,237	67,398	84,040	98,188	109,494	125,330	142,249	158,033

B. PERCENTAGE CHANGES IN M2 AND IN FACTORS AFFECTING IT (1971–1977)

M2	1971	1972	1973	1974	1975	1976	1977
Percent change due to changes in	24.3	24.7	16.8	11.5	14.5	13.5	11.1
Foreign assets	5.2	2.3	−3.7	−2.2	−0.8	0.6	1.3
Credit to prvt sector	23.5	26.4	19.1	13.1	12.8	11.9	9.0
Credit to central govt	−0.7	1.1	−0.6	2.7	5.9	4.0	2.6
Credit to local govts	0.6	0.8	0.7	1.2	0.7	0.4	0.9
Others	−4.3	−5.9	1.3	−3.3	−4.1	−3.4	−2.7

SOURCES: Bank of Japan [1(1977), pp. 15–18: table 15]. OECD [24(July 1975), p. 40; (July 1977), p. 38; (July 1978), p. 42], reprinted with permission.

In partial conflict with the OECD, the Bank of Japan—after looking at the total public sector—came up with a verdict that downgraded the stimulus provided. Pointing out that local financial difficulties had caused a drop in local spending, the bank stated, "It can be assumed that public finance as a whole did not have much power in stimulating business activity in 1975" [3(1975), p. 23].

There could be less dispute about Japan's relative success in reaching her two goals of stability and recovery. By year's end, statistics showed that GNP in 1975 was up 2.5 percent over 1974. While consumer prices rose 11.8 percent compared with a target of 10 percent, wholesale prices rose only 3.0 percent and export prices fell 2.9 percent [24(July 1976), p. 19]. In 1975, and again in the next two years, Japan performed relatively well in holding down wholesale prices. (*See* Exhibit 11.)

THE INSTITUTIONAL IMPACT OF HARD TIMES

Like inflation in 1973 and 1974, recession in 1974 and 1975 posed social as well as economic problems. Many of Japan's most distinctive practices were especially suited to times of rapid growth: for example, "lifetime" employment, businessmen's heavy reliance on debt, the willingness of the establishment to come to the rescue of its troubled members if state policy wanted this done, and the very high propensity to

Exhibit 10

Monetary Trends, Illustrated

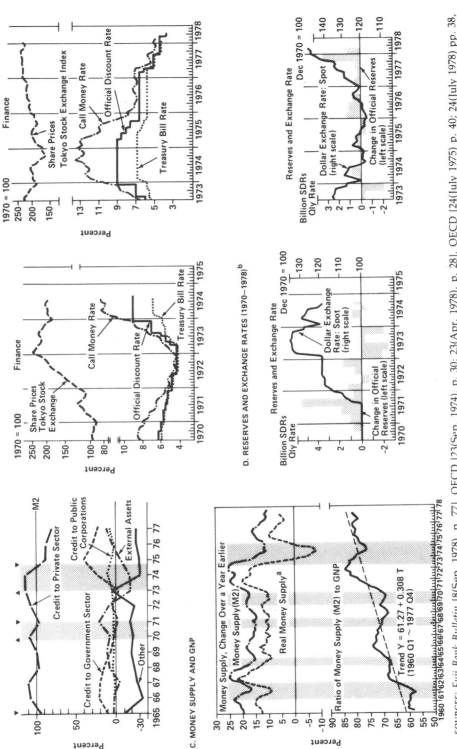

A. CHANGES IN THE FACTORS AFFECTING M2 (1965–1977)

B. MOVEMENT OF MAJOR INTEREST RATES AND SHARE PRICES (1970–1978)

C. MONEY SUPPLY AND GNP

Trend Y = 61.27 + 0.308 T
(1960 Q1 ~ 1977 Q4)

D. RESERVES AND EXCHANGE RATES (1970–1978)[b]

SOURCES: *Fuji Bank Bulletin* [8(Sep. 1978), p. 77]. OECD [23(Sep. 1974), p. 30; 23(Apr. 1978), p. 28]. OECD [24(July 1975) p. 40; 24(July 1978) pp. 38, 42, 43], reprinted with permission.

NOTE TO PART A: Percentage share in increase money supply.   NOTE TO PART C: Shaded areas indicate periods of monetary restraint.

[a] Real money supply is defined as money supply (M2) deflated by the GNP implicit deflator.
[b] Year-end exchange rates for the yen against the US dollar were as follows:

1970: ¥356.0 to $1	1972: ¥302.5 to $1	1974: ¥301.6 to $1	1976: ¥293.7 to $1
1971: ¥315.7 to $1	1973: ¥281.0 to $1	1975: ¥306.2 to $1	1977: ¥241.1 to $1 (up from ¥268.2 at the end of August)

Exhibit 11

Year-to-year Percentage Changes in Wholesale Prices for Manufactures, 1974–1977

Period	Japan	US	France	W Ger	Italy	UK
1975–74	1.5	11.0	−5.7	3.3	8.2	24.2
1976–75	4.4	4.6	7.4	2.5	22.7	16.4
1977–76	1.7	6.2	5.6	2.7	17.3	14.2

SOURCE: U.S., Department of Commerce [28(Sep. 1978), p. 23].

save. What had happened to these practices during two years of hard times?

Outcome for Lifetime Employment

Although unemployment in Japan was reported lower than in western countries, it rose as the recession lengthened and failed to fall with the recovery (*see* Exhibit 2). Real unemployment in Japan, moreover, was officially admitted to be higher than official figures indicated. For one thing, Japan (unlike the United States) did not count laid-off workers as unemployed. For another (unlike Germany and Britain) Japan inflated the size of the workforce against which unemployment was measured by including self-employed and family workers in it. For a third point, Japan's women workers (unlike their western sisters) tended to drop out of the workforce in hard times, and thus out of unemployment statistics [13(1974/75), pp. 11-13]. For a fourth point, questions could be raised about how many who left the workforce between the ages of 55 and 65 did so on a voluntary basis. With so much unemployment "disguised," the "actual" level reportedly was put at twice the official figure by the Ministry of Labor and at three times the official figure by the chairman of the Japan Chamber of Commerce and Industry [10(1976), p. 30]. What job loss or reassignment might mean in human terms showed up in an episode reported as far away as the *New York Times*:

> Toshinobu Aburao, chairman of the labor union at Yashica Camera Company's factory in Kanagawa prefecture, tried to commit suicide by hari kari after signing a labor agreement with the company that allows it to lay off workers. Under the agreement, 900 workers . . . were to be transferred to other plants or given incentive pay to voluntarily retire [22(Oct. 24, 1974)]. © 1974 by The New York Times Company. Reprinted by permission.

Under all these circumstances, the *Industrial Review of Japan* argued that the "long severe recession" was "shaking the myth of lifetime employment" [10(1976), p. 30].

On the other hand, enterprises had not dropped enough workers to relieve themselves of "the burden of overemployment caused by the drop of production." Thus, in 1976, "The surplus labor force latent in existing employment [was] estimated by the Japan Federation of Employers' Association . . . at two million and by the Labor Ministry at 500,000 to 700,000 workers" [10(1976), p. 30]. In 1977 it was estimated by the Sumitomo Bank at "nearly a million" [31(Dec. 21, 1977)]. According to M. Matsuyama, senior economist at the government-sponsored Economic Research Institute, "Unless the seniority-based wage system and over-all personnel management are revised, Japanese companies won't be able to survive" [31(Dec. 21, 1977)].

Outcome for Corporate Reliance on Debt

Besides the tradition of secure employment, Japanese business had a tradition of heavy reliance on debt. The fact that high fixed-interest charges raised the breakeven point had posed no problem in years of rapid growth, but such was not the case in a recession. In the words of the OECD, "The danger of excessive dependence on external funds became conspicuous . . . when extremely low rates of capacity utilization coupled with rising fixed costs resulted not only in a very serious profit squeeze and an almost complete exhaustion of accumulated internal reserves, but also in a marked increase in the number of business failures" [24(July 1977), p. 22]. (For selected data on business results and investment trends, see Exhibits 12 and 13.)

After noting that "one out of four companies went into the red in the first half of fiscal 1975" [14(1976), p. 38], the Economic Planning Agency demanded a more cautious pattern of financing. "Enterprises are now called upon," it said, "to restructure their financial foundations so as to even withstand economic upheavals." In addition, when making loans hereafter, "Financial institutions will need to pay greater attention to the earnings rate and financial structure of enterprises, rather than to the sales amount as before" [14(1976), p. 20].

Outcome for Savings and Investment

Comparing the recent recession with others, the Economic Planning Agency noted that "private equipment investment used to lead business recovery," but "this time, it showed no sign of upturn" even two years after the trough [14(1977), pp. 56, 57]. On the other hand, Japanese households

had actually raised their rate of saving. Always relatively high, this had peaked in 1974 at 24.3 percent of disposable income [24(July 1976), p. 10]. Putting these disparate trends together, the Planning Agency was disturbed: "One of the basic reasons for the current slow recovery," it said, "is . . . the growing imbalance between savings and investment" [14(1976), p. 67]. Thus, tasks for the future would include "lowering the ratio" of household savings and "reawakening . . . enterprise investment zeal" [14(1976), p. 118]. The latter, especially, was considered vital: "Whether the Japanese economy will be able to embark on a smooth road to recovery or shift to stable growth depends after all upon private investment in plant, machinery and equipment" [14(1976), p. 55].

Outcome for Mutual Supportiveness

One reason Japan was sometimes referred to as "Japan, Inc." was the mutual supportiveness of the establishment. During the recession of 1974–1975, one well-publicized example of this was the "rescue" of Toyo Kogyo, Japan's number three auto maker and Hiroshima's biggest employer.[5] Under the headline, "Hanging Together—Japan's Establishment Rushes, More or Less, to Aid Mazda's Maker," the Wall Street Journal reported as follows:

TOKYO—Toyo Kogyo Co., developer of the rotary-engine Mazda and Japan's No. 3 auto maker, has its back to the wall. Slack sales and swollen inventories have created a serious cash shortage. An American company in this shape might fold or go into receivership. Certainly it would lay off

[5] Toyo Kogyo employed 35,000 people, and perhaps another 250,000, including workers' families. Subsidiaries and suppliers might also be dependent on it. "If the worst befell Toyo Kogyo," wrote one Japanese magazine, "it would be like a second atomic bomb for Hiroshima" [31(Mar. 24, 1975)].

Exhibit 12

Japanese Corporate Performance

A. TRENDS IN COST AND PROFIT RATIOS, PRINCIPAL ENTERPRISES[a]

	All Industries: *Ratios to Net Sales*					*Manufacturing:* *Percentage Breakdown of Major Costs*			
FY *Half*	*Net* *Profit*	*Labor* *Cost*	*Finan* *Cost*	*Deprec*	*FY*	*Matrls* *Cost*	*Labor* *Cost*	*Finan* *Cost*	*Deprec*
1970 I	3.92	7.69	3.32	3.10	1970	72.5	15.4	5.8	6.1
1970 II	3.35	7.65	3.45	3.15	1971	70.2	16.7	6.5	6.6
1971 I	2.73	7.89	3.63	3.24	1972	69.6	17.7	6.2	6.5
1971 II	2.72	7.97	3.80	3.30	1973	71.6	17.3	5.6	5.5
1972 I	2.71	8.24	3.66	3.28	1974	72.8	16.6	6.0	4.6
1972 II	3.36	7.61	3.25	2.94					
1973 I	3.76	7.70	3.11	2.65					
1973 II	3.01	7.08	3.14	2.28					
1974 I	2.48	7.50	3.35	2.08					
1974 II	1.52	7.41	3.66	2.11					

	All Industries: *Ratios to Gross Sales*					*Manufacturing:* *Ratios to Gross Sales*			
FY *Half*	*Net* *Profit*	*Labor* *Cost*	*Finan* *Cost*	*Deprec*	*FY* *Half*	*Net* *Profit*	*Labor* *Cost*	*Finan* *Cost*	*Deprec*
1975 I	0.84	7.99	3.84	2.16	1975 I	0.76	13.39	5.03	3.55
1975 II	1.39	7.51	3.67	2.19	1975 II	1.96	12.52	4.81	3.57
1976 I	1.91	7.65	3.52	2.04	1976 I	3.06	12.46	4.47	3.20
1976 II	2.15	7.34	3.44	2.12	1976 II	3.15	12.13	4.34	3.28
1977 I	2.12	8.03	3.28	2.05	1977 I	3.01	12.76	4.03	3.08
1977 II	2.09	7.81	3.03	2.13	1977 II	2.82	12.33	3.68	3.25

B. DISTRIBUTION OF CORPORATE PROFIT AND LOSS (FISCAL YEARS)

	All Industries					*Manufacturing*			
	1973	*1974*	*1975*	*1976*	*1977*	*1973*	*1974*	*1975*	*1976*
Sales (billions of yen)	355,309	440,414	456,562	529,780	556,538	120,120	145,705	148,291	173,417
Sales (%)	100.0	100.0	100.0	100.0	n.a.	100.0	100.0	100.0	100.0
Cost of goods sold	82.2	82.7	83.0	83.1	n.a.	78.5	80.2	81.8	81.6
Selling, gnrl & admin exp	12.6	12.7	14.0	13.7		13.5	13.5	14.4	13.8
Operating profit	5.2	4.4	3.0	3.2	3.0	8.0	6.3	3.8	4.5
Other profit & exp (net)	−1.6	−1.9	−1.7	−1.4		−2.4	−2.7	−2.6	−2.1
Recurring profit	3.6	2.5	1.3	1.8		5.6	3.6	1.2	2.4
Extraordinary P&L	−0.2	—	0.2	—		−0.6	−0.2	0.4	—
Pretax profit	3.4	2.5	1.5	1.8		5.0	3.4	1.6	2.5
Taxes	1.5	1.3	1.0	1.0	n.a.	2.3	1.8	1.2	1.4
Net profit	1.9	1.2	0.5	0.8		2.7	1.6	0.4	1.1
Officers' bonus	0.1	0.2	0.1	0.1		0.1	0.1	0.1	0.1
Dividends	0.5	0.4	0.4	0.3		0.7	0.6	0.5	0.5
Retained profit	1.3	0.6	—	0.4		1.9	0.9	−0.2	0.5

Exhibit 12 (continued)

C. SELECTED CORPORATE FINANCIAL RATIOS (FISCAL YEARS)[b]

	All Industries				Manufacturing			
	1973	1974	1975	1976	1973	1974	1975	1976
Total assets (billions of yen)	258,006	293,910	319,890	352,878	104,206	117,259	130,355	140,048
Net worth (billions of yen)	37,131	42,123	44,614	48,479	18,934	21,005	22,096	23,777
Ratios								
Own cap/total cap	14.4	14.3	13.9	13.7	18.2	17.9	17.0	17.0
Oper profit/total cap	7.2	6.5	3.5	4.8	9.1	7.8	4.3	5.6
Recurring profit/total cap	5.0	3.7	1.5	2.7	6.4	4.5	1.4	3.1
Recurring profit/own cap	34.5	26.1	13.4	19.9	35.2	24.9	8.2	18.2

D. TRENDS IN CORPORATE FAILURES (CALENDAR YEARS)

	1970	1971	1972	1973	1974	1975	1976	1977
Number of failures	9,765	9,206	7,139	8,202	11,681	12,606	15,641	18,471
Total liabilities (billions of yen)	719.2	712.5	497.8	705.4	1,649.0	1,914.6	2,765.8	2,978.1

SOURCES: Bank of Japan [2(July 1972), p. 121: table 89; (May 1974), p. 127: table 89; (Sep. 1976), p. 134: table 91; (July 1978), pp. 131 and 134: tables 90 and 91]; Japan Ministry of Finance [17(Dec. 1978), unpaged chart]; and Japan Ministry of Finance [18(Mar. 1978), pp. 44–47, 50–51, 56–59: tables 1-2, 1-3, and 1-6].

[a] About 450 companies selected for each survey out of those listed on the stock market with a capital of ¥1.0 billion or more.

[b] Owing to discrepancies in the reported operating figures and ratios, these data should be taken as only approximately correct.

many workers. Any government assistance would come only after prolonged congressional debate over federal giveaways and the free-enterprise system.

Things work differently in Japan. Toyo Kogyo's problems have prompted the biggest corporate rescue in recent Japanese history. That unusual combination of business and government interests colloquially called "Japan, Inc." is giving Toyo Kogyo a lot of tender loving care in the form of experienced management advice, loans, special tax breaks and big fleet-size purchases of Toyo Kogyo's slow-selling cars [31(Mar. 24, 1975)]. Reprinted from the *Wall Street Journal.* © Dow Jones and Co., 1975.

Reporter Nathan Pearlstein then went on to tell how the company's major banker got members of his "group" to promise support, persuaded fifty other bankers to join in giving Toyo a "stop-gap" loan of $119 million (even though the company's total bank debt already exceeded $1.1 billion), and also persuaded a major trading company (that owed his bank some $37.5 million) to handle the sales of Mazdas overseas. Next, Shigeo Nagano, prestigious chairman of Japan's Chamber of Commerce and Industry and former chairman of Toyo's steel supplier, offered to become the "supreme advisor" of the troubled company. As analyst James Abegglen pointed out, "Mr. Nagano has a quasi-official position in Japanese society." As another analyst put it, "Nagano's coming in means that all of Japan is standing behind Toyo Kogyo." At another level, suppliers waited

Exhibit 13

Trends in Investment and Savings by Source (Calendar Years)

	1970	1971	1972	1973	1974	1975	1976
Total savings or investment (billions of yen)	28,520	31,008	35,146	44,224	49,107	46,911	52,926
Savings by source (%)							
Depreciation, etc.	33.3	34.2	35.2	33.4	35.0	38.9	37.3
Private corporations	16.5	14.3	12.5	6.3	−3.5	6.2	8.4
Households & nonprofit institutions	32.7	34.7	37.2	43.1	49.4	58.9	56.7
Government	19.2	19.2	18.1	18.9	18.0	8.6	6.3
Statistical discrepancy	−1.6	−2.3	−3.0	−1.7	1.1	−12.5	−8.7
Total	100.0	100.0	100.0	100.0	100.0	100.0	100.0
Disposable income of households (billions of yen)	45,605	52,011	60,278	75,771	94,221	110,106	123,463
Savings ratio of households (%)	20.4	20.7	21.7	25.1	25.7	25.1	24.3

SOURCE: Bank of Japan [1(1977), pp. 316–318: table 175].

to be paid, employees turned to selling cars, and townspeople raised Mazda's sales from 20 percent of the Hiroshima market to 34 percent [31(Mar. 24, 1975)].

Still another rescue was that of Chori, Inc., one of the "big three" in the domestic wholesaling of textiles. On sales of slightly more than $2 billion, Chori's anticipated operating loss was about $15 million. With encouragement from the Bank of Japan, four banks and three suppliers postponed interest payments of $21 million and made a new loan of $36 million. The *Wall Street Journal* explained:

> Chori is being rescued . . . because [it] is regarded as an essential component of Japan's complicated distribution system. The company is active at every stage of the textile production and sales process, often supplying raw materials or intermediates and buying back semifinished or finished goods to and from the same customers [31(Sep. 8, 1975)]. Reprinted from the *Wall Street Journal.* © Dow Jones and Co., 1975.

Not all big companies, however, got help. In 1974 and 1975 several bankruptcies were

so large as to be reported in the US press. This list included a "major" air conditioner firm that had once been the "darling" of Japanese investors, a "large" textile concern whose collapse would "strain" a South Korean bank, a trading company, a "major" shipbuilder, a "medium-sized" steel producer, and the diversified Kohjiin Co. (paper, chemicals, and synthetic fibers). Kohjiin's debts were estimated at $490 million, and its collapse was the "biggest since the war." In explaining why some of these companies got no help from the establishment, the *Wall Street Journal* said, "This firm's failure didn't imperil other companies"; it wasn't "an established member of the corporate hierarchy"; it was "somewhat peripheral" [31(Nov. 13, 1974 and Aug. 27, 1975)].

POPULATION DYNAMICS AS A THREAT

If some of Japan's most distinctive practices were threatened by recession, others were threatened in a more basic way by population dynamics, especially as reinforced by education trends (*see* Exhibits 14, 15, and 16). According to analyst Peter F. Drucker, this factor was the "villain" in Japan's horoscope—far more important than "the petroleum cartel, Japan's dependence on raw materials imports, or the world recession"—although these were the "monsters" commonly identified in the "popular demonology" [6, p. 565].

Elaborating on this theme Drucker noted that Japan's postwar baby boom had been followed by a "baby bust" in the mid-1950s. Meanwhile, longevity had risen to western standards. Thus, as in the West, a falling proportion of workers was having to support a rising proportion of dependents, mainly oldsters. The significance of this trend was heightened by the common Japanese practice of tying pay to age. "For every year by which the average age of the labor force in a plant goes up, the plant's labor costs rise by five to seven percent," Drucker stated [6, p. 568]. Japanese figures for average monthly contractual cash earnings (*see* Exhibit 14, Part D) are roughly in line with these figures, at least for males to age 35 or so.

The coming dearth of young, and thus of relatively low-paid workers would be aggravated by education trends. According to Drucker, "The best available Japanese study concludes that university graduates make up 58 percent of the males now entering the labor force" [6, p. 567]. If so, the supply of manual workers would be inadequate to support the growth Japan would need to offset the impact of seniority pay as the average age of her workers increased.

Besides leading to a dearth of manual workers, education trends also added to Japan's existing surplus of persons trained only for high-level jobs. If these persons failed to find suitable work, especially in view of the hardships undergone to prepare for management or one of the professions, Japan

stood to suffer human as well as economic costs. According to a government study, it was "normal" for children aged 12 to 15 to do homework or attend a cram school for "almost nine hours each day *after* school" and even "to take a sample test of the high-school examinations every Sunday for years on end." "The pressure was becoming more and more intense, with the suicide rate among teenagers and even among preteens reaching alarming proportions" [6, p. 573].

In addition to threatening the labor supply, "population dynamics" also threatened "Japan's traditional capital supply." Given that the old consume but do not save, Japan's high rate of personal savings would fall as the proportion of oldsters increased. Thus, "government economists" had reportedly calculated that "the Japanese savings rate would be lower by at least one-third, if not a full half . . . if Japan today had the same age structure as the United States . . . where there are 32 million people who are on social security, including eight million 'survivors,' as against a working population of 92 million." Even at one-half to one-third of normal, Japan's savings rate would be relatively high (*see* Exhibit 13), but it would be "a low rate for Japan" and "perhaps too low" in light of "future needs" [6, p. 569].

Suggesting what he saw as the major implication of his findings, Drucker argued that the "basic issues facing Japan" were not "economic" but "social."

> Everyone I met in Japan last fall [1977] . . . talked economics and only economics. Even the theoretical mathematician and the elderly abbot of the famous Zen temple were obsessed with the dollar/yen exchange rate, the export surplus, and the cost of petroleum. Japan is indeed undergoing traumatic economic changes. Yet the basic issues facing Japan are not economic. They are changes in social structure and social values. Social policies that have served Japan superbly well for a cen-

Exhibit 14

Selected Data on Japanese Population, Education, and Cash Earnings by Age Group

A. PERCENTAGE OF WORKING-AGE POPULATION AND DEPENDENCY RATIOS, 1950–1977

Year	Working Age Popn (15-64)	Young Ages (1-14)	Aged (65 up)	Dependency Ratio[a]
1950	59.7	35.4	4.9	67.5
1955	61.2	33.4	5.3	63.3
1960	64.1	30.2	5.7	55.9
1965	68.0	25.7	6.3	47.1
1970	68.9	24.0	7.1	45.1
1975	67.7	24.3	7.9	47.6
1976	67.6	24.3	8.1	48.0
1977	67.4	24.2	8.4	48.4

B. PERCENTAGE OF SCHOOL GRADUATES WORKING OR ATTENDING ADVANCED COURSES[b]

Graduates	1955	1970	1976
Jr high school graduates			
Jobs	42.0	16.3	5.2
Advanced courses	51.5	82.1	92.6
Sr high school graduates			
Jobs	47.6	58.2	42.2
Advanced courses			
Males	20.9	31.6	32.8
Females	14.9	23.5	35.1

C. POPULATION BY FIVE-YEAR AGE BLOCKS, PERCENTAGE BREAKDOWN, 1950 AND 1975[c]

Year	0-14	15-29	20-24	25-29	30-34	35-39	40-44	45-49	50-54	55-59	60-64	65 and up
1950	35.4	10.3	9.3	6.6	6.2	6.1	5.4	4.8	4.1	3.3	2.8	4.9
1975	24.3	7.1	8.1	9.6	8.3	7.5	7.3	6.6	5.2	4.2	3.8	7.9

D. AVERAGE MONTHLY CONTRACTUAL CASH EARNINGS BY FIVE-YEAR AGE BLOCKS IN TOKYO, 1976 (IN THOUSANDS OF YEN)

	17	18-19	20-24	25-29	30-34	35-39	40-44	45-49	50-54	55-59	65 and up
Males	73.0	85.1	104.4	134.9	173.3	202.4	222.7	233.4	240.8	204.2	152.1
Females	70.8	81.9	94.2	107.4	118.5	119.7	124.2	123.3	123.3	121.7	105.0
Percent difference											
Males	—	16.6	22.7	29.2	28.5	16.8	10.0	4.8	3.2	−15.2	−25.5
Females	—	16.0	15.0	14.0	10.0	1.0	4.0	−1.0	0.0	−1.0	−13.0

SOURCES: Part A: Oriental Economist [26(1978/79), p. 68], reprinted with permission. Parts B, C, and D: Japan Ministry of Labour [19(1976), pp. 202, 203: table 86]; Japan Office of the Prime Minister [20(1978), pp. 28, 29 and 581: tables 14 and 415].

[a] Young plus aged divided by working-age population. For forecasted future trends, *see* Exhibit 15A.

[b] Remainder listed as without occupation or "other."

[c] The 1950 total includes persons of unreported age, so subtotals do not add to 100. The total population was 83.2 million in 1950, 111.9 million in 1975.

Exhibit 15

Selected Data on Japanese Population and Labor Force Participation

A. ESTIMATED POPULATION GROWTH AND DISTRIBUTION OF POPULATION BY AGE GROUP (1980–2050)

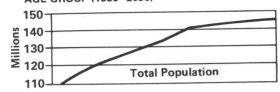

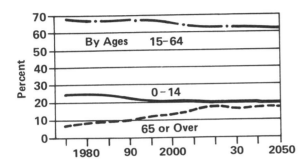

B. LABOR FORCE PARTICIPATION RATE BY SEX AND AGE GROUP (1968 AND 1977)

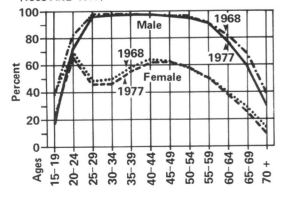

SOURCES: Part A: Oriental Economist [26(1978/79), p. 67], reprinted with permission. Part B: Japan Office of the Prime Minister [20(1978), p. 48: chart 4].

Exhibit 16

Selected Dependency Trends

Year	Age of Population (in percent)			Persons at Work Per Person Aged 65+
	65+	0–14	15–64	
1970	7.1	24.0	68.9	6.9
1977	8.4	24.2	67.4	5.6
1990[a]	11.0	22.5	66.5	3.9[b]
2000[a]	14.3	20.0	65.7	2.9[b]

SOURCES: Japan Office of the Prime Minister [20(1978), p. 13: table 8 and p. 9: table 31]. Calculated from data in Oriental Economist [26(1978/79), pp. 68, 69].

[a] Estimates.

[b] Figure assumes that the proportion of the working-age population *actually working* would remain at the 1977 level of 63.2 percent.

success is rendering them obsolete and is turning them into dangers to Japan's social cohesion and her ability to compete economically [6, p. 564]. Excerpted by permission from *Foreign Affairs* (April 1978). Copyright 1978 by Council on Foreign Relations, Inc.

PUMP PRIMING DOMESTIC DEMAND—1976, 1977

After two years of stagnant real growth in which industry and labor had suffered, these interest blocs urged vigorous action to reflate domestic demand. Miki and Fukuda went part way—but at first only part way—to meet their demands in 1976. On the one hand, the stated purpose of the initial budget was to insure a "sustained recovery and improve the labor market situation." In addition, the government proved willing to plan a deficit of ¥7.3 trillion, which would be even higher than the mostly unplanned deficit of FY 1975. Moreoover, expenditures would emphasize public works, social security, and other welfare-related purposes. On the other

tury are rapidly becoming untenable. These policies were designed to change Japan from a poor, and poorly educated, rural society with low life expectancies into a wealthy, highly educated, industrial society with high life expectancies. Their very

hand, taxes would grow a little faster than estimated GNP; prices for "many" state services would rise, and, "in sharp contrast to the past," no income tax reduction would be granted [24(July 1976), pp. 36, 37]. The OECD later applied the term "cautious" to this initial budget and to monetary policy, too, since "no important new measures were taken" in this area in 1976 [24(July 1977), p. 36].

Before year's end, however, and still more in 1977, demands for an expansive policy were to get a more responsive hearing. One reason was the widening trade gap. From $1.5 billion in 1974, Japan's export surplus soared to $5.0 billion in 1975, $9.9 billion in 1976, and $17.3 billion in 1977.

Other related reasons for reflating were continued unemployment at home and low production levels in some industries (*see* Exhibits 2 and 3). Both reflected weakness in home demand. As shown in Exhibit 1, private consumption had not been buoyant since 1973, and investment (particularly private investment) had been particularly slow. Looking behind the figures for a reason, analysts noted that consumption had been held down by relatively small wage increases (only 8.8 percent being won in the spring wage offensives of 1976 and 1977); the steady rise of consumer prices (at about 9.0 percent a year); the high propensity to save, reinforced by the still low level of publicly financed pension payments (*see* Exhibit 17); the near saturation of home demand for many consumer durables (92 percent or more of all households had electric washing machines, refrigerators, and TV sets in 1972; 44 percent had passenger cars); and continuing fears of unemployment (which, at 2.1 percent of the workforce in August 1977, was at its highest rate in eighteen years) [2(Sep. 1977): table 117; 14(1976), p. 20; 24(July 1977), pp. 7–9; 26(1977/78), p. 68; 31(June 15, 1977 and Sep. 8, 1977)]. Business investment had been held down by the still discouraging trend of profits, the rising cost of plant and equipment, the high level of inventories, the high proportion of unused capacity, fears about the impact on exports of sudden surges in the value of the yen, and prospects of slow growth in the future (*see* Exhibits 18, 19, and 20).

This situation was unsatisfactory from both domestic and foreign points of view. Domestic discontent led to a setback for the LDP in elections for the lower house of the Diet held in December 1976. Miki, in effect, was forced to resign, and Fukuda was enabled to win the premiership. Foreign discontent showed itself in increasing trouble with trade partners. At the end of 1977 this culminated in a so-called US "ultimatum," which demanded that Japan reduce her huge trade surpluses and shift her current balance from black to red.

In response to these pressures, fiscal policy turned reflationary in the first half of FY 1976. Thus, public works expenditures were again moved forward or "front loaded." Late in the second half of the fiscal year (November 12, 1976 and March 11, 1977), two special business-propping programs were announced, one with seven parts and one with four. While the second speeded up rather than increased planned state expenditures, the first was believed to involve additional outlays of about ¥1.8 trillion. (As pointed out by the EIU, it was not always possible to tell how much was really "extra" in these cases [7(IV 1976), p. 3].) Apart from one provision that permitted the national railway and tel & tel companies to invest ¥0.4 trillion, the aims of both programs were couched in general terms. The programs proposed to finance and speed up public works; to finance, encourage, and facilitate new housing; to encourage private plant and equipment investment "through administrative guidance"; to encourage Japan's rising exports of whole plants; to increase employment; and to support small- and medium-sized enterprises [7(IV 1976), p. 3; 7(I 1977), p. 10; 24(July 1977), pp. 36, 42].

Exhibit 17

Public Old Age Pension Plans in Japan

Public Pension Plans	Number Persons Covered (000)			Number Pensioners (000)			Avg Annual Pension (¥000)			Pension/Cash Earnings in Industry (%)[a]		
	1970	1975	1976	1970	1975	1976	1970	1975	1976	1970	1975	1976
Annuity Insurance[b]	22,260	23,649	23,847	520	1,031	1,235	171.2	667.7	826.3	18.8	31.4	34.4
Annuity Fund[c]	(389)	(5,341)	(5,395)	42	302	371	21.4	44.6	52.4	2.4	2.1	2.2
Natl Pension Plan[d]												
Contributory	24,337	25,884	26,469	None	2,731	3,395	—	169.3	197.1	—	8.0	8.2
Noncontributory[e]	}			3,454	4,613	4,381	28.5	130.7	146.0	3.1	6.1	6.1
Seamen's Insurance	262	244	237	14	23	26	229.8	873.4	1,089.6	25.3	41.0	45.4
Mutual Aid Assns, workers in:												
Natl govt	1,149	1,162	1,163	120	201	216	332.2	1,005.2	1,170.0	36.7	47.3	48.7
Local govt	2,536	3,004	3,033	228	374	414	401.4	1,114.8	1,294.2	44.2	60.9	53.9
Public corps	789	787	802	170	212	221	371.4	1,061.8	1,226.0	40.9	57.7	51.0
Prvt schools	194	270	282	4	6	7	236.8	787.4	918.0	26.1	43.1	38.2
Primary sector corps	407	445	450	18	38		202.5	658.7	776.0	22.2	36.5	32.3
Govt pensions	n.a.	n.a.	n.a.	1,495	1,429	n.a.						
Natl civilian				101	81		223.4	691.2		24.6	32.5	
Natl military				1,256	1,234		51.4	154.4	n.a.	5.7	7.3	n.a.
Prefectural				138	114		250.6	779.8		27.6	37.6	—
Total	51,934	55,455	56,283	6,065	9,646							

SOURCES: Office of the Prime Minister [20(1977)], pp. 390, 391, 513, 515: *esp.* tables 281, 351, and 353]; U.S., Department of Health, Education and Welfare [30(1977), pp. 124, 125]; and D. E. Woodsworth [32, pp. 114–122].

NOTE: Benefits available at age 60 (55 for women and miners) under Annuity Insurance; at age 65 under National Pension Plan.

a Average annual cash earnings for regular workers in industry were ¥908,400 in 1970, ¥2,126,400 in 1975 and ¥2,402,400 in 1976. For males alone the figures were ¥1,078,800, ¥2,451,600 and ¥2,772,000.

b This plan compulsory for workplaces with five or more employees. Financed by equal wage-based contributions from employer and employee (totaling 7.6 percent for males), plus a government subsidy of 20 percent of benefits paid.

c Optional for companies employing 1000 or more workers. The benefits provided by the Fund are additional to (adjusted) benefits provided through National Annuity Insurance and private company plans.

d This plan compulsory for all workers not otherwise covered. The contributory plan financed by workers and government only. No employer contribution.

e Designed for persons unable to contribute because of age or low income. Entirely state funded.

Exhibit 18

Major Industrial Indicators

1973 = 100

SOURCE: *Oriental Economist* [25(Jan. 1978), p. 5]. Reprinted with permission.

Concern for small business and industry structure also showed up in a more specific measure that went into effect late in 1976 entitled the *Provisional Law for the Business Conversion of Small Enterprises*. This measure prescribed "full government aid" for small-scale companies that wanted to change their field of operation because of structural difficulties in their present line of business. Permissible reasons were spelled out to include:

1. Increasing competition from developing countries

2. Declining demand due to the appearance of a new product

3. Difficulty in obtaining raw materials

4. An intrinsic tendency to cause pollution [29, p. 10].

More and larger reflationary steps were taken in FY 1977. Thus, monetary policy eased from March onward. For example,

the discount rate was cut in several steps from 6.0 percent to 4.25 percent, its lowest level since the troubled aftermath of World War II. Fiscal policy followed suit. While the initial budget was officially assigned the "double task of putting the economy on a long-term sustainable growth path and improving the public sector's financial position," specific provisions called for an income tax cut of ¥653 billion and a planned deficit of ¥8.5 trillion. At 29.7 percent of planned expenditures, this deficit would nudge a long-term 30 percent-of-expenditures ceiling, self-imposed by the Ministry of Finance [24(July 1977), pp. 41–43; 24(July 1978), p. 44].

Soon after this reflationary budget was passed, Fukuda made his celebrated promise that Japan would grow at 6.7 percent during the on-going fiscal year, and would thereby cut her current balance from $3.7 billion to *minus* $0.7 billion.

When it later became clear that both of Fukuda's targets were likely to be badly missed, two further business-propping programs followed, each financed by a supplementary budget. The first, announced on September 3, 1977, appeared to call for added expenditures of ¥2.0 trillion: ¥1.0 trillion for national public works, ¥150 billion to finance public works at the local level and ¥870 billion for housing [17(Sep. 1977), pp. 12–14; 25(Oct. 1977), p. 4].

Other proposals in the September program were less easily quantified. These included:

1. Seeking to reduce interest rates

2. Promoting private plant and equipment investment—specifically, by accelerating power plant construction, promoting the construction of oil stockpiling facilities, and promoting "large-scale overseas investment"

3. Promoting personal consumption by relaxing the terms of installment credit on automobiles and household electrical appliances as well as by making efforts to ex-

Exhibit 19

Official Japanese Real Growth Targets for FY 1977 and FY 1978 Compared with Actual Outcome for FY 1976 and FY 1977

A. PERCENTAGE CHANGES IN REAL GNE, PRICES AND PRODUCTION

Item	FY 1976–75 Actual Change	FY 1977–76 Official Targets	FY 1977–76 Actual Change	FY 1978–77 Official Targets
	Percentage Changes in Selected GNE Components at CY 1970 Prices			
GNE, total	5.8	6.7	5.5	7.0
Prsnl consump	4.4	5.4	3.7	5.3
Prvt housing	3.5	8.3	3.9	9.8
Prvt plant & equip invstmt	1.1	6.9	1.3	6.7
Increase, prvt stocks	593.0	63.6	−9.3	21.3
	Percentage Changes in Price and Output Indices (1975 = 100)			
Wholesale prices	5.5	5.7	0.4	2.7
Consumer prices	9.4	8.4	6.7	6.8
Mining & mfg prodn	10.8	9.2	3.2	6.8

B. CHANGES IN BALANCE-OF-PAYMENTS ITEMS ($ MILLIONS)

Item	FY 1976 Actual	FY 1977 Official Targets	FY 1977 Actual	FY 1978 Official Targets
Trade bal	11,148	7,300	20,335	13,500
Exprts	69,394		83,363	85,000
Imprts	58,246		63,028	71,500
Current bal	4,682	−700	13,996	6,000
Long-term cap bal	−1,606		−2,441	−7,000
Basic bal	3,076		11,555	−1,000

SOURCES: Bank of Japan [2(Mar. 1978), pp. 172, 173: table 122]. *Oriental Economist* [25(Feb. 1977), p. 5; 25(Jan. 1978), p. 6; 25(Mar. 1976), p. 6; 25(Dec. 1978): tables 4, 7, and 10 in statistical section], reprinted with permission.

pand the amount and reduce the interest rate on consumer loans made by private financial institutions

4. Beefing up various programs for public and private loans to small businesses in difficulties

5. Monitoring prices

6. Taking a variety of measures to assist companies and workers in "structurally depressed" industries. Under this heading, specific proposals included the creation of cartels to maintain prices or cut back production, "administrative guidance to scrap or freeze excessive equipment," and the utilization of loans available to small and other companies for "business change-over" [17(Sep. 1977), pp. 12–14].

Exhibit 20

Trends in Export Growth

A. TOTAL EXPORTS

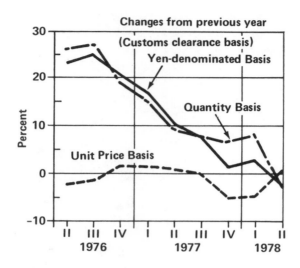

B. TRENDS OF MAJOR EXPORT GOODS

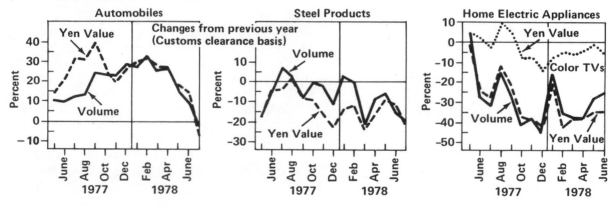

SOURCE: *Oriental Economist* [25(Oct. 1978), p. 7]. Reprinted with permission.

December's business-propping program seemed to call for extra outlays of ¥1.3 trillion. Further financing of local public works and further assistance to small- and medium-sized enterprises were the two objectives emphasized [24(July 1978), p. 46]. The structural problems of larger industries were not, however, to be ignored. Toward the end of 1977, government was known to be working on a bill that would facilitate the formation of cartels—perhaps cartels with teeth—in order to reduce excess ca-

pacity in a number of large industries, probably including shipbuilding and steel [29, p. 10].

Along with December's business-propping program and a second supplementary budget by which the program was to be financed, the government also made public the general outlines of a tentative budget for upcoming FY 1978. One purpose of this "extraordinary" step was to encourage business by enabling it to look at fiscal policy fifteen months ahead, and to see that policy would be stimulative. Thus, the stated aim of the budget was to promote "economic recovery through a strengthening of domestic demand" [24(July 1978), p. 46]. For the first time ever, the initial budget's expenditure figure was expected to exceed that proposed in the last initial budget by more than 20 percent, and the planned deficit would exceed "the long-guarded 30% limit" for dependence on bonds for revenues [15(Jan. 15, 1978), p. 1; 33, p. 138].

This acceptance of mounting deficits contrasted sharply with earlier intentions. Thus, as late as 1976 an official projection had looked forward to cutting the general account deficit to 15 percent of outlays by 1980 [24(July 1976), p. 45].

CRITICAL ASSESSMENTS AND ALTERNATIVE PROPOSALS

As Fukuda's government made promise after promise, followed by program after program, various critical assessments were evoked. The OECD, for example, pointed out that business-propping so far had produced only brief upturns, and it suggested several reasons for this outcome:

POLICY CONCLUSIONS. In spite of the expansionary measures taken by the Japanese authorities on several occasions, the recovery of economic activity from the recession [of 1974-75] did not prove self-sustaining. As in other Member countries, successive doses of temporary fiscal stimulus . . . have not reduced very considerably the large amount of slack inherited from the last recession. The overhang of excess stocks has limited the impact of reflationary policies. And the generally uncertain economic climate has dampened the spending propensity of enterprises and households. . . . There have been short periods of strong growth of output, due often to the coinci-

dence of a sharp rise in exports and the impact of higher public expenditure, followed by a marked deceleration of activity as the exogenous stimuli petered out. Until the autumn of 1977, the risk of rekindling inflation represented a constraint on the relaxation of demand management. Concern about future budget deficits has limited the size of counter-cyclical fiscal measures, especially before the self-imposed rule of the "30 percent limit" was abandoned at the end of [1977]. Phases of abrupt variation in the exchange rate have increased business uncertainty. And worldwide depression in particular sectors, together with the general problems of structural adjustment, have compounded the difficulties of economic management [24(July 1978), pp. 55, 56].

More sharply, the EIU wondered if Japan was seriously trying to reflate. The following comment was made apropos of the $7.5 billion program of September 1977.

The first reaction to this package . . . is that if it were implemented with the same degree of enthusiasm as was implied by the way in which it was presented to the world, it would have a marked effect on the growth of the economy, possibly pushing it above the government's target of 6.7 percent. However, experience shows that reflationary schemes, introduced partly in response to foreign pressure, are not always what they seem to be and the indications are that the latest package is no exception. More specifically, about a half of the $3,350 million increase in housing loans, said to be sufficient for the construction of an additional 100,000 units, relies on extra funds from the private sector which may or may not be forthcoming. Furthermore, because of the nature of the budgetary system, only a proportion of the proposed additional public expenditure need result in the creation of additional funds and most observers feel that the true impact of the measures during the current fiscal year will be nearer $4.5 billion [than $7.5 billion]. As for the steps put forward in relation to investment and small business these can mean almost anything and the safer assumption is that they will not mean much, at least not during 1977-78 [7(IV 1977), p. 2].

Others criticized official economic projections (*see* Exhibit 19). Was it reasonable to suppose that the various components of GNE would move as predicted to bring about growth of 6.7 percent in FY 1977 and 7.0 percent in upcoming FY 1978? Even if so, was it also reasonable to assume that the trade and current surplus would decline as planned? In this connection, it was pointed out that the forecasts for FY 1977 were being proved wrong by events, especially the trade and current balance forecasts. It was also noted that most private forecasts for 1978 put growth in the neighborhood of 5.0 percent, not 7.0 percent, as officially proposed [25(Jan. 1978), p. 2]. It was further noted that the United States had asked Japan to grow at 8.0 percent in the upcoming calendar year, while the International Monetary Fund had, in effect, suggested that a 7.5 percent growth target would be an appropriate contribution for Japan to make toward a worldwide upturn by 1979 [12(May 8, 1978), pp. 139-141].

The idea that Japan should raise her growth target and pursue growth more aggressively had proponents at home as well as overseas. Thus, both business and labor had often voiced doubts that the business-propping programs so far introduced would suffice to meet their stated goals. These interest blocs had accordingly demanded higher state expenditures, plus substantial tax cuts [5(Oct. 1967), p. 122; 15(Nov. 15, 1977), pp. 1, 3].

Drawn up on the opposite side in this battle was the Ministry of Finance. Pointing to trends in inventories, profits, and operating ratios, this ministry reportedly argued that the "water table was too low for pump priming to be effective" [25(Aug./Sep. 1978), p. 26]. Pointing to the recent rapid rise in the national debt and in the ratio of debt to GNP (*see* Exhibit 6, Part C), this ministry also reportedly warned its peers of the long-term risks of repeated stiff doses of deficit financing. One observer summed up the ministry's self-appointed task by stating:

> With the politicians thinking only of the next election as they clamor for more treasury disbursements or tax cuts, it is up to the Ministry of Finance to courageously resist these wantonly irresponsible demands for ever-greater budget deficits, for too-easy approval of fiscal policy initiatives will have a long-run adverse effect on Japan's economic future [25(Aug./Sep. 1978), p. 26].

Those who doubted that Japan could or should pump-prime her way out of stagnation and imbalance pointed out that the country must consider some alternative way or ways whereby the trade surplus problem would be met. As one observer put it, three options, no matter how unpopular, might turn out to be "inevitabilities":

1. Acceptance of import curbs by its partner nations

2. Enforcement of a curb on its own export sales

3. Toleration of another skyrocketing of the yen exchange rate against the dollar [25(Jan. 1978), p. 6].

Indeed, to some extent these outcomes were occurring already. Fukuda mainly blamed the "wild surge" of the yen (*see* Exhibit 10, Part D) and the adverse impact of this surge on business confidence and export volume growth for Japan's anticipated failure to reach his 6.7 percent growth target for FY 1977 [15(Nov. 15, 1977), pp. 1, 4; 15(Dec. 15, 1977), p. 6; 15(Jan. 15, 1978), p. 1]. (For an overview of trends in Japan's export growth *see* Exhibit 20.)

NEW INITIATIVES

Besides disagreeing about how much to spend and whether pump-priming could be made to work, by 1977 Japan was seeking other solutions to her foreign and domestic problems.

Whatever domestic changes might be made, in the foreign sphere it appeared likely that Japan might once again have to seek new answers to the old, familiar questions of the 1880s, the 1930s, and the 1950s: What to export? Where?

In this connection, one issue that was being examined had to do with Japan's role vis-à-vis the developing world, particularly vis-à-vis those neighboring countries that, back in the 1940s, she had once sought to weld into a Japanese-led East Asia Co-Prosperity Sphere [31(Sep. 25, 1978)]. Already some of these countries were being developed, largely by foreign capital, to serve Japanese companies and others as sources of non-polluting factory sites and of plentiful low-cost labor. By the same token, however, these countries were being developed not just as markets but as competitors, with new industries geared to producing certain goods for worldwide export at a lower price than goods made in Japan. Population and GNP data for some of these so-called "new Japans" are presented in Exhibit 21.

Exhibit 21

Selected Asian Areas: Population (mid-1975), GNP (1975), and Growth Rates (1960–1975)

Location	Population (million)	Est Total GNP (US $ billion)	Est Per Capita GNP (US $)	Growth Rates 1960–1975 Population	Growth Rates 1960–1975 Real GNP Per Capita
China (mainland)	822.8	315.3	380	1.6	5.2
China (Taiwan)	16.0	14.9	930	2.8	6.3
Pakistan	69.2	11.3	160	2.9	3.3
Philippines	42.2	15.9	380	3.0	2.5
Thailand	41.9	14.6	350	3.1	4.6
South Korea	35.3	19.9	560	2.3	7.1
North Korea	15.8	7.1	450	2.8	3.8
Sri Lanka	13.8	2.6	190	2.1	2.0
Malaysia	12.3	9.3	760	2.8	4.0
Hong Kong	4.4	7.7	1760	2.2	4.2
Singapore	2.3	5.5	2450	2.0	7.6
Asia (excluding Japan)	1957.0	556.0	280	—	—
Japan	115.6	496.3	4450	1.1	7.7
Indonesia	132.1	29.1	220	2.2	2.4

SOURCE: International Bank for Reconstruction and Development [11(1977), pp. 10, 16, 23].

REFERENCES

1. Bank of Japan. *Economic Statistics Annual*. Tokyo.

2. ——————. *Economic Statistics Monthly*. Tokyo.

3. ——————. *The Japanese Economy in 1975*. Tokyo, annual.

4. ——————. *Money and Banking in Japan*, translated by S. Nishemura. New York: St. Martin's, 1973.

5. *Business Japan*. Tokyo, monthly.

6. Drucker, Peter F. "Japan: The Problems of Success," *Foreign Affairs* (April 1978), pp. 564–578.

7. Economist Intelligence Unit. *Quarterly Economic Review: Japan, South Korea*. London.

8. *Fuji Bank Bulletin*. Tokyo, annual.

9. Gibney, Frank. *Japan: The Fragile Superpower*. New York: W. W. Norton, 1975.

10. *Industrial Review of Japan*. Tokyo, annual.

11. International Bank for Reconstruction and Development. *World Bank Atlas: Per Capita Product and Growth Rates*. Washington: 1977.

12. International Monetary Fund. *IMF Survey*. Washington, bimonthly.

13. Japan Economic Planning Agency. *Economic Survey of Japan*. Tokyo: Japan Times Ltd., annual.

14. Japan Economic Planning Agency. *White Paper on the Japanese Economy*. Tokyo, annual.

15. *Japan Economic Review*. Tokyo, monthly.

16. Japan Institute of Labour. *Japanese Industrial Relations Series: Employment and Employment Policy*. Tokyo, 1979.

17. Japan Ministry of Finance. *Monthly Finance Review*. Tokyo.

18. ——————. *Quarterly Bulletin of Financial Statistics*. Tokyo.

19. Japan Ministry of Labour. *Yearbook of Labour Statistics*. Tokyo, annual.

20. Japan Office of the Prime Minister. *Japan Statistical Yearbook*. Tokyo, annual.

21. Keidanren (Federation of Economic Organizations). *Economic Picture of Japan, 1976*. Tokyo, 1976.

22. *New York Times*.

23. Organization for Economic Cooperation and Development. *Main Economic Indicators*. Paris, monthly.

24. ——————. *OECD Economic Surveys: Japan*. Paris, annual.

25. *Oriental Economist*. Tokyo, monthly.

26. Oriental Economist. *Japan Economic Yearbook*. Tokyo, annual.

27. Tanaka, Kakui. *Building a New Japan: A Plan for Remodeling the Japanese Archipelago*. First English ed. Tokyo: Simul Press, 1973.

28. United States, Department of Commerce. *International Economic Indicators*. Washington: Government Printing Office, quarterly.

29. ——————, Department of Commerce, Industry and Trade Administration. *U.S. Export Opportunities to Japan*. Washington: Government Printing Office, 1978.

30. ——————, Department of Health, Education and Welfare. *Social Security Programs Throughout the World*. Washington: Government Printing Office, trienniel.

31. *Wall Street Journal*.

32. Woodsworth, David E. *Social Security and National Policy: Sweden, Yugoslavia, Japan*. Montreal and London: McGill-Green's University Press, 1977.

33. Yoshino, T. "The Japanese Economy and Its Problems," *Intereconomics* (May/June 1978), pp. 136–139.